Magazine Writing

▶ WHAT DOES IT TAKE TO LAUNCH A CAREER WRITING FOR MAGAZINES?

In this comprehensive, up-to-date introduction to magazine writing, students will learn everything from the initial story pitch all the way through to the final production, taking with them the essential tools and skills they will need for today's rapidly changing media landscape.

Written by a team of experienced writers and editors, *Magazine Writing* teaches the time-tested rules for good writing alongside the modern tools for digital storytelling. From service pieces to profiles, entertainment stories, and travel articles, it provides expert guidance on topics such as:

- developing saleable ideas;
- appealing to specific segments of the market;
- navigating a successful pitch;
- writing and editing content for a variety of areas, including service, profiles, entertainment, travel, human interest, and enterprise.

Chock-full of examples of published works, conversations with successful magazine contributors and bloggers, and interviews with working editors, *Magazine Writing* gives students all the practical and necessary insights they need to jump-start a successful magazine writing career.

Christopher D. Benson is Associate Dean of the College of Media and Associate Professor of Journalism at the University of Illinois at Urbana-Champaign. He has written for the magazines *Chicago, Savoy, Jet*, and *The Crisis*, and has contributed to *The Washington Post*, the *Chicago Tribune*, the *Chicago Sun-Times*, and *Reader's Digest*. He has worked as Features Editor and Washington Editor for *Ebony* magazine.

Charles F. Whitaker is Helen Gurley Brown Magazine Research Journalism, Northwestern University. He was a senior editor at *Ebon*, *Miami Herald* and the *Louisville Times* (KY), and he has written fo cago Sun-Times, Chicago, Jet, Essence magazine, The Philadelphia I. Post, Chicago Parent magazine, and Folio.

Magazine Writing

Christopher D. Benson

Charles F. Whitaker

Routledge
Taylor & Francis Group

NEW YORK AND LONDON

Acquisitions Editor: Erica Wetter
Development Editor: Mary Altman
Editorial Assistant: Simon Jacobs
Production Editor: Emily How
Text Design: Emily Johnston at Apex CoVantage Ltd
Copyeditor: Sarah Fish
Indexer: Alan Rutter
Cover Design: Gareth Toye
Companion Website Designer: Natalya Dyer

First published 2014
by Routledge
711 Third Avenue, New York, NY 10017

and by Routledge
2 Park Square, Milton Park, Abingdon, Oxon OX14 4RN

Routledge is an imprint of the Taylor & Francis Group, an informa business

© 2014 Taylor & Francis

Library of Congress Cataloging-in-Publication Data
Benson, Chris, 1953–
Magazine writing / Christopher Benson, University of Illinois at Urbana-Champaign,
    Charles Whitaker, Northwestern University.
        pages cm
  1. Freelance journalism.   2. Freelance journalism—Vocational guidance.   3. Feature
writing—Vocational guidance.   4. Journalism—Authorship.   I. Whitaker, Charles F.
II. Title.
  PN4784.F76B46 2013
  808.06′607—dc23
  2013022567

ISBN: 978-0-415-89276-6 (hbk)
ISBN: 978-0-415-89277-3 (pbk)
ISBN: 978-0-203-08436-6 (ebk)

Typeset in Warnock Pro
by Apex CoVantage, LLC

Printed and bound in the United States of America by Sheridan Books, Inc. (a Sheridan Group Company).

Contents

▶ **5 Sharpening the Angle**

▶ **6 Pitch Perfect**

▶ **7 Research: The Foundation of Good Storytelling**

▶ **8 Structure: The Building Blocks of Good Storytelling**

▶ **9 Structure II: The Mortar for Storytelling Blocks**

▶ 10 Self-Edit

▶ 11 Literary Non-fiction: Storytelling at Its Best

▶ 12 The Profile: Where Life Stories Come to Life

▶ 13 Service: "Hey, I Can Do That!"

▶ 14 Arts and Entertainment

▶ 15 Sports

▶ 16 Travel

▶ 17 Essay

▶ 18 B2B: The Ultimate Service Journalism

▶ 19 Writing for the Web and Tablets

▶ 20 Legal and Ethical Considerations

List of Boxes

Beginning the Journey: An Overview

1

▶ INTRODUCTION

Welcome to the world of **magazines**. This is the beginning of an exciting journey of discovery for the emerging writer who wants to get published. As we will see, arriving at that destination takes a good dose of skill and understanding. Equal parts art and science. What we hope to accomplish on these pages is to help you sharpen your critical thinking skills, as well as your writing ability. What we will see here is that establishing and maintaining a successful magazine writing career is as much a matter of analysis as it is creativity, with a good deal of determination and hard work.

Our focus in this book will be on the magazine article—from conception to publication. This is a fascinating and unique area of journalism, one that can allow considerable freedom of expression, even while it demands structure according to a set of well-established conventions, which we will cover. Our objective is to help you understand the field of magazine publishing, as well as the process—what it takes to get your story published as a freelance writer. Our hope is that at the end of this journey, you will have taken great strides in developing the skills necessary for any writer to draw the right kind of attention in this highly competitive area. Of course, the right kind of attention means getting published. The suggestions and assignments here are designed to help you develop your ability to conceptualize a publishable magazine piece, sharpen your idea, market the story, and finally understand what it takes to produce it—the research, the writing, the editing.

LEARNING OBJECTIVES

1. The nature of the modern magazine.
2. The things a freelance writer should know to get published.
3. How a magazine is organized around content.
4. How a magazine is organized around key staff.
5. The things to consider before pitching a magazine story idea to an editor.

Thinkstock / Zoonar

Without question, understanding the dynamics of this field requires an appreciation of the special qualities of the magazine story. For example, the difference between a magazine article and a news article is clear. But what might not readily be apparent are the distinctions between magazine articles and newspaper features. You must consider these distinctions as you begin to formulate your concept of the magazine article, learn how to develop it, how to write it, and—as important as anything else—how to sell it.

That is why this book basically is organized around four concepts, although there is some measure of overlap. First, we will set the context for everything that comes up during the writing process. It is important that you understand the marketplace you might want to enter as a freelancer. Accordingly, we will take up the basics. We consider the nature of a magazine, as well as the history, the development, and the current state of the industry in which an editor has to make professional judgments about your work. You will consider who might be interested in publishing your article and why. What are the interests of particular magazines and their readers? In what ways will you reach them with the piece you propose to write?

Second, we deal with story development. This process begins, of course, with conception. We will discuss the sources of good magazine story ideas, and the enterprise it takes to recognize and refine them. Ultimately, you will think about what makes an idea a good topic for publication in a specific magazine aimed at a particular readership. What makes it appealing? Again, what makes the story marketable?

Third, no matter how effectively you develop the story, and no matter how good you might think your work happens to be, you must be able to approach editors and show them that the idea is perfect for their publication. How well you do that will go a long way toward your success in getting published.

Finally, there is the writing. A substantial portion of the material presented here focuses on the writing process. Information gathering, of course, is key to your success as a writer. We will examine the critical sources of information you will need to complete your assignments successfully. We also will consider the essential elements of the interview, from mechanics to substance. The small and large stories you hope to develop over the course of your journey through these pages will give you the opportunity to refine your writing skills. It is important to note that even the lesser writing assignments you might undertake will increase your knowledge and ability in a few key areas. Hopefully, you will gain a deeper appreciation of quality magazine writing on multiple levels and you will make appreciable progress toward producing it. Throughout this book, you will be exposed to writing selections we believe set good examples of particular aspects or categories of magazine writing, or simply represent some of the best writing that has been published. We will guide you through a critical appraisal of these excerpts.

Additionally, it is important that you read magazines on a regular basis in order to apply the lessons you learn here, see how the guidance in this book springs to life in published articles, and to analyze for yourself why certain pieces work or don't work; why certain stories are published in particular magazines; and how story ideas are generated. Not only will you become familiar with the focus of some of the leading publications, but you can learn quite a bit about effective writing by reading the stories that get into print or are produced for online magazines. You also can begin early on to focus on a particular magazine to which you would like to submit your work. The information on these pages certainly will help in setting your own writing strategy. But, first, there are some basic questions that must be answered.

▶ WHAT IS A MAGAZINE?

A magazine is a publication that typically is produced and distributed *periodically*. In a previous age, we thought about magazines largely as printed publications that were distributed monthly, weekly or bi-weekly. But in the digital age—when many online magazines are updated daily and have no print component—our notions about the frequency of magazine publication and the method of distribution have changed dramatically.

But what does it publish? As a glance at any magazine might suggest—whether you find that magazine at the checkout counter in a grocery store or on the shelves of a bookstore or the racks of a corner newsstand or, increasingly these days, online—the scope of content appears to be unlimited. The range of offerings has been defined and refined by editors and publishers over more than 200 years, as we discuss in Chapter 2. But this brings us to the very definition of "magazine."

MAGAZINE:
A collection of stories published and distributed periodically for a specific audience.

The word "magazine" comes from the French word "magasin," which means "store" or "storehouse," often used in connection with storage of weapons or ammunition. In the case of periodicals, it means a collection of stories. As we begin to see in Chapter 2 and continue in Chapter 3, these stories can be framed in a number of ways and directed at a number of communities, based on specific characteristics and interests. So, we should begin to think about the magazine as an assortment of content (long articles and short ones) that is curated and/or aggregated to appeal to a community of readers or users who are bound by the similarities of their characteristics, their affinity for a subject area, and their perspective, or point of view. The audience for the "zine" is key to many of your considerations as a freelance writer, just as it is to publishers, editors, and—importantly—advertisers.

In its 2003 Magazine Reader Experience Study and a subsequent 2005 User Engagement Study, researchers at the Media Management Center at Northwestern University conducted a survey of magazine readers and web users to help identify those characteristics that most engage an audience.

Among the qualities noted by the nearly 11,500 survey respondents to the print magazine study was that engagement in magazines—especially for women—was highly personal. Respondents noted that they spent time with magazines because:

- It makes me smarter.
- It's my personal time out.
- The stories absorb me.
- It's relevant to me.
- I trust it.
- I talk about it and share it.
- I learn things here first.

Among the qualities noted in the survey of web users:

- It connects me with others.
- It touches me and expands my views.
- It helps and improves me.
- It's tailored for me.
- It's my personal time out.
- It gives me something to talk about.

What's interesting about those characteristics is that they're applicable to both the **lean-back** experience of reading a print magazine and the **lean-forward** experience of digital presentation. That digital presentation increasingly is part of the "delivery" system for many zines.

Lean-back vs. lean-forward   When we talk about the lean-back experience, we're addressing that "personal time out." It's the experience of kicking back and relaxing with a media property, whether that means being engrossed in a long-form narrative piece or poring over the pages of a fashion layout or a home decorating ("shelter") magazine spread.

The lean-forward experience is largely about service. It's all about seeking information and sharing it through individual searches online, hyperlinks embedded by **aggregators** of previously published content, and through social networks. It's about connecting with people in the "community." In the lean-forward experience, the user is in control. She determines in what order she wants to experience the content. Unlike the lean-back experience, where writer and editor control the narrative and guide the reader through the content, the lean-forward experience is not linear, allowing the user to hopscotch through the content in any way she chooses. Although we tend to think of print as a lean-back experience and digital as lean-forward, the advent of the new digital readers and tablets (spearheaded by the Kindle and iPad) has made it possible for people to replicate the print experience in a digital format. The tablet also creates opportunities for people to surf the net for multiple **platform** presentations, even while reading magazines in traditional form. Best of all for writers, it means many opportunities to create content across multiple platforms.

It's important for emerging magazine writers to understand how content is curated and used in the magazine, whether digital or print. Understanding the magazine environment is just as important as understanding the audience, tone, and point of view of the magazine.

As we shall see, good magazines have strong identities that are made apparent by way of an easily discernable **voice**, look, and worldview. Editors are the

AGGREGATOR:
A person or media organization that collects and assembles previously published material and distributes in its own collection, mostly online.

PLATFORM:
A method of delivering information, whether by traditional print, broadcast or audio, or digitally on computers, tablets, and smart phones.

guardians of those identities, but it is vital for the emerging magazine writer to try to understand the editor's goals and objectives for reaching her audience with content. This is vitally important in that the rejection rate among freelance writers is exceptionally high. All this will become clear as we dig deeper into producing and pitching your story ideas. But coming to understand the industry, as well as sharpening your writing skills, is imperative in moving beyond "no," as the experienced freelancer is quite adept at doing.

Clearly, knowledge is the key. In fact, we suggest that there are five "knows" to get to "yes"—the successful magazine assignment.

▶ GETTING THE ASSIGNMENT: THE FIVE THINGS EVERY FREELANCE WRITER SHOULD KNOW

As stated, there are five "knows" that get you to "yes." Quite simply, you must:

1. Know the magazine.
2. Know the audience.
3. Know the history.
4. Know the story.
5. Know the voice.

Know the magazine   Even where magazines might appear to present the same subject matter (as in zines that are aimed at women readers), there are distinctions you should come to understand before developing story ideas and submitting them for consideration. As we discuss in Chapter 2 and Chapter 3, magazine publishers and editors have worked at shaping their publications to speak with a clear and distinctive voice and to appeal to a very select audience. So, knowing the magazine—as you might know a friend—is the first step in navigating a way into the conversation you want to engage as a freelance magazine writer.

Getting to know the magazine involves some preliminary research. Even if you think you already know a magazine because you have seen it on newsstands, read it periodically, browsed online, or even subscribed to it, there are additional steps you must take to really get to know the magazine intimately. *Writers Market* is a great first step in zeroing in on magazine profiles, the departments, and other sections of the magazine that are most likely to provide "break-in" possibilities for new writers. It also provides information and instructions for submitting a query—pitching your story idea to an editor. But don't stop at this resource. Check out the magazine's website and the magazine's guidelines for writers. There is information you will glean from a careful read of the publication, but also from the way the editors describe it and set out their vision in these accessible resources. We discuss other steps in Chapter 5.

Know the audience   As stated above, it is imperative that the successful writer understands the readers for whom he is writing. We discuss reader characteristics in Chapter 2 and you will come to appreciate the fine distinctions among the people who are reading magazines even when these readers seem at first to be substantially similar. Who are these people? What are their characteristics, their needs, their interests? How do you take this background knowledge and shape your story to meet their expectations, their needs, their interests in certain information and presentation? Understanding all this will help you enter into a conversation with these readers, successfully moving from observations about everyday occurrences to stories that resonate with an audience—beginning with the editors who curate the content for that audience, and decide whether to include you in the lineup.

Know the history   Before you ever get started, it is vital to know whether the target magazine publishes pieces like the one you might want to produce. But there is more, even after you have determined that your kind of story fits in. Here, and in Chapter 5, we suggest that it is important to know whether a magazine already has published the piece you want to pitch. Still, your examination doesn't even end there. You also must consider whether the magazine has published something so substantially similar that the editor is unlikely to accept your story idea and give you the assignment. Clearly, knowing the publishing history of your target magazine—as well as that of its competitors—will help you avoid an automatic "no" when you make your suggestion.

Know the story   Although it might seem obvious that you should know something about the subject you want to propose, too many writers have their pitches rejected simply because they fail to identify the critical elements of the story that connect with the specific readers of the target magazine. We discuss the importance of conducting preliminary research in Chapter 6, and then in Chapter 7 we go further into the need and techniques for conducting thorough overall research of documents and probing, revealing interviews. But a clear understanding of the subject matter you intend to cover and the key sources connected to that story have to be established early in the process—when you first pitch the piece to prospective editors.

Know the voice   The style and tone of presentation in a specific magazine are part of its distinctive identity. It is essential that you recognize this voice and demonstrate that you can match it in your writing. This demonstration begins with the query, or story pitch, which we discuss in Chapter 6,

VOICE: The style and tone of presentation that form a distinctive identity for the magazine and for the writer.

and then it continues as you produce the story, which is treated in varying degrees in the subsequent chapters on writing skills and styles.

It is important to note that there will be a sixth "know" once the assignment has been granted. It certainly is important for the successful writer to know her rights. We take a look at practical legal and ethical considerations for the freelance writer in Chapter 20. A seventh "know" is vital as you close in on the end of the writing process. If you know what works (and what doesn't) you will perform your self-edit efficiently and effectively, producing magazine copy that is as tight as it is informative and creative. The result will be an article or department piece with great impact, no matter what the length or format.

Long before that happens, of course, you have to determine where you are most likely to find success in placing a story—getting it published.

▶ MAGAZINE CONTENT ORGANIZATION

It is important to take a long hard look at those magazines that interest you. Break them down into their component parts. How are the magazines organized? What is the **architecture** of the magazine? Many are still organized in the traditional three-well format, which includes a front section, a feature well, and a back section. Study this **break-of-the-book** to determine the types of stories that are presented and, as important as anything else, how they are ranked. The **front-of-the-book** typically is built around a news or consumer orientation. (For good illustrative examples, see *New York, Chicago, Glamour, Essence,* and *Esquire.*) This front section has departments—style, grooming, gadgets, travel—and columns that are focused on service and current events. Often, the service pieces are tied to current events in that they focus on the latest offerings of certain items.

BREAK-OF-THE-BOOK: The organizational **architecture** of a magazine, usually around a front section, a middle feature well, and a back section.

The feature well often is the home of the cover story, as well as the major and lesser features. One way to tell you're in the feature well of many magazines is that you likely will see fewer advertising pages in this section. Many publishers keep the ad-to-editorial page ratio lower in the feature well not only to maintain the design integrity of the well (avoiding "clutter"), but also in order to avoid conflicts between advertising content and editorial content, as we discuss in our presentation on ethical considerations in Chapter 20. Try to discern whether the feature well has a number of related stories, or "packages." How are they pitched to the reader with respect to titles and decks (the subtitles and epigraphs that are featured at the beginning of major features)? These all come together in ways that can be instructive, helping to establish the voice of the publication, and suggesting ways for you to frame the angle of the story, as we discuss in Chapter 5.

If there is a **back-of-the-book** section, what is its focus? Some magazines use the back-of-the-book merely for story "jumps" (continuations of articles from the feature well). Others fill the back-of-the-book with additional departments and columns. Nearly every magazine ends with some sort of "outro" or closer—a one-page department that signs readers out with a smile or a provocative thought, image, or message.

Consider, too, the editorial strategy that might be apparent in the way the front and back sections are planned. Marketing is a key consideration at all levels of the magazine publishing business. There is something of a "thumb-through" strategy at work in pitching the magazine to potential readers at the newsstand. Notice the behavior of people who "thumb through" magazines at the rack (either from the front of the book or the back) and how they are attracted to certain features that pull them into the magazine and, ultimately, to the checkout counter to purchase it!

As a writer, your understanding of the architecture of the magazine will help you determine whether a story would be best suited as a smaller department piece or a longer article for the feature well, and then how it might be framed and enhanced (with illustrations, photos, or other graphic elements) to attract reader attention. This will help you think not only about points of entry, but also about developing an angle that will resonate with the editor who is responsible for a particular department or column, or the articles editor who assigns features. It also will help you make the case for your story in a way that is most appealing to the reader, at least as the editor sees the reader.

▶ MAGAZINE STAFF ORGANIZATION

In the preceding section, we mentioned titles of certain editorial positions. While these can vary from one magazine to the next, the staff positions generally are designed to handle the vital functions in putting the magazine out each publishing cycle. Their specific roles should be familiar to the emerging writer in order to make sure the right people are contacted for the right story suggestions. Knowing how to address a story suggestion can go a long way toward avoiding getting lost in the shuffle, or getting a "no" merely on a technicality. You will find the magazine staff listed in the **masthead** somewhere in the front section of the book.

In the chain of story consideration, most magazines have some variation of the organizational hierarchy you will see set out in the box. Often there are assistants who might or might not be part of the vetting process for submissions. Getting to know how your target magazine handles these inquiries—which means knowing the right person to contact—is essential.

MASTHEAD: The listing of magazine personnel, including the editorial, design, advertising, and other business staff.

FINDING THE RIGHT EDITOR ON THE MAGAZINE MASTHEAD

IMPRESSIONS

"NO SECOND CHANCES"
VOLUME 8, NUMBER 5

Editor-in-Chief	Joanna O'Neil
Executive Editor	Nathan Chan
Managing Editor	Carter Garret
Senior Editors	Craig Cawley, Betsy Coin, Ashley Collins, Samantha Morton, David Sorrell
Associate Editors	Danielle Cooper, Kimberly Fry, Bob Levy, Scott Parker, Dana Walsh
Assistant Editor	Sarah Fine
Editorial Assistant	Anjali Bishop
Creative Director	Tiffany Hester
Art Director	Jamie Bernstein
Digital Editor	Ahmed Mahir
Photography Editor	Victoria Cavalli
Contributing Editors	Melanie Brooks, Glenda Bush, Gary Collier, Derek Divittorio, Karin Hecht, Aaron Preis, Victoria Sward, Andrea Waldron
Production Director	Lauren St. John
Research Editor	Kristin Nakamura
Copy Chief	Maria Veneta
Assistant to the Editor	Taylor Lawson

The masthead for the imaginary magazine Impressions (above) is typical of the listing of editorial personnel. Often, there will be a separate masthead listing the personnel from the business side, including such people as the publisher, the advertising director, sales staff, and circulation director. But this editorial listing tells an important story for the freelance writer. It tells the story of the people responsible for determining content of the magazine. As we have discussed, often the people who will have something to say about assigning a story to you will be at the senior or associate editor rank.

Among the five "knows" that get you to "yes" is a requirement that you know the magazine. And here, you should know the editorial mission, the style of presentation of the magazine, as well as the editors and their responsibilities for reviewing pitches and assigning articles. Generally, magazine mastheads all have some version of the editorial hierarchy listed below.

EDITOR. This is the person who ultimately is responsible for making sure the publication consistently fulfills its editorial mission, its purpose for publishing. Sometimes this person will have the title editor-in-chief. An executive editor title is used to designate the person who is second in charge, and most frequently when the publisher also carries the title editor, or where there is, in fact, an editor or editor-in-chief. The point here, though, is that, given the level of responsibility of the top editor (and even the editor next to the top), it is not likely that people in these positions will screen story pitches for relatively new writers. If they are involved in the nuts and bolts of story development at all, this involvement likely would be limited to work on major pieces and with established writers. So, they will not be the persons who generally will read story ideas submitted by those freelancers who do not already have relationships with the magazine.

MANAGING EDITOR. This person is responsible for tracking editorial schedules and usually will work with a production coordinator, with the design staff, and with the advertising coordinators to make sure the pages of the magazine are processed in a timely fashion and that the magazine is published and distributed. Not likely to be the person who reads story pitches.

SENIOR EDITOR. Depending on the structure of a given magazine, this person might be in charge of a section or subject area of the magazine, such as food, fashion, or entertainment. Some senior editors are responsible for particular departments, such as financial information or politics, or might be responsible for the entire front-of-the-book or back-of-the-book, assigning and compiling all the short pieces that appear in these sections. This editor, or her assistant, might review story pitches in her designated areas.

ARTICLES EDITOR. This person might handle specific subject areas for major features that are assigned, usually to regular contributors. While articles editors can work alone, and with their assistants, they sometimes work in groups of editors on special packages and features. Articles editors often will review story pitches.

CONTRIBUTING EDITOR. This person is a writer for the magazine, usually on retainer, and likely is among the highest paid freelancers for the publication. Sometimes contributing editors carry the title editor-at-large. They can handle special subject areas or departments, but are not part of the assignment chain and do not read story pitches, as a rule.

ASSOCIATE EDITOR. Depending on the structure of the magazine, an associate editor might have responsibility for editing a section of the magazine, or for handling a particular subject area. If so, he will review story suggestions as part of his work. Usually, though, this person works with one of the senior level editors in managing the creative team (including photo, design, and research staff) to put an assigned story together.

ASSISTANT EDITOR. Typically, this person handles a good deal of the administrative work as part of the editorial team. Permissions, scheduling, fact-checking, and other similar functions might be part of the portfolio. Sending "nice" rejection notes also might be included. But an ambitious assistant editor also might want to get advancement points by bringing fresh story ideas to the attention of more senior level editors.

EDITORIAL ASSISTANT. Usually this person only handles administrative duties tied to the production process. Likely not the person who will be able to vet a story proposal. Sometimes, though, as with the associate editor, this person might have responsibility for reviewing and summarizing story pitches for a more senior level editor.

▶ A FINAL WORD

Clearly, finding success as a freelance magazine writer is all in what you know.

Among the goals we hope to reach in the following pages is providing that knowledge: familiarity with a range of magazines and their editorial missions; an appreciation of reader interests and how best to satisfy these interests with solid story ideas; and an ability to apply certain proven writing techniques in telling rich and engaging stories. Achieving these objectives will require critical thinking skills, which will be sharpened in reading and analyzing some of the best magazine articles published in recent years. It also will require critical appraisal of your own writing.

There is an added value of our considerations here. It is consistent with our commitment to helping to develop well-rounded professional journalists who are prepared to meet the increasing challenges of our diverse society. To do so, we all must come to appreciate the value of differences based on race, ethnicity, gender, nationality, sexuality, ability, religion, and class, rather than seeing these differences in oppositional terms. Although there is a heavy emphasis on marketing when it comes to succeeding in the freelance magazine world, it is important for students to understand early on that—in every way conceivable—magazine writing is a form of journalism. As such, writers in this form still must be guided by all the principles and values of journalism, along with the best practices when it comes to skillful expression. What that means is that magazine writers must be guided by values of accuracy and fairness in gathering and presenting information—even while expressing more freedom in giving voice to these stories. In that context, appreciating the value of diversity—especially with respect to reflecting multiple perspectives—is a foundational goal. Indeed, it is organic to journalism excellence. Hopefully, in the pages that follow, you will find ways to cross your own boundaries in search of that untold story, reflecting fresh perspectives, generating new knowledge. In so doing, you not only will be rewarded with rich and entertaining narrative possibilities, but you also will go a long way toward enlightening readers in areas they otherwise might not have considered. That is journalism of the first order, and a goal of the best writers.

WRITER'S WORKSHOP

Here are some suggestions for you to apply some of the central points of this chapter as you begin to develop article ideas.

The first step along the way to successful magazine writing is to know certain things about yourself and the magazine. So, start by thinking about the magazine you have the greatest interest in reading. Now think about what it is that attracts you to this magazine. Make a list. Next, consider the stories you might anticipate appearing in the magazine, based on your own reading experience and interests. Finally, think about how you might consider these stories as a staff editor reviewing submissions by writers, such as yourself. What would you want to see? If you begin your writing process with this exercise, you will take a big step toward establishing a conversation with readers of particular magazines. In the following chapters, you will pick up additional tips that—in connection with the "Assignment Desk" exercises—will help you internalize certain practices that one day will become second nature to you.

Chapter One Review

ASSIGNMENT DESK

1. Take a look at the magazine rack at your local newsstand, bookstore, or supermarket checkout line. Consider the range of offerings and note your own impressions of the various ways these "storehouses" of information distinguish themselves right on the cover. How would you describe these distinctions?

2. Select a magazine (preferably one you have not read before) and "thumb through" the front-of-the-book section. How would you describe this front section in terms of the type of information presented? Does it seem to have a news peg, tied to current developments on products or trends? Is the focus more on service, or consumer interests, presenting information on goods and services? Does it have more of an entertainment focus? Is it a combination of these approaches? Which stories attract your attention in the front-of-the-book section? Write down the reasons you are attracted to these stories. How might these considerations shape your own story suggestions to this magazine?

3. Flip through the entire magazine and note how content is organized. Consider the distinctions between the kinds of stories that are published in the front and back sections from those presented in the feature well. Describe this "break-of-the-book" in terms of the emphasis presented for readers.

4. Read the names of the editors in the masthead. Identify the titles of people you might consider contacting with your story suggestions. Provide a rationale, giving reasons for the selections you make.

5. Check out *Writers Market* online at www.writersmarket.com, or pick up a copy of the latest edition from your campus library. Find the listing for the magazine you selected at the newsstand. What does the entry tell you about the people most likely to review your story suggestion, and the section most likely to present break-in possibilities for you as a writer?

▶ KEY TERMS

- aggregator
- architecture
- back-of-the-book
- break-of-the-book
- front-of-the-book
- lean-back
- lean-forward
- magazine
- masthead
- platform
- voice

▶ **SUGGESTED READINGS**

Peck, Abe; Malthouse, Edward C. *Medill on Engagement.* New York: Hampton Press, 2010. Peck and Malthouse edited this volume in which 17 faculty members from Northwestern University's Medill School of Journalism and its Media Management Center explore how content creators, including magazine editors, provide rich, engaging experiences for their audiences.

▶ **WEB RESOURCES**

http://www.writersdigest.com/ Home page for *Writer's Digest*, an online and print resource for writers working in a variety of genres, from fiction to journalism.

http://www.mediamanagementcenter.org/ Website of the Media Management Center at Northwestern University, a research center that focuses on the growth, sustainability, and content development strategy of a variety of media.

http://stateofthemedia.org/2012/magazines-are-hopes-for-tablets-overdone/magazines-by-the-numbers/ The annual "State of the Media" report of the Pew Research Center's Project for Excellence in Journalism. This section of the website focuses specifically on the magazine industry.

2 The Inside Story: A Look at the Magazine Industry

▶ OVERVIEW

It is pointless even to begin considering writing for magazines without weighing the opportunities to get published. What are the chances? The process of recognizing the opportunities and taking advantage of them begins with an understanding of the industry, the people (the publishers and editors) who operate in it, and the consumers (the readers) whose interests must be served. Thus, fitting in requires an appreciation of the dynamics of the magazine publishing industry and the characteristics of magazine readers. What is the motivation of publishers and editors in putting out magazines? (What is their editorial purpose? What is their advertising purpose?) What is the motivation of the reader in buying and reading them? (What are their interests, their needs?) These are vital considerations for the magazine writer to make in developing a successful writing strategy that is as much about marketing as it is about solid reporting and writing. The first step in getting to "know" the magazine and its readers, of course, is in coming to understand the nature of the magazine publishing business.

LEARNING OBJECTIVES

1. How to begin to "know" the magazine and "know" the audience.

2. How magazines are categorized according to their subject matter, and how these categories have become more specialized through history.

3. How magazine publishing is distinguished from other media production.

4. The reasons people turn to magazines to read the stories you will write and how you can connect with them.

5. How best to tell stories in a contemporary environment across platforms to satisfy the needs and interests of readers.

▶ MAGAZINE CATEGORIES

One of the first things to recognize is that there are many categories of magazines—categories and sub-categories. While commentators increasingly are setting out sub-categories that include custom magazines, literary reviews, and even comic books, for purposes of considering freelance writing, contemporary magazines fall generally into one of two broad categories: consumer and trade (also known as Business-to-Business publications). The two categories are distinguished not just by their editorial content (though there are vast differences in editorial approach between consumer and B2B publications). But they also are distinguished by their advertising. **Consumer magazines** feature advertisements for goods and services aimed at a general consumer. **B2B publications** feature advertisements for goods and services aimed exclusively at the business owners and managers engaged in the industry targeted by the publication.

Consumer magazines likely are the ones most familiar to the general public. These are the magazines we tend to see at the checkout counters, on newsstands, and in our mailboxes, if we have subscriptions. They are aimed at readers generally looking for information about events, people, trends, and culture, among other areas. These days, the broad area of consumer magazines is broken down even further into categories that include entertainment (*Rolling Stone*), commentary (*The Nation*) or cultural elite (*Harper's*), business and finance (*Fortune*), fashion (*Vogue*), beauty (*Glamour*), health and fitness (*Shape*), shelter (*Architectural Digest*), travel (*Condé Nast Traveler*), service (*Family Circle*), and so on. They can be broken down still further into such categories as gender (*Cosmopolitan, Esquire*), race (*Essence*), and ethnicity (*Latina*). Finally, they are sorted by range of age of the readership.

As we soon will see, recognizing these fundamental distinctions is vital to shaping your content in ways that will resonate with a contemporary magazine readership. And that audience has become more sophisticated and more focused, while the magazine publishing industry has responded by moving increasingly to more targeted marketing.

B2B MAGAZINES: Sometimes referred to as trade publications, these are aimed at business owners, managers, and other professionals who need specialized information.

In the B2B category, we find magazines that are aimed at business owners, managers, and professionals who want more specialized information, which they need for success in their industries. These magazines—which generally are only available by subscriptions directed to highly targeted readers—provide information about technical developments in various fields, performance of specific businesses, profiles of business personalities, and legal and legislative developments. And, as with consumer magazines, B2B publications are broken down still further. Here, though, the breakdown is sorted according to vertical and horizontal categories. **Vertical publications** generally refer to those that deeply focus on specific businesses or professions, or are aimed at specific job titles within an industry. Examples of vertical publications include *Landscape Professional*, *Pharmaceutical Executive*, and *Dentistry Today*. As this list suggests, vertical publications provide information that targets the relatively narrow interests within a specific field. **Horizontal publications**, on the other hand, still cover specific areas or industries, but may cut across several job titles within the industry, or cover areas that could be pertinent across a number of different fields. Representative titles among the horizontal trades include *Hotels*, which is aimed at everyone in the hospitality industry, from the managers of hostels to travel agents. And then there is *Advertising Age*, whose audience includes everyone from advertising content creators to ad sales people and account managers.

To further illustrate the difference between vertical and horizontal publications, let's take a look at a specific industry populated by a wealth of B2B titles: restaurants. A number of B2B titles target various segments of this industry. *Nation's Restaurant News* is a horizontal book that cuts across a wide swath of the industry and targets managers of both chain restaurants and fine-dining establishments, as well as individuals in charge of the front of the house (food and beverage managers) and food preparation (everyone from fry cooks to executive chefs). On the other hand, *Plate* magazine, a vertical book, only targets "table cloth" restaurants and, even in this sector, only those people—executive chefs, sous chefs, pastry chefs—involved in the preparation and presentation of food.

▶ MAGAZINE DEVELOPMENT: A BRIEF HISTORY

The sorting of magazines into all the categories and sub-categories is the result of years of development of an industry that has been quite adaptable to changes in our society. Indeed, magazine publishing has experienced a number of highs and lows over its more than two-hundred-year history. Prohibitive printing costs, high cover prices, low literacy rates, and mailing problems and costs well into the nineteenth century created problems to be sure. At its most critical moments, though, the industry has adapted. By the middle of the twentieth century, according to the late Theodore Peterson, the magazine industry had overcome significant challenges. These challenges were created by four periods of modern development that had caused many observers to wonder if the medium could survive. The first period came immediately after World War I when wide distribution of automobiles threatened to take people out of their homes (and away from their magazines). The second period came in the mid-twenties, when radio became a pervasive—and live—medium, attracting reading audiences. The third period began in 1927 when sound was added to motion pictures. And the fourth period, Peterson notes in *Magazines of the Twentieth Century*, began in the 1950s with the advent of television and its images and immediacy. Most recently, the speed, pervasiveness, and appropriation of published material by Internet aggregators (often provided free of charge to people surfing the net) also have created challenges that Peterson well might see as the fifth period of challenge—one raising concerns about whether magazine publishing remains viable as a business option. Yet, magazine boosters point out that the industry has survived and flourished during all past periods of innovation. This is largely because publishers have been able to assess the changing needs of the reading consumers in order to adapt and fulfill editorial missions. Appreciating this development—understanding a bit of the history and the editorial mission of magazines—helps considerably as writers determine just where and how they might fit in.

The early years   The modern magazine, according to Peterson, was born in the last decades of the nineteenth century. But American magazine publishing began in February 1741 with the launch of two publications—and the dawn of the country's first magazine publishing war—in Philadelphia. Andrew Bradford launched *American Magazine, or a Monthly View of the Political State of the British Colonies* on February 13, 1741 with a January 1741 publication date. Bradford was a chief rival of Benjamin Franklin, who had been working on the production of his own new publishing venture. Bradford beat him to market by three days. Yet undeterred, Franklin launched his *General Magazine and Historical Chronicle for all of the British Plantations in America* on February 16, 1741. It also bore a January 1741 publication date. Neither magazine was a tremendous success. Franklin's *General Magazine* hung around for six issues before the statesman and inventor folded it in favor of other pursuits. Bradford was even less patient. He only produced three issues of *American Magazine*. But, as brief as these early experiences might have been, they marked the birth of the American magazine.

Benjamin Franklin

Thinkstock / iStockphoto

Modeled after the elite British magazines of the period, these, and other American magazines that were published into the early nineteenth century, similarly were aimed at an elite group of land-owning readers, and engaged many of the significant issues of the day. But with low literacy rates and high publishing and shipping costs, building readership beyond such a small, exclusive group was a problem. As with the efforts of Bradford and Franklin, many of the early magazines did not last very long. The important distinguishing qualities of the magazine, though—its format as a "storehouse" of features and commentary, coupled with unique perspective and voice, as with such nineteenth-century cause publications as *The Emancipator*—continued to characterize the magazine publishing form as the medium emerged into the modern period, which Peterson noted.

Several factors spurred the development of the contemporary magazine. Industrialization led to improvements in printing quality and illustrations (engravings, photographs, and eventually color), and created more leisure time for people to read magazines. Improved postal delivery and special postal rates for periodicals extended the national distribution reach of the publications. And the increasing need for advertisers to establish "brand" identity among the growing numbers of consumers expanded a source of revenue for magazines that, in turn, led to the development of an entirely new business model for the successful modern magazine. As a result, magazine publishers were able to manage the costs of production and distribution, and expand overall circulation, charging advertisers for exposure of their messages to these consumers. The new business model for modern publishing even impacted newspaper profits.

MUCKRAKING MAGAZINES ADD BITE TO THE PRESS WATCHDOG ROLE

As the magazine solidified its position as the first national medium, by the turn of the twentieth century it also would develop a quality that would rise above the presentation of service, entertainment, and lifestyle articles. It would develop a voice, one that would come to distinguish magazines from each other, even while reflecting one common theme: advocacy. While the drive to increase circulation and advertising revenue already had driven big city newspapers to slug it out with sensational and often-irresponsible **yellow journalism** stories, magazines would take a more elevated approach, winning readers and influencing public policy with long-form investigative stories.

In a way, this investigative form of reporting began with the infamous 1887 undercover expose written by Joseph Pulitzer's *New York World* newspaper reporter "Nellie Bly" (Elizabeth Cochran) on abuses in New York's insane asylum. But, given their nature as national in scope, their long lead time to publication, and the greater amount of printed space they could devote to articles, magazines would become the desired venues for serious-minded journalists who wanted to add bite to their watchdog roles.

In 1902, *McClure's Magazine* set in motion a period of **muckraking**—intense magazine scrutiny of unfair business practices, public frauds, political corruption, unsafe labor practices, race, and, of course, unhealthy food processing. It began with the 19-part series on the Standard Oil Company written by Ida Tarbell for *McClure's* beginning in November 1902 and running through October 1904. The series later was published in a two-volume book, *The History of the Standard Oil Company*, all leading to the anti-trust breakup of John D. Rockefeller's huge monopoly in Standard Oil.

There also was Lincoln Steffens' 1904 "Shame of the Cities" series for *McClure's*, focusing on the negative impact of urban corruption on immigrant groups. And there was Samuel Hopkins Adams' 12-part series "The Great American Fraud"

YELLOW JOURNALISM: Takes its name from the popular late nineteenth-century newspaper comic strip and refers to newspaper sensationalism.

Theodore Roosevelt

Thinkstock / Photos.com

on patent medicine "quackery" for *Collier's* beginning in October 1905. *Ladies' Home Journal* editor Edward Bok also weighed in, publishing exposes and illustrations of medical hoaxes and banning patent medicine ads in his magazine. The *LHJ* expose and the one published by *Collier's* contributed to Congressional passage of the Pure Food and Drug Act of 1906.

Then, there was the series that led to historic political reform. Shortly after Pulitzer's archrival William Randolph Hearst purchased *Cosmopolitan* in 1905, the new publisher directed that a muckraking series be published on abuses in the selection of U.S. senators. He wanted the magazine to become an advocate of direct election. U.S. senators under the constitution were selected by state legislatures, creating serious problems with corruption and graft, as industrialists and financiers peddled influence. In 1906, *Cosmopolitan* published the series "The Treason of the Senate," exposing the corruption and leading to adoption of the Seventeenth Amendment to the U.S. Constitution in 1913, establishing direct election of U.S. senators by popular vote.

While the journalists and editors of the period relished the "muckraking" term as a badge of honor, it was coined in an April 14, 1906 speech delivered by President Theodore Roosevelt that was meant to criticize their practices and methods as a warning against press excesses, even while supporting the desired public outcomes.

In "The Man With the Muck-rake," Roosevelt used the metaphor of the character in "Pilgrim's Progress" who tended only to look downward as he raked the muck:

> the man who in this life consistently refuses to see aught that is lofty, and fixes his eyes with solemn intentness only on that which is vile and debasing.
>
> Now, it is very necessary that we should not flinch from seeing what is vile and debasing. There is filth on the floor, and it must be scraped up with the muck rake; and there are times and places where this service is the most needed of all the services that can be performed. But the man who never does anything else, who never thinks or speaks or writes, save of his feats with the muck rake, speedily becomes, not a help but one of the most potent forces for evil.

The period of intense muckraking only lasted for the better part of the first decade of the twentieth century, but its influence on magazine form and content still can be felt. In a direct way, we see it reflected in what magazine historian Ted Peterson called the "cultural elite," magazines like *The New Yorker*, *The Atlantic*, *Harper's*, *The New Republic*, and the more recent arrival *Mother Jones* that take a detailed, probing look at issues. But, in effect, it also can be seen in all magazines that express their unique voice and, through their advocacy of ideas, as well as the presentation of trends and the provision of balanced consumer information, address the needs and concerns of their communities of interests—the readers.

A new publishing model   Frank Munsey long has been credited with developing this new publishing paradigm as early as 1893 for his *Munsey's Magazine*. He figured that, by cutting his cover price—even below what it cost to produce and distribute the magazine—he could expand circulation. Increasing the number of people reading the magazine would mean increasing the number of people exposed to the advertising carried by the publication. Advertisers then would pay (eventually on a cost per thousand basis) for exposure of their goods and services to the increasing numbers of magazine readers. As a result, advertisers wound up paying enough to enable magazines to meet the costs of production and turn a profit. For the first half of the twentieth century, magazines experienced tremendous growth, with many of the most popular magazines reaching millions of readers and earning hundreds of millions of dollars a year. Given the amount of printed space they provided, the longer lead time for production, and significant fees they were able to pay, magazines also were able to attract the best writers and photographers in the country—people who came together to strengthen what would become the first national medium of entertainment, service, commentary, and issues.

By the 1950s, though, the magazine publishing industry had begun to transform once again. The emergence of television would change everything. As a new national medium, television would displace the general interest magazine with respect to audience appeal. Television was immediate and had great impact with its moving pictures. Moreover, television delivered a significantly larger audience to advertisers at a much cheaper cost per thousand.

LEADERSHIP FROM A "COPYCAT"

The editorial meeting started, as it often did, with a discussion of cover concepts. Typically a tense period in these meetings as *EM: Ebony Man* editors would try to sell the publisher on the stories they eventually would try to sell to the public. The late publisher John H. Johnson, always impatient at these times, finally broke in when an editor oversold, describing a story he was pitching as "cutting edge."

"I don't want to be cutting edge," Johnson admonished. "I've built a fortune on being the biggest copycat around."

Perhaps. But even though Johnson had established an African American media empire with Black interpretations of *Readers' Digest, Life,* and *TIME* magazines, he also helped usher in a new period of segmented magazine marketing that eventually spawned even more specialized racial and ethnic offerings. In the process, he promoted a strong and positive Black image to the nation and the financial viability of the African American consumer market among national advertisers.

In November 1942, *Negro Digest* was launched by Johnson, providing a collection of significant stories in the "Negro" experience, much as *Reader's Digest*

© 2014 THE ASSOCIATED PRESS

had been doing with a collection of general stories for its national audience. It was quite a financial struggle to get the new magazine off the ground, as Johnson had to borrow $500 on his mother's furniture for promotional postage. The investment paid off, as the first edition sold 3,000 copies, largely in its Chicago hometown. But the magazine would get a huge boost when Johnson convinced former first lady Eleanor Roosevelt to submit the first of a series of columns titled "If I Were a Negro," sympathizing with African American impatience for social change. The subsequent success of *Negro Digest* provided the cornerstone of a publishing house that would be worth an estimated $400 million in annual sales by the turn of the twenty-first century.

The pillar of the company would become *Ebony* magazine, launched in November 1945, with its oversized picture magazine format, much like *Life*. Unlike the other established magazines, though, *Negro Digest* and *Ebony* presented a positive picture of Black American life. In a way, this was in keeping with the tradition of the Black advocacy press, the newspapers, that for 115 years had promoted intellectual and social merit of the African American community in their push for social justice. The Johnson mission was summed up by his editors in the "Backstage" column of the inaugural issue of *Ebony*:

> We're rather jolly folks, we *Ebony* editors. We like to look at the zesty side of life. Sure you can get all hot and bothered about the race question (and don't think we don't), but not enough is said about all the swell things we Negroes can do and will accomplish. *Ebony* will try to mirror the happier side of Negro life—the positive, everyday achievements from Harlem to Hollywood.

In celebrating everyday Black achievement, commentator bell hooks later would say, the photo pages of *Ebony* became a site of resistance to the negative portrayal of African Americans that had characterized mainstream media coverage of Black people, when it existed at all. In addition to middle-class African Americans at work and at play much as any other middle-class families might be depicted, celebrities (with their impressive homes and pools and maids) also became a staple of the magazine. As a marketing matter, African Americans—as a racial minority—were seen as a very specialized segment, even though *Ebony* reached a general, family oriented audience. It was special because it was Black.

It is important to note, though, that the positive depiction of African American life and the great potential for success as shown by celebrity stories did more than simply inspire African Americans. It also helped to reframe the narrative on racial difference in America. Once national advertisers began to see Black people as potential consumers of washing machines and televisions and cars (with a great deal of personal prodding by Johnson), they began to advertise in *Ebony*. Then (again with a push by Johnson) they began to understand that

African American consumers were more likely to pay attention to ads that featured positive African American images. Black models began to appear in ads that increasingly were produced by a growing number of Black ad agencies and booked by an emerging group of Black modeling agencies. Thus, not only were the Johnson publications instrumental in framing a new narrative on racial identity, they also were transformative in related business areas.

Owing to *Ebony's* success, Johnson Publishing Company eventually would publish as many as a half dozen magazines (including the newsweekly, *Jet*), produce television shows, operate three radio stations, launch a book division and a cosmetics division, and erect a sleek multi-million dollar headquarters building in downtown Chicago, the hub for company offices in New York, Washington, Los Angeles, London, Paris, and in post-Apartheid Johannesburg.

While Johnson Publishing Company for years dominated the world of Black magazine publishing, it eventually would become a victim of its own success. With an increasing movement toward magazine specialization—a movement Johnson helped to lead—other publishers and advertisers began to see that the African American community was not monolithic. Much like all magazine readers, there were more specific communities of interest within the larger general Black consumer market *Ebony* reached.

By the 1970s, other magazines began to further segment the Black reading audience. Within months of each other in 1970, *Essence* (for African American women) and *Black Enterprise* (for African American professionals) were founded. For Johnson, once a pioneer in market segmentation, this development would present a new challenge. That challenge intensified with changing **demographics** and a social and political movement of the 1960s and 1970s that made younger African Americans less interested in stories merely about Black celebrities and achievement.

By the turn of the twenty-first century with even more specialized African American offerings like *Vibe*, a Black urban cultural magazine, *Ebony* struggled to remain relevant. For example, *Essence* (which called itself "a socially aware woman's service magazine whose purpose in life is to raise the level of expectation of black women and improve their self-esteem") and *Black Enterprise* ("For Black Men and Women Who Want to Get Ahead" in business and the professions) clearly were cutting into Johnson's readership and advertising base. Paid circulation for *Ebony* slipped from a high of 1.8 million to a reported 1.3 million and the price for advertising rates, once quoted at nearly $60,000 per page, was adjusted downward.

The problem was worsened by the company's slow transition online—as with so many other traditional print publications—starting first with a limited promotional site and eventually moving to provide full editions through an iPad app.

By 2011, new management and new editorial leadership had been installed (with former White House Social Secretary Desiree Rogers as CEO and former *Harper's Bazaar* editor Amy DuBois Barnett as *Ebony* Editor-in-Chief), helping to secure a new infusion of cash from minority investor JP Morgan, and raising hopes that the proud "copycat" that once helped lead the movement to segmentation once again could move forward in meeting future challenges.

Increased specialization   The magazine industry responded to the threat posed by television by turning increasingly away from general interest editorial content to a more specialized approach to both audiences and editorial. For the first half of the twentieth century, a golden age for magazines when popular publications like *Life* and *Look* could be found in 1 in 5 American homes, magazine publishers attempted to appeal to as broad an audience as possible with wide-ranging editorial content. The magazine truly was a mass medium.

But television delivered even greater mass—many more millions than even the biggest magazines. And even though the cost of thirty seconds of television advertising was far greater than the cost of a color page in the largest-circulating magazine, the cost for reaching a thousand of those television viewers made the new medium a much more economical buy.

Magazine publishers responded by narrowing their editorial approach and zeroing in on specific readers. Their argument was that, while 30 seconds of advertising on the popular TV show "Gunsmoke" might be a cheaper buy on a cost per thousand basis, an advertiser—say Maytag appliances—may not be interested in reaching all the "Gunsmoke" viewers. Yet, Maytag might find a more appealing audience and a more compatible editorial environment in a women's service magazine like *Good Housekeeping* or *Family Circle*. That appeal worked, ushering in yet another radical shift in magazine industry's business paradigm. Publishers touted their specialized editorial environment and the special characteristics of their audiences, which aligned with those precise qualities sought by advertisers, who increasingly wanted to target consumers.

It is essential for the aspiring magazine writer to understand the special interest business model that serves as the very foundation of the modern magazine—whether traditional print version or the emerging online editions. Knowing who the magazine is targeting and how its editorial content creates this specialized environment that appeals to both readers and advertisers is key to developing story ideas and writing in a voice that will appeal to very specific readers. Indeed, this understanding is where the writing process begins.

Let's take a closer look at the two targets of magazine publishers: readers and advertisers.

► MAGAZINE READERS: A SOPHISTICATED AUDIENCE

In developing an understanding of magazine readers, it is important first to have an appreciation of the differences between magazines and newspapers. Several of these differences are quite apparent. Magazines are printed on higher quality paper than are newspapers and tend to be valued more highly by readers and kept around longer. In fact, each copy sold likely is read by at least five additional people. (This **pass-along rate** is seen by advertisers as an added value.) Magazine articles are longer, provide greater depth and detail, take more time for writers and editors to prepare, and take more time for readers to absorb. Thus, there is an expectation that more thought, time, and research will be provided in magazine articles. This, in turn, means these pieces will be held to a higher standard of evaluation.

As important as anything else is the distinction between magazine and newspaper focus. While newspapers—for the most part—are focused on a specific geographical community, magazines are aimed at **communities of interests**. Magazine readers are connected by their values, beliefs, needs, and desires, more than their physical location.

When we speak of magazine readers, we think of two broad areas: demographics and psychographics. **Demographics** are characteristics. **Psychographics** are interests. As we will see, both areas of consideration are vital in developing an understanding of how best to reach these consumers—whether as an advertiser marketing products or services, or as a freelance writer marketing story ideas.

DEMOGRAPH-ICS: Reader characteristics, such as age, gender, and race.

Demographics   When it comes to magazine readership, demographics tell us something about the characteristics of the people who are consuming the magazine. There are general considerations with respect to the characteristics of all magazine readers. Then there are the specific characteristics of particular magazine readers. As we have seen, the move to greater and greater specialization in magazine production means that the readership for a given magazine increasingly has become narrowly defined. Each magazine has developed its editorial mission around the need to reach very specific groups.

PSYCHOGRAPH-ICS: Reader interests.

So, with demographics, we consider such variables as age, race, ethnicity, education level, and income level of the readership. Generally speaking, magazine readers tend to be better educated, better paid professionals, according to industry research. Each magazine readership, though, will have its own specific demographic profile within that broader range.

Psychographics   Here we consider the needs, interests, and attitudes of readers, particularly as they translate into lifestyle choices and consumer behavior. Ultimately, these all connect to the information demanded by a particular group of people. Key to their connection are the values they share. Understanding how this plays out in the connection of individuals to a community of interests requires a quick look at how people identify themselves by the values they share. There are two levels of consideration here, according to social scientists, for there are both primary and secondary values. **Primary values** go to such areas as political disposition (liberal or conservative); financial and economic attitude (cautious or aggressive); social outlook (inclusive or exclusionary); and lifestyle preference (reserved or adventurous). With **secondary values**, we consider the needs and interests of persons within the set of primary values. These secondary values would include information; entertainment; service; motivation/inspiration; social bonding; and health, fitness, and grooming.

It is important to note that publishers and editors consider both the primary and secondary values in continuously thinking about the audience makeup and needs. The primary values go to the reader characteristics, which will be considered in the overall approach of the magazine. For instance, people with more conservative political views, who are more cautious economically and reserved in their lifestyle choices, likely will be more comfortable with a more sober tone and serious-looking magazine that likely is dominated by text rather than art. With respect to the secondary values, editors always are mindful of the interests and needs of the readers in order to shape content—specific stories—that will serve those interests, and meet those needs. These often are referred to as the **pillars** of the magazine, because they form the very structure that holds the entire book together for a specific audience—the content that must be present in order to maintain the appeal.

PILLAR: The editorial composition of the magazine—those topics that make up or are touched on in every issue, like celebrity, fashion, travel, food, grooming.

So, the primary values set the context for the entire magazine in which the secondary values, or pillars, provide the guidance for content. In other words, if you value entertainment, there will be distinctions between the type of entertainment you appreciate depending on your political disposition, financial outlook, social attitude, and lifestyle preference. Although there might be some overlap between conservative and liberal consumers, there often are differences with respect to specific choices that are made.

TINA BROWN: GAME CHANGER

During the last quarter of the twentieth century, no magazine editor wielded more influence or had a greater impact on the industry than the British ex pat Tina Brown. At a time when American magazines were becoming increasingly specialized and long-form narrative writing was nearly given up for dead, Brown presided over the re-imagining of two general interest titles in the Condé Nast stable—*Vanity Fair* and *The New Yorker*—that offered sprawling articles on a relatively wide range of topics. In the process, she also is credited with breathing new life in the magazine form and ushering in the industry's second golden age.

Brown rose to prominence in her native England when she was tapped at the tender age of 25 to be editor-in-chief of the British glossy magazine *Tatler*, which Condé Nast had purchased in 2002. As the legend goes, Brown ramped up the publication's youth appeal by infusing its coverage of the UK's celebrities with wit and style. Wit, style, and youth appeal were just the qualities Condé Nast chairman S.I. Newhouse was looking to inject in his revival of *Vanity Fair*, which was a fashion magazine in its early twentieth century incarnation.

The old *Vanity Fair* was shuttered in 1936, but in the early 1980s, Newhouse sought to resurrect it as a general interest magazine focusing on America's glitterati—a term that also became central in the magazine's vocabulary. But Newhouse needed the right editorial steward to pull off his vision. Two editors were hired and dispatched in rapid succession after the magazine's re-launch in 1983. Following Brown's successful remaking of *Tatler*, another venerable publication took on an entirely new form in the late twentieth century. Newhouse whisked Brown from London to take the *Vanity Fair* helm. Though British (or maybe because of her British pedigree), she proved to have impressive instincts for what Americans wanted in high-toned, well-reported gossip and scandal.

Under Brown, *Vanity Fair* quickly became the most talked-about magazine of the 1980s and early 1990s. She hired famous writers—Gail Sheehy, William Styron, Peter J. Boyer—and some who'd never written before, like the movie producer Dominick Dunne. And she paid them exceptionally well, ratcheting up the market value for blue chip magazine writers across the industry. They, in turn, produced salacious stories about problems and peccadilloes of the rich and celebrated presented as lilting literary works that read more like fiction. Brown's *Vanity Fair* may have trafficked in the same editorial waters as *People* and *Us Weekly*, but its stories were exhaustively reported and buffed to a high gloss.

But Brown's *Vanity Fair* was not all froth. She also infused the book with coverage of politics and foreign affairs. An issue of *Vanity Fair* was like eavesdropping on a chic dinner party where the guests discussed everything from the messiest million-dollar divorce to crisis in the Middle East.

With a flair for generating buzz, Brown also turned cover shoots into editorial events. She allowed celebrated photographers like Annie Leibovitz, Herb Ritts, and Bruce Webber to spend freely and coax American movie stars and high-profile performers into poses and scenarios that poked fun at their own celebrated images. Two of the most provocative of these were a Leibovitz portrait of the actress Demi Moore, who in 1991 appeared on the cover naked and very pregnant (starting something of a trend in magazine publishing). One year later, Moore was naked again on a *Vanity Fair* cover, only this time *sheathed* in a painted-on body suit by artist Joanne Gair.

The magic Brown had worked on *Vanity Fair*—in three years circulation rose from an anemic 200,000 to nearly 1.2 million—made her the toast and the envy of the magazine industry. *Vanity Fair* won four National Magazine Awards during her reign and ad pages increased 220 percent. But S.I. Newhouse didn't allow Brown to rest on those laurels. Another Condé Nast title was in need of saving.

In 1992, Newhouse asked Brown to take the reins of *The New Yorker*, the venerable general interest title known for its long literary tradition and sardonic cartoons. Though the magazine—which was credited with inventing such journalistic staples as the personality profile—had a loyal and very vocal following of intellectuals and academics, its readership and ad pages were dwindling, and its editors seemed content with the magazine's detachment from and disdain for almost anything remotely related to popular culture.

Brown's charge was to drag the magazine into the contemporary cultural conversation while retaining its elegant literary tone and intelligent approach to long-form narrative non-fiction. Her arrival sparked a wave of defections and firings of some of the magazine's stalwart writers and editors. But Brown also enlisted a raft of new writers, including David Remnick, Henrik Hertzberg, Malcolm Gladwell, Jeffrey Toobin, and Anthony Lane, all of whom would stamp their mark on the magazine and give it a fresh, new, culturally and politically relevant voice. She enlivened the magazine's pages and ramped up its buzz factor by adding photography and commissioning controversial illustrations that pushed *New Yorker* covers beyond their traditional posture of whimsy and satire into the realm of in-your-face social commentary.

The changes worked. Under Brown, *The New Yorker* became a cultural and journalistic success (winning 10 National Magazine Awards during her tenure), though still a money loser. She decamped in 1998—lured away by Bob Weinstein of Miramax to start her own magazine from scratch. At that time, *The New Yorker* was still losing $11 million a year, though circulation was nearing 1 million.

Brown's next venture, *Talk*, was designed to shake up the media world with its mix of high and low culture, featuring high-profile individuals from the worlds of politics, letters, and entertainment. With frank revelations from its lineup of luminaries, *Talk* was supposed to be a conversation starter. But the conversations—along with the economy—ground to a halt following the terrorist attacks of September 11, 2001. The magazine fell victim to both a recession and the changing mood in a country ramping up for two wars.

Following her first high-profile failure and her dabbling in book publishing and television, Brown emerged once again, this time in the digital sphere. In 2008, with backing by broadcast mogul Barry Diller, *The Daily Beast* was launched. It is an online magazine that is a storehouse of news, commentary, and content culled from a variety of new and legacy media. In late 2010, *The Daily Beast* merged with the floundering *Newsweek* magazine, providing cache for the former and a lifeline for the latter whose demise seemed imminent. Brown was installed as the editor-in-chief of the newly dubbed The Newsweek Daily Beast Company. The combination was not enough to change the fortunes of *Newsweek*. In July 2012, it was announced that the company would cease production of the print magazine in December of that year. And while some blame Brown for the ultimate demise of *Newsweek*, most acknowledge that the title was a lost cause well before the merger and Brown's valiant, though ultimately unsuccessful, attempt to rescue it does not dim her influence or import as one of the most important magazine makers of the late twentieth and early twenty-first centuries.

▶ VALUES MODEL

In determining an editorial lineup that appeals to readers month after month, we have developed a Values Model that helps to visualize the connection between audience values and content designed to address those interests and needs. In developing this model, we have looked at those secondary values that will bring readers to a specific magazine. Then we connect specific content areas to those values to make sure we are providing something of interest to the reader each and every issue. As a visual, consider a bar graph where the vertical axis represents "values" and the horizontal axis represents "content." On the vertical axis, you can plot the secondary values that reflect the readership interests of a particular magazine. For example, if information, entertainment, service, and health are key secondary values, they will be listed along this vertical line. Then, on the horizontal axis, there will be a list of broad content areas that correspond to the identified secondary values. For example, music, television, film reviews could be content listings that correspond to entertainment. Investment advice might be a financial content area that corresponds with service. Medical content could correspond with information, service, and health.

Table 2.1 provides an illustration of how the process works for a hypothetical magazine that is built around service values, or pillars. An articles editor for this magazine is aware of the reader interest in current information about such areas as, say, entertainment offerings and health and fitness, among the topic areas identified along the values axis. In planning

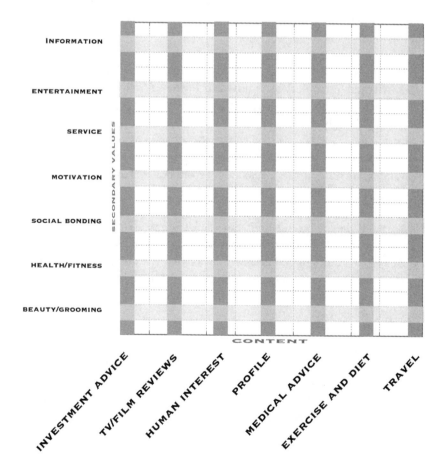

each issue, there will be a great deal of consideration given to serving this interest by scheduling specific articles, identified along the content axis. While this type of graphic might not necessarily be used by the editor, he will be aware of the points of intersection between specific story ideas that match up with needs and interests of his readers. In so doing, he will continue to satisfy those needs and interests and keep the readers coming back for more. The successful writer also must consider these variables in order to develop story ideas that get published.

Obviously, the specific content areas are determined on the basis of the demographic and psychographic profile of the readership. While one group might value financial content under service, another might be more interested in service stories about food preparation, or auto repairs. Also, the primary values will set the overall (liberal/conservative; reserved/adventurous) voice and tone of the magazine, the context of its presentation and style.

Reading between the lines   It is important to *know* the magazine before beginning to shape story ideas. The better you come to understand the magazine, the better prepared you are to develop story ideas and produce them successfully for publication in that magazine. But how is that done?

Certainly, you can learn a great deal about the readers of particular magazines by reading the blurbs submitted to *Writer's Market* by the magazine editors and, of course, the articles that are published in the magazine. In some ways, though, these can be abstractions in that they are subject to your interpretation. We suggest that you check all sources of reader information cumulatively. First, read the descriptive blurb that is published either in *Writer's Market*, on the magazine's website, or included in the writer's guidelines that are put out by most magazines.

Next, look at the magazine's online media kit. These are promotional materials designed to tell advertisers who the magazine is targeting, but they can be helpful guides to potential writers as well. The media kit will contain the magazine's mission statement, which will define the audience and suggest the magazine's editorial pillars—the coverage areas that it deems most important to its readers.

You also should take a look at the articles and the way they are framed. Absorb the language that is used, the imagery employed, the length of the sentences, and so forth. All of this information will tell you something about the level of sophistication of the audience, as well as the type of information the audience demands from the magazine.

SLATE AND SALON USHER IN A BRAVE NEW WORLD

While the digital sphere is chock full of websites that borrow heavily from the magazine publishing playbook—with their curated content and niched audiences—it is two pioneering, broad-based media properties that helped shape the digital magazine landscape. *Slate* and *Salon* are general interest webzines that cover everything from politics to pop culture, and, as such, are something of a throwback to earlier magazines. Their coverage is eclectic, touching on the most topical news, people, and events of the day. But they do so by employing a combination of traditional storytelling techniques and the interactive tools and multi-media that differentiate the lean-back print experience from the lean-forward web experience.

As important as anything else, these two publications set the example for other magazine publishers to follow. Once upon a time, the online presence for most magazines was limited to promotional sites, designed merely to sell single copies of the magazines or, perhaps, subscriptions. Now, thanks to the example of success of *Slate* and *Salon*, publishers, like Hearst, have entire divisions dedicated to developing new content, as well as "re-purposing" content from print editions, and adding the full range of media—including video clips—to augment storytelling. New digital delivery systems—like the wildly successful Zinio—have made it possible for digital readers and tablet users to have both a lean-back and lean-forward experience all at once.

For the writer now, the brave new challenge is thinking of the full range of storytelling possibilities across platforms.

SLATE. Founded in 1996, by Michael Kingsley, a former editor at *The New Republic, Slate* is updated daily with news, features, slide shows, and a variety of interactive essays. Its roster of contributors has included high-profile writers like the late Christopher Hitchens, as well as Anne Applebaum, Tim Wu, and other notables like former New York Governor Eliot Spitzer. Its focus on assembling the glitterati under its URL makes *Slate* an unlikely destination for up-and-coming writers. This is an invitation-only virtual party, and you have to write your way in climbing the ranks of traditional media or establishing yourself as an expert in a particular domain.

SALON. Though it bills itself as an arts and culture webzine, *Salon* is much more. Like its chief competitor, *Slate*, it covers a wide variety of current affairs, from books and music to politics. *Salon* launched in 1995 and established the model for commercial Internet ventures—a model built largely on the support of advertisers, as is the case with traditional print media. It has yet to turn a profit and often has struggled to stay afloat. While *Salon* has its share of celebrated contributing writers, it also has attempted, with varying degrees of success, to cultivate and curate new voices, on both its blogs and comment boards. Though robust, these efforts have sometimes proven to be unwieldy, with discussions spiraling out of control and comments degenerating into vicious attacks. *Salon's* finances and future are uncertain, but it remains an influential presence in the digital space.

There is another step, though, and that is to "read between the lines," in a manner of speaking. This is done by "reading" the ads that are published in the magazine and analyzing them. Certainly, the types of products and services featured say something about reader interests, but this will be just the beginning of your analysis. It is important also to consider the kind of language that is used to reach the reader. What kind of imagery is used? If there are people included in the ad, who are these people? What can you determine about their age, diversity, lifestyle? By the time you review a dozen or so ads, you will have a profile of the reader that brings you so much closer to understanding how you, the writer, might engage in a conversation with her. After all, advertisers have spent considerable amounts on market research to make sure they know exactly how to reach the specific audience they seek. This is an easy way for you to take advantage of that research in determining your own strategy for reaching that audience with insightful articles that are designed to appeal to readers.

As we will see in subsequent chapters, it is important to develop this ability to "read" the reader in ways that will facilitate the conversation you will have as a writer. You will come to understand where these conversations can be conducted—specific magazine markets, how to focus the topic, and, as important as anything, how to convince an editor that you are capable of handling it all.

Chapter Two Review

▶ KEY TERMS

- B2B
- community of interests
- consumer magazines
- demographics
- horizontal publications
- muckraking
- pass-along rate
- pillar
- primary values
- psychographics
- secondary values
- vertical publications
- yellow journalism

▶ SELECTED READING

Abrahamson, David. *Magazine Made America: The Cultural Transformation of the Postwar Periodical.* Cresskill, NJ: Hampton Press, 1996. Abrahamson provides a comprehensive examination of the history of the magazine industry since WWII.

Blanchard, Margaret A. *History of the Mass Media in the United States.* New York: Routledge, 1998. Blanchard's wide-ranging survey of American media covers everything from the founding of the nation's first newspaper in 1690 to the media impact on culture and conflict up to the dawn of the twenty-first century.

Janello, Amy; Jones, Brennon. *The American Magazine.* New York: Harry N. Abrams, 1991. Janello and Jones explore the history of American consumer magazines in this lavish pictorial volume that was commissioned by Magazine Publishers of America and the American Society of Magazine Editors.

Johnson, John H. *Succeeding Against the Odd: The Autobiography of a Great American Businessman.* New York: Warner Books, 1992. Autobiography of the influential publisher and entrepreneur.

Peterson, Theodore A. *Magazines in the 20th Century.* Champaign-Urbana, IL: University of Illinois Press, 1964. For many years, Peterson's was the definitive examination of twentieth century magazines.

▶ WEB RESOURCES

http://www.magazine.org/ Official website of the Association of Magazine Media (formerly the Magazine Publishers of America), a non-profit organization that represents more than 170 American and 30 international media companies that publish across print and digital platforms.

http://www.magazine.org/asme The website of the American Society of Magazine Editors, an offshoot of the Association of Magazine Media. ASME members are editorial leaders of the nation's major business and trade publications.

http://www.abmassociation.com/abm Official website of the American Business Media Association, the non-profit organization of business-to-business media.

http://journalists.org/ The official website of Online News Association, a non-profit membership organization for writers and editors working in the digital sphere.

Magazine Markets

▶ OVERVIEW

As discussed in the previous chapter, the magazine industry has undergone a number of significant changes over the course of its more than 200-year history leading to, among other things, a much more specialized focus among the many offerings. Even within certain categories, or "markets," we see fine distinctions that set one magazine apart from all others in its group. An editor is keenly aware of his magazine's well-honed identity and the very selective readership—the community of interest—attracted to that magazine. It is imperative that the freelance writer also becomes aware of the distinctions in successfully navigating a path to publication.

In the interest of helping to sort it all out, we have set out in this chapter a discussion of a few magazine markets, which will illustrate the nature of modern magazine publishing. Broadly speaking, these are areas that can be welcoming to freelance writers, although you will note that some listings here are considered "destination markets" and only accessible to proven writers—those with a record of published material up the chain of related publications.

Appreciating this dynamic will help an emerging writer operate a lot more efficiently in developing a strategy for publishing success.

LEARNING OBJECTIVES

1. The distinctions between certain leading magazine categories or "markets."

2. How editors work to distinguish their magazines from others in the same categories.

3. The importance of fine-tuning topics for specific magazines within certain markets.

4. How to begin shaping your writing strategy.

5. The importance of charting a path up the chain of related magazines to your ultimate destination market.

▶ SELECTIVE MARKETS

No matter where you wind up publishing, it is essential that you know something about the leading titles in certain categories, as the editors you deal with are going to expect that you know how the competition is sizing up. Approach this new level of understanding with complete openness. An important consideration to keep in mind in this regard is that you don't have to be a man to publish in a men's magazine, or a woman to publish in a women's magazine. Nor do you have to be a waste management worker to write for special publications in this field. Certainly, the magazine is a focused, targeted medium. But the rules of journalism apply and good reporting in researching an idea—along with the ability to appreciate distinctive magazine voice in telling the story—will be much more important than gender, occupation, or even locale in getting published.

HITTING THE TARGET

It is important to keep in mind that contemporary magazine publishing—and by extension freelance writing—is all about targeting. Industry observers agree that there are four factors to consider in determining the selective market appeal that magazines strive to achieve. They are the **magazine focus**, the **magazine niche**, the **audience composition,** and the **audience interests**.

MAGAZINE FOCUS. Another way to consider the focus is to think about category. So, the focus would be whether the magazine is categorized as a men's or women's magazine; or a business, entertainment, travel, or service magazine, among other categories.

MAGAZINE NICHE. Within the category, there often will be special topic areas covered by the magazine. So, a men's magazine might look topically at sports, fashion, or health. Its style of presentation also would be considered here, so that a hip, irreverent style would distinguish one men's fashion magazine from one that is more traditional or serious in its presentation.

AUDIENCE COMPOSITION. Here, we consider the demographics of the audience; the characteristics that include gender, age, race, and ethnicity.

AUDIENCE INTERESTS. Here, we consider the psychographics of the readers to determine whether, within a specific niche, a particular audience will want to read a particular story about a specific topic.

▶ MEN'S MAGAZINES

The men's magazine market is about more than babes, booze, and balls. The myriad titles in this category also present some of the most elegant literary non-fiction and the most incisive journalism in all *magazinedom*. True, you'll find plenty of service in these books—everything from how to shave to how to make the perfect martini—but writing for these magazines also means knowing which topics will appeal to the erudite *Esquire* man and which are better suited for the *ab*sessed *Men's Health* guy.

In the upper echelon, these magazines rely heavily on nationally known writers to fill their feature wells. The front of these books is the entry point for new writers, usually through short, service-oriented department pieces. But tight, witty essays that are novel expressions of what it means to be a modern man have a shot—no matter how long a shot—at getting attention and helping you get a foot in the editor's door at both the big glossies and their online brethren.

Getty Images

Esquire   Literary, but not exactly stuffy, *Esquire* considers itself a guide for the contemporary man of the world. Or, as the magazine's time-honored motto boasts, "Man At His Best." Not as bawdy as *Maxim*, nor as fashion-obsessed as *GQ* or *Details*, *Esquire* is where au courant men (although 30 percent of its audience is female) turn to discover what they should be doing, reading, and wearing. Yet it also covers the major issues and personalities of the day. Traditionally, its tone definitely has been more sophisticated. No surprise, given its established reputation early on as a book for tweedy intellectuals. But since the advent of *Maxim* and *Men's Health*, both of which were game-changers in the men's magazine category, *Esquire* has learned to let down its hair. These days you'll find more hip, urban vernacular, and trendy references throughout its pages. Even here, though, the jargon is used in clever, intelligent writing appropriate for the specific subject matter.

Breaking into *Esquire* isn't easy. Its feature well, which is home to award-winning narrative non-fiction, is dominated by big-name writers who cover topics and people of national significance. But new writers can elbow their way into *Esquire* with shorter pieces in the front-of-the-book (which takes its name from the magazine's "Man at His Best" or MAHB motto). In this section, service reigns supreme. Here *Esquire* tells its readers how to cook, how to dress, as well as how, when, and where to make love. The editors are always looking for fresh takes on men's lifestyle. New products, as well as up-and-coming designers, chefs, architects, and other artists, also are featured. Successful publication in other magazines also can provide a path to the *Esquire* destination. For example, *Chicago* magazine, one of the most successful city publications, has provided a gateway to *Esquire* for several writers.

Esquire.com also can be a viable entry point for newbies. Service prevails here, too, but because the website is so voracious and is updated frequently, its editors are far more willing to consider short, topical features from writers who've yet to have a breakthrough piece in another national magazine.

GQ   Originally known as *Gentlemen's Quarterly*, *GQ* is more than a style bible. While it is true that looking good is the magazine's principal preoccupation, the magazine covers more than just Versace suits and Ferragamo shoes. *GQ* editors see the book as a comprehensive men's lifestyle magazine, but its target reader is definitely a man who places a premium on looking good, which is why the feature well and most of the back-of-the-book are splashed with lavish fashion spreads. Even the mini-profiles of the young actors and athletes sprinkled through the book are merely excuses to swath these celebs in designer threads.

Like *Esquire*, *GQ*'s narrative features are presided over mostly by writers who regularly win National Magazine Awards. While fashion and style are *GQ*'s bread and butter, the magazine also serves up a healthy helping of their in-depth coverage of national affairs and world events. These readers may be clothes horses, the editors seem to maintain, but they want to be kept abreast of more than just Alexander Wang's latest line. They also want the smart, literary storytelling for which *GQ* also has become known.

The magazine's celebrity cover stories (basically an excuse to showcase a well-known personality in trendy attire) are typically awarded to writers with a track record of chronicling the lives and careers of A-list actors, musicians, and athletes.

But new writers can crack *GQ* with a fresh take on the lifestyle topics that fill its front-of-the-book departments, many of which are subsumed under the "Manual" heading. Manual is all about what to do or not do to be a chic and sophisticated twenty-first century man. There's also "The Punch List," a roundup of pop culture tidbits that includes everything from movies and books to sports and cars.

Men's Health   Sex and six-pack abs are the lifeblood of *Men's Health*. The essence of this magazine is the notion that guys who are fit and healthy live longer and get laid more often. Though much of the magazine is devoted to exercise routines, diet tips, and advice columns touting how to perform the perfect dumbbell curl or how to perfect the surefire pickup line, the editors view *Men's Health* as a holistic lifestyle magazine. Its editorial pillars include fashion, gadgets, travel, and entertainment. In addition to its cover story on a celebrity who embodies the *Men's Health* ethos, the feature well includes essays and narrative stories that demonstrate how to improve your life mentally, physically, and sexually.

The tone of *Men's Health* is casual and fun. The editors certainly are serious about living healthily. That commitment is embodied by *Men's Health* editor David Zinczenko, the face of the magazine and a former round mound whose *Eat This, Not That* books are popular entreaties to give up processed sugar and saturated fats. But the *Men's Health* voice is not that of your nagging significant other; it's your best bud encouraging you to join him in the gym and maybe for a quick drink afterward.

The editors of *Men's Health* are more likely than the editors of other high-profile men's magazines to consider over-the-transom feature ideas from aspiring contributors. If you have an original take on a topic that is in this book's wheelhouse, you have a good shot at muscling your way into *Men's Health*. And, of course, the success you experience with published articles in this magazine becomes the steppingstone to others up the line.

Maxim   *Maxim* is as lustful and as beer-drenched as a frat house. You can tell that from the covers, which always feature a scantily clad starlet gazing seductively into the camera. Make no mistake about it, this magazine is all about the things, experiences, and relationships that make being young and male fun—hot girls, hot cars, sports, video games, and booze. But beyond the toys and the T&A, there's a method to this madness. The *Maxim* man wants to live life to the fullest and views this book not as a preachy guide to achieving that, but as an acknowledgment and affirmation that it's okay to cling to your animal house attitude for a little while longer.

The key to the door of *Maxim* is to understand the voice and its rapid-fire delivery of one-liners. The joke is vital here. *Maxim* editors look for ideas that combine service delivered with a witty, racy take. Think of a Judd Apatow movie in print form and you pretty much have the tone of *Maxim*. Bro' speak abounds, but it can't seem forced. Yet the editors realize that writing funny is hard, which is why they are known as the most heavy-handed rewriters in the industry. And they'll tell you that, too.

Don't be discouraged, though. Getting in the book—mostly in the front—is not as challenging as it may seem. Think babes, brew, and cool playthings—the more expensive the better—and you're in the *Maxim* zone. Just don't get married to every word in your original draft. Chances are, it will get *Maximized* before it's finalized.

Men's Journal   Take a dash of *Esquire*, mix in a bit of *Men's Health*, and layer that over the high-toned adventure magazine *Outside* and you have *Men's Journal*, a combination of experiential travel and literary lifestyle packaged for the Baby Boomer who enjoys golf, skiing, and whitewater rafting, or at least hopes to enjoy those things one day.

The *Men's Journal* man aspires to have the heart rate of Lance Armstrong and actually would consider dropping three grand for a Cannondale Synapse Carbon 3 racing bike if he ever really decides to take up biking again. The *Men's Journal* guy is serious about his adventure sports—though maybe not as serious as the *Outside* guy (or woman), who tends to be a bit younger and probably a bit more inclined to actually participate in the activities—running, biking, water sports—that are the staples of that magazine. The *Men's Journal* man's attachment is a bit more romantic. He fancies himself as still active, and still hits the links or the tennis court, but he also loves *reading* about adventure, which explains the magazine's heavy emphasis on sterling, experiential prose.

Here, the feature well is all about the experience—first-person accounts of man conquering mountain, water, desert, forest. The narratives are thrilling, capturing in vivid detail the sense of danger and accomplishment in the journey. The writers are the story and their objective is to take the reader along for every step of the gripping voyage.

But *Men's Journal* is a lifestyle magazine as well. The front-of-the-book is filled with tips on cooking, dressing, and staying fit, filtered through the lens of the youngish Baby Boomer. There's also a wealth of reviews of the very expensive gear and gadgets required for adventure travel—from kayaks and canoes to tents and tennis rackets.

And there are the essays and short FOB takes about men of adventure, as well as treatises on being a man old enough and successful enough to afford this pricey lifestyle but struggling to make time for it in his high-pressured world. While the experiential features and celebrity profiles may be out of reach for most writers who are new to the magazine (unless you happen to be or know of an adventure traveler with a great tale to tell), the service pieces and short essays and profiles provide an opportunity for new writers to break into *Men's Journal.*

Details   Often considered the younger brother of its Condé Nast stable mate, *GQ*, *Details* has a slightly more salacious and a hipper tone. It features a raft of personal offerings about the unusual *sexcapades* of young men about town—some of them writers who are new to the book. Pop culture is a huge editorial pillar, too. Trends in music, art, culture, and fashion play a huge part of the editorial makeup. The magazine's pages are replete with adoring images of metrosexual pop and music stars and androgynous models. But its humor veers toward the locker room variety.

Unlike *GQ*, which features only well-established writers, *Details* is a bit more accessible to writers who are trying to break into the big time. Its celebrity cover stories and fashion spreads are out of reach for newbies. But anyone with a novel pop culture piece and/or a good sex story could crack these pages.

► WOMEN'S MAGAZINES

Women's magazines dominate the industry. The offerings range from venerable giants like *Ladies' Home Journal* and *Good Housekeeping* to third-wave feminist titles like *Bitch* and *Bust*. The landscape breaks down into three categories: women's service; women's lifestyle, fashion, fitness; and the relatively new "magalogs." But there is so much editorial overlap that the distinctions among these magazines have become increasingly blurred. Still, if you're going to try to write for one of these titles, it's important to understand approximately where they reside in the magazine universe.

Women's service   These are among the oldest and most celebrated titles in the business. They were once referred to as the **Seven Sisters** at a time when, obviously, there were only seven of them: *McCall's, Ladies' Home Journal, Good Housekeeping, Redbook, Women's Day, Family Circle,* and *Better Homes & Gardens*. Gone now is *McCall's*, but its surviving sisters have been joined on the newsstand by a pair of eponymous celebrity magazines, *Martha Stewart Living* and *O, The Oprah Magazine*, and a juggernaut from Time, Inc., *Real Simple*.

Bloomberg via Getty Images

SEVEN SISTERS: The seven original women's service magazines.

Ladies' Home Journal   *LHJ*, like most of its sisters, is more than just a guide for homemakers. From its start, *LHJ* has tackled a wide range of issues pertinent to the wives and mothers who comprise the bulk of its audience. (As far back as 1906 the magazine published an article on the scourge of venereal disease. And, as we write in Chapter 2, the magazine was front and center in the muckraking investigative exposes of the turn of the twentieth century with its examination of medical hoaxes.) Yes, homemaking, child-rearing, recipes, and beauty tips are editorial pillars. But *LHJ*, considered the more serious of the traditional women's service books, also traditionally tackles issues like recovering from breast cancer, coping with a child who has Down syndrome, and, more recently, families struggling to get back on their feet during the recession.

The thing to remember when writing about serious issues for *LHJ*—and this is the case with most of the women's service books—is that stories need to offer hope to the readers. Tragic endings won't fly. Service is the hallmark of these magazines, so readers want to know that they (or a loved one) can overcome the adversities depicted in the stories.

Boxes with how-to tips and resource recommendations are also staples of the magazine. It is essential that aspiring *LHJ* writers consider the service aspect of any proposed story.

Good Housekeeping   From its inception, *Good Housekeeping* set out to be an advocate of the American homemaker. But the magazine is more than its famous seal of approval. It also has been a champion of women's issues, particularly as they related to the goods and services women buy for their families. It was an early champion of product testing and stumped for things like safe food. It features personal stories about women's trials and triumphs with dieting, parenting, marriage, and illness. And it strives to make the modern homemaker's life easier and safer. *Good Housekeeping* relies on a stable of regular contributors for most of its print content.

Women's Day and *Family Circle*   Both of these books focus pretty exclusively on domesticity. They're full of recipes, do-it-yourself decorating tips, diets, fashion and beauty tips, advice about child-rearing, party planning, health and nutrition. *WD* is a little easier to break into, as it does feature the occasional personal story and relationship/sex stories—especially in its online edition (the print product is much less racy).

Martha Stewart Living   The doyenne of domesticity, Martha Stewart has stamped her name and her signature guidance on this magazine. It is a wish book for those women who aspire to be like Martha. It is full of Martha Stewart's ideas for sprucing up your home, your recipes, your holiday, and everyday celebrations. Don't expect to break in, though. These ideas are all vetted and tested by the *MSL* staff.

O, The Oprah Magazine   Oprah bills her self-titled magazine as a guide to "living your best life." Essentially that means trying to replicate Oprah's life on *your* budget. The emphasis is on finding the resilience within yourself to be the best you can be. The editors try to capture in print the spirit of Winfrey's now-departed talk show. In addition to featuring the lineup of experts Oprah made famous—Dr. Phil, Nate Berkus, Suze Orman—the magazine also features stories by real people who successfully have seized their destinies or tapped into their reservoirs of inner strength and spirituality to live their best lives. Often, these stories are contributed by writers who are new to the magazine, with the "LYBL" front section providing a great break-in possibility. The key is to focus on Oprah's philosophy of making the most of your personal gifts and, of course, your personal connections. Imagine a magazine changing the entire masthead for a June (Father's Day) edition to pay tribute to dads with references to the relationships, like the one for the top spot, Founder and Editorial Director, "Vernon Winfrey's daughter." (That would be Oprah.)

Real Simple   This is the ultimate how-to book. Its clean and simple design mirrors the clean and simple life it tries to help its readers achieve. A cross between a lifestyle and a service book, *Real Simple* provides tips on maintaining order and balance in a life complicated by work, family, and social obligations. In many ways it is the anti-Martha Stewart. *Real Simple* tries to show its audience that there are better ways to spend one's time than weaving your own placemats and churning your own butter. Like *MSL*, however, the ideas in *Real Simple* are largely staff generated and the stories are staff executed.

Women's lifestyle   The women's lifestyle magazines include some of the most celebrated and denigrated titles in all of *magazinedom*: celebrated because many of them are hugely successful and have withstood tremendous changes in fashion and taste to remain cultural touchstones; denigrated because they often are accused of promoting inaccessible beauty standards and notions of happiness based on getting and pleasing a man. But these magazines continue to connect with their audiences in ways that other magazines might only hope to.

Glamour   Glamour is the modern young woman's guide to fashion, dieting, grooming, relationships, and careers. Its target audience consists of rising professionals who are attempting to navigate life in the city (and these are largely city girls). *Glamour* attempts to provide her with role models whose success she can emulate, and with tons of tips for looking her best as she climbs the career ladder. Its *Glamour* Dos & Don'ts are the ultimate how-tos for looking good.

Glamour is heavy on service—lots of charts, charticles, and tip boxes. In addition to its celebrity cover stories, the feature well includes personal stories of women on the move and tips for surviving life's great challenges: being a broke bridesmaid; asking for a raise; getting over the guy who cheated on you. The senior editors have specific coverage areas, such as health, beauty, or lifestyle. And they each get thousands of story pitches each month. They rarely assign any of those ideas to writers with whom they've never worked. But many young freelancers break in by demonstrating in their pitches that they understand the *Glamour* reader and the editors' approach to reaching her.

Cosmopolitan   Cosmo catches a lot of flak for its unabashed emphasis on sex, specifically for its focus on getting and pleasing a man. But if you think that's all this Hearst publication is about, you're actually missing the point. Underneath its obsession with orgasm is a belief that young women can take control of their own sexuality, that they needn't wait for a guy to make the first move. It's not exactly a feminist message (though some have

Getty Images

made the case that *Cosmo's* ethos is rooted in feminism), but there is an underlying message about empowerment that runs through the magazine.

In between the sex, the magazine covers fashion, diet, nightlife, and careers. Most of the story ideas are generated in-house and assigned to writers with whom the assigning editor has an ongoing relationship (usually from her work at a previous magazine). Story pitches can get you on the magazine's radar, however, so don't be afraid to pitch. Just keep the *Cosmo* girl and her active libido in mind.

Marie Claire   *Marie Claire* is Hearst's other women's lifestyle magazine. It is not as sex-crazed as its sister, *Cosmo*, but like a lot of women's lifestyle magazines it does devote a fair amount of editorial real estate to sex and relationships. Its other main editorial pillar is fashion. No big surprise there, since the magazine was born in France and is featured heavily in Lifetime Television's design competition series "Project Runway." But as a lifestyle magazine, *Marie Claire* also features a wide range of stories about lives and challenges of young, professional women. Many of those stories are submitted by relatively unknown writers. *Marie Claire* is a slightly easier book to break into than some of its competitors, including its sister publication, *Cosmo*. And, of course, publication here can lead to future publishing possibilities in other magazines.

▶ SHELTER MAGAZINES

The shelter magazine category has been especially vulnerable to the fits and starts of the nation's volatile housing market. Several high profile titles— *Metropolitan Home*, *Domino*, and *Cottage Living*—were shuttered as the early twenty-first century housing boom went bust. But the closing of some traditional print titles has resulted in opportunities online as new digital shelter magazines have arisen to fill the void.

There are few opportunities for new-to-the market writers in the world of traditional shelter magazines. Most of those editors rely on a steady stream of writers with experience covering home décor and gardening. The newer digital offerings, however, have a broader scope—some incorporate fashion as well as home décor—and are more open to contributions from feature writers and bloggers new to the sphere.

Architectural Digest   *AD* is a showcase for the well-appointed palaces of the nation's elite. It is a Condé Nast title and, like a lot of titles in the CN stable, it features the work of the nation's most celebrated individuals, in this case architects, contractors, and interior designers. Wealth and status are on display here, and it takes a certain degree of status to break into the book as a writer. *AD* is considered a "dream book" for a good portion of the readership that can only fantasize—not realize—the lifestyle and homestyle featured on its pages. To an extent, the same might be said of emerging freelance writers, who might have to set their sites on other markets in this category.

House Beautiful   *HB* is Hearst's big entry in this category. It also features well-appointed homes, but the owners, architects, and decorators are not as important as the end result. *HB* tries to show its readers how they, too, can turn their homes into the showplaces featured in its pages. It targets an upscale audience, but *House Beautiful* is as much aspirational as inspirational. Unlike *AD*, it is not necessarily the picture book for the well heeled and well connected.

Traditional Home   Meredith is probably the biggest player in this category. In addition to *Better Homes & Gardens*, it publishes a raft of special interest titles (magazines with infrequent publishing schedules) devoted to remodeling and home décor. But its main entry in the category is *Traditional Home*, the best-selling magazine in the category. Though it targets an affluent audience, like *House Beautiful*, it is not viewed as the magazine where the rich and influential show off their homes and lifestyles. It is a guide to inspiring home décor, with big pictures to inspire readers.

▶ **FASHION MAGAZINES**

A lot of people fail to distinguish the women's lifestyle books from the fashion magazines. It's easy to see why. Fashion and beauty are such important editorial pillars in the lifestyle books—making up as much as 40 percent of the content in some cases—that at first blush it appears that

Popperfoto / Getty Images

those magazines are all about fashion. But when you open the pages of the real fashion books you see the difference. While the lifestyle magazines traffic in everyday looks for regular women, the fashion magazines feature Hollywood glamour and couture—looks that its readers aspire to achieve.

EN *VOGUE*

It is the very definition of high fashion. In fact, the name of the magazine, *Vogue*, has come to represent the very best and very latest of looks, models, and designers. The term "vogue" has been incorporated in contemporary urban vernacular and pop culture to mean striking the pose, as represented by singer Madonna's huge hit by the same name. But it hasn't always been that way.

Vogue began in 1892 as a high society magazine. Fashions were not emphasized, unless there were references to the appropriate garments to wear to social events. Condé Montrose Nast changed all that when he bought the magazine in 1909. Nast (a former advertising manager who would later buy *Vanity Fair*, *The New Yorker*, *Glamour*, and *House and Garden*) transformed *Vogue* into the premier fashion magazine that over the years would come to reflect the changing culture, as much as the seasonal styles. "Fashion can tell you everything that is going on in the world with a strong fashion image," *Vogue* editor-in-chief Anna Wintour noted in a special HBO documentary celebrating the 120th anniversary of the magazine.

In particular, over the years, we have seen a steady forward movement of women's culture in the pages of the magazine, from that high society image of the early days through the radical transformation of women in the 1960s and 1970s and into the new millennium. High fashion to ease in dressing, to street and designer blends (that "high-low mix of fashion" Wintour introduced in the magazine in the late 1980s), even to grunge (just once) and to high fashion again.

Although the magazine intentionally has taken on controversial substantive topics, as with the publication of Lee Miller's photographs of Dachau following World War II, and such contemporary issues as environmental concerns, the magazine also has been controversial in ways that appear unintended. Consider the presentation of a white model in blackface, another with eyes taped to appear Asian, large hoops referred to as "slave earrings," and, of course, basketball superstar LeBron James posed aggressively holding model Gisele Bundchen in what critics charged was a bit too reminiscent of a King Kong movie poster.

Inside, these days, the magazine pages are filled with the trendiest looks on the hottest models put together by the hottest designers as captured by the hottest photographers. In fact, largely because of *Vogue*, photographers, models, and designers have become superstars in their own right. (Vera Wang once worked at the magazine as an assistant to Fashion Editor Polly Mellen.)

Text is minimal here; pictures reign. A few essays and mini features on art and culture dot the front of the book (where one is likely to find the bulk of the text). But the pieces are rarely assigned to unknown freelancers. Every so often, though, *Vogue* does surprise with a small, lifestyle- and culture-focused feature that is well within the reach of any competent writer. That certainly makes pitching their articles editor worth the shot—even if it's a long shot. But the thing to keep in mind always is that the critical distinguishing mark of *Vogue* over the years has been its signature tie-in of fashion and culture. "Fashion to me is a reflection of culture," *Vogue* Fashion Editor Camilla Nickerson noted in the HBO documentary. "It's not about whether everybody is wearing a trench coat. It's there to report on the world at large."

Helpful hints for the aspiring fashion writer.

Harper's Bazaar   Slightly more accessible than *Vogue, Harper's Bazaar* is nonetheless a high fashion magazine. Its emphasis is on trends that make it from the runways of Paris, Milan, and New York to the streets of Philadelphia, Chicago, and Seattle. Its focus is almost exclusively on fashion and beauty (including hair and makeup tips) with very little editorial veering out of that territory. In addition to including the requisite fashion spreads, the feature well does spotlight celebrity profiles (of entertainers, designers, and other jet-setters), typically produced by an established writer.

FASHION, BOLD AS *ELLE*

More than any publication in the women's fashion category, *Elle* has been hailed for its embrace of an international beauty standard that is all-inclusive, embracing women representing the spectrum of ethnicities and skin tones. Founded in France in 1945 by a pair of influential journalists (Pierre Lazareff and his wife, Hélène Gordon), *Elle*, from its inception, announced to the world that it intended to be not just an arbiter of taste and style, but the definitive word on what fashion-forward young women should think, be, and wear. Its slogan trumpeted the belief by *Elle* editors that their magazine was central in the lives of its readers. "If she reads, she reads *Elle*," they declared.

It long has been considered the most exotic of the fashion magazines. It's become more domesticated as it settled into a more American vibe, but it retains a bit of continental flair. There is more pop culture here than in some of its competitors. *Elle* features cutting edge and up-and-coming artists, actors, musicians, and designers, and is always on the lookout for the next big thing, which provides an opening for new writers who are plugged into what's hot.

By the time *Elle* reached the shores of the United States following the 1981 purchase of its owner, Hachette magazines, by French publisher Daniel Filipacchi and his businessman partner, Jean-Luc Lagardère, the magazine was struggling. But its reputation as a style guide with an appreciation for beauty in all its shades was cemented by its use of models of African and Asian descent in its avant-garde and radically chic fashion spreads.

In 1997 the magazine advanced the concept of beauty even further when it put Sudanese model Alek Wek on its cover. With her magnetic smile and close-cropped hair, Wek was the first African model to grace the cover of *Elle*, or any American women's magazine for that matter. It was a bold and ultimately profitable move. For not only were readers intrigued by Wek's striking looks, they were drawn to her dramatic backstory.

Wek, the seventh of nine children, was born in 1975 in Wau, Sudan. Her father was the minister of education in Wau; her mother was a homemaker. When civil war broke out in the country in the mid-1980s, the family was forced to flee their home on foot, hiding from rebel forces in the bush as they tried to make their way to Khartoum, the nation's capital in the North.[1] Her father, who had suffered a hip injury years before, contracted an infection during the journey. He died four years later.

With the civil war raging, Wek and one of her sisters emigrated to London. Their mother joined them two years later. Wek's modeling career began in 1995 when she was discovered by a talent scout while strolling through an outdoor market in South London. The 20-year-old art history student was uncertain about the prospect of entering the foreign world of haute couture, but within a year she was signed with the prestigious Ford modeling agency and strolling the catwalks of Paris, Milan, and New York draped in creations by the likes of John Galliano, Donna Karan, and Calvin Klein.

She was already a much-in-demand runway presence when *Elle*'s international creative director Gilles Bensimon stirred up the fashion world by featuring her on the cover of the magazine's November 1997 US edition. Bensimon, a noted photographer in his own right, shot the cover himself. Stylist Jon More swathed Wek in a tailored snow-white suit jacket that was buttoned tightly at the waist. She wore no blouse. The contrast of the gleaming white fabric against Wek's flawless ebony skin made for an arresting image that proved to be a commercial and critical success. Most of the letters that poured into the magazine in the ensuing months applauded the editors for celebrating a different standard of beauty. None other than Oprah Winfrey joined the celebration by inviting Wek on her show. "If you'd been on the cover of a magazine when I was growing up, I would have had a different concept of who I was," Winfrey told Wek.[2]

The Wek/*Elle* example demonstrates that fashion and beauty standards are not carved in stone. Aspiring writers who hope to enter this realm should consider pushing at traditional boundaries to explore the beauty in the unconventional. As *Elle* has shown, stepping outside of the usual beauty box can pay dividends and set you apart from the pack.

InStyle   *InStyle* is the newest kid on the fashion magazine block, but it burst onto the scene like gangbusters. With its focus on translating the style of Hollywood's elite into fashion and beauty tips real women can emulate, it took fashion magazines off the runway and onto the red carpet. It ushered in the trend that kicked supermodels off the covers of women's magazines in favor of starlet-of-the-moment types. Yet for all its focus on celebrity, *InStyle* still straddles a line between aspirational and accessible fashion tips. Its theme: You, too, can look like the stars. There's not much in the way of features here. It's mostly tip boxes and *charticles* on how to achieve a certain look. Occasionally there's a celebrity Q&A, but the content is mostly staff-written.

▶ FITNESS MAGAZINES

The explosion of magazines devoted to health and fitness reflects the desire of Americans—particularly Baby Boomers—to live longer and healthier. Nearly every lifestyle magazine, whether it is aimed at men or women, has a column or department devoted to exercise, diet, and/or living a more active life.

This emphasis on fitness has spawned magazines and websites devoted to specific activities—hiking, biking, backpacking, running, and weightlifting—and more holistic books that aim to help its audience achieve better mental and physical well-being. That is particularly true in the sphere of women's magazines, where a fierce battle among three major fitness titles is being waged.

Self   It is a little unfair to call *Self* a fitness magazine. In many ways it is so much more. Its old tag line promoted the magazine as being a guide for the mind, body, and spirit of its active women readers. Inside the book you'll find editorial devoted to each of those aspects of a woman's well-being. *Self* includes all the traditional editorial pillars of a typical women's lifestyle magazine—fashion, beauty, relationship advice—and provides an additional overlay of health and fitness tips. Its readers are made up of a broad range of women, from singles to mature wives and mothers. The magazine not only instructs them in yoga and dieting, it offers a wide range of health tips and provides inspiring stories about women who have seized control of their health.

Self also is one of those rare major women's magazines with several entry points for new writers. The editors pride themselves on maintaining a relationship with the magazine's vast audience and are more open than many other magazine editors to accepting ideas—particularly inspiring stories—from readers and new writers.

Self.com also is a robust and interactive website that allows opportunities for tremendous contributions from readers and new writers. The website is a forum for a variety of ongoing dialogues about diet, weight loss, and exercise. Readers can contribute as participants in the conversations. Writers can submit articles or features highlighting inspirational stories for the audience.

Shape   *Shape's* emphasis is largely on diet and exercise, though like *Self* it tends to touch on some traditional women's lifestyle pillars—fashion, beauty, relationships. But the bulk of *Shape's* editorial revolves around weight loss tips and exercise. This is the book for women seeking tighter buns, slimmer thighs, and tips on turning back the aging clock. The text largely consists of how-to exercise instruction (with big photos) and recipes, leaving little room for contributions from freelancers.

Women's Health   *Women's Health* is the newest entry in this category, but it entered with a big splash. It was originally billed as the distaff version of Rodale's hugely successful *Men's Health*, but the content here is not nearly as salacious. Where many have long considered *Cosmopolitan* as *Men's Health*'s female counterpart (both are orgasm obsessed and have similarly cheeky tones), *Women's Health* is much more subdued. Like *Men's Health*, exercise, diet tips, and recipes comprise the bulk of the editorial, but there is a good deal of the women's mag staples—fashion, beauty, relationship advice—here as well.

And like *Men's Health* and its main competitor, *Self*, *Women's Health* revels in personal stories about the diet, health, and weight loss triumphs of real women. The focus is on success. These are inspirational stories, so aspiring *Women's Health* contributors must always focus on stories where the end is positive.

▶ SMALL, INDEPENDENT WOMEN'S MAGAZINES

Ms.   *Ms.* is the grandmother of all of the small magazines devoted to presenting stories about women's equality and empowerment. The original feminist magazine (second wave), it flirted for a brief while with providing traditional women's magazine fare but reverted back to its bread and butter issue: how to advance the causes of women in societies where they still remain victims of overt and subtle forms of discrimination. The magazine takes essays and articles from a wide range of contributors, both newbies and veteran writers.

Bitch   *Bitch* is a media property that includes both a robust website and quarterly magazine. Though it bills itself as a vehicle for feminist expression, *Bitch* is much more. Online and in print it covers a wide range of issues, from pop culture to politics, from the perspective of third-wave feminists. The editors welcome contributions from new writers—anything from articles to essays—that examine pop culture from the point-of-view of this feminist audience. The magazine accepts reviews, reported pieces, Q&As, roundups, but no fiction or poetry. Though the emphasis is on culture, that subject area is defined broadly to include takes on everything from movies and television to peccadillos of public figures.

Bust   Like *Bitch*, *Bust*'s emphasis is on pop culture, but it bills itself as the "magazine for women with something to get off their chests." The tone is not as didactic as that slogan might imply. It is a lifestyle magazine that stands as an alternative to the big New York glossies in its competitive universe. It does cover a wide range of topics, including fashion, beauty, food, celebrities, and sex, but it purports to be more cheeky and honest than its bigger competitors. The editors are very open to submissions, preferably to specific departments. The six issues a year are arranged thematically. The themes are announced in advance on Bust.com, *Bust* media's highly interactive website.

WRITER'S WORKSHOP

Here is a suggestion for you to apply a central point of this chapter as you begin to develop article ideas.

Consider the freelance strategy as something of a chess match. The champion chess player always focuses on the immediate move, but is mindful of the impact of that move on every move that will follow in the game. As a matter of your own personal writing strategy, you might want to consider this technique. Always stay focused on the article you are contemplating, but never think only about that article. In other words, you always should consider what has been suggested throughout this chapter: that the best strategy is built on charting out a path from a freelance-friendly market—particularly a magazine that is open to considering work by new writers—that will connect you in a chain of magazine writing opportunities ultimately leading to your destination market. So, consider the range of magazines summarized in this chapter, sorted by categories. Think further about the groupings according to their focus and then the niche they fill in these categories. Now begin to consider a point of entry with a mind to where it ultimately might lead you. In this connection, consider whether the best point of entry will be the online edition, the front-of-the-book in the print edition, or some other position in a magazine. But always think about the next move.

Chapter Three Review

▶ KEY TERMS

- audience composition
- audience interests
- magazine focus

- magazine niche
- Seven Sisters

▶ SUGGESTED READING

Abrahamson, David. *Magazine Made America: The Cultural Transformation of the Postwar Periodical.* Cresskill, NJ: Hampton Press, 1996. Abrahamson provides a comprehensive examination of the history of the magazine industry since WWII.

Blanchard, Margaret *A. History of the Mass Media in the United States.* New York: Routledge, 1998. Blanchard's wide-ranging survey of American media covers everything from the founding of the nation's first newspaper in 1690 to the media impact on culture and conflict up to the dawn of the twenty-first century.

Janello, Amy; Jones, Brennon. *The American Magazine.* New York: Harry N. Abrams, 1991. Janello and Jones explore the history of American consumer magazines in this lavish pictorial volume that was commissioned by Magazine Publishers of America and the American Society of Magazine Editors.

Endres, Kathleen L.; Lueck, Therese. *Women's Magazines in the United States: Consumer Magazines.* Westport, CT: Greenwood Press, 1995. This reference guide contains profiles of 75 American women's magazines, some dating back to the eighteenth century.

▶ WEB RESOURCES

http://www.magazine.org/ Official website of the Association of Magazine Media (formerly the Magazine Publishers of America), a non-profit organization that represents more than 170 American and 30 international media companies that publish across print and digital platforms.

http://www.magazine.org/asme The website of the American Society of Magazine Editors, an offshoot of the Association of Magazine Media. ASME members are editorial leaders of the nation's major business and trade publications.

▶ NOTES

1. Wek, Alek, "Supermodel Alek Wek's Bittersweet Return Home—to a Free South Sudan," *The Daily Beast*; August 28, 2012.

2. "Retro/Alek Wek, Elle Cover, November 1997," Beauty is Diverse.com, August 21, 2011.

4   The Big Idea

As we discussed in the first chapters of this book, there is a certain amount of knowledge you must have long before you begin working on a specific writing assignment. Of the "Five Knows" we believe will get you to "yes," several will be important just in generating the story idea itself. You must know the magazine (its focus and its niche); know the history (whether your story idea already has been handled by the target magazine); and know the audience (who the readers are and whether they have an interest in your particular story idea and have an interest in having it told in a specific way). Here, though, for good measure, we will add a couple of additional "knows" as sub-parts. For it is important to know something about yourself before embarking on this writing journey. Your motivation for taking on each new writing assignment, as well as your interests and capabilities, are critical pieces of the decision making process. Knowing your writing strategy also is important in determining whether a particular story makes sense to undertake. In the end (as in the beginning), you would do well to start with what you know when it comes to the basic story idea, because, as we will show, the best story ideas are in a place you just might be overlooking: right there in front of you.

LEARNING OBJECTIVES

1. Develop resources that continue to generate marketable magazine story ideas.

2. Recognize story ideas in everyday occurrences.

3. Develop techniques for matching observations to ideas and ideas to stories.

4. Consider matching story ideas with readers who will want to read them.

5. Consider ways to cross your own boundaries in search of the untold story.

▶ IDEAS ARE EVERYWHERE

The late Pulitzer Prize winner Gwendolyn Brooks, longtime Poet Laureate of Illinois, is reported to have said once that she could gaze through her window and see a poem going by. Classical music composer Ludwig von Beethoven quipped that he tripped over ideas getting out of bed in the morning. What can freelance magazine writers learn from a celebrated poet and a master composer? Everything. Especially when it comes to getting started. That is because everything starts with conception. But the idea— the marketable and writable idea—often is the most challenging part of the magazine writing experience.

Here is one vital area where contrasts between newspapers and magazines are most apparent. While newspaper writing often is a matter of covering what *has* happened, magazine writing just as often can be a matter of covering what is *about* to happen. Unlike writing for newspapers, where stories frequently are handed to writers—a news conference is called, a fire breaks out, a music concert is scheduled—in magazine writing, you must discover the story, develop it, sharpen the angle, and present it for a very select group of readers. But how do you do that? How do you get to a point where story ideas are generated with the kind of apparent ease Brooks and Beethoven suggested? How do you begin to see stories passing by your window? How do you begin tripping over all the ideas that pile up at the foot of your bed? The key is in what you know—starting with what you know about making the critical connections: connections between observations and ideas; between ideas and stories; between these stories and markets; and between the markets and actual writing assignments you can execute successfully. So, where do ideas come from? They come from enterprising writers, people who keep an eye wide open and an ear to the ground.

Gwendolyn Brooks

Getty Images

Start in your own backyard The best place to begin recognizing the potential story ideas is right there where you live. Too often, people who don't reside in larger metropolitan areas tend to think that nothing of note goes on in their communities. In fact, things are going on all the time. The key is in recognizing that there are potential stories in these things and the places where these things occur.

Somewhere in places like these, there is a factory that is retooling to meet future challenges. There is a farm raising llamas or ostriches. Maybe an antique shop with unique collections. A furniture manufacturer who takes weeks to create a single piece. A watch manufacturer who continues a family tradition. Perhaps these kinds of places and activities merit stand-alone stories. Maybe instead they spark ideas for something larger, something they might help illustrate—something national in scope. Is the activity at the factory or the stock raised at the farm representative of some economic trend that could be of interest to a magazine? Does it demonstrate the need for reassessing longstanding practices—thinking of new ways to manufacture or new sources of food and clothing? On the other hand, is the antique factory or watch repair shop a mark of our need to hold onto tradition, to keep alive a neglected art?

Perhaps the entire town becomes the source of an idea for a story. A travel piece. Small towns as destinations for weekend getaways. The charm of a bed-and-breakfast; an antique safari; a drive-in theater; a pass through a covered bridge; and a stop at a diner along the way. What about your college town? Doesn't a tour of Big Ten college towns sound like a story idea that will resonate with editors and readers? Well, it did, and netted one writer a nice assignment.

In addition to interesting places and people, *events* in your hometown might spark ideas. One of the authors once attended a library book presentation and signing by the late Eleanor Taylor Bland, a mystery writer living in Waukegan, Illinois, near Chicago. By day, she worked as an accountant. By night, she did her duty as a grandmother, who periodically would turn away from the babysitting and cooking chores just long enough to cook up new ways to "kill" people. The author's story idea that flowed from that lecture, "Murder, She Wrote," was purchased by *Chicago* magazine.

Read all about it   As thorough as newspaper coverage of a particular topic might be, there often is room left for more—the kind of in-depth, textured storytelling that magazines are uniquely well suited to provide. Stories that explore the human element to a greater degree. Stories that can focus on compelling aspects of a news story that might not be developed otherwise. What stories are the local papers reporting that might lend themselves to longer treatment, or narrative form?

A few years ago, one of the authors happened upon a story in the *Chicago Tribune* business section regarding a sex harassment lawsuit against the CEO of a major Chicago-based corporation filed by a much younger woman he had recruited and mentored before allegedly developing a much more personal connection with her. The story seemed to have some potential for longer treatment. The writer's instincts told him there was something there, although he wasn't exactly sure just what at the time. It was clipped and placed in a "futures" file. You never know.

Even a huge national news story has room for a more expansive treatment as a magazine story. When news broke about the plagiarism of *The New Republic* writer Stephen Glass, something occurred to writer Buzz Bissinger. He saw the possibility for an in-depth character study of Glass, the person who had violated the fundamental trust of his publication, profession, and public. The result was a revealing 1988 *Vanity Fair* article, "Shattered Glass," which later was adapted as an acclaimed feature film under the same title. (See our list in Chapter 11.)

New York-based writer and editor Erin Scottberg recalls similar experiences when she was research editor at *Popular Mechanics*. "I was out having drinks with my editor one night and we were talking about how ridiculous the whole cattle auction industry is," she recalls. The next day, there was a story in the newspaper and she and her editor knew immediately they should do a piece for the online edition of *PM* to get it up right away. But, instead of going big, as with the "Shattered Glass" *Vanity Fair* piece, they decided to go smaller with a special "charticle" of sorts. "That was something we knew right off the bat would be the most interesting presentation; a picture of the cow, pointing things out," she notes. "We decided we would develop a short intro blurb and present the details graphically." The result is "The World's Most Expensive Cow" published at popularmechanics.com on March 1, 2010, showing graphically just how the sum of the many cow parts is even greater than the whole, when it comes to market value.

As with published stories in newspapers, television news stories can provide ideas for much longer treatment. They contain great visuals, and public relations firms often pitch stories and angles to television that are not always offered to print, for various strategic reasons. But these stories can serve as the foundation for good magazine ideas, too. Beyond that, PR representatives are always "shopping" ideas to writers with whom they have a relationship (even those who merely happen to be on their extensive mailing lists). While we never want to be "fed" stories, somewhere within the ideas that are being pitched by PR professionals are the seeds of new "takes" on stories we can nurture with our own independent reporting.

That is what Erin Scottberg did when a public relations representative pitched a story to her related to the release of the Batman film, "The Dark Knight." "So I figured out the *Popular Mechanics* angle of the story I wanted to cover," Scottberg notes. As the conversation with the PR rep progressed, Scottberg fixed on the "Bat-Pod," the high-tech motorcycle, which seemed a natural fit for her audience. "I mean, you don't get more *Popular Mechanics* than cars and motors and engines and talking about how something like that works."

In addition to general publicists, there also are organizational press professionals—press secretaries for elected officials; corporate communications officers for businesses; and news bureau staff for colleges and universities—who can be great resources in magazine story development. Keep in mind, though, that the only mission for public relations representatives or press aides is to promote the event, company, individual, or policy initiative in their portfolio. So, while they will have a wealth of helpful background information and can help set up interviews (as the film rep did for Scottberg, who wound up talking with the film director and stunt coordinators for "The Dark Knight"), you always must take care to maintain your journalistic independence even in the exciting field of magazine writing.

When it comes to sources of ideas, keep in mind that, as a student, your backyard includes your campus. Colleges and universities maintain "experts" lists of faculty who are doing groundbreaking research and provocative scholarship. These are the people who are trotted out as "talking heads" for news shows when important stories break in their areas. They also can be the sources of magazine stories in many significant ways.

Richard Powers, a MacArthur Fellow and National Book Award-winning author, also was an English professor at the University of Illinois at Urbana-Champaign, where he maintained a campus office. But it was not in the English building on the campus quad with his other department colleagues. No, his office was in the University's Beckman Institute—an interdisciplinary center of cutting edge science and technological research on the school's fabled engineering campus to the north. That is because Powers' novels focus on themes that engage human interaction with science and technology. Walking the halls of Beckman, absorbing the intellectual energy—and the story ideas—was a vital part of his research. But his work also is the stuff of magazine articles, like the one *Chicago* magazine bought from one of the authors for the October 2009 edition focusing on Powers' tenth novel, *Generosity: An Enhancement*, about a blissful Algerian refugee who is discovered to have a mysterious "happiness gene." And, of course, there is the piece Powers wrote about himself for the October 2008 edition of *GQ* when, inspired by the deep knowledge production all around him at Beckman, he became only the ninth person in the world to have his genome sequenced. You might say, he lives his work. Certainly, that level of absorption and being tuned into your surroundings can lead to fascinating storytelling possibilities.

Additionally, in academic communities, abstracts and journals are part of the scholarly network. But they also provide a wealth of information about academic research and thought that can be "translated" for a consumer magazine audience, so long as you are able to find the significant popular angle.

Then there are trends. If something happens once, it is news. If it happens two or three times, it is a pattern. If that pattern is repeated, it just might amount to a trend. Successful writers—those who know how to mine occurrences for story ideas—become quite good at *trendspotting* and turning these observations into publishable story ideas. If you are right, then you get quite a bit of credit for being the first to recognize the significance of what so many others scarcely noticed. But, even if you are wrong, an article in this regard can be framed as speculative so that it still can be a thought-provoking read. What are some of the trends you can spot in your own community? College-age drinking has been a longstanding issue. But what can you observe on your own campus that might suggest something different, something shifting? An increase in activity? A decrease? Cultural activities (beer pong)? Consumer information? One night on their own "intellectual" crawl, a group of professors began a robust debate about the relative alcohol content of beer (light and regular), ale, and stout, with plenty of sampling for, well, the sake of discourse. Of course. That night, one of them—a writer—got on the Internet to begin putting together a story with surprising results. (Guinness has less alcohol content than Miller *Lite*? No way!) Possibly a front-of-the-book story for a trendy men's magazine. What about social alternatives to drinking? One of our former students took note of an increase in popularity of Hookah bars among students and began hanging out to explore these non-alcoholic, culturally diverse settings for an engaging narrative story.

Many commentators have advised that you should listen to what your friends and family say are things they care about. There are story ideas in these conversations if you are a *purposeful* listener. One of the authors prefers to have his hair cut in barbershops—as opposed to new wave unisex salons—because he feels they are great places for provocative conversation. You can learn about the topics people want to engage in barber shops—beauty shops, too—which often can feel like town squares. It is all about the need for "conversational currency," the capital of the curious, that grows in value as it is passed along to increasing numbers of other people. Magazine readers, after all, tend to be more highly educated and engaged in public affairs. It often is important to people in this demographic group to be able to engage in the discourse underway all around them. This is true of a range of topics from lifestyle and entertainment to geopolitical affairs and social justice.

In that connection, lunchtime conversations with the right people also can be rewarding—from a storyteller's perspective. Over lunch one day with a lawyer friend of one of the authors, the conversation turned to interesting projects they were handling. After the author finished talking about a book project, the attorney talked about a fascinating case she was handling. It was a sex harassment case against the CEO of a major Chicago-based corporation. The lawyer was representing the woman who filed the suit. The much younger woman. This was starting to sound familiar. As it turns out, the twenty-something woman had been having an affair with the sixty-something CEO, who summarily fired her and . . . Wait a minute. Hang on. Instantly, the author recalled that *Chicago Tribune* clip in his futures file and ordered another round of drinks. What developed during this conversation was a plan to let the author do the equivalent of a **ride-along**, observing the behind-the-scenes maneuvering of the lawyer as she moved toward settling the case. Clearly, such a story would be rife with compelling narrative possibilities, as well as a wealth of information on the substance of sex harassment as a compelling issue in the workplace. As the author expected, *Chicago* magazine expressed interest right away in publishing the piece.

Anniversaries always present interesting storytelling opportunities. But it is important to consider the essential questions before getting too deeply involved in developing the idea. What is the historical significance of the original event or occurrence? How are we affected by it in the contemporary moment? There is the story of the writer who, while combing through digests, discovered the approach of the 100th anniversary of the invention of the Ferris Wheel and was able to get that story published. Typically, people think in terms of five-year increments when it comes to anniversary stories, but even the first anniversary of a significant event—as with the death of pop star Michael Jackson, or Whitney Houston—can resonate. Political events, wars, battles within wars, inventions, birthdays all can provide rich storytelling ideas—either relating the historical facts surrounding the event, or some related issue that can serve as a story in and of itself. In the case of the Michael Jackson or Whitney Houston deaths, perhaps a look at what might have developed in the ensuing years. What new knowledge have we acquired about the circumstances surrounding the events? What about the survivors? How have their lives changed? The point here is not necessarily to focus on these specific events, but to recognize the storytelling possibilities that can arise whenever we pause for a moment to reflect, as people tend to do on anniversaries. As a writer, how can you connect with these people through stories, helping them see even larger significance in the anniversary?

"What's up?"   Good ideas often come when you're not trying to think up good ideas. The process involves not only being observant, but also inquisitive about those things we observe. There is a term from the vernacular that seems appropriate in covering this process: *"What's up?"* These observations can come when you're working out at the gym. Notice how often men and women wind up comparing workout notes and tips in going through the exercise regimens. What's up with that? Are health clubs becoming the new singles bars? Two people are seen walking on your campus quad, each talking on separate cell phones. What's up with that? Are people connecting *and* disconnecting through technology? And what about changes in technology and popular trends? As former web director for Hearst Men's Network at Hearst Digital Media, Eric Gillin recalls seeing story possibilities for esquire.com even as he was riding to work on the subway. He started noticing that those

RIDE-ALONG: A technique whereby writers are given full access to observe behind-the-scenes activities to add the depth of first-hand observations to narrative structure. Usually done with police on duty.

ubiquitous white ear buds were giving way to the larger and often bulkier stereo headphones as people carved out their own private space in public. A closer look revealed one brand was emerging as the most popular. It was "Beats By Dr. Dre," developed by the hip-hop impresario and highly successful Grammy-award-winning producer of artists like Snoop Dog and Eminem. What Gillin saw as an astute observer was the beginning of a ground-shifting trend. What he saw as an editor was a story about a ground-shifting trend. It all can start with asking that simple question—"What's up?"—and remaining open to multiple possibilities in considering answers and explanations.

Ideas can come while you're shopping at the mall, or even going to a movie. In 1996, *New York Times* Pulitzer Prize-winning writer Michiko Kakutani spotted something intriguing outside a museum. African American teens were sporting *"preppywear"* while White teens were going urban contemporary— baggy jeans, sweats and all. What's up with that? "Common Threads," was Kakutani's answer in the *New York Times Magazine*. It was an insightful piece about how White kids look to Black kids for cues about what is "cool" and how Black kids look to White kids for emblems of "success." (See our discussion in Chapter 17.)

How about a walk along Lake Michigan in Chicago? One of the authors once saw something curious during such a walk on the first pleasant day of spring. On the Lakefront bike path in Chicago's Hyde Park community, there was an ambulance, a paramedic crew, and a small crowd of onlookers. Moving past his foreboding and the crowd, he was able to glance at the lifeless body of a man being lifted onto a gurney and into the ambulance. Scattered around the ground, where the man apparently had fallen, were a bicycle, a tennis racquet, and an airline ticket. The man, who clearly was overweight, apparently had wasted no time in getting out on the bike path, on the court, on the move all at once. And maybe a bit too quickly after a long lazy Chicago winter. What's up with that? Is there a health risk in becoming too physically active too soon? Is there a "spring tune-up" regimen people should follow before physical exertion during the milder weather? Is there a warm-up routine everyone should undertake before becoming active at *any* time? What might cause us to overcompensate for that "cabin fever," the despondency that sets in during the cold, dark, depressing months?

Roseanne Barr

Getty Images / WireImage

As the doors of the ambulance closed, the people in the crowd—a culturally diverse group—began exchanging hugs and cell numbers. Somehow, the tragedy of this stranger had brought other strangers together in a heroic humanitarian effort. What's up with that? Points of connection for an otherwise disconnected people? A warm heart at the core of what might seem to be a heartless big city?

This "what's up" process continues, even after an assignment is negotiated. (See box.)

MULTIPLE POSSIBILITIES

Mike Sager, who has been called the "Beat poet of American journalism," is a writer-at-large for *Esquire*. He is a former *Washington Post* staff writer and *Rolling Stone* contributing editor. As a long-form writer, he has brought the best of literary techniques to his presentation of contemporary culture and especially to revealing and textured celebrity profiles. For *Esquire*, Sager was assigned to interview comedienne Roseanne Barr for the magazine's regular section, "What I've Learned," a short bio format he pioneered. After the end of the session, as they were just sitting around, Barr made a passing reference to the fact that she suffered from Multiple Personality Disorder. *Wait. What?* Next thing he knew, Sager was working on a much longer piece on Roseanne's condition—in addition to his one-pager. Here, in a presentation format similar to the "What I've Learned" page in *Esquire*, Sager discusses the discovery and the persistent follow-through that led to the August 2001 feature, "I Am Large, I Contain Multitudes."

Roseanne basically was just one of those "What I've Learned" interviews. It was set up by *Esquire* as a one-hour session. I got there and everything was pretty standard—even though she was six hours late. I found her to be sweet and very intelligent beneath her prickly exterior.

After the interview was done, her people wanted me to stay with her for a little while because they had to go shopping. We were just hanging out at that point and I had proven myself to be a good human being with a good ear who appreciated her and saw what a genius she was.

I appreciate unconventional people. I was able to turn off my tape recorder and stop being a reporter and just listen. So that was the reason for all that revelation.

I don't play cards, but I have a great poker face. No reaction at all. But I remember when she told me, "I have MPD." On the outside I had a face of stone. But on the inside I was thinking "Holy Cripes! This is so freaking weird! What a great story!"

I went home and talked to my editor. Then I called her up and said: "You know, we should do this story." It took a bit of prodding, but after a time, she agreed to proceed.

It took four months of reporting to do the long-form story. There was tremendous approach avoidance with her. She would invite me up to visit her at her house outside LA, and I would spend a few days at a time, I would follow her around, we would go here and there. Then I'd come back again and do the same thing.

Finally, I said, "I've got to meet the personalities." At first she didn't want to do this. But she did give me permission to talk to her therapist. He told me everything. What an amazing story.

And then I got to meet the people, the personalities. I'm a pretty skeptical guy, but man, I was pretty convinced. I felt like, either she's the best actor on the planet, or this really exists, she really has multiple personalities. As she brought out the different personalities, there was a distinct shift. Each one had its own mannerisms and voice and speech patterns. I wouldn't have believed it if I hadn't been right there, taking it all in.

If I hadn't seen that little opening and kept my foot in there and pursued it a million times with her, it never would have happened.

Among the many poignant scenes in the Academy Award-winning film "A Beautiful Mind" is one where John Nash (Russell Crowe) takes Alicia, the future Mrs. Nash (Jennifer Connolly), out on the terrace, points to a billion stars in the nighttime sky, and urges her to name a shape. She says, "Umbrella." He responds by taking her hand and connecting a collection of stars to form the shape of the umbrella. "Do it again," she says in rapt amazement. And we, the audience, share that "aha" moment. That is what the best magazine writers do for readers. We take the random assortment of everything in the universe and recognize shape and form and—ultimately—stories. If done right, the stories that are revealed will connect the dots for people in ways they, too, can recognize, just as "John Nash" revealed a form, the umbrella narrative, in the billions of stars.

AIM TO SERVE

While many observations of daily events might be good ideas that can be worked into viable and marketable stories, clearly it will take some further consideration to determine whether your observation has the potential to develop into a publishable piece. In thinking through the possibilities, consider what purpose your story might *serve*. Indeed, "SERVE" is a useful acronym to help in sorting the key qualities inherent in a good idea—one that has the potential to become a published magazine article because it connects with readers in vital ways.

It is important in this regard to consider whether the idea has **Significance**. What meaning will the story have to the reader? The measure of such significance will be found in part by reviewing the reader profile you have developed in order to determine interests and needs.

The second quality of the good idea is **Enlightenment**. Will it provide information that is elevating? Will it educate, that is, provide new knowledge? In this connection, you should reflect on the freshness of the piece. The idea should provide something that is original.

The third quality of the good idea is **Relevance**. How well is the story idea tied to reader needs and interests? A Chicago radio station news director once hung a sign on the newsroom wall that read simply, "Affect." He wanted his news team always to focus on how each story impacted listeners. That, he believed, would be the determination of their willingness to stay on past the music segments to listen to the news. The same can be applied to magazine article ideas. How does the story in development affect the reader? Among the top ten words direct mail marketers have learned will have the greatest impact on people are the words "you," "save," and "money." Notice how often these words are used in direct mail promotions (not to mention magazine cover lines). The point, though, is that, in magazine writing—as in promotional writing—you must consider how your idea relates to those things that are uppermost on people's minds. These are the things readers consider most relevant and worthy of their time and consideration. And, let's face it, ultimately, the story is being *sold* to the reader in the sense that we want her to read it.

The fourth quality of the good idea is **Value**. Here, we're talking about value in terms of worth to the reader (as opposed to the values model, which goes to reader characteristics). What is the "take-away," the one or two things the reader will continue to process after reading the piece? The story could provide a service in solving a problem that clearly is identified and connected to the reader's interests. This could be in the realm of consumer information regarding products and services. It could provide financial information regarding investments and home mortgage refinancing. It could provide public policy information that enables people to make enlightened choices among elected officials and their initiatives. Or, it simply could provide that "conversational currency," which can be of considerable "value" to the reader. Information as information can have its own intrinsic value.

The fifth quality of the good idea is **Empathy**. To establish empathy with the reader requires that the reader does not necessarily have to see herself as the central character in the story, but she has to connect in some way with the conflict, the cause, the circumstance that we're covering in the story. A former student of one of the authors got a front-of-the-book assignment from *Chicago* magazine. It was a short piece on a noted furniture designer who had moved his showroom to an old boatyard. The student writer focused on the move, which seemed to have elements of significance and enlightenment (even entertainment). The editor saw it all differently. It was set in motion by a throwaway line about how the furniture designer had been an attorney, who had decided to chuck it all to follow his passion. That became the story. The editor saw the connection with her readers—many of whom were successful professionals, who longed for the more romantic lifestyle of the artisan. She knew they would be in empathy with the subject of the story.

▶ SETTING STRATEGY

Assuming you have mastered the writer's vision and can see stories moving past your window, or maybe you trip over them at bedside in the morning, how do you break in? One possible writing strategy is to target a particular magazine. For example, *Vanity Fair* is a destination market—a magazine to which the best writers aspire to contribute. Clearly, *Vanity Fair* contributors have a great deal of experience in order to rise to that level. As we suggested in the previous chapter, they are at the top of their game. That means they also have something tangible that has opened the door to consideration by *Vanity Fair* editors—a track record of performance as indicated by notable writing samples from magazines *Vanity Fair* editors respect. If you want to write for *Vanity Fair*, you might begin to consider the paths to that destination. Most magazines will consider front-of-the-book sections for break-in opportunities for new writers. But even here, it is important to show that you have contributed in certain subject matter areas (so that you have some level of expertise and access to sources) with experience with those magazines *Vanity Fair* editors will take seriously. City and regional magazines have provided gateways of opportunity in this regard. For example, a number of *Chicago* magazine writers have been published a few times in *Esquire*. But *Chicago* itself is a destination market. So you would want to consider the path that might lead to *Chicago* opportunities, say, in the "Arena" front section. A small local publication might provide that opportunity. In the "City of Brotherly Love," the *Philadelphia City Paper*, an award-winning alternative newsweekly, can serve as an opening to *Philadelphia*, the prestigious regional magazine that has been the recipient of numerous National Magazine Awards. Feature articles published in your community newspaper or in your campus newspaper can provide opportunities for gateway publications.

Front-of-the-book pieces, if done successfully, can create opportunities for more assignments. For one thing, a short piece in a front section will enable an emerging writer to develop a relationship with a section editor that turns into opportunities to write major features for that editor as she rises up in the masthead, or for other editors at the magazine, based on her recommendation. Additionally, online publishing assignments—which might not pay much—can open the door to longer print publication possibilities that do pay and to bylines in bigger, more prestigious digital magazines. In fact, blogging and short

Ta-Nehisi Coates

Getty Images

critiques have created opportunities for a number of emerging writers, particularly as magazines move increasingly toward strengthening their online presence with original material. A former student of one of the authors created an online "magazine" blog covering campus entertainment and turned that into an internship opportunity with *Esquire*'s online edition.

THINKING OUTSIDE THE BOX

Ta-Nehisi Coates is senior editor at *The Atlantic* and a contributing writer to *The New Yorker:* For years, he said he was interested in doing a story on the city of Detroit. He had this gut feeling that there was more to Detroit than what was depicted in the traditional narrative played out in the media. "Being that I'm from Baltimore, a city that also has a rep that's not so good," he says, "I felt like there was a story in Detroit that wasn't being told."

Coates reveals that when he's developing stories he tries to take a contrarian view. "I'm always looking for the story that defies the conventional wisdom."

In this instance, he wondered if Detroit was truly the vast wasteland of foreclosed homes and abandoned businesses that he'd always heard about or if there was more to the story than this "stale stereotype."

So he arranged to go to Detroit to visit friends and scope out the city. He asked his friends to drive him around. He had no agenda, no plan. "I just wanted to see the city through the eyes of some people who live there."

They drove around for a couple of days, and nothing really jumped out at him. He saw a lot of the established Detroit narrative: some desolate neighborhoods with boarded-up homes, some stretches of urban blight that reminded him of his native Baltimore. But on the third day—the day he was planning to leave—they stumbled across a bucolic tract that looked like a suburban oasis. As it turns out, this was the Arden Park Historic district, a neighborhood of stately homes on broad lots sprouting tall oak trees.

"If you had blindfolded me and dropped me off there, I would have thought I was in some suburb far outside of the city." He had his friends drop him off so he could walk around the neighborhood and talk to residents. They told him about the history of the neighborhood, its rich tradition of diversity, its inhabitants' fierce dedication to their much-maligned city.

"This neighborhood defied everything you'd ever heard about Detroit. It wasn't this tract of desolate, abandoned homes. It was beautiful. The people who lived there were proud, hard-working people."

Coates pitched a story to *New Yorker* editor David Remnick who agreed that "The Other Detroit," indeed, was worth a 5,000-word assignment for the magazine.

"The thing I try to remember when I'm looking for stories is to be skeptical," Coates says. "I try to look for the countervailing evidence that might disprove what everybody thinks they know is true. I usually find that there's much more to the story than what we've heard."

Know it all   It cannot be stressed enough just how important the "knows" can be. In addition to knowing the magazine, you also will have to *know* its history. Here, we mean the publication history. Has the target magazine published anything along the lines of the idea you are considering? That means you must consider *everything* that is directly on point, as well as *anything* that might be considered so substantially similar as to preempt your idea. Moreover, you will want to consider whether a similar idea has been taken up by any other magazine that is considered to be competitive with your target magazine. If so, your editor might consider that the idea is not fresh enough for consideration. After all, *Details* and *Maxim* will not want to be seen as copying each other. Nor will *Cosmopolitan* and *Marie Claire*, or *Condé Nast Traveler* and *Travel & Leisure*. Knowing the magazine will clarify this notion of "freshness." It has been asserted that there is a finite number of ideas in the publishing universe. Certainly, Hollywood has discovered this in recycling the seven basic storylines in multiple presentations. While magazine editors like to think they are always bringing something new to the reader, some topics might get dusted off, updated, and essentially recycled from time to time. That time period depends on the magazine mission, its readership, and the creativity of its editors in finding new dimensions of story ideas that can be presented. Thus, in knowing the magazine, it is important to consider just what the cycle of repetition might be. With some publications, you might see recurring themes several times a year. With others, maybe only once a year. Some have much longer cycles. As we advise, anniversary stories create great potential for story ideas. But how many anniversaries of the same event can you possibly present? One of the authors once proposed a magazine story on the 1969 assassination of Black Panther Fred Hampton. In looking at the calendar, the author saw the approaching date of the fortieth anniversary of the murder (which had caused a tremendous public scandal, led to the electoral defeat of a once-powerful state's attorney, and resulted in a successful nearly two-million-dollar wrongful death suit). The editor saw the merits in the idea. But, he pointed to the story that had been written on the subject for his magazine in commemoration of the thirtieth anniversary of the shooting. In the editor's view, ten years was too soon to explore even a new, contemporary dimension of a story based on the same event.

PITCHING FORWARD: Planning magazine stories for timely publication by tying in to events that will occur later.

Typically, reviewing a year or two of your target magazine should suffice, if you make sure that you also have identified and reviewed the magazines that might be seen in competition with your magazine. So, as we indicated above, while *Marie Claire*, *Cosmopolitan*, and even *Glamour* appeal to different niches, the similar focus—that connection generally to a young female audience—would suggest that an idea for a story for one of these magazines (on, say, getting the most mileage out of five set pieces in your wardrobe) would be diminished if it already has been published by one of the others.

In setting strategy, don't forget the importance of timeliness. Although magazines have longer lead times than other media (constantly shrinking thanks to technological advances), timeliness is still a value. So, how do you make sure a story is going to be timely a few months down the road? In magazine parlance, it's called **pitching forward**. Remember, newspapers tend to publish what *has* happened. Magazines tend to publish what is *about to* happen. Anticipate where the world is going to be at the point of publication. Is a recording artist going to drop a new product in March (Music Month)? What about a movie release? Magazine writer and book author Greg Lindsay methodically anticipated the release of the film "Up in the Air" for the opportunity to write about a frequent flyer group and its international marathon of air travel. (See box.)

SOARING SUCCESS WITH AN EYE TO THE HORIZON

For the better part of a year, New York writer Greg Lindsay tracked the advance stories about the 2009 film "Up in the Air." He knew he had a story that would tie into the release of the picture featuring George Clooney as a corporate hit man, a termination expert who, among other things, is addicted to air travel and all its associations—especially the mega-million-mile perks he has amassed in "Airworld," the elite space he occupies.

Lindsay, a contributing writer for the business magazine *Fast Company*, had been writing about air travel and knew about a group of frequent flyers who, like Clooney's Ryan Bingham character, "stockpile miles for currency."

The group is FlyerTalk, an Internet forum designed for information sharing on airline frequent flyer and hotel loyalty programs. With more than 17 million posts and more than 20 million page views a month, the group has become quite an influential voice in shaping frequent flyer programs.

"I had been aware of FlyerTalk for years and I found their whole culture fascinating. So I always wanted to write about them," notes Lindsay, co-author of the book *Aerotropolis: The Way We'll Live Next*.

"The problem was that they were totally insular, which always is a problem with subcultures. I needed a major sort of mainstream culture tie-in to justify it," he recalls. That tie-in came with the release of "Up in the Air." But Lindsay needed more. He needed to have all the colorful characters for his story—people who are scattered all over the country—in one place at one time. "It just fell in my lap when I was online and I found out they were going to be chartering a jet with 200 of them flying all over. It was perfect."

The result was a nearly 10,000-word article for the February 2010 edition of *Condé Nast Traveler*, in which, among other things, Lindsay was able to join the madcap mystery tour, as you can read in the following excerpt from his article:

For some time last year, a driven, delirious group of air warriors had been planning a kind of convention that would climax in a paroxysmal celebration of Airworld mania in Frankfurt in which champagne would be drunk, fuselages would be stroked, first-class lounges would be plumbed for pleasure. It would be the ultimate miles reward. When I asked to jump aboard, they embraced me. My expedition was led by Tommy Danielsen, a ruddy-faced Norwegian who had amassed millions of transatlantic miles. I joined them in Chicago. We were to start at O'Hare, fly to Newark, connect to JFK, and then . . . on to Frankfurt! After a day of rest and champagne, we would hop a chartered flight to Oslo, then Toulouse, and then back to New York in 24 hours. We were never to leave the airports. Some people like Paris, Prague, and Vienna. Control towers, hangars, kitchens, and first-class lounges were the sights this group wanted to see.

▶ WHAT'S MY MOTIVATION?

Even before you begin the search for the story idea, most professional writers and editors advise, you should consider why you are doing this in the first place. *Know* yourself, in other words. What is your motivation? There are a few possibilities, and coming to understand your motivation will go a long way toward shaping the story you undertake and the time you spend developing it. It all comes down to strategy and the approaches that might be dictated by the strategy that is set.

Clearly, there is an interest in the money. Without question, compensation is a key motivating factor. And the cost of earning that compensation is measured as much by the time you spend working on the piece, as it is in any of the other hard costs associated with this type of work. How does that affect the idea and the amount of time you spend developing it? Simply put, time is money in the area of freelancing. The time you spend working on one story is time away from another in the zero-sum world of the magazine writer. It wouldn't make sense to spend an inordinate amount of time on a story that is paying less than the story it is keeping you from working on.

This is goal-oriented writing. Clearly, your goal is to get paid. How much work you do compared to how much you are earning in the end just might determine the scope of the idea you develop. A story that only pays $450 but requires twenty interviews would not be cost effective. Or, would it? Sometimes there are reasons to consider the greater long-term benefit of taking a short-term hit. There are circumstances where even taking a lower fee will make sense in spending time shaping an idea. The question, again, goes to motivation, which should flow from your overall strategy.

FRESH IDEAS, GOOD STORIES

Terrance Noland has served as Deputy Editor, *Men's Journal*, and a former articles editor for *Esquire*. In those roles, Noland always would look for different things when vetting story ideas from freelancers, depending on which part of the book they were pitching. For department pieces in *Men's Journal,* a lifestyle magazine aimed at active men who enjoy adventure, sports, and travel, he looked for novelty or a new approach to familiar ideas.

"The front of the book is all about service—new gadgets, new techniques for doing familiar sports. We generally take story ideas from people who are immersed in an activity either as participants or spectators. I tell people to get deeply involved in something, really immerse yourself in it. Having that deep background not only allows you to come up with ideas, it allows you to write with more authority when you get an assignment."

For the feature well, Noland would look for ideas that have narrative potential. "We're about adventure and exploration, so our features need to take the reader on a journey. They need to be stories with rising action and tension, with a definite beginning, middle and end."

So, how do you find those?

I think there's a narrative somewhere in every topic, but a lot of new writers don't think about how to tease it out. I think you have to find the person who is going to carry the story, who's going to be the central character whose perspective will be the one the reader experiences the story through.

In that connection, a story idea might be good for your portfolio. Here you have a key strategic choice. The best way to get future assignments is to show that you are capable of handling stories within certain subject areas. If you wanted to handle a story in the area of high school basketball, it would be necessary to show that you have written such stories before. So, taking an assignment for less money in this area makes sense if it is aimed at showing a future editor your understanding of the subject matter and that you have some source contacts who would be cooperative in building a new story—one that well could result in wider exposure, more money, and even more opportunities for future writing assignments. Thus, generating publishable story ideas to expand your portfolio becomes a very important career-building strategy. Perhaps, even a vital part of your compensation. This is true whether you intend to continue working as a freelance writer or plan to become a staff researcher, writer, or editor for a magazine.

Perhaps you have a passion for a compelling issue of public concern. Certainly your sense of social responsibility as a journalist might drive you to tackle issues in magazine story development that ultimately help people make enlightened public policy choices. It is likely that you will spend more time working on a piece for which you have great passion, despite the relatively low level of compensation such an assignment might net.

Relationships are vital in the publishing business. As you develop a reputation as a freelance magazine writer, you will have the chance to cultivate relationships with editors. These relationships, in turn, will be fruitful to you in netting an assignment that you never had to pitch yourself. One of the authors was pitching a story to a senior editor at the *Chicago Tribune Magazine* over lunch one day, when she changed the subject and began to discuss the problem she was having pulling in a writer to handle a different kind of story. It was a piece on male vanities for an upcoming issue. She wanted a male writer to experience the full range of pampering treatment for guys—spa, hair, manicure, pedicure—and then write a story about it all. Even though it was not what the author had in mind, he jumped at the chance to do something the editor would appreciate (and, of course, the makeover was an added benefit). The writer earned gratitude points and was able to maintain access to the editor for future pitches. The point is that so much is built on relationships. Editors will determine that you are good with narrative detail, or personality profiles, or human interest or service, or even—yes, this, too—male grooming and fitness. Whatever your strength, it will be recognized and editors will come back to you repeatedly to engage your unique voice in presentation of stories that are important to them. And they will listen to you when you come with ideas of your own.

WRITER'S WORKSHOP

Here is a suggestion for you to apply a central point of this chapter as you begin to develop article ideas.

If the path you choose to publication is targeting a specific magazine and developing ideas for that market, you will have to do a considerable amount of homework. You must *know* the magazine—becoming completely familiar with its focus (lifestyle, business, sports, shelter, city) and its niche (women; African American; business professionals; 18–34; college educated). Create your own fine-tuned reader profile, and determine whether the reader will have an interest in the idea that is formulating. Even more important, consider whether the editor you will pitch to will be able to see your idea as one the reader will have an interest in seeing.

Chapter Four Review

ASSIGNMENT DESK

Take time to consider how you might move from making observations about the world around you to generating story ideas.

1. **Observe.** Find a relatively busy place (student union, dorm lobby, health facility, shopping mall, public park). Take notes—just a sentence or two—on the activities you observe, the things people are doing. Then write a sentence or two about what these activities might indicate about the interests and needs of the people you see.

2. **Infer.** Look at your list from #1 above. What's up? What kinds of topical ideas might you suggest that flow from these observations? Be open and expansive as you consider the kinds of stories that are suggested by the things you observe.

3. **Process.** Develop a list of potential readers and magazines that might match up with the story ideas you develop in #2 above.

4. **Strategize.** Select a magazine for which you would like to write. Now develop a strategy for getting published in that magazine. Determine whether there are special departments that are ripe for "breaking in," and specific publications that might be highly regarded by the editors of your target magazine. Now expand your strategy, discussing in a few lines how you will successfully pitch the ideas you have developed here to each magazine in the chain.

▶ KEY TERMS

- empathy
- enlightenment

- pitching forward
- relevance

- ride-along
- value

▶ SUGGESTED READING

Kent, George E. *A Life of Gwendolyn Brooks.* Lexington, KY: University of Kentucky Press, 1993. Kent offers the first full-scale biography of the late Pulitzer Prize-winning poet.

Powers, Richard. *Generosity: An Enhancemenet.* New York: Farrar, Straus and Giroux, 2009. Powers' ambitious novel explores the nature of happiness and the ethics of scientific inquiry and human experimentation.

Sager, Mike. "I Am Large, I Contain Multitudes," *Esquire.* New York, August 2001. Sager's long-form profile of the alleged multiple personality disorders of comedienne and television personality Roseanne Barr.

▶ WEB RESOURCES

http://www.vanityfair.com/magazine/archive/1998/09/bissinger199809 "Shattered Glass," by Buzz Bissinger. *Vanity Fair*, September, 1998.

http://www.popularmechanics.com/science/health/genetics/4346386 "The World's Most Expensive Cow," by Erin Scottberg, *Popular Mechanics*, March 1, 2010.

http://www.popularmechanics.com/technology/digital/visual-effects/4273883 "Dark Knight's Bat-Pod Took Up-Armored Road From Garage to Set," by Erin Scottberg. *Popular Mechanics*, July 17, 2008

http://www.chicagomag.com/Chicago-Magazine/October-2009/Futurama/ "Futurama," by Christopher Benson, *Chicago*, October 2009.

http://www.gq.com/news-politics/big-issues/200810/richard-powers-genome-sequence "The Book of Me," by Richard Powers. *GQ*, October 2008

http://www.nytimes.com/1997/02/16/magazine/common-threads.html "Common Threads," by Michiko Kakutani. *New York Times Magazine*, February 16, 1997.

http://www.esquire.com/features/what-ive-learned/what-learned-roseanne-0301?click=main_sr "What I've Learned: Roseanne," by Mike Sager. *Esquire*, February 28, 2001.

http://www.esquire.com/ESQ0801-AUG_ROSEANNE_rev?click=main_sr "I Am Large, I Contain Multitudes," by Mike Sager. *Esquire*, August 2001.

http://www.cntraveler.com/travel-tips/flying/2010/02/Triumph-of-the-Air-Warriors "Triumph of the Air Warriors," by Greg Lindsay. *Condé Nast Traveler*, February 2010.

5 Sharpening the Angle

▶ SHARPENING THE FOCUS

The initial idea—whether it's based on an observation, a PR tip, an anniversary, or just plain luck—is only the beginning of the story development process. You must sharpen the basic idea into a focused and workable story suggestion (understanding that the sharpening and development will continue beyond this point). In order to do that, to move to a story suggestion, you have to know what story you are suggesting. Recall the process we have undertaken up to this point. Let's say you have observed something, an activity, a behavior, something apparently mundane that just might have some larger meaning, or something newsworthy that may merit deeper exploration. You have begun examining that observation by asking a question about it, making inferences about its meaning. For any observation you make, there might be a half dozen topics. For every topic, there might be a half dozen particular stories.

Each one of those stories will be organized around a particular **angle**, a theme that connects all of the elements of the story into a cohesive whole and, ultimately, connects the story itself with an audience interested in reading it. Even before that, you will have to connect with an editor interested in presenting it to that audience. "It's fascinating to realize that writers don't write for publications," notes Greg Lindsay. "They write for editors." He certainly knows from his experience writing for some of the leading magazines, including *Fast Company*, *The New York Times*, *Bloomberg Businessweek*, *Travel & Leisure*, and *Slate*.

ANGLE: The focus of a story, sometimes referred to as the slant or theme.

SLANT: A key element of the consideration of the angle, looking at the potential audience.

THEME: The central topic of a story, which can be summarized by a concrete topic statement, or simply understood by the reader based on the presentation of material.

What determines the story you pick is the angle (the **slant**, the focus, or the **theme**). Here, there is a clear distinction between newspaper writing and magazine writing. In newspaper writing, slanting is a sin. In magazine writing, it is a virtue, as every magazine has a point of view or perspective that resonates with its audience. In newspaper writing, you want to balance, providing (to the best of your professional ability) equal weight to all factors. Magazines generally will highlight one facet of this "truth," one that interests the reader and thus meets the expectations of that reader. A good newspaper reporter will spend years sharpening a nose for news. A good magazine writer will spend years developing a keen ability to sniff out feature angles.

So, what is a good angle? Put another way, what is your particular story about? What is it *really* all about? We can look at movies for examples of storytelling angles. The film "Amadeus" is about the creative genius Wolfgang Amadeus Mozart. But only partly. This quirky prodigy and rock star of his moment really becomes a vehicle through which playwright and screenwriter Peter Shaffer tells a story that is both larger and smaller than Mozart himself. This is a story about jealousy and its destructive power. Similarly, "The Godfather" appears to be a story about the mob. In fact, it is a story about family and more specifically (and ironically) the destruction of the family in an attempt to save it. The "X-Men" series uses the action-adventure superhero genre to tell us a story that really is allegorical. It is the story about individualism as a source of empowerment. It presents to us the value of difference and, in the process, addresses the angst of the teenager (struggling with being ostracized, marginalized for being different).

In the last chapter, we shared the experience of Mike Sager, writer-at-large for *Esquire* when he recognized an altogether new story rising out of his pre-scheduled short bio interview with comedienne Roseanne Barr. When she revealed that she had multiple personality disorder, a light bulb illuminated for Sager, and he wound up with a story he never would have anticipated when he set out to do the short bio.

One of the authors was assigned to do a story for *Chicago* magazine on the anticipated campaign of Chicago Congressman Bobby Rush for mayor of that city. Rush, a former Black Panther, was destined to become a fascinating story, but the interview never was granted and the author had to retool. He proposed a new angle on the story: he would interview all the other African Americans who had run for mayor of Chicago, discussing the issues a unique candidate like Rush would face, perhaps even offering advice through the magazine on how he should run, what he should look out for, what we all might expect. The editors agreed. But then, the story changed again, in the course of the first interview. The late R. Eugene Pincham was a former Illinois Appellate Court judge, whose most recent reputation in Chicago was that of a gadfly and political opportunist, given to making inflammatory political statements. That was the public image. What the author saw in the privacy of Pincham's study was something much different. As the interview went on, Pincham was on the phone constantly. He was being asked for legal referrals, which he would rattle off the top of his head. It was as if he knew every lawyer in Cook County, as well as every lawyer's precise specialty. And he was getting calls from reporters, including those who had helped to shape that unkind public image. These reporters were calling for insight on complex legal matters they were covering. Hold on, wait a minute. The *Chicago* editors agreed on the new story, one that revealed how Pincham, much maligned in the contemporary press, had a rich history of advocacy, a lawyer's lawyer, the man every other lawyer in town wanted to watch deliver his closing arguments. Ultimately, in "The Defiant One," published in the July 1999 edition of *Chicago*, he was presented as something of a metaphor for the local African American community, which, much like the man himself, had been terribly misunderstood.

CHANGING COURSES, NAVIGATING THE ANGLES

New York magazine contributing writer Will Leitch certainly understands how to change course in the middle of an assignment. Leitch, the enterprising founding editor of Gawker Media's *Deadspin* sports blog, was working on a *New York* story on the upstart Twitter. "It was early enough in their development that I was able to hang out at the office all day and interview the founders and go out drinking with them—stuff I could never do now," recalls Leitch. And then things changed, as he writes in "How Tweet It Is," published in the February 8, 2009 edition of *New York*.

> The first day I was in the Twitter office, I sat in the corner, playing with my own Twitter page, taking notes (it feels somewhat silly to write in a notebook there), and waiting to talk to Williams. [. . . .] And then I noticed something on Twitter Search. The first person was "manolantern," who, at 12:33 local time, posted, "I just watched a plane crash into the hudson rive (sic) in manhattan." After that, the updates were unceasing. Some fifteen minutes before the New York Times had a story on its website (and some fifteen hours before it had one in print), Twitter users who witnessed the crash of US Airways Flight 1549 were giving me updates in real time.

In the instant of a *Tweet*, the Leitch story was transformed from one considering how Twitter could succeed to one ending with the conclusion that it could not fail. "There are two major ideas that were fascinating to me about this," recalls Leitch, who also is a contributor to *The New York Times, GQ, Fast Company,* and *Slate*. "One is the idea that Twitter can't help but succeed if we live in a world where someone sees a plane crash right in front of them and the first thing they do is to take a picture of it and show it to the world," Leitch insists. "The second idea is that, while this is going on, at the Twitter offices, they were having some boring meeting about their server," Leitch recalls. "They had no idea a plane had crashed until like five hours after their server had broken the story. This was the new medium."

Hugh Jackman
Getty Images

So, once again, what is your story about? What is it really all about? Answering these questions helps to define the story clearly, to sharpen its focus. This, in turn, will give editors a sense of connection between the reader and the story you are suggesting. Remember our values model. Which one of those values have you addressed? How well have you connected with one of the pillars of the publication? What audience need will your story satisfy? The editor will consider that all-important thing readers will gain from the piece in determining whether your story fits into the lineup of the book. Here is where the *SERVE* device (discussed in the last chapter) can intersect with the values model in helping you sharpen your focus. Given the profile of the readership of the magazine, what is the level of significance, enlightenment, relevance, value, and empathy your piece will provide to this very specific group? What will the reader take away from this story?

Another way to approach your angle is to consider who your story is about. Who is affected by the events, issues, or phenomenon that you have observed? Who are the characters through which you can tell the story and whose experiences can provide you with a narrative arc? People help illustrate and illuminate stories. They provide a face with which the audience can identify, a pulse that beats in sync with the rhythm of the reader. Finding the right face, the right heart for the story, then, will help you find the right audience for the story, too. You will begin to think about this person, his plight, her triumph. Considering who the story is about—the right face, the right audience to connect with that human element—also will help you identify a magazine or group of magazines that would provide an appropriate home for your story. There is the popular story about how an editor at *Parade* magazine rejected a pitch from a freelancer about cardio pulmonary resuscitation techniques being taught in middle schools. In one of those unusually lucky situations, the writer got a second chance to talk up the story and in the process told the editor about a five-year-old who saved his grandmother. Finally, the editor reportedly responded: "Why didn't you tell me this story was about kids who save lives?"

What is it all about?   In magazine writing, we reach an answer to the ultimate (What is this story really all about?) question in effect by asking others. Who is interested in reading this piece? Who is interested in publishing it? Is it the right idea for that publication and its readers? In answering these questions, you must be sure your treatment is on the mark in terms of:

• Subject (broad topic)
• Slant (direction, angle)
• Scope (breadth of coverage).

Essentially, you must fine-tune the basic idea into a workable story suggestion with all these considerations in mind. Sharpening the angle and finding the right magazine go together. What constitutes a good angle just might depend on the publication considering it. There are calculated steps you can take to carry you a long way in getting there.

Examine the magazine in order to determine how to refine the topic idea into a sellable article. Read several back issues in addition to the magazine's writers' guidelines in order to get a sense of how the magazine engages with its readers.

Next, you will want to review the four factors we set out in Chapter 3, using them to evaluate the publication:

1. The magazine's focus
2. The magazine's niche
3. Its audience composition
4. The interests of its audience.

Focus   As we discuss in Chapter 3, we generally think of the focus as the category. So, generally speaking, we are talking about focus in terms of men's and women's magazines, as well as business, entertainment, lifestyle, service, travel, and commentary. But there are other factors that are important in sharpening your analysis. Consider whether the magazine is a horizontal book—one that cuts across a variety of demographics and topics–or a vertical book—one that drills deeply into a topic and has a fairly uniform demographic. *Essence* magazine is a horizontal African American women's service book that cuts across a wide swath of categories, from lifestyle to home décor, and appeals to African American women from age 18 to 49.

Forbes magazine is a vertical business title with a fiscally conservative perspective and an audience that consists mostly of executives (most of them men) in upper management positions.

Even these categories are sorted according to the niche the publication fills, as measured partly by its style or presentation.

Niche   When we consider the style of the magazine, we are talking about its presentation, or voice. Is it hip and irreverent, as with *Rolling Stone* or *Cosmopolitan*? Is material presented in a more serious or traditional voice, as with *Ladies' Home Journal,* or more serious still, as with *Harper's*? Does the magazine have a service orientation, as characterized by *Self* and *Essence*? Are stories framed in a how-to format as one might find in *Good Housekeeping*? As you read back issues of the magazine, take note of how it speaks to the audience. First person suggests a familiar and personal connection, such as that established in Elizabeth Foy Larsen's July 2012 *Family Circle* article "Risk Management" on child rearing and adopting more relaxed supervision techniques—with certain limitations, of course:

> I'd be lying if I said my husband's and my approach to independence is always an unqualified success. Last summer I was working late in my home office while Walter was putting Luisa to bed. That's when Henrik and Peter decided it would be fun to sprits several of our neighbor's garages with cooking spray. Walter caught them mid-high jinks, and the next morning the boys were marched to the neighbors' to apologize and clean up.

That conversational first-person style is characteristic of a magazine that forms a close bond with readers and is an important factor to consider in shaping up the story that will be proposed.

Direct address—use of the second person—also suggests a more conversational, and often how-to, service tone. Here, the writer David Tamarkin speaks directly to the reader in a package on local bars presented in the March 2013 edition of *Time Out Chicago*. After setting up this segment on bar desserts with references to so many mundane offerings, he gets to the point of it all in a way that makes the important connection to the magazine's demographic: "Listen, we have nothing against a big cookie that tastes like warm Toll House dough. But you can do better."

A more elevated tone is suggested by use of vocabulary—arcane or esoteric phrases—or an assumption of a certain level of historical, cultural, or artistic knowledge. Notice Owen Edwards' opening to a front-of-the-book piece on a photo exhibition in the October 2011 edition of *Smithsonian*:

Spin doctoring—the art of turning bad news into good and scoundrels into saints—goes back a long way. How far back is subject to debate: The bust of Nefertiti? Roman bread and circuses? Jacques-Louis David's heroic paintings of Napoleon? An exhibition of photographs from the dawn of the 20th century, now at the Arthur M. Sackler Gallery, provides a look at spin, Qing dynasty-style.

Owens opens confidently aware that he is having a conversation in the pages of *Smithsonian* with people he knows—people whose interests he understands, just as with Tamarkin in *Time Out Chicago*, and Larsen in *Family Circle*. Similarly, they all assume a certain background of experience and knowledge of their readers. Clearly, style connects to the makeup of the readership and what readers tend to understand and value. Knowing how to appeal to specific readers requires that you know who these readers are. As we discussed in Chapter 3, there are a couple of key areas to consider in this regard.

Audience composition   Without question, in sorting demographics, understanding the age range, gender, and race is vital to understanding how to speak to that audience and, by extension, how to get that conversation started by way of a story idea. Here, as we have seen, specific groups will have specific desires for information that is pertinent to their lives. These desires are part of their connection as members of specific communities of interest and translate into the interests that are considered in our fourth category of analysis. What is the education level of the audience? Is it made up of individuals who have completed some college or none? Do they have advanced degrees? This information helps determine the voice the magazine employs. What is the average household income of the audience? Is this, by and large, a group of wealthy, well-established readers or a group of young professionals who are just starting their careers? The demographic profile of the readers will dictate the magazine's approach and yours as well. In looking at even the excerpted passages above, you might be able to discern fairly quickly something about their characteristics—most especially the age. In this connection, it is important to note that, when it comes to age, the 18 to 34 range generally is one preferred by many magazines, given the heavy emphasis of this group on consumerism. Think: *"advertising."*

Audience interests   When we speak of audience interests—psychographics—we are including those values, needs, and motivations of the readers. The interests of the target audience well could be connected to the demographics. Age, education level, and gender especially could serve as the basis for the things to which a particular group is most connected. Is this an audience of skiers, bikers, or power shoppers? Do they regularly entertain at home, like to travel, or collect art? These are the factors that advertisers consider not only in deciding on their media buys (the television shows, radio programs, newspapers, and magazines they select to run their ads), but also in sharing their messages. Advertisers want to make sure they are speaking directly to an audience that is engaged in the process and has an affinity for the products or services they are marketing. But they also are the factors that editors consider in scheduling assignments. The audience's psychographic profile speaks not only to what these readers *already* do, but what they *aspire* to do as well. Not all of the three million readers of *Vogue* can afford one of the $2,500 Hermes handbags clutched by the models in its pages, but they are all *fashionistas* of a sort, and the younger, less well-heeled among them certainly aspire to stroll the boulevard one day with an expensive purse on the arm. These interests and aspirations are what bind the audience. Thus, they are the factors you need to keep uppermost in your mind as you begin to sharpen your focus, shaping up your idea with an angle that will appeal to this group.

▶ PROCESS

Look at several related magazines as potential targets for your idea. Remember, we said you should narrow your approach to several similar magazines. A look at any magazine's online media kit will give you a sense of what other magazines are in its competitive set and are ripe targets for your idea. A trip to the newsstand to see how magazines are grouped on store shelves also will provide some insight.

As you develop the idea, hone in on a category of magazines. For example, if you have made an observation about men and women making social connections at the gym, you first might consider whether this piece is best suited to a male or female audience, and then whether it should be slanted for a magazine with a focus on health and fitness or one on lifestyles or relationships. How you sharpen your focus might be a function of whether you see the story as a trend and whether that trend is situated more logically in an exercise environment (*Shape* or *Men's Health*) as an interesting byproduct of working out, or in a lifestyle environment (*Cosmopolitan* or *Details*) as a service-oriented piece on ways to "hook up." In a way, this becomes circular. You have an idea and want to sell it to a magazine. But, just as advertisers will consider the values, needs, and motivation of readers, so, too, will editors of the magazine you decide to approach. The magazine's focus and niche ultimately determine the angle on the idea you pitch, because you're going to fine-tune your article for publication. In so doing, you will convince the editor that you know what's appropriate for that particular magazine, what fits the format, the personality.

Here's how it works. After making an observation, you'll need to do some initial reporting to flesh out the idea. If you think this is a trend, what statistics can you gather to support that assertion? Peruse the Internet and other publications for information that will help you develop a level of expertise about the topic. When possible, try to find some initial subjects engaged in this enterprise who might be main characters in your story. All of this information will help to flesh out your pitch once you've identified the appropriate magazines.

As we have discussed, when searching for a home for this idea the first question you ask is who is interested in reading this piece? Relatedly, who is interested in publishing it? These are two distinct questions. Who is interested in reading will be a much larger group than the circulation of any given magazine. Determining who is interested in publishing will force you to narrow the material.

This leads to a third important step: distill. Once you have identified a potential market (a category of magazines) and have done enough preliminary reporting to understand the scope of the topic in the context of these magazines, it is important to ask yourself a couple of questions that, at first, might seem contradictory. First, ask yourself how big can I make it? Then ask yourself how small can I make it? In considering how big the story is, what the writer is asking is whether there are universal elements in the topic idea that make it right for a magazine with a horizontal focus and audience. Or is the idea best suited for a vertical magazine with a more narrow focus and audience. Consider what there is about this topic idea that cuts across all groups. Or what makes it perfect for a very specific audience. Then begin to consider ways to connect those elements to specific needs and interests of the targeted group. Let's consider the workout/dating story: if that story was pitched to a traditional women's fitness magazine like *Shape* or *Self*, the writer might take a vertical approach. The angle of the story might be solely on the health benefits. Pitched to a women's lifestyle magazine like *Cosmopolitan*, which has a very specific audience but an all-encompassing lifestyle focus, the angle of the story might emphasize the sexual benefits, or the dating opportunities created by working out.

Finally, you will want to conduct your own test of the idea. In working to sharpen those elements of the story idea to appeal to specific reader groups, consider what it is about your story that makes it different, and that makes it unique. A helpful way to do that is by crafting a short title and deck for the story. The title can be three to five catchy words that get to the essence of the story. The deck, which is like a subtitle, should be 30 words or fewer to highlight the news and sum up the angle of the story. For example, a piece about the soaring prices of the work of the late Mexican artist Frida Kahlo and the recent resurgence in fascination with her life might have the suggested title: "The Kahlo Connection." Its deck might read: "Collectors and celebrities have resurrected Mexican Artist Frida Kahlo, now a posthumous post-modern hit." Clearly, the angle of this suggested story would be more than simply the resurgence in popularity of Kahlo's works. It would go to the celebrity connection to that resurgence.

The discipline required to sum up an idea with a limited number of words—as you do with a title and deck—also will be helpful in focusing your effort on sharpening the angle. On the other hand, as commentators have noted, the less focused piece might require many more words to describe, and likely cannot lend itself to a clear and concise title. A working title will force you to think of an angle instead of just a subject. Remember to get the most salient elements of the story in your headline and deck to heighten an editor's interest.

There is the story of mega-hit-making record producer Kenny "Babyface" Edmonds who was once asked by a magazine interviewer how he knew when he had a good song to produce (for the likes of stars like Toni Braxton). He said that his test of his music was to imagine it playing on Top 40 radio. If it sounds like something he might hear on the radio, then he knows he has a hit. Test yourself. Consider a working title for your piece and imagine it on the cover of a magazine. Does it look and sound like something people might be attracted to? If so, it just might be a hit.

▶ COVER

Experienced magazine writers and commentators suggest that a good technique for considering sharper story angles for particular magazines is to think about the way stories are pitched by the editors of your target magazine. As important as the break-of-the-book is the way stories are marketed to regular readers and potential readers. Magazine industry analysts will

Thinkstock / Ingram Publishing

tell you that it all begins on the cover of the magazine. What does the style of cover presentation say about the magazine's attitude, its philosophy, as well as the stories it features? Is there a photo or an illustration? What about the cover lines, the blurbs selling the readers on the stories inside? What kinds of stories are these and how are they framed? For years, editors of *Ebony* magazine would meet on a regular basis to pitch the "hot" stories that might be featured in the coming months. By "hot" stories, they meant those stories that could grab a reader's attention as a cover blurb. They moved from the topics (universal elements) to specific title ideas (angles) that they believed would appeal to their market and move newsstand copies. In sorting the stories that would make it to the cover, there also was discussion of the way these stories would be framed. The themes that would be most attractive to readers. Based on what you see in looking at the magazines you have selected as potential targets, what kinds of stories do you think that magazine's editors believe are hot? How do they express their ideas, sell the readers, pitch the stories? This is a good indication of what the editors see as the important topics and—just as significant—the angles on the stories that rise from these topics.

▶ CONTENTS

The contents pages of magazines also can be quite revealing, not just about the stories that are featured and where they can be found inside,

IMPRESSIONS

VOLUME 8, NUMBER 5
MAY 2013

CONTENTS

The table of contents can provide a wealth of useful information to the freelance writer when it comes to shaping the angle and the pitch for a story. Here, we learn how the editors have interpreted their editorial mission for a magazine that clearly appeals to young, upwardly mobile professional women. The readers of Impression *are interested in service articles that help them stay healthy and become smart consumers. They also are interested in career advancement, but also life-work balance, with an eye to recreation and relationships. And, of course, they can be stargazers and will pay attention to the magazine's celebrity offerings. The language used in shaping the titles also can be helpful in understanding the voice of the magazine in engaging this book's audience in the conversation that develops in your magazine piece.*

but also about the focus of these stories. Often magazine editors will build to the presentation; pitching a story on the cover, blurbing it on the contents page, and then adding even more dimension with the title, subtitle, and deck on the story's title page. What can be determined regarding the breakdown of stories based on a reading of these elements? What especially is revealed on the contents page about the types of stories that are sorted among the front and back sections, and the feature wells? As important as anything else, how might the same stories be sharpened, refined, trimmed, or enlarged to move from one section to the other? For example, is a story on an upcoming music festival best suited for the feature well of *Rolling Stone*, or in the more topical front section?

▶ EDITOR'S PAGE

Most magazines will have a page devoted to musings by the editor or publisher. Many writers feel that reading this page will tell you what the top editorial person thinks about her book, the stories that are featured in a given month, and why they are significant to the reader. Making this reading exercise a habit, they say, can provide a great fix on the best angles on stories, as well as the philosophical approach of the magazine. After all, the editor or publisher is using the column to have a conversation with the reader. You should get in on that conversation. Eavesdrop. After all, there is familiarity in the language—*how* something is expressed, as well as *what* is expressed. Importantly, the editor is telling readers things about the articles appearing in a given edition of the magazine and doing so in a way that suggests what she thinks about the stories and how they connect to the reader. As industry observers advise, valuable insights are provided on these pages for the freelance writer interested in making that connection by way of the assigning editor.

▶ LETTERS TO THE EDITOR

Though some magazines shamelessly salt this section with only the most fawning letters, *The Economist* uses letters to the editor as a method for establishing an ongoing dialogue with the magazine's highly intelligent readers, who often challenge the magazine in their eloquent, beautifully written, and thoroughly researched epistles. Like *The Economist*, other magazines that maintain a robust and candid dialogue with their audiences through the letters also can provide you with an idea of reader interests, the level of education and sophistication, as well as the way readers have responded to particular stories that already have been published. Have the readers liked the stories? What exactly did they like about them? Are the readers critical of certain aspects of the stories? It is important to go back and read those articles and determine whether there are ways to be responsive to reader comments in addition to the points raised by the readers. In so doing, writers will go a long way toward sharpening their ability to focus the angles on stories that can be developed for publication. As important as anything else, though, a good writer will tune her ear to the voice of the publication and come to understand the reader as one might understand family and friends. As we have said before, it is essential that writers improve the ability to enter into conversations with readers. Ultimately, this is the goal.

It is important to note here, though, that published "Letters to the Editors" should be distinguished from the public comments that accompany online editions of magazines. Since the online edition can be read and commented on by anyone surfing the Internet, there is no guarantee that these comments are made by regular, loyal readers of the magazine, or instead by casual unique visitors who hyperlinked onto the site—maybe even accidentally. Understanding the magazine and its focus in order to fine-tune the angle on a proposed story is in large measure a matter of connecting with the people who have formed connections with the magazine—the regular readers.

Chapter Five Review

ASSIGNMENT DESK

1. Select a magazine and read the cover lines, contents page, editor's or publisher's column, and published letters to the editor. Based on this review, write a summary of types of stories that are published in the magazine. Looking at the analysis you have developed here, what can you determine about the angles on stories that appear in the magazine?

2. Take a look at several magazines in the same category (for example, women's magazines; health & fitness; or fashion). How are similar topics "framed" by editors of each of these magazines to appeal to specific audiences?

3. Take the observation you made in Chapter 4 and develop an angle for a story that might be published in a specific magazine.

4. Write a headline and deck for the idea that you have developed. Now write a separate headline and deck for the same idea, but slanted for several specific magazines.

5. Take a news story and develop an angle for a feature story based on that event or issue.

▶ KEY TERMS

- angle
- slant
- theme

▶ SUGGESTED READING

Brewer, Robert Lee. *Writer's Market 2013*. New York: Writer's Digest Books, 2013. Annually updated guide to a number of freelance writing opportunities.

▶ WEB RESOURCES

http://nymag.com/news/media/54069/ "How Tweet It Is," by Will Leitch. *New York*, February 8, 2009.

http://amsaw.org/ Official web page of the American Society of Authors and Writers, an association of North American (mostly) non-fiction writers that provides references to agents, editors, and other resources.

6 Pitch Perfect

▶ INTRODUCTION

As we have seen, there are a number of steps that must be taken before a writer is ready to craft an article for publication. An estimated 90 percent of all **pitches** are, well, pitched—rejected by editors. This statistic should not be daunting to the emerging writer. The percentage is so high because so many stories are proposed by people who don't have a clue about how to frame a story, sharpen the angle, and, as important as anything else, make the most effective presentation to editors using a few well-established techniques to gain favorable attention. That will be the focus of this chapter.

▶ MARKETING YOUR WORK

The discussion in the preceding chapters has been designed to guide you through a methodical approach to making the approach to editors. Certainly knowing what you need to know before making your pitch is vitally important. Let's review the steps taken so far:

1. You have made an observation of something (whether an occurrence in your daily routine, an item currently in the news, or one you discover through your search of archives or in discussions with persons you know).
2. You have identified the basic story idea that can flow from this observation or research.

> ### LEARNING OBJECTIVES
>
> 1. Develop strategies that put you on the right path to your target magazine.
> 2. Navigate paths to editors who are receptive to your ideas.
> 3. Develop an understanding of what editors are looking for in queries from writers.
> 4. Translate your story idea into a pitch that will be read by editors.
> 5. Develop a checklist of elements to include in your query.

PITCH: The presentation of a story idea to an editor.

3. You have done some additional research to flesh out people and begin to identify an angle for your story.
4. You have identified several publishing possibilities, several magazines that appear to publish the kind of story you have in mind.
5. You have examined the magazines and their online media kits and writers' guidelines to determine their focus and niches.
6. You have evaluated the magazines' readers to determine their needs and interests, as well as their characteristics.
7. As a result of these steps, you have fine-tuned your basic story idea, sharpening the angle further to appeal to particular readers.
8. Now you must approach magazine editors to pitch the story you want to sell.

What is the best approach to pitching the idea—making the case for the story and your ability to produce it? In this chapter, we will discuss the various approaches to framing a pitch to editors and the elements that are essential to include. Here we outline the process that is most likely at least to gain favorable attention, if not the assignment itself.

▶ BREAKING IN

As we have discussed in earlier chapters, it is very rare that an emerging writer breaks into a major magazine with a feature story. Typically, a new writer's entrée into a magazine for which she's never worked is a short department piece in the front- or back-of-the-book, or an online piece for the digital edition of the magazine. These ideas are pitched to a senior or associate editor who is responsible for filling that space, or, in the case of the online magazine, to the managing editor for digital, or someone in his chain of responsibility. It is always best to check, as each publication is different in this regard. Developing relationships with these up-and-coming editors is key to getting a foot in the door of the publication and launching your career as a freelance magazine writer. The magazine business is an itinerate one. Editors advance their careers by moving from book to book, taking a step up the masthead with each transition. As these young editors rise up the ranks—from assistant editor, to associate editor, to senior editor, to articles or features editor—they take with them their "*Rolodex*" of writers who successfully produced department pieces for them during their ascent. As the editors gain more responsibilities and get bigger stories to edit, they assign bigger stories to the writers who produced for them most consistently.

To discover which junior editors are responsible for which sections, examine the magazine's masthead. Determine whether the editorial categories include the editors' names. Lifestyle magazines typically have a health editor, a fashion or style editor, and, perhaps, an editor responsible for technology. If the masthead offers no clue—often editors are simply listed generically as "associate editor" or "senior editor" with no sense of an area of specialty—check the magazine's writers' guidelines or call to ask which editor handles the departments named in the magazine.

Before pitching the editor, read several back issues to get a feel for the kinds of stories used in the department and how they are treated. Does the department consist of "high concept" pieces that abandon traditional narrative format in favor of a heavy use of graphics and info boxes? Many departments consist of several short pieces, some no more than 250 words. Does the magazine use a lot of Q&As in the front-of-the-book? (See our discussion in Chapter 12.) Editors often are desperate for ideas to fill these spaces, so pitch several ideas instead of just one. It will demonstrate that you have an eye for the kinds of pieces that fit the department. Being able to deliver consistent spot-on ideas to a young editor will endear you to her and ensure that you ride her coattails to bigger stories down the road. Remember our earlier discussion about motivation. One of the goals of your writing strategy is to build relationships. "It's fascinating to realize that writers don't write for publications; they write for editors," notes Greg Lindsay, a contributing writer for *Fast Company*. "I'm a big believer in relationships," says Lindsay, a visiting scholar at New York University, who also has written for *The New York Times, The Wall Street Journal, Travel & Leisure,* and *Condé Nast Traveler.*

Of course, every so often new writers are able to break into a magazine with a feature article. This is more likely to happen at smaller magazines. There are several possibilities available to emerging writers who want to break into a magazine with a feature. You might just prepare the manuscript, send it unsolicited and unannounced to the editor, and then wait for her to respond with a contract. The concern here is that editors are exceptionally busy people who are not likely to carve out time to read 2,000 plus words of an article they were not expecting from a writer they don't know. The other drawback to submitting an unsolicited manuscript is that—assuming they see it at all—editors will have a tendency to see such an unsolicited story only as the writer has framed it. As creative and imaginative as they might be, they just might fail to recognize other rich possibilities for developing (or redeveloping) a story you already have put together.

In fact, if an editor spends any time at all with an unsolicited manuscript, she just might see a small part of the manuscript she doesn't like and then reject the entire document, without reading on to discover some very rewarding material for her readers. It is important to understand, as discussed earlier, that editors want to have a hand in shaping the stories they assign. You should want that, too, because you and the story will benefit from this engagement. This is not simply a matter of ego gratification. Editors see themselves as the guardians of the style and tone of their magazines. They pride themselves on knowing their readers and what those readers want.

As well as writers might think they know the market and the voice of the magazine, the editor is going to feel she has an even better understanding of all this and more. That is what she gets paid to do—knowing the reader, the reader's interests, and how best to satisfy these interests.

Additionally, at any given moment in any given month, the assigning editor will be engaged in the long-range editorial plans for the magazine. In other words, she will know how even a kernel of a story idea fits into future stories and packages of related stories that are merely in the planning stages at the time of your pitch. The best editors, after all, have risen through the ranks because they are well practiced at seeing stories and angles that can match up with their reader interests and needs months in advance. So don't be discouraged if an editor wants to refashion your approach. An editor can be a very good partner in the story development process, beginning with the conception of the idea. (See our discussion of the process in Chapter 10.)

Finally, there are litigation concerns that make editors reluctant to read unsolicited manuscripts. Some editors refuse to read stories that come over the transom in order to avoid a big fight with someone who might claim later to have inspired something that wound up getting printed. As a legal matter, ideas and even story titles are not subject to copyright protection and without more evidence of actual copying an idea cannot serve as the basis of a winnable claim. But it can be a costly nuisance to have to defend a claim that gets past the first legal hurdle and survives a motion to dismiss. (See our discussion in Chapter 20.)

One such case once arose at *Ebony* magazine, where a story titled "25 Ways to Find Your Perfect Mate" brought a claim from a woman who argued that she had written a book with a similar title. The author claimed she had sent the book to *Ebony* for story consideration. After the tedious (and successful) defense, a new policy was implemented at the parent company of *Ebony*: all unsolicited manuscripts were to be returned unread (preferably unopened) with a form letter stating the company's practice of not reviewing such manuscripts.

SLUSH PILE:
The unsolicited manuscripts that are received by editors and usually ignored or assigned to a junior staffer for review.

Book publishers have a similar policy so that editors likely will not consider a manuscript from a writer unless submitted by an agent known by the editor. In this way, book editors create another layer of vetting by the people (agents) they reasonably believe can spot good stories before they're submitted. Even those magazines that do not have "return unread" policies likely will just let unsolicited manuscripts accumulate in the **slush pile**, so-called because it takes on the character of all the unsightly and annoying slush we want to avoid in frigid winter months.

There are exceptions to the manuscript submission rule. Certain kinds of material can only be evaluated in finished form. If the piece you are proposing is a humor piece, an essay, or a work of opinion or fiction, it is likely that editors will want to see the completed work if only to make sure you can deliver what you promise. Plain and simple, in these categories editors just can't tell that your humor piece will amuse, that your essay will elevate, or that your work for fiction is literate until they actually see what you can do.

Again, the point here is that, unless a submission falls into one of these categories, editors will not have time to review a fully developed piece that, based on their experience, likely will not be on point for the magazine. They also will want to have a role in the total development of the piece they're interested in buying. Don't circumvent the editor's role in providing this guidance. So, with that in mind, sending an unsolicited manuscript is not likely to be fruitful.

Some people will try to make a direct telephone pitch. This might seem like a good idea to establish personal contact so that the editor will remember you. But, if the editor remembers anything—assuming you even get through on the phone—it is likely that the most distinguishing feature of the recall will be annoyance. Editors are extremely busy and simply don't have the time to field phone queries, even if you are convinced that you have the perfect idea for the magazine. So unless you have an ongoing relationship with an editor, it is best to avoid making phone pitches—at least as a matter of first impression. Even when you know an editor, it is better to make a phone appointment ahead of time. Most editors have their own preferred time to screen pitches. Some like late afternoon, or early evening. (One former editor used to set aside the 4 p.m. hour for such review, after handling the more urgent matters of the business day.) Some editors might like to review pitches first thing in the morning, before getting started on the business of the day, and before any scheduled editorial staff meetings where ideas are discussed. Others prefer weekends. The pitch that provides such freedom of choice is more likely to get a non-prejudicial read.

Obviously, the point of working our way through these "pitch" considerations is to illustrate why the **query** letter is the best way to make a pitch—particularly if this is your first contact with a particular editor. There are a number of reasons why a query letter is beneficial. Essentially, the query—the industry standard—is quite familiar to editors, who prefer a concise summary that can help demonstrate a few key factors: a story idea that connects with readers; the writer's access to the information and people to make the story happen; your professionalism in presenting the idea; and an idea of your writing style (your voice). The query also is the most efficient tool—for both the writer and the editor—to determine whether a given story will be a good fit for a particular magazine. If it is not, then the writer can retool quickly and re-shape the pitch for another magazine.

QUERY: A letter to a magazine editor proposing a story idea.

The idea   As we have discussed, the initial steps in the story development process, if executed properly, should increase the likelihood that the story idea that emerges will resonate with a particular editor at a particular magazine.

First, before you actually approach a magazine you have to flesh out the story. Your preliminary research will help you identify the scope of the story you want to propose and the likely sources of interviews to be included. What are the issues that are presented by the story? Who are the key people whose views on this subject should be expressed? Is there any anecdotal information (potential narratives) that might help to illustrate the story and bring it to life?

But preliminary research is about more than just setting out the scope of the story and sources. It is essential to look at the target magazine(s) thoroughly to make sure the story you want to pitch has not already been published. Clearly, a writer needs to have a very intimate understanding of the magazine, its editorial mission as defined and expressed in its pages, as well as its audience makeup and interests.

It also is important to understand the cycle of your target magazine(s). In other words, if a magazine has published a similar story, how likely is it to come back to that subject? Is your piece substantially distinctive so as to warrant new treatment, a fresh angle, or an update? How often does a magazine "refresh" similar subject matter? Clearly, *People* will revisit topics much more frequently (sometimes a couple of times a year) than *The New York Times Magazine* (possibly only once every few years).

Further, special topics deserve special effort in conducting background research. In Chapter 4, we mentioned the writer who pitched a fortieth anniversary story about the assassination of Black Panther leader Fred Hampton to a magazine that already had done a similar article on the thirtieth anniversary. The editor passed on the idea just for that reason. Clearly, ten years was too soon to return to this subject in his view. Usually, it is a good idea to review at least one year's back issues of your target in order to make sure you are not duplicating what already has been done. Obviously, though, there are those times when—depending on the magazine or the subject matter—a couple of years is not nearly enough.

In addition to reviewing past issues of a particular target publication, it also is important to review a similar lineup of the magazine's key competitors. If *Cosmopolitan* already has published a story on the five fashion components every woman should have, it is unlikely that an editor at *Glamour* will find a similar piece fresh and exciting. Similarly, editors of *Details*, *GQ*, and *Esquire* are not going to want to be seen as copying each other, even though all these magazines purport to have distinctive audiences.

Access   A good story idea that connects with a specific market is the beginning of the process of getting a magazine story assignment. It is imperative that the pitch shows that the writer will be able to produce the story. Having access to good sources is an important first step. The preliminary research also will help identify the significant people to interview. It is important to keep in mind, as we will discuss in a later chapter on interviewing, that the key person might not necessarily be the top official in a government agency or the top executive in a corporate setting. An essential goal of the preliminary research is to identify the person who will have the most to say on the proposed story or who embodies the trend or issue you have observed. And the person should look like the kind of source the target magazine would respect and would want to include in the lineup. This signals to the editor that you have carefully considered the specific approach and voice of the magazine, as well as the needs, interests, and expectations of the readers. Preliminary research would show, for example, that *Ladies' Home Journal* might expect to see experts who have written (magazine articles or books) on a given topic, while *Marie Claire* might want to see much more anecdotal content, the personal experiences of people affected by the issue. What does your targeted magazine prefer to show—expertise or personality—and how does it prefer to show it? This understanding will shape your interview list.

Related to this is the writer's ability to reach specific persons and get the interviews. If access to key sources already has been established, then that will be an important point to include in the pitch. If you haven't established contact with potential sources at the time of the pitch, it will be important to show that you have ready and reliable access to sources. It would be a mistake at this stage of your writing assignment to make promises you have no hope of keeping. If you have never met George Clooney and have never written a story about anyone at his level of notoriety, then it might not be a good idea to suggest that you will include an interview with him. It is not likely his publicist will provide access.

Thinkstock / iStockphoto

There is a value-added benefit you can bring to the "sourcing" of your stories. It is the value of presenting multiple perspectives with an eye to finding new voices of authority. Even though the editors might have certain people in mind as "experts" in certain areas, there are fresh faces and experiences and opinions that can help to inform readers on multiple levels. A number of media organizations have been looking at ways to expand the range of voices that come through their media. Consider the example below, cited in Tom Witosky's article on Gannett, published in the Fall 2003 edition of the *Nieman Reports*:

> Gannett publications use two procedures to assure that mainstreaming and diversity become a part of the newsroom culture. Each newspaper must establish a list of minority experts for use by its reporters. These lists, often divided on the basis of subject, are to be used by reporters and editors to expand the pool of sources. Benge acknowledges that these lists produce varying levels of success. In some newsrooms, reporters turn to them constantly; in other newsrooms, they are largely ignored.

In crossing boundaries to find someone other than an older white male to speak about, say, a financial issue, an enterprising writer will introduce readers to other credible sources of information, who also represent the value that people from different racial, ethnic, gendered, and religious backgrounds can bring to topics of interest. Such an effort can be transformative as the first important step in helping people to develop new attitudes.

Writing   Of course, access to sources is only one factor in demonstrating that a story can be completed successfully. Writing ability—and particularly, the ability to write well for specific markets on deadline—is vital. Published writing samples should be included in your submission package. But the letter itself should be considered a writing sample. As such, it should be prepared with great thought and care.

Presentation   It is essential to recognize that the query letter is a professional contact and says a lot about the writer in its *form*, as well as its content. Editors get dozens of letters. What will make yours stand out? Clearly, if it is executed in a sloppy manner, or if it looks like a form letter sent to multiple parties, it will not make the most favorable professional impression. To begin, some form of letterhead (even if generated on a computer) would be good. As with any letterhead, it should include a return address, telephone number, and email address. Avoid garish colors. They might attract attention, but it is guaranteed to be the wrong kind. White works just fine. At most, you might consider a buff or ivory color, but in general, keep it plain and simple in order to project a look of professionalism. This is your first impression and it will say a great deal to the editor about the kind of first impression you might make with sources for your story when you introduce yourself as a freelancer on assignment from his magazine.

Checklist   Double and triple check the information about the editor you are pitching. Confirm his position and the correct spelling of his name. Some editors won't read even one line of a query if their names are misspelled in the salutation. *Writer's Market* can be quite helpful as a first step in determining which editors are responsible for various sections, but even *Writer's Market* might not have the most current or the most complete information. Sometimes magazine editors will submit *Writer's Market* forms hurriedly and neglect certain details that might be vital to new writers. Sometimes staff changes have occurred in the lead time between submission of these forms and actual *Writer's Market* publication and distribution. Certainly, by the end of the publication cycle, a personnel change might have occurred.

You may also use the magazine's writers' guidelines (often online, or available by mail) to confirm name spellings and titles. But double check the information you find there as well. Like *Writer's Market*, the magazine's own writers' guidelines sometimes are not updated as quickly as editors change jobs.

Just to make sure, given all these possibilities—or in the event *Writer's Market* is not entirely clear on the editor's identity—it is best to check with a phone call. Here is where telephone contact really can help you. Sometimes, in the course of checking with an administrative assistant on the correct name, spelling, and title of the appropriate editor, you just might strike up a special relationship. Learn that person's name. Address the person in any follow-up calls (although it still is best to keep such calls to a minimum). As any professional journalist will attest, administrative assistants sometimes can be your best friends in getting through to sources at their companies or organizations. The gatekeepers, they often can have the discretion that might open doors and put through phone calls.

The good thing about this process is that, unlike the unsolicited manuscript, someone is going to read the query. It might not be the person to whom you address it. That person well could be merely the official point of entry. Quite possibly, it will be an editorial assistant or assistant editor. But somebody will read it. And somebody will respond to you.

Voice   As important as anything else is the way your idea is expressed in the query. As noted above, the query is a writing sample—the one writing sample an editor can be sure has not had the benefit of some other editor's graceful touch. In other words, you should bear in mind that this is an opportunity to impress the editor with your writing flair and to demonstrate that you fit into her magazine and can hold your own amongst all the other writers. But don't sacrifice clarity and precision of language for too-cute phrasing in your query. Be creative, but don't overdo it.

▶ ELEMENTS OF THE QUERY

BACKGROUND: The research conducted to document facts that form the substantive structure of a story.

One of the first things a query can show is your ability to do research, to **background** a story. A certain amount of background is needed for the query—even before you get the assignment, let alone begin writing the story. Clearly, this is to be considered preliminary research that covers a number of areas; it is not the research for the entire story. But the preliminary research has to be thorough enough to provide the foundation you need to make a strong pitch and convince an editor that you will be able to produce the article.

"I do hours of research and probably 10 one-hour phone calls before I pitch a magazine story," freelance writer Jennifer Kahn told attendees at the Stanford's Future of Freelancing Conference in 2010. "I know who my main character is going to be and roughly what the structure is before I pitch, and I probably have 25 percent of the reporting done before I pitch," said Kahn, a journalism professor at the University of California, Berkeley, who has successfully pitched stories to *The New York Times Magazine*, *The New Yorker*, *Wired*, and *Sports Illustrated*, according to a report on the conference written by Kathryn Roethel.

Focus on the key elements of the story idea. In broad terms, there are four areas that matter here (and a fifth that will be added later). What is it about? Who is it about? Who is affected? Who will you include as sources? There should be enough here to support what you say you'll produce. Look at the articles published in the magazine. As we have discussed before, you also need to make sure there is nothing similar in competing magazines. Offer a brief synopsis of the subject. Explain what the article will cover. Editors want facts, so give them the facts. Explain who will be interviewed and why. Tease out a brief anecdote about these individuals that may flesh out and humanize the concept.

People matter. Think through the sources you will use. Begin to compile a list of experts to be interviewed. You definitely will want to refer to some of these people in the query. Look for real people who are examples of or affected by the phenomenon you've observed and can help illustrate the idea. They needn't be the individuals who will find their way into your final version, but identifying some of these people will help an editor conceptualize the story.

In terms of your presentation, there are certain elements to be included no matter what form your query takes. The query is a combination story summary and sales pitch. Think "headline," as one editor advises. Here's where your working title will come in handy, and have some additional utility. How you frame the story by way of your working title will show some creativity and will sharpen your angle. It helps the editor see the story—and see it especially in her magazine. (But don't get your feelings hurt if your title doesn't survive the production.)

Then there is a final area that is important to consider. An additional "who." That "who" is you. Who are you, and why should an editor trust you with an assignment? To a large extent you should demonstrate the reason with the nature and quality of your query. But you also need to set out a couple of points about yourself to help illustrate your ability. You should conclude your pitch with a summary of any special knowledge or background experience that makes you the best writer for the article. To an extent, the fact that you have come up with the idea helps in this regard. After all, if you have done your job right, you have set yourself apart just because you have identified a story no one else has done. That alone should give you a measure of credibility. But there are important points to be made about your ability to see it through. Show that you have unique access to sources. If not unique, then at least show access: anything in your personal background, in similar stories you have covered—even if only for your campus publication—or special projects you have worked on for journalism or other courses.

▶ FORM OF PRESENTATION

While there is nothing written in stone when it comes to the query letter (in fact, it is written on your computer, and printed on paper, which means you can experiment until you get it right), there are certain elements every successful query will include: your opening, a synopsis of the story, the sources who will be featured, and a bit of your bio.

Opening   Many editors suggest that, in addition to coming up with a working title to frame your piece, you also treat the opening of your query as something of a lead in the story itself. This might not be the actual lead you end up writing. In fact, it probably won't be, but it will set the tone for your query and demonstrate your writing ability. We'll talk about effective story openings in a later chapter, but it doesn't hurt to begin thinking about one at this stage. Just as with the working title, a good lead helps to focus you, if it's done right. It effectively will hook the editor and tell him what the story is all about. This is what makes for impacting story openings. They hook the reader and give him a reason to read on. Make the editor want to do that. "Get my attention," advises Eric Gillin, former web director, Hearst Men's Network and Hearst Digital Media. "Grab me by the throat."

The same rule applies for traditional print pitches as for the online zines, like esquire.com, which Gillin managed. A similar tip can be taken from promotional writing, where the rule is to make the sale in the first 1 to 25 words. Think about that in crafting an opening to your query letter. If you'd like to start with an anecdote, make sure it is tight and bright. It can't be a long, convoluted story that takes several paragraphs to get to the point.

Synopsis   What is this story all about? This is also called a "nut graph." It is like the lead of a traditional news story in that it includes all the salient details about the story—who, what, where, when, why, and how. A good nut graph might have a "killer stat"—some number or bit of detail about the subject that suggests its importance or significance to the readership. The story mentioned earlier about exercise and dating might include a statistic on the rise in gym memberships or, if you can find it, some suggestion of the number of people who say they met their mate or significant other at a gym. Look for that kind of detail to give your query weight and to show the assigning editor you've done your research.

Sources   Who will be featured in this story and why are they important in setting it out? It is vital in this connection that you show you will have special access to the people who will be important in telling your story. It can be difficult to get potential sources to cooperate before you've been assigned a story. Some may be reluctant to talk if you cannot guarantee that the time they've spent with you will bear fruit. Other experts, however, are more than willing to share their knowledge with a writer who shows an interest in their work or research. Check with local universities and colleges for professors who might be conducting research in the area you are interested in pursuing. They are often fonts of information and usually willing to engage with reporters.

Bio   The query letter is not your resume, which should be included in the package. So don't restate the resume here. But the key to this section of your query is to arouse interest in the editor in looking deeper into your submission package. Include just enough personal information to show that you can handle the story assignment and to make the editor want to look at your clips and your resume. So consider those parts of your background that are most pertinent to closing out this pitch. It might be certain writing credits, which you will suggest the editor can look for in your package. It might be an internship in which you had solid relevant experience dealing with the precise issue at the core of your story, or during which you met and interacted with experts in the field. Keep in mind that you only have a limited amount of space to make your points in the query. How might you best make them?

Packaging   Every submission (if you are writing to an editor for the first time) should include: the letter; your resume; and relevant writing samples. Relevant here is a relative concept. If you are pitching a story on a new restaurant opening, show a sample of a restaurant piece you already have had published. If a restaurant story is not in your portfolio, then provide a story on food preparation. If not that, then a critical review. If you have no reviews, then perhaps a personality profile, or a lifestyle or entertainment or nightlife feature. The point is that, if you don't have a writing sample that is on point, then submit anything you have written that touches on some *component* of the story you are pitching. But make sure to include a line in your letter to show the editor what is most pertinent about the writing sample. Don't assume the connection will be obvious. The editor, after all, is quite busy and just might only get those things you call to his attention. Also, it helps to focus his attention if you send samples that are similar to what the magazine publishes. The point here is that you should give the editor what he is used to seeing in his magazine and what he would expect to see in your completed work. Help the editor picture you as a contributor. If you have not written in this area, send pieces that show the depth of your reporting (even if you're proposing a short department piece) and the quality of your writing, particularly if you think your writing style matches the tone of the magazine. You may send samples from competing magazines if you think the competitor is held in high regard by the magazine you are targeting with this query. Editors are sometimes turned off by samples from publications with a dubious reputation for accuracy or ethics, so try to be conscious of that when submitting clips for consideration.

THE QUERY

The query should only be a page, and no longer than a page and a-half, long and can take one of several forms, as described below.

BUSINESS FORMAT. This is a straightforward approach that states right up front what you want to write. Here you will set out the topic, followed by a discussion of the elements of the story and the sources you will include. The letter ends with a brief discussion of your credentials and a cordial invitation to contact you. Your clips are especially important here because this approach does not necessarily show any writing flare, although it should be competently and professionally written!

STYLISTIC FORMAT. This approach likely would use something of a sample lead to a story. This "lead" might include a colorful anecdote, quote, or statistic. The point, though, is to hook the editor and demonstrate what you can do even with a short, one-page presentation. The body of the query should convey the information to be provided in the article, along with any trends that might be pertinent and, as with all forms, an idea of the people who will be interviewed. The last paragraph will summarize your writing experience and any credentials or other experience that might qualify you to write the piece.

OUTLINE FORMAT. This is an approach to query writing that is best used when there are quite a few points to be made in the article and where a one-pager would not be sufficient in setting it all out. Here, a short opener (probably around two or three sentences) would be used to set up a series of highlights or bullets of the major points of the article, ending again with the pertinent personal information.

The most effective approach clearly will depend on the nature of the proposed article, the style of the magazine, and your own writing style. But the key to success is in setting out the idea quickly and efficiently in a style that is suitable for the magazine. Again, a sample lead can be quite effective because it grabs the editor "by the throat," as Eric Gillin suggests. It also shows what you can do in an unedited form.

Always think of the query as an audition. What are the elements of your presentation that will allow you to put your best foot forward? Typically, they might include an anecdote, a provocative quote, surprising information, and context that provides meaning to a busy editor.

▶ APPROACH

Since most editors only want a page or two (preferably a page) it might be hard to get all those great ideas in. The best approach is to decide on the format you want to take and get it all down. Just write until you get it out of your system. Once this is done, you can edit. After all, it's always easier to cut it down to size later. This also will make for a much tighter presentation.

Don't forget to include your resume and writing samples. Remember, too, that with these documents included, you will not need to spend a great deal of space setting out your qualifications, which will save you some valuable space to do other things. Focus on the killer stats, the experts you'll include, and the access you have to people and information pertinent to the story. Don't be afraid to express your qualifications with confidence. "I believe I am well-suited to handle this assignment for several reasons. As my resume shows . . ." Then use your background to make a few choice points. Again, focus on the precise aspects of your experience that make the case for you to get this assignment.

▶ DRAMATIC CONCLUSION

As promotional writers are taught, always end on the action you want an editor to take. With promos, that might be to write a check, return the enclosed coupon, call today, call right now. Here, it is a little different. But you still want to suggest some action, establish the expectation. That is not to say "I'll call your office next week." Most editors will simply think "Thanks for giving me a heads-up to avoid that call." The preferred professional closing might be "I look forward to talking with you about the possibilities." Or, "I look forward to expanding on this idea as soon as you have had a chance to consider this topic." Of course, this always leaves open the option to call if you haven't heard anything in a reasonable amount of time.

So, what is reasonable? How long do you wait? Just what constitutes a reasonable amount of time depends on a number of factors. The first is what the editor determines is a reasonable amount of time. Often you will see references to response time in *Writer's Market*. That can be anywhere from a couple of weeks to a month or more. In the absence of an indication, some commentators advise you to wait four weeks, while some say six weeks. The point is to wait a "reasonable" amount of time. But, again, there are factors to consider in determining what is reasonable. If your pitch is for a time-sensitive issue, or for a seasonal topic, then this sort of consideration might cause you to cut the waiting time short. However, if you are submitting a story with a seasonal peg, you must be cognizant of the magazine's lead time. A story with a Thanksgiving angle needs to be submitted some time in the spring to get strong consideration for that year's issue. Most magazines require about six months' advance notice for seasonal work. But, again, check the magazine's blurb in *Writer's Market* or on its online guidelines.

If you have submitted your query in a timely fashion and have allowed a "reasonable" interval to pass without any word, you can consider contacting the administrative assistant—your new best friend—just to make sure the package was received. That person likely will give you an idea of the turnaround time. Best to wait at least a couple of weeks after such a contact before calling again. Sometimes a follow-up letter with additional selling points can be a helpful approach. But only if there really is a new development. Not everybody wants to get multiple pitches on the same subject. One thing to avoid is sending a copy of the original letter stamped "Copy" or "Second Notice." This can be a real annoyance to editors.

Many impatient writers want to consider simultaneous submissions. This is something to consider only if the magazine makes it clear that it will accept a pitch that you are sending to multiple markets. Few are so accepting. Think about it: every magazine editor is going to believe that his book is unique and satisfies special needs and interests in a precise market niche. So, if you are pitching multiple editors, then you obviously don't understand that distinctive quality of the magazine and your story does not deserve attention. Further, silence from an editor can be due to any number of factors that do not amount to rejection. As noted, some editors have special periods set aside from story consultation, editorial planning, and production, just to review queries. Your letter might have arrived off cycle. Once an editor reads your query and likes the idea, she is not going to want to learn that five other editors also might be considering the pitch. Most editors will want the exclusive from start to finish.

With respect to compensation, it is best to leave all such considerations out of the query. This is a matter best left to the negotiation discussion (which we take up in Chapter 20). There are standard rates that will be offered to first-time writers in certain sections of the book.

Don't overlook the basics. Maintain a business-like appearance of your letter. Check for grammar, word choice, and spelling. Nothing will prejudice an editor's read more than a typographical error in your letter. Certainly anyone can make a mistake, but you have the chance to proofread your letter before it goes out. If you fail to do that and fail to recognize mistakes once you do it, then you are essentially telling the editor that you also are not careful enough to check the facts of the story you are asking to write.

Confirm the information of the person to whom you are writing. Consider delivery instructions. While most first-time contacts through the query letter should be mailed, increasingly editors are accepting pitches in other forms. Check whether a fax or email query would be accepted. Often, email is fine once you have developed a working relationship with an editor. Increasingly, editors are willing to accept in multiple ways. "I don't care how you get here," Eric Gillin advises. "Fax me, if you can find a way to fax me. Send me something in the mail. Just get it to me. The problem isn't *how* it's delivered, it's *what* is delivered." In any event, it always is best to check first. At the Stanford Future of Freelancing Conference, writer Jennifer Kahn suggested a preliminary email contact of just a couple of sentences to check whether an editor is interested in your story idea and asking for a reply. This is a useful tactic, as she noted, because an interested editor will then write to you asking you to pitch.

Finally, if you submit through the mail and want your writing samples and any other materials returned, you also must include a self-addressed stamped envelope (SASE).

WRITER'S WORKSHOP

Here is a suggestion for you to apply a central point of this chapter as you begin to develop article ideas.

In her presentation at the Stanford Future of Freelancing Conference in June 2010, writer and journalism professor Jennifer Kahn gave a useful organizational tip that tracks the advice most writers share. Try keeping the entire pitch to five paragraphs. The first, she recommends, should set out that compelling case for the story (perhaps through a sample lead, as some writers and editors suggest). The second paragraph should explain very clearly, and concisely what the story is about. The third paragraph should expand on the reasons why the editor (and her readers) should care about the issue presented. The fourth paragraph should provide some information on the sources you will consult. The final paragraph should say something about you that will help the editor see your ability to handle the piece. This is a useful approach to keep in mind in framing a query presentation.

Chapter Six Review

ASSIGNMENT DESK

This assignment will be in three parts. Take another look at the idea you have considered over the course of the earlier chapters (having made an observation, sharpen that observation into an angle for a category of magazines). Now write a query letter to pitch that story idea to your target magazine using the three most common styles of presenting the pitch:

1. Business Format

2. Stylistic Format

3. Outline Format

In completing this assignment think about different ways you might empha-size the various aspects of the query in adapting to the styles of presentation. What will you stress in working with a business over a stylistic format? How does the outline expand or limit your ability to make the case for your story and yourself?

▶ KEY TERMS

- background
- pitch
- query
- slush pile

▶ WEB RESOURCES

http://www.nieman.harvard.edu/reports/article/101008/Mainstreaming-and-Diversity-Are-Gannetts-Core-Values.aspx "Mainstreaming and Diversity Are Gannett's Core Values," by Tom Witosky. *Nieman Reports*, Fall 2003.

http://freelance.stanford.edu/reports/pitch/ "The Science (Not Art) of the Magazine Pitch," by Kathryn Roethel. "The Future of Freelancing: Redefining Journalism. Reinventing Yourself," June 2010.

http://freelance.stanford.edu/ Reports of the two-day Future of Freelancing Con-ference at Stanford University in June 2010, at which 120 freelance writers and 50 editors, agents, and other experts met to talk about writing, marketing, and future prospects.

www.mediabistro.com Comprehensive website whose listings include jobs and freelance opportunities for budding freelance writers.

www.writersmarket.com Official website of the subscription-based guide to writing opportunities.

http://amsaw.org/ Website of the American Society of Authors and Writers, an association dedicated to helping new and established writers connect with agents, publishers, and editors.

7 Research: The Foundation of Good Storytelling

▶ INTRODUCTION

In this chapter, we discuss the vital elements of story development that are special to magazine articles. In essence, as experienced hands have attested, there are two broad areas of research consideration: documents and voice. With documents, we discuss the importance of reviewing all published material pertaining to your assigned subject matter (newspaper and magazine articles, scholarly works, books and online entries, blogs and public comments). How much background information is enough? What is too much? Ultimately, we consider what is crucial to the particular story being produced. And, as we will show, everything depends on the nature of the magazine and the expectations of the audience, as well as the scope of the story. The bottom line is that the research should be as narrowly drawn as the angle, as focused as the target audience, and as extensive as necessary to cover the subject matter thoroughly. We will show how important it is to begin the research process even before drafting the query and certainly before the first interview is scheduled. Voice is where the interview material is considered first. Here, we will show contributors the importance of obtaining both expert opinion for factual context, and personal stories for illustration. Not only does voice help to humanize the subject matter, according to industry observers, but it also helps to show what all the background information actually means—through interpretation and by way of example. That is why, as we will discuss, magazine interviews must be immersive and can

LEARNING OBJECTIVES

1. The two types of focused research needed to write strong stories.

2. How to determine the amount of background needed to conduct interviews.

3. How to approach the interview process with different types of interview subjects.

4. How to determine the proper weight to give to background research for particular magazine audiences.

5. How to begin thinking about the presentation of research and interviews in dynamic magazine stories.

take substantial time to conduct even after the substantial time spent in preparing for them. Readers should walk away feeling they know the people who are presented in the story—their needs, their motivations, their conflicts. And that is true even when the focus of the story is not on an individual.

▶ DOCUMENTS

Whether you are writing a service piece for *Woman's Day* or an issue-driven narrative for *Vanity Fair*, the need for background research is vital. No matter how well you write, you must have the right stuff about which to write. It all starts with research. And that process, as we explained in Chapter 6, should start before you even frame your story pitch. After all, you want at the very least to make sure you have set out the right scope of the story you want to write and you need to make sure your story has not been published already by your target market—the magazine you are considering for your piece. As important as anything else, though, you want to make sure you are well grounded in the subject matter in order to frame your story persuasively for initial discussion with the editor, but also to frame the scope of the second level of research you will conduct—the interviews.

Without question, good research techniques are essential when writing articles for the select and highly informed audience, which magazine readers tend to be. First, factual substance is the basis of all good writing. This is true whether you are dealing with investing, city planning, weight loss, education, exercise regimens, sports controversies, spousal abuse, home decorating, or the personality profile. Whatever the topic, there must be content. There also must be context. They are both established by the factual background obtained through solid research.

There are additional benefits that flow from good background research. As Professor Peter Jacobi has written, the mass of research also gives you, the writer, a more authoritative voice, as we discuss in Chapter 9. That is true even when you don't use everything that turns up in your research. Indeed, as we will discuss later, you should not use it all in the story.

The first step is to be able to separate what is crucial from what is just basic information. So, what is crucial to this story? To answer that question, you must start with a clear understanding of the magazine focus and the audience needs and interests. Does the magazine stress personality? Does the magazine stress fact-laden issue-oriented presentation? This is the most basic first question to answer. Most research questions are going to flow from that answer. Compare *Marie Claire* and *Ladies' Home*

Journal on a health story. October is "Breast Cancer Awareness Month" and both magazines are likely to consider stories on women and cancer. But the approach will be different with respect to framing the issue. *Marie Claire* is much more likely to present a story that is personality driven; a human interest approach that will appeal to its younger demographic. *Ladies' Home Journal* pushes facts and documentation for a slightly older audience of professionals and parents. These determinations are made by editors who clearly are aware of their editorial mission and—as important as anything else—the interests and needs of their readers. *Ladies' Home Journal* readers are women who likely are going to demand more supportive information, while *Marie Claire* is aimed at aspiring professionals who, according to the market research, have a particular interest in the stories, experiences, and accomplishments (including the cancer survival) of other people. In the personality-driven approach of a *Marie Claire* piece, issues will serve as a backdrop for the presentation of anecdotal narrative—a case study of sorts. Thus, more research time will be devoted to identifying people than to obtaining documentary evidence. In an issue-oriented *Ladies' Home Journal* piece, people stories will serve as examples to illustrate the documented facts that will be presented in a lengthy article, citing books as well as medical professionals, and will include two or three sidebar boxes with related substantive information. Thus, more time will be devoted to researching the subject matter itself—collecting facts and medical data to summarize the issues presented in a thorough manner. Although time will be spent documenting the personal stories, they will occupy a smaller percentage of the total background research for the story. Note how the magazine presented short references to personal stories to set up an article related to breast cancer by writer Sharlene K. Johnson:

> Patty Nersesian, an at-home mother of three in Manlius, New York, was 31 when she had a bilateral mastectomy last year, followed by reconstruction with saline implants.
>
> Lee Mirrer, a 49-year-old office manager for a Santa Barbara, California, dental office, had three surgeries on her left breast in the past year before she and her doctor were both satisfied that she could safely forgo follow-up radiation therapy.
>
> What do these two women have in common? Neither of them had invasive breast cancer.

In the article, each of the women is quoted only once, while the writer's substantive research and interviews with experts takes up the majority of the space devoted to the story about ductal carcinoma in situ (DCIS) and how DCIS—a pre-invasive, or Stage 0 breast cancer—is treated medically.

There are other questions to consider in setting the scope of your background research. Does the magazine tend to focus on elements of political drama or legal fights, the competing forces surrounding an issue or the consequences of these battles on people affected by them? Is the magazine more service oriented than issue oriented? An article on binging (periodic overeating), drinking, relationship disorders would take this focus into account. So, while background information is important in setting out the issue (presenting an overview of the problem and its consequences), more research time will be devoted to sorting viable solutions to the problems that are identified. This might involve more interview time with professionals and academicians for opinions.

Clearly, then, knowing your target market is a critical first step in knowing how much that audience is going to want to know about the subject, and the sources of that information that will be valued the most. This, in turn, will determine how much time you devote to obtaining certain types of information. Research for factual presentation? Research for expert opinion? Research for anecdotal narratives in case studies? The point here is that there is a limited amount of time to devote to the research process. You must spend that time wisely. How do you strike the balance? The research has to be as focused as the target market, as sharp as the angle you have polished for the story.

Thinkstock / iStockphoto

▶ VOICE

No matter which magazine you have targeted, your story ultimately will have to reflect a balance of the structural elements (background facts; anecdotes; quotes; and examples), as we discuss in Chapters 8 and 9. Just how these elements are balanced depends on the magazine focus and audience expectations. But in the presentation, there must be voice, as well as documentation. Certainly, as you develop your writing style, your writer's voice will emerge as something of a signature in your articles. But here, we speak of voice in terms of the human element that breathes life into the story.

There are several ways to include this element in the magazine article. To the extent that your research has turned up leading published works in a particular area, you might consider citing these works, and even quoting select (and very limited) passages, as reviewed by your editor and fact checkers for copyright purposes. Most often, though, the people you quote will be the people you interview in the course of gathering information for the story. The interview is a significant part of the information gathering process in that it provides authoritative detail to the factual presentation and it can add personal experience—even human drama—to illustrate these details. And, as you might expect, the interview also is important in preparing the personality profile, although not always essential, as we discuss in Chapter 11.

Expert and personal sources   Generally, the interviews for most stories tend to fall into a couple of categories. There is the expert perspective and there is the personal, or anecdotal, experience.

In the effort to provide support and dimension for the assertions in the story, you will want authoritative, well-positioned people with expertise in your topic area. As discussed earlier, a number of your experts likely will be identified in your preliminary research. The articles and other documents that turn up either will be authored by people who are knowledgeable, or will cite these people and the work they have done in the relevant fields. These are the people who have some connection to your story by virtue of their experience (professional, political, or otherwise), or their research (scientific, academic, or otherwise). Some names also will rise to the top simply because they have been in the news. These sources usually have significant reputations, often national in scope and recognition, which, for national magazines, can be important. Editors often will not want just anyone's opinion on a subject. They will want *the* expert. Don't hesitate, though, to start with "who" you know. Determine sources you're familiar with through work, school (professors), and social relationships. Think critically about the points of connection between the people you know (or sources you already have cultivated) and the information you seek to present. There are those occasions when you will have to "educate" your editor, convincing him of the significance someone brings to your story—especially where the editor has not heard of the expert before your introduction.

Identifying and cultivating sources   Other efforts to develop sources can be quite fruitful. Contact associations in the field of inquiry. There are trade, professional, and social action associations and organizations in Washington, DC, for example, that are staffed by lawyers and researchers charged with the responsibility of lobbying federal agencies and lawmakers on policy considerations. Contact these organizations, ask for the press office, or public affairs, explain the scope of the article, and get a referral. These people are quite knowledgeable in their subject area (and everything related to it). But keep in mind that they are in business to represent a specific point of view.

Keep in mind, too, that each contact you make can lead to additional contacts. A name is mentioned, or additional unpublished research is cited. You also can be proactive and ask for other people, whether they support your source's position or contradict it. Obviously, that conflict also adds a dimension to the story. What you will find, in other words, is that your connection to one source can start something of an expert "tree" leading to others, and on and on. As we suggest in Chapter 6, there is nothing more gratifying than finding a new voice on a particular topic, someone with a fresh perspective who can provide an altogether new dimension to your story. After all, the best person to quote is not always the person with the highest title, a bunch of letters behind his name, or a name that often appears in print. Sometimes it's the assistant to the assistant who's got the goods, the person who actually has done the scientific research or the legislative drafting.

Clerks and secretaries also can be helpful. It is important to recognize these people. Assistant staffers grow up to be chiefs of staff. It is the nature of politicians to move to higher and higher offices throughout their careers. One of the authors obtained the Chicago home telephone number of the late Harold Washington when he was an Illinois State Senator. The number stayed the same when Washington was elected to the U.S. Congress from Illinois. And it stayed the same even when Washington was elected as the first African American mayor of Chicago. Obviously, that contact information became increasingly significant. Similarly, David Axelrod freely gave out his cell number when he was a political consultant representing mostly Illinois politicians, like rising star Barack Obama in his successful run for the U.S. Senate. One of the writers held onto that number and used it when he wanted Axelrod again (by then a White House senior political advisor to President Obama), for a Chicago-related story. When the writer called, Axelrod answered the cell—as he was boarding Air Force One to travel to California with the President.

Clearly, sources can and should be cultivated over time. It is important in this regard to build relationships of trust and confidence. Establish credibility with new sources right from the start. Get a referral by someone they care about. Make the connection to something they care about, whether the subject matter or the magazine. Is it prominent enough to get their attention? Does it cover areas that are important to their work? Does it reach an audience that is important to their election or for sales of their products?

When enough is enough   The scope of research also must be considered when it comes to determining how far to take the interviewing process. For example, how many sources do you need? A lawyerly response we always give to students: "It depends." What is the story you are planning to tell? What is the market for that story? What will your target magazine most likely present and what will the audience—the readers of that magazine—expect to take away from that story? As important as anything else, the experienced magazine writer will be open to new discoveries in the course of conducting research and interviews. These discoveries just might lead to new considerations for the scope of the story that is being written. This, in turn, might cause you to modify your initial determination of sources to interview.

One of the authors once was assigned a story on African American head coaches in the NFL for *Ebony* magazine. The assignment called for a "roundup," which was basically a snapshot profile of the three Black head coaches to appear at the beginning of football season. For such a short piece, the writer decided that only background information and a couple of quotes from each of the coaches would suffice. Three interviews. But in the course of interviewing the three head coaches—Tony Dungy, Indianapolis Colts; Herman Edwards, New York Jets; and Marvin Lewis, Cincinnati Bengals—the writer discovered that they all had been represented by the same sports agent; were all advanced through the NFL as a result of a successful Minority Coaching Fellowship Program; and were all good friends. The writer pitched a larger story to the *Ebony* editors, was granted more space, and proceeded to expand the interview list to include—among others—the sports agent and the late attorney Johnnie Cochran, who had filed a successful lawsuit to push the NFL to create more head coaching opportunities for African Americans. The new story about the competitive pressures to win team victories (against friends) and the moral pressures to help create new opportunities for more African Americans required more perspectives, more voice, more interviews to tell the complete story. In other words, the story will tell you what is required.

As with this NFL piece, you must be open to the evolving story. There are times when the shape of your story might change with new information you might never have considered at the onset of your work. Research can be a dynamic process. And the experienced writer will see opportunities for richer story development, or even the production of an altogether new story.

In Chapter 4, we showed the example of *Esquire*'s writer-at-large Mike Sager's discovery connected to his interview of comedienne Roseanne Barr for the magazine's "What I Have Learned" one-page bio. As a result of her revelations regarding her multiple personality disorder, Sager's work grew from the initial one-source mini bio piece to a story that involved interviews with Barr's family and with medical experts.

The reluctant interviewee   There are special considerations with interviewees who are a bit reticent, as Sager reports Barr was when he first brought up the expanded MPD story possibility. When the reluctant source is the focus of the story—as with a profile—there can be unique challenges, which we discuss in Chapter 12. But here we look at the people you might need to add that important voice to your story of multiple perspectives. Unlike sources on breaking news stories, who might feel some obligation to talk, there are people who don't necessarily feel quite so obligated to help you out on a magazine feature story. It is important to appeal to the need to be included. "I want to get your side." Appeal to the ego. "You are the only person who can help clarify issue X." Appeal to the sense of altruism. "I need your help in understanding this subject." One of the writers had to interview one of the cousins of Emmett Till, the 14-year-old Chicago teen who was lynched in the Mississippi Delta in 1955 for whistling at a White woman. The cousin had been there as a 12-year-old—in the same bedroom—when Till was abducted. Reached by telephone, some 50 years later, the cousin said he did not want to talk about the tragedy, and especially did not want to relive the events leading up to the torture murder of young Till. Before he let the cousin hang up, the writer implored him to help him understand something else about life in the South. What was it like, the writer asked the former sharecropper, to pick cotton? The cousin went on to reminisce about that experience and what it was like to swim in the nearby river and to go "uptown" for summer treats and eventually he was coaxed by the writer on the momentum of the conversation to keep moving forward from the cotton fields to the river to the town and then back to the house on that fateful night. In the end, the writer was able to walk the cousin through the horrific events surrounding the grisly death of Emmett Till that sprang from one of those uptown visits—a journey he adamantly refused to make at the onset of the conversation.

The pre-interview checklist   The point is that getting the interview sometimes can create challenges. That is why you want to be clear at the very beginning what you are looking for and how the information will be used. Introduce yourself as a writer, and, as mentioned, specify the magazine you have targeted for your article. If time permits, mention any expertise that might be useful in persuading the interviewee to talk with you—past experience, or another article you've written on a related topic.

Specify the angle you are pursuing and, of course, the amount of time you think you will need. Clarify whether the interview will be done by telephone or in person. Telephone interviews can seem more convenient to some sources, because they tend to think of these sessions as shorter commitments. Keep that in mind. Request background information (either from the source or the assistant/secretary) that might not be available online. Of particular interest in this regard would be the resume or curriculum vitae (which should include all published titles, books, which you at least will want to review prior to the interview, even if the source is widely known). It is important to have all this information beforehand. It might be included in your story. It can help your understanding of the expert you will interview. It also is useful in loosening up the subject during the interview. Flattery can go far in smoothing the way to a successful interview. Finally, make sure you confirm the interview the day before it is scheduled to take place.

PREPARATION MAKES PERFECT

Review all background information and write out your questions beforehand. It is important to consider that writing out your questions helps to establish a roadmap for the discussion. Once the questions are written and logically ordered, it is much easier to recall even without looking at notes.

Develop the five-to-ten questions you've got to have answered by each particular source. Pretend you will only have time for these questions. But always have more questions than you need. We can't stress how many times writers have been granted 15 minutes only to wind up sitting around for a couple of hours in highly successful interviews.

Often sources will grant you shorter time so they can break off if it is not going well. If they like you, however, if you stroke them, massage the ego by being prepared with their background and the significance of their work, they wind up going on. So, know that you will get the essentials in the short time granted, but be prepared for more just in case.

Don't waste time with questions in areas you can either get from another source or from background documents. The exception here is that there are times when you want to ask the same question of several different sources just to get differing opinions or perspectives on an issue. What is each person's spin or take on the question?

We mentioned that the questions should be written out. But that does not mean you should read them. Write them, memorize the things you want to cover but let the session flow. The best interviews are more like conversations than interrogations. You will find sources much more willing to offer information and spend more time in such settings. You also will get quotes that are much more colorful in that they come in a more relaxed conversational style. This obviously is especially valuable in the personality profile.

▶ CONDUCTING THE INTERVIEW

As mentioned, the interview for magazine articles should be much like a conversation with give-and-take, and periodic shifts in direction to pursue those unexpected bits of information that invariably will come up in such a talk. In other words, even though you have prepared for the interview with a range of questions, there are times when you want to allow the conversation to flow a bit in order to capture information you might not have anticipated. There also is an ancillary benefit of being in face-to-face conversation with someone in that you have the chance to observe the other person who is talking. The most accomplished magazine writers do not rely solely on what people say. They also make observations about what is said, about the way in which it is said, the body language, the rise and fall of the voice, the overall mood. Later in our discussion of literary non-fiction in Chapter 11 and profiles in Chapter 12, you will see how important these observations can be in establishing a sense of immediacy and in developing characters that leap off the page for readers. In such cases, the writer becomes something of a personality analyst as well as magazine interviewer. But even where a person is not the focus of the story and is only contributing vital information to it, there is a value in making key observations about demeanor and the like. Such insight can be helpful in guiding the writer toward the truth, by indicating whether there is reason to question what is being said, whether points that are raised in the conversation need to be verified by additional sources.

So, how is all this accomplished? Clearly, one of the first things to consider is how best to document this kind of interaction to make sure not only that the words of the conversation are captured accurately, but also that the context for the words is established. Here, we consider the best way to ensure accuracy and make the observations you need to make to keep it all in perspective. Do you write notes during the session, do you bang out notes on your laptop, or do you use an electronic device to record? There are pros and cons with each process.

Handwritten notes   For news reporting, handwritten notes always are preferred, as there is great pressure in the news business to move quickly from reporting on the story to actually writing and submitting it. In the long-form writing process for magazines, where the conversations with your subjects could be quite comprehensive and where you want to be able to respond, shift directions unexpectedly, and make the kinds of observations discussed above, note-taking might pose a problem. Either you are absorbed in the process of writing and miss some of the subtlety that can be so telling, or you are distracted by these observations to the point where you miss the precise words of the quote. There are writers who can sit through an entire interview without ever taking notes and still capture every detail and the most significant words. One of the writers here once conducted an interview with Barack Obama's barber to gain perspective on the President's persona for a magazine piece. Clearly, the best way to interview a barber is in the barber's chair—getting a cut and taking part in a time-honored ritual: barbershop gossip. No way to take notes under these circumstances (particularly under the barber's smock!). The writer had to keep the conversation going smoothly, while trying to remember the key quotes to illustrate the point, finally running around the corner after it was all over to write the notes on a napkin while the conversation still was fresh. This technique can only work for short conversations or where only a few precise quotes and facts might be needed. More detail will be needed for lengthy and precise comments. Still, writing copious notes can interfere with all the other things that must take place during the interview.

To the extent writers want to maintain a lengthy conversation flow and make the observations that are so vital to magazine perspective, there are techniques that can be helpful. Some writers develop their own shorthand "coded" references to capture as much of the wording as possible. The problem here is that it can be distracting to engage in multiple steps between what is said and translating it to your code in order to document what is said. You can get so caught up in thkg abt alt sp 4 wds that you lose track of the significance of what is being said. This takes you out of the interview, and out of the interview is not where you want to be. Another technique many people use is simply to skip words allowing you to focus on the key words of what is being said, either for quotes to preserve or significant factual information for the exposition. A final consideration with respect to note-taking is simply to allow lapses in the session to finish writing a particular passage or thought. Clearly, this can disrupt the pacing of the conversation to the extent you are stopping and starting. It is never a good practice to allow your subject to sit there watching you with your eyes turned down to your note pad, while she waits and waits and waits for the next question or comment.

In conducting telephone interviews, some writers will use a speaker phone in order to free up hands for note-taking. This is not the best idea. It can be annoying to the person on the other end of the line. Often there is an echo, or a delay (with parties on either end of the conversation stepping on each other's lines), and there could be sensitivity on the part of your subject that there is less privacy in these situations—that anyone passing by on your end might overhear the conversation. Again, you do not want to allow any distractions that might take the interviewee out of the session even for one self-conscious moment.

Increasingly, writers (and just about everybody else) will use their computers for note-taking. Often this is done in telephone interviews and can be useful to the extent you are proficient enough to keep track of the conversation while you are typing away. Even in phone conversations, though, the clicking keys might be a distraction to the person on the other end of the

Medioimages / Photodisc

line, causing him to pause to weigh his words, feeling that they are subject to some kind of transcription process as in a court of law. Without question, taking notes on a laptop during a face-to-face interview can be off-putting.

As we have suggested, the key in making the right choices in documenting the interview is in considering the best option for accuracy, for ease of conversation and for allowing you, the writer, to make the important observations that are critical to good magazine storytelling. Obviously, these considerations are set against the need to avoid obtrusiveness. As we have seen, certain techniques for documenting the session can be distracting and can take the subject—or you, for that matter—out of the moment, which can be costly from the writing standpoint.

Electronic recording   With all these considerations in mind, many writers opt for electronic recording devices. Assuming all precautions are taken, a recorder allows you to maintain a comfortable pace with the conversation, be responsive to shifts in direction, and make the observations you will need in order to gain perspective. Additionally, editors and legal counsel increasingly want to maintain records of all information gathering and will want recordings in order to document that quotes are accurate. The value of all these benefits outweighs what might seem to be the potential distraction of a recording device in the session. Some people might be concerned about having every word—and grammatical error—captured on the recording. Experience has shown, though, that people tend to forget that a machine is present when they get absorbed in the conversation. That is the responsibility of the writer—to ensure that level of absorption. You must make sure your source is so caught up in the conversation that the entire focus is on that event, and not the process of recording.

As with other methods of documenting the interview, electronic recording has a few challenges. Transcribing the interview can take time. If you use a service, there are fees to consider. Some writers even have concerns about confidentiality, although transcription services tend to try to maintain integrity in that regard. Transcription software is not all that helpful in that most programs are designed to recognize one voice, not two, at a time. There is a benefit for you to handle your own transcriptions, though. You have the chance to review the interview, begin sorting how particular quotes will fit the story, and identify additional areas that need to be clarified in ways that were not possible during the actual interview. "I transcribe myself because I get a lot out of it," Mike Sager notes. "I realize that I haven't asked every question I need to have answered." The long-form literary non-fiction form of his writing requires a great deal of detail. "I will find an incomplete scene that I want to write, and then I realize there are a lot of things that are left out," notes Sager, writer-at-large for *Esquire*. "So, I call the person back a million times. I might call and ask, 'What shirt were you wearing that day?'"

Of course, the real downside is the possible technical glitch, like running out of power. Most writers will change batteries with each new interview. That certainly addresses the most common technical problem! Recording clarity and volume can be concerns. It doesn't hurt to carry ear buds or headphones at least to monitor the beginning of the interview to make sure there is sufficient volume and no interference. Mike Sager famously uses a lavalier mic with his recorder to make sure he gets good audio from the subject. But his lav has an "on-off" switch. During a critical session with Roseanne Barr while working on that multiple personality disorder piece, the comedienne was absently fiddling with the mic and accidentally turned it off! The gap in recording wasn't discovered until long after the interview. Obviously, as Sager will attest, it makes sense to check the counter and the sound level periodically to make sure the session still is being recorded.

QUESTIONS OF THE MOMENT

As we have advised, it always is a good idea to write out your questions before the interview. In so doing, you will have to consider the scope of your interview in connection with the information you need to write your story. But you also will be able to think through a logical trajectory for your conversation. In most cases, writing the questions helps to commit them to memory. So it likely will be unnecessary to read them during the interview. But it is good to know they are there in the event you lose track in the twists and turns of the conversation. In thinking through your approach, it is as important to consider the *way* you will ask as the *what* you will ask. In this connection, there are several types of questions to consider.

OPEN-ENDED QUESTIONS. These are questions that allow for a certain freedom of movement in answering that quite possibly will lead to something you did not anticipate. "What do you think about the problem of school closings?" Such questions give the subject a chance to stretch out, loosen up a bit, and go through a little verbal throat-clearing, providing enough material for you to zero in on with follow-up questions.

FOLLOW-UP QUESTIONS. The follow-up question is important to clarify, specify, and illuminate. Moreover, invariably, something will be said that opens up a new line of questioning as much as it responds to the initial question asked. It is your job to make sure all points are covered. Keeping track of what still needs to be answered (even while keeping track of all those other questions you wrote down) can be challenging. But in the flow of the conversation, it certainly is manageable. There also is an ancillary value. You know how much time you have been granted and how much you need to cover in that time. You must stay in control of the interview session and the follow-up question helps in that regard. It says to the subject "I am in control here," and maintains a comfortable pace. Finally, there is the chance to forge personal connections that can be fruitful. The psychological cliché, "How did that make you feel?" (in one of its many forms), can be useful as a follow-up question that engages the interviewee on a different and more personal level that can provide a new dimension to the story. Always leave the door open at the end of an interview to contact your source for additional follow-up questions. Invariably something will occur to you later. No matter how much focused attention you devote to the interview session, something will rise up from your notes or your recording, or something will develop in subsequent interviews that begs for a follow-up with this particular person. Make sure you keep this option open.

CLOSED-ENDED QUESTIONS. These are questions that typically call for a "yes" or "no" answer, or a simple confirmation of a fact. These, obviously, are used for specific information designed to confirm or contradict material that has turned up in your preliminary research or in other interviews.

LEADING QUESTIONS. These are hybrid forms of the closed-ended questions that suggest a response, in effect, putting words in the mouth of the interviewee. In a leading form of the "How did that make you feel?" question, the circumstances might suggest a feeling, which you can observe in your follow-up. "Wasn't that frustrating?" Even while suggesting the answer, these questions also can help a subject frame a response. If they yield a closed-ended "Yes" or "No" then you can follow up with a simple open-ended "Why?" If used effectively, a sequence of open-ended, closed-ended, leading, and follow-up questions can wind up yielding some great quotes, or references. All these techniques must be handled with care, however, to avoid offending a subject and shutting down the session.

TOUGH QUESTIONS. There are a couple of things to keep in mind when considering the tough, or potentially embarrassing, question. Is it necessary? Clearly, you will not want to ask gratuitous questions just to show how tough you are as a writer. Make sure there is some substantive storytelling purpose behind every question—particularly the tough ones—before putting them on your list. The second consideration is one of timing. When do you need to get the question into the conversation? Typically, you hold the tough question until close to the end of your session. Obviously, that question just might wind up being the last one you ask, as it can end an otherwise successful session. But it also can shift the tone of the interview, coloring anything else that might come up. Harrison Ford once sat at a table with a half dozen writers to talk about his role in the second "Star Wars" feature, "The Empire Strikes Back." A writer asked Ford about an unsuccessful picture he had made between the first and second "Star Wars" installments. It was the first question in the encounter. There wasn't much the other writers could get out of Ford for the rest of the session. Even while you time the provocative issues to come close to the end, you should plan for a follow-up in the event you get the chance to expand on the response.

ENVIRONMENTAL QUESTIONS. As mentioned earlier, it is important to pay attention to everything going on during the interview. Watch your subject's body language. A hand gesture can be revealing, either as a "tell" regarding the veracity of a comment, or as a character trait for the personality profile. Note the rises and falls in voice and inflections. Observe the subtlety and nuance in the conversation. The interviewee might be signaling that he wants to go down a certain road, wants to reveal something you didn't expect. On the other hand, he might be indicating that he does not want to go there. Either way, he is telling you something. You also should note whether the subject is being evasive because he doesn't want to answer or simply cannot find the right answer at the time. Judgment is key under all circumstances. Nailing a subject with a tough question at this point might not be in the best interest of the interview. It might be better to come back to the point later. It also might be useful to frame the follow-up as a leading question. But the environment includes everything in the room—everything you can observe. If there is a curio on the desk, or a unique decorating style, these things reveal something about the person. In an interview with former Tuskegee, Alabama, mayor Johnnie Ford by one of the authors, gold-colored ceremonial shovels were observed in a corner of the mayor's office. The obvious inference was that this was a man known for being bullish on development, always ready to break new ground. In an interview with wealthy investor Chris Gardner ("The Pursuit of Happyness"), an abstract painting of Miles Davis (with a disembodied face) led to the question about social masks that led to an especially sensitive side the "rags-to-riches" Gardner was concealing behind his blood-on-the-streets tough-guy image as a Wall Street financier. The point is that the story exists everywhere—in the words of the interview responses, in the meaning between the words, and in the air surrounding them. Pay attention.

ANECDOTAL QUESTIONS. Clearly, these are related to the environmental questions. As suggested, there are stories that are connected to every aspect of a person's life. But most people are not natural storytellers. Few of us think or speak in the kind of richly embroidered detail that makes for compelling narrative. To get that kind of detail in a story, the writer typically has to coax it out of her subject. One way to do that is to ask your subject to walk you through their actions at a moment in time. "Let's talk about that last day of the trial. What did you do that morning, as you prepared to go to court for the closing argument?" And, as the story progresses, you must be ready for the "pop-ups," those questions that drill down for the details that also can be ripe for stories and quotes and revelations. "What did you pick out to wear that morning?" "Why that outfit?" "What were you thinking as you got ready to go?" Getting your subjects to tell you what they *did* in addition to what they *thought* will trigger more anecdotal recollections, the kind that can animate an otherwise boring narrative.

CATCH-ALL QUESTIONS. "Is there anything I haven't asked you that I should know?" "Anything else that you might want to include in the story?" Some people believe this to be an amateurish type of question. After all, if there is anything you should know, then you should know what you should know. Still, you can't be expected to think of everything. The first time that question yields a bombshell of a response, you will appreciate its value.

CLEANUP QUESTIONS. Is there a preference for title? Is there a preference for affiliation? Is there a preference for name ("Bob" or "Robert") and middle initial? Don't assume that others have gotten this information right in previous reports. Usually, you will have the answers to these questions early on, but make sure you have this information before you leave.

PRIOR REVIEW. Sometimes the subject will have a cleanup question for you. "Will I have a chance to review before you publish?" The questions created by this question are: What are you being asked and what will your response mean to the interviewee if you agree? Are you being asked to check the accuracy of quotes? Are you being asked for review rights of the whole story? If the whole story is being reviewed, does that mean the subject wants approval rights? This is a potentially perilous area for the writer, as we discuss in Chapter 20.

▶ GETTING IT RIGHT

As the discussion above demonstrates, interviews are unique information gathering opportunities in that they have the potential for depth and dimension that is not possible with information collected in a document review. They also create certain pressures in that they take place at an appointed time and—in only rare cases—cannot be recreated if information is missed. So, we cannot stress enough how important it is to prepare in every way possible—advanced research, deciding on the method of documenting the interview, and, of course, the conduct of the interview, including facilitating the conversation and designing questions that are most likely to net the kind of information you need.

Facilitating the conversation is important and includes everything from ensuring the comfort level of your source (vital to a successful session) to keeping things on track (essential with respect to time management). Maintaining the comfort of the session requires a good assessment of your source. If she is interview savvy, then you can get right down to the business of the interview. If she is an interview neophyte, then there might be a need for periodic coaxing to help get through certain points in the conversation—especially if there are sensitive areas to be covered. If you just plow right into the subject at hand, you might get things off to an awkward start that well could set the tone for the entire interview. Although the ambush interview has its place in confronting a subject with embarrassing information that is designed to gauge honesty or dishonesty, guilt or innocence, most of our interviews for magazine purposes are designed simply to document facts, gain perspective, and capture personality. So, it is in your interest as a writer to make sure you create the circumstances that are conducive to the free flow of information and revelation.

Small talk is useful, unless it is contrived. An icebreaker can be helpful. This doesn't have to be as mundane as the weather, unless there is something so unusual going on outside—an ice storm in July—as to make it topical. But nothing in the interview should be wasted. Even small talk. The key to a good icebreaker is that it not only can be used to put a subject at ease, but also can be used to segue to the substantive conversation you want to facilitate. In an office setting, if you notice new furniture, or a sudden flurry of activity in the suite, or your subject balancing multiple calls as you wait to begin, these are observations that can give rise to certain inferences that also can lead into the conversation. Is there an indication of a business expansion, or a particularly busy day? Are there connections to some other aspect of your interview? Anything can be tied in. An interesting photo or painting on the wall. A reference to a recent article or television interview featuring the subject. The point is to find something that can be used to establish a positive connection (which can be flattering to the subject) before beginning to engage in the substantive conversation. During the interview, there are tested ways to show the source that you're not threatening, that you are reliable, that you are trustworthy. A nod here, a smile there, a well-placed response like, "I see your point," or "That's interesting, and it leads to my next question."

▶ FINAL CONSIDERATIONS

There are a few things to consider at various stages of the process. Immediately after completing each interview, you should review your notes or your recording for a couple of reasons. Obviously, when it comes to the recording, you want to make sure there were no technical problems. But in both cases, it is good to do a quick review while the interview experience still is fresh. This will enable you to consider anything that was missed, and anything that might help to guide interviews with additional sources. Make sure your record keeping is in order. Magazine editors (and particularly fact checkers) will want lists and contact information for all interviewees. They also will want all of your notes, interview transcripts, and, quite possibly, the digital download of the actual interview. Also, there is the increasing likelihood that your target magazine will consider an online presentation of some aspect of the story. This well could be a slide show with audio excerpts from the interview. Keep these multi-platform possibilities in mind as you proceed. Finally, it always is a good idea to send copies of the published magazine to your sources. Often, the magazine's promotion department will handle this sort of thing. Work with that department to include a "Compliments of . . ." note from you. After all, relationship building is key to future writing success.

WRITER'S WORKSHOP

There is a way at least to get an idea early on in setting the scope of interviews to conduct—making sure you are contacting enough sources, and not too many. Some have suggested that it is helpful to start by making a list of the top five or ten things you need to cover in the piece. Of course, writing the query always helps you with this process. Next, under each of those items, list all the things you would have to present in order to clarify those five or ten things. Now consider the potential sources of that information. As you begin to determine general categories of experts for a story on multiple sclerosis (neurologist, psychologist, social worker, patient) to represent the various aspects of the story you want to write, your list will evolve to more specific practitioners and finally specialists in the area you are exploring, leading quite possibly to the University of Chicago Hospital, where a new trial is underway for MS treatment designed to forestall the onset of symptoms. Of course, as with the NFL story cited in the chapter text above, one source often will mention something that opens the door to further inquiry, new sources of information, and so on, until your list of possibilities is quite vast. At a certain point, you will know you have reached the saturation point with interviewing when multiple sources are pretty much saying the same thing. Minimize the risk of such time wasting effort by considering very carefully the information a particular source is likely to provide ahead of time. Make your list of points to include in the story, and match that list with the people likely to add substance (background facts) or warmth (the personal experience) to bring your story to life.

Chapter Seven Review

ASSIGNMENT DESK

1. You are a writer for the alumni magazine at Your State University. For the October edition—the month of Homecoming—the magazine wants you to write a 2,500 word article on the historical significance of the football stadium. Consider and list at least five areas you would want to cover in this story and explain briefly why these areas would be important.

2. Review your topic list and now consider five people you would want to interview for the story. Specific names are not needed here, but you should consider the categories of persons who might lend important perspectives to your piece, in connection with the points you want to make. Provide a brief rationale for these choices.

3. Develop three to five critical questions you would want to ask each of the persons on your interview list.

4. Now assume you have begun the interviewing process and learned from one of your sources that the stadium locker rooms are in desperate need of renovation. Keep in mind that you are writing for the alumni magazine's homecoming edition at a state university. List at least two additional sources you will want to interview to explore this renovation issue and explain why you have selected them.

5. Finally, list the three to five questions you will want to ask the new sources and explain your rationale.

▶ KEY TERMS

- anecdotal questions
- catch-all questions
- cleanup questions
- closed-ended questions
- environmental questions
- follow-up questions
- leading questions
- open-ended questions
- prior review
- tough questions

▶ SUGGESTED READING

The Playboy Interviews. New York: M Press, 2006. A five-volume series that features some of the most compelling of *Playboy* magazine's legendary interviews. The volumes include *They Played the Game*, featuring athletes such as Jim Brown,

O.J. Simpson, Lance Armstrong, and Dale Earnhardt Jr.; *Movers and Shakers*, featuring the likes of Donald Trump, Bill Gates, and Malcolm Forbes; and *The Directors*, which includes Orson Wells, Stanley Kubrick, Francis Ford Coppola, and Spike Lee.

Wenner, Jann. *The Rolling Stone Interviews*. New York: Back Bay Books, 2007. Wenner, *Rolling Stone* founder and editor, has collected some of the best *Rolling Stone* interviews conducted between the end of the 1960s and the mid-2000s. The book contains interviews with rock stars, movie stars, and cultural icons, including John Lennon, Oriana Fallaci, Jim Morrison, Tina Turner, Bill Clinton, the Dalai Lama.

▶ WEB RESOURCES

http://www.lhj.com/health/conditions/cancer/are-we-overtreating-breast-cancer/ "Are We Overtreating Breast Cancer?" by Sharlene K. Johnson. *Ladies' Home Journal.*

http://www.esquire.com/ESQ0801-AUG_ROSEANNE_rev?click=main_sr "I Am Large, I Contain Multitudes," by Mike Sager. *Esquire*, August 2001.

8

Structure: The Building Blocks of Good Storytelling

▶ INTRODUCTION

In this chapter, we take a look at one aspect of story structure—the most visible part of it. In broad strokes, we will discuss the beginning, middle, and end of the story; the factors that link the opening and closing; and everything between these two critical sections that should fit together into one cohesive thematic whole. There are important considerations for the contributor to make with respect to these components in successfully planning and building the solid structure for a magazine story. In the beginning, we discuss the two vital parts of a strong story opening: the lead and the nutgraf. Each functions in unique and important ways to hook the reader, set the tone and pacing for the story, and explain what will unfold. Without question, the theme of the piece has to be established here. For the middle of the story, we discuss the options available for exposition, which involves key elements of story development. In that connection, we consider the key components of the story: anecdotes; background facts; examples; and quotes. We show how the best-structured articles are balanced presentations of all these elements in ways that keep the reader engaged in the story, even while she is being elevated by it, and continue to serve the purpose of reinforcing and clarifying the theme. This is a very important point because along with the need to maintain balance in the presentation of material in the story is the equally important need to thread the theme of the article through all the elements—the bricks—of the

LEARNING OBJECTIVES

1. The components of the story and how they all fit together tightly.

2. The important circular connection between the beginning and end of the story.

3. How to set up a theme for your story in two stages.

4. How to thread the theme through all of the storytelling components.

5. How to bring the story to a close, providing the all-important "take-away" value for the reader.

story. In the end, we show how the two vital parts of the closing (the setup and the payoff) relate back to the opening in ways that ultimately help to reinforce the theme. What is it that we want the reader to carry away from the reading experience? That is the meaning of it all. Now let's see how it all comes together.

▶ THE OVERALL STRUCTURE

Although we will discuss multiple components of magazine storytelling here, all stories basically come down to three broad structural elements— the beginning, the middle, and the end—which have been handed down since Aristotle's day. If composed effectively, these broad structural areas support each other in such a way as to achieve cohesive storytelling and impact. That is why it has been said that the best-written magazine articles use all elements of good storytelling, in effect, to "tell you what we're going to tell you, then to tell you, and finally to tell you what we told you." Put a different way, good storytelling should establish, develop, and reinforce the central point that is being made. The opening should "tell you what we're going to tell you" by *establishing* the story with a lead that first attracts the attention of the reader. The middle should "tell you" by *developing* the story through anecdotes, background facts, examples,

Thinkstock / iStockphoto

and quotes. The closing should "tell you what we told you" by *reinforcing* the theme, tying it all up, tying it all together. Thus, at every juncture the accomplished writer will consider what the story is all about—what it *really* is all about—and use every storytelling component to inform the reader of that significance. To see how this works, we must start at, well, the beginning.

▶ THE BEGINNING

Often, the opening of the story is referred to as the "lead" (or in classic newspaper reference, the "lede"). Quite literally, the opening of the story is the leadoff paragraph. And, if handled properly by the writer, the opening should lead the reader into the next component part of the story for more information. Here we refer to the beginning section as the opening, because we see the lead as only one of two essential parts of this first section of the magazine story. The second part of the opening is the "nutgraf," or what some writers refer to as the "billboard" paragraph, where the theme, the point of the story, is clarified in a concrete way.

There is a point of distinction here between magazine writing and news writing. In news writing, we learn that the lead of the story must do quite a bit of work to establish the news peg or the most important aspects of the story—the who, what, when, where, and why. That is because the classic structure of the news story is the "inverted pyramid." The news story is structured so as to provide the most important information first and then everything else in descending order of importance or significance. Magazine writing is different. Magazine readers have to be drawn into a story. For stories that do not have an apparent "peg" to a news event—as is so often the case with magazine writing—readers will have to be made to want to read on. They will have to be shown that the information is important or significant to them either because it will inform, enlighten, engage, or entertain them. The magazine story tends to be longer and the key information is not always at the top. Instead, it will be threaded through the piece. The process of absorbing it all takes much more reader time, and the writer has to justify that time right at the beginning. How is that done?

While commentators have offered a number of visual metaphors for magazine structure to rival the newspaper inverted pyramid, the one that strikes us as most useful (given its simplicity) is the building block, or brick. Structurally, as has been asserted by industry observers, a magazine article is constructed by an assembly of tightly fitted blocks, with those close to the end of the story carrying elements that well could be as significant as those presented earlier. The first of these **copy** blocks comes right at the beginning.

COPY: All text that makes up the editorial—not advertising— content of a publication.

The lead   The lead of the magazine article serves multiple functions. For reasons discussed above, it must attract attention; establish the pacing; and set out the story, establishing what it is all about.

First, as we have suggested, it should "hook" the reader. We have discussed marketing in other contexts of magazine publishing (publishers market to specific advertisers for revenue; editors design content to attract specific readers to sell to advertisers; and freelance writers sell story ideas to editors through queries that are aimed at appealing to readers who appeal to advertisers). It is important to understand that the marketing does not stop. When you write a story, you are *selling* it to the reader. The point is that you must reach out and convince a reader that a story is worth the time to read. As you review the best-written magazine articles, you will note that writers often use an attention-grabbing opener. This can be a provocative summary line or question meant to surprise; a powerful quote that can intrigue; or a narrative anecdote that will engage.

An example of a good summary opener can be seen in a breast cancer story, "Protect Your Breast Health Now," published in the October 2005 issue of *Ladies' Home Journal.*

> One in eight women will develop breast cancer over the course of their lifetimes, and almost all of us spend a lot of time worrying that we might. A recent survey by the Society for Women's Health Research found that 22 percent of women named breast cancer as the disease they fear most, more than twice as many who said heart disease.

Writer Paula Dranov draws the reader in with a startling statistic aimed directly at the *LHJ* audience of women readers. And she connects with the reader right away with an empathetic note, "almost all of us spend a lot of time worrying," thus establishing both an emotional and intellectual hook.

In a similar way, a health piece on the value of organic foods titled "Natural Selection" published in the December 2012 issue of *Vogue* draws on news headlines as a way of attracting attention.

> The news was enough to make organic devotees hang up their Whole Foods eco-bags: In September, a group of Stanford researchers sparked an uproar when they reviewed 237 studies and concluded that organic food had no nutritional benefit over conventionally grown food. All those years of sifting through barrels of mottled apples (and paying more, to boot) were for naught?

Right away, the writer, Jancee Dunn, grabs the reader's attention with a hook—based on a news report, no less—that connects with an issue that certainly has wide appeal to the style-conscious and, yes, health-conscious reader of *Vogue*. In fact, the central issue posed here likely has universal appeal in that most consumers probably have wondered at some point whether organic selections provide enough benefits to make them worth the higher prices. It certainly is an opener that draws the reader in to learn whether green matters. The writer, flipping the lead on its head, goes on to show that it does matter in select ways that are discussed in the article.

While the effect of the summary lead is clear in these examples, many writers opt for the anecdotal lead largely because it can accomplish all the goals of the lead, if executed properly, and provide a much more satisfying writing experience. Narrative, as we will see in Chapter 11, is storytelling of the first order. It can create a sense of immediacy; not just setting a scene for the reader, but actually placing him directly in a scene by creating atmosphere, adding life to the story, and engaging in ways that serve the critical first purpose of the magazine lead: to hook the reader by creating a sense of shared experience.

The point is that anecdotes can provide their own allure in drawing readers into the setting and even the drama of a situation we come to experience, as we see here in the opening of "Live on TV: The Fall of Greece," published in the December 2012 issue of *GQ*. The writer sets the stage with a brief summation of what is about to take place on the video he reviews, and then segues into the narrative description of it all.

> The participants, seated in an arc, are arguing. They are arguing in a language you don't understand. In the center is a man who clearly should be moderating the conversation, though he appears to have little control over what is going on. The panelists talk over one another, as though the faster and louder you say something the truer it becomes.

> Then, far to the moderator's left, an animated blonde woman says something that clearly riles a short-haired young man on the opposite end. This lurch—from heated debate to something much crazier—happens in a flash. The short-haired man picks up his glass of water and, rising to his feet, throws its contents in the blonde woman's face. It's a direct hit. She seems to freeze, but after that it's all so fast, so frantic.

What is "all so fast, so frantic" is a slugfest among the lawmakers before the video-recorded scene comes to an abrupt end. Although writer Chris Heath begins this narrative by revealing that we are watching a video clip, the pace and description of his writing effectively place us right in the scene watching it all unfold in disbelief before reminding us once again with the payoff that we are watching as he watched on TV. By this time, the reader is drawn by the curiosity—if nothing else—just to see where the story will go.

As the *GQ* excerpt shows, narrative can take up a lot of space. It is important to know whether a magazine will accept such a long way into the story before planning to undertake such an opening. But the anecdotal opener can be as short as you might be able to write it effectively. Take this example, "Why You Can't Ignore Kanye," from the August 29, 2005 issue of *TIME*.

> The first time Kanye West asked folks at Roc-A-Fella Records to let him rap, there was an uncomfortable silence.

Writer Josh Tyrangiel goes on to weave together background and narrative to show why the "authentic" rapping community did not embrace the preppy West right away, only to watch him eventually become a huge success tapping into the middle-class connection to hip-hop.

It is important to keep in mind that the opening also has to clarify the substance of the story. An anecdote—by showing—quickly illustrates an element of the story and a representative character (a significant person) in it in a way that both intrigues and demonstrates for the reader just what will follow. It is important to understand in this regard that the anecdote is something of a mini-story itself. As such, the best-crafted anecdote will have a beginning, middle, and end, much like the story it is being used to illustrate and set up. But developing a good anecdotal opening can take time and space, which just might cut against the effectiveness of the story you are writing.

In addition to hooking the reader, the lead must establish the pacing for the story. Even while grabbing the reader's attention, you must do so in a way that is consistent with the nature of the story. Its length and use of language will signal to the reader how the entire story will flow. You wouldn't want to tag a long narrative lead onto what basically is a fact-laden service story. So, sometimes the well-crafted anecdote might seem out of place for a crisply written shorter magazine piece, one that might be better served by a provocative opening line. A cautionary note is in order here. Often it is tempting (perhaps mostly for writers in a hurry) to rely on a quote to open a story. Certainly quotes can perform all the essential functions of a good magazine lead—grabbing reader attention and setting things in motion. But you must make sure that the quote you select is absolutely the best opener with these essential purposes in mind. That does not mean simply the best quote. It means that a quote is the best way to start the story, and the quote you select must set out what we can expect to follow in the rest of the story. In so doing, you will maintain control of your story and not simply rely on your interviewees to write it for you.

Consider the following opener for a June 2007 *Parade* magazine story on Angelina Jolie.

> "I am my mother's daughter," Angelina Jolie tells me, with a proud smile. "I mean," she adds quickly, "I hope but don't think I'll *ever* be as good as her."

Here, writer James Kaplan immediately fixes our attention on the tension that existed in Jolie's life at the time of the interview for this story. She was struggling with the recent death of her mother, from whom she drew inspiration to move from her "bad girl" past to a life of social commitment—a struggle effectively captured in the aptly titled story, "A Life That Matters."

This point brings us to a third important function of the lead, and that is that it must set the theme for the story—again, telling what this piece is *really* all about, which only you, the writer, can do in deciding strategically what it takes to establish, develop, and reinforce it all. In other words, by utilizing the most cohesive structure. But you first must set it up effectively. And that, in turn, leads to the second part of the two-part opener: the **nutgraf**.

The nutgraf The nutgraf in magazine writing is what some have described as much like the "topic sentence" in a school composition. It effectively tells the reader—in a "nutshell"—what the story is all about and where it will go. It does this both by explaining the meaning of what the reader has just experienced in the lead and by outlining for the reader what to expect (what issues will be addressed, what questions answered) in the story to follow. So, while an anecdotal lead might connect with the reader's feelings, the nutgraf that follows that lead should connect with the intellect, adding a rational basis for the initial emotional reaction and working together with the lead to motivate the reader to go on into the story. The nutgraf has been called the "Billboard" because of its pronouncement function, but more aptly it also has been called the bridge in that it connects the — *The nutgraf.* lead to the rest of the story.

Whether you opt for what amounts to a provocative summary lead, or the longer narrative anecdote, you still will have to explain to the reader very clearly the thrust of the story. The point to keep in mind is that, whatever choice you make for a lead, you must—in the very next paragraph or section—include the all-important nutgraf.

In the *Vogue* health piece, after raising the question whether there really is a difference between organic foods and those grown with the help of pesticides, the writer follows the crisp, news-peg-of-a-summary lead with the following point:

> Putting nutrition aside (and the inarguable fact that organic food tastes better), the way these two groups of food are produced has the biggest impact on our health.

This beginning of the nutgraf makes it clear that the writer parts company with the studies cited in the lead and likely will provide information to back up that position. Clearly, the two-step process of the lead and nutgraf in this case adds to the interest in finding out how this conflict will be resolved.

NUTGRAF: The section of a story that follows the opening section and sums up the point of the story that will follow.

As we saw in the lead of the *LHJ* story on breast cancer, the writer points to the widespread anxiety among women about the possibility of developing breast cancer, and then bridges to the very next paragraph with the line: "Is the fear founded?" She goes on to provide background to show that it might not be.

In the *TIME* magazine story on Kanye West, the writer weaves quite a bit of background into the opening before finally reaching the nut of the story.

> Throughout, West careered between the Protestant ethic and street fantasies, revealing himself to be wise and stupid, arrogant and insecure, often in the same breath. But by baring his flaws and being self-critical—and daring listeners to do the same—he created a fresh portrait of African-American middle-class angst, and you could dance to it.

In the *Parade* piece on Angelina Jolie, the writer works the nut of the story into the same opening paragraph as the quote he used to get it all started. Immediately following that quote, he writes:

> Jolie's mother, Marcheline Bertrand, lost her seven-year battle with ovarian cancer in January, at just 56. Angelina Jolie clearly still mourns her mom. But the 32-year-old actress is also saying something more complex about who she's been, who she is and what she aspires to be.

He then goes into a background discussion of the mother's commitment to social good to establish the foundation for Jolie's public spirited work, which was getting wide coverage at the time.

It is important to recognize that writing an effective opening for a magazine article can be the most difficult part of your assignment. Sometimes you can be so overwhelmed by the sheer volume of material you have gathered in your research and interviews that you face the uncertainty of how best to set it in motion for the reader. What does it all mean?

That is why, in crafting a good lead, it can be helpful to start before you ever sit down to write the story. After all, you start out knowing the direction you have set for the story (as you explained in the pitch to your editor and in each request to sources for interviews). Things begin falling into place during the process of information gathering. Each document, each interview, has a potential gem that can be used in polishing your piece. Listen for interesting stories in the interviews. Tune your ears to the kinds of anecdotes that will leap off the page, grab reader attention, and—as important as everything else—illustrate your story. One of the authors of this book was assigned to write a profile of the late federal judge James Parsons, who was named by President John F. Kennedy as the first African American federal judge. At a news conference attended by a number of newspaper reporters documenting his long career, Parsons mentioned in passing that he had been informed about his historic nomination to the federal bench in a phone call placed by President Kennedy himself. No one followed up on that question, but the author sensed there was a story—a magazine-friendly anecdote—about that phone call. More questions would be asked later—at a safe distance from the other reporters. What were the circumstances surrounding the call? What was said? What was the reaction? How did that make you feel? These are the kinds of details that make for a good narrative anecdote—the kind of anecdote that provided an engaging opening for the magazine piece on Parsons.

Once you have identified such gems, you can begin to work them into subsequent interviews with other sources to flesh them out. The process might take time and might even take you off point periodically, but it will be worth the effort when you strike gold, as with the surprise call to Judge Parsons from the President of the United States.

Finally, it is important not to get stuck on writing the perfect lead at the beginning of the writing process. No matter how organized you are as a long-form writer, some points will become even clearer as you begin sorting them throughout the piece you are writing. The best advice in this regard came from a former magazine editor, who often counseled writers to use a makeshift lead just to jumpstart the writing process and avoid getting blocked. His all-purpose lead, which sets up a nutgraf quite nicely: "Everybody knows (fill in the blank), but what they don't know is (fill in the blank)." Clearly, this is a placeholder and is not likely to serve as the opener for any story worth reading. But it gets you started and helps to crystalize the essential point you are setting out to make. The polished opener can come after you have sorted through all of your material to generate a first draft of your story. Once you have organized your material and know what you are writing (partly because you know what you have written), you are in a better position to set out the direction—by way of a lead and nutgraf—for the reader. This is why the best advice here just might be that the lead is the first thing you think about and the last thing you write.

▶ THE MIDDLE

After you effectively have set up your story with your opening, telling us what you are going to tell us (with the thematic lead and nutgraf), you begin to tell us—developing the theme throughout the body of the story, that middle section that comprises roughly 90 percent of the entire piece. This is what is known as the "expository" section of your story. Exposition basically is where the information and meaning you are trying to convey in the story are "exposed." This exposure, this development, requires certain elements of storytelling, including background information to provide the history of the story, analysis to provide meaningful context, and illustration to help clarify through example and anecdote. All of these storytelling elements constitute the essence of the basic building blocks of your article: anecdotes, facts, examples, and quotes. As we will see, the best structure for the magazine article is one that successfully balances the use of these blocks of copy in a well-paced alternating presentation.

Anecdotes   As mentioned earlier, anecdotes should be seen as little stories within the story. They engage readers with their immediacy of scenes that add so much life to the storytelling. As with any story, anecdotes have a beginning, middle, and end and should be shaped in a way that fits the overall structure of the story with respect to pacing and length.

Facts   In order to establish the validity of your story, key facts are needed. They include the historical background material as well as the contemporary development of your topic. This information is vital to reader comprehension, adding detail, dimension, and, of course, significance to your piece.

Examples   These are illustrations that are used to support the factual points made. Examples are used to document that factual assertions really are true. They add credibility to the piece, which ultimately contributes to your authoritative voice in presenting the material.

Quotes   As we have discussed, voice is essential to good magazine writing. Your writer's voice certainly will come through as you develop a signature style for your writing. But, here we speak of the voice of your subjects—the people you have interviewed—and, whether they are included to add factual substance or colorful reflections, they infuse your story with a human presence that will make it much more relatable to readers. Keep in mind the multiple functions of quotes, providing substantive information and personality, while advancing the story—adding another critical building block to complete the structure and lead the reader forward.

Weight and pacing   There are a couple of things to keep in mind regarding your presentation—the assembly of these copy blocks—that go to weight and pacing.

With respect to the weight of factual content, take measure of the amount of material you have collected and the amount that really is needed to tell your story effectively. The amount of factual material needed to tell your story will depend on the magazine and audience, as well as the nature of the story itself. If the magazine leans toward more personality focused pieces, then less factual information and more illustration—more human affect—will be needed. In the next chapter, we discuss the notion of factual compression that can help cover a great deal of background in a smaller area of copy space. If, however, your magazine tends toward more thoughtful substantive presentation, then a greater amount of factual material will be required to meet reader expectations.

The particular story—its nature and length—will set a framework for the presentation. Space and time constraints certainly will set limitations on the amount of material you can consider including. A story on managing retirement accounts requires more factual consideration. Still, you should never lose sight of the human element. Even an issue-driven piece should show impact on people. Though facts are stressed, anecdotal information can engage people. At times, even magazines on business and finance use personalities to help illustrate specific topics. After all, people are attracted to other people, and they are attracted to stories about other people. They might be more inclined to read stories about issues they otherwise might not read if these stories are centered on a personality or group of people. Ultimately, with respect to the weight of material, it is imperative that you keep the theme of the story uppermost in mind. Once that theme has been established in your opening, it must be reinforced by every element, every building block of your story. When it comes to factual presentation, think "key" facts—those that are most relevant to the thematic point of it all. Not every related fact should be included. But certainly the relevant facts should be. Relevance is relative. Similarly, "illustrative" anecdotes, "contextual" quotes, and "significant" examples are all considered for the story on the basis of their connection to the point of the story. In other words, thematic relevance always is the consideration in deciding on material to include so that your anecdotes will add life, your quotes will add depth, and the examples will add meaning to it all.

Pacing also is critical in maintaining reader interest in your presentation. Consider how evenly the story moves. If a story gets bogged down in factual recitation, then you are likely to lose a reader. Similarly, if a narrative anecdote goes on much longer than is needed to make a point, or simply is too long in relation to the rest of the story, then the writing is not effective.

Try balancing the presentation with alternating blocks. For example, a block of factual copy followed by a quote helps move the story forward, and the reader through that story. Consider the various building blocks as coming together as scenes in a film. Just as each scene has to move the story forward, so, too, do the elements of your storytelling. The order of this presentation is strictly a matter of writer choice. There are no hard and fast rules on this aspect of expository writing. Typically, you would want to set out a key fact (whether historical or contemporary). You then could illustrate that fact with an example. After that, you might consider following up with a quote. An anecdote could well add dimension to the quote by illustrating the experience of the person being quoted. Alternatively, you could begin a section of your story (a scene, if you will) with an anecdote. Then you might segue to a factual discussion that will explain the significance of the anecdote. An example can follow, ending with a quote to help contextualize it all. In this kind of structural approach you effectively are dividing your story into topical component sections and providing something of a beginning, middle, and end to each section.

Consider the structure used by Ray Quintanilla for the story "Small Wonder," an April 7, 2002 *Chicago Tribune Magazine* piece on the Earhart school and its effort to improve student test scores. Quintanilla sets up the story with a narrative anecdote, tracking a class of eighth grade students. Notice how Quintanilla moves comfortably and seamlessly from a quote to an anecdote to a background fact in a way that keeps the reader moving forward.

> "Did you study for the Constitution test last night?" [one student] asks a classmate as he removes his coat and sits down. "I bet you were watching TV all night. Didn't do a thing. You'll be here next year," he teases.

> Across the room, an energetic [girl] is at her desk, grumbling about "having to be sitting down all the time." She and her classmates are expected to remain in their seats the entire six-hour day, unlike some schools where children change classes. Gym class, the only way for these adolescents to burn off energy, comes only once a week.

Then Quintanilla moves back into the anecdote, showing us the teacher's movement from one activity to the next, as she "begins scribbling a sentence on the blackboard," and engages the students in the interpretation.

> "I did not weep: I had turned to stone inside," [the teacher] wrote in large letters on the blackboard. "The writer, Dante, wanted to convey a message about emotions, that they are strong," she explains.

Quintanilla has done a remarkable job of pulling together his background reporting with the interviews and personal observations to enrich this story and develop a pace that keeps the narrative flowing. Importantly, he recognizes the need to provide some factual context for the one student's comment about having to sit down all day. That context is important to this story because of the unique nature of the Earhart school as a model for disciplined and focused work that ultimately pays off with improved test scores.

The best articles will be thoughtful, yet imaginative in structure. You will have opportunities to take certain risks, once you recognize the rules of engagement. But, as the *Tribune Magazine* excerpt shows, sometimes the basics—if done right—are all you need.

▶ THE END

As with the opening, the closing of your story should be constructed in two parts. Here we consider a *setup* and a *payoff*, in telling the readers what you have told them, drawing everything together, and restating the theme once more in such a way as to reinforce it. In this connection, magazine writers are urged to consider the payoff of the story—that all-important takeaway value for the reader, the enduring point of your story.

The setup   The setup is included in the closing paragraphs of the story that can do one (or all) of a few things. These grafs can summarize the significance of everything discussed in the story; touch on details regarding the future impact of an issue presented; resolve a problem set up in the story, or recommend possible solutions; and, of course, restate the theme.

The payoff   The payoff is the real conclusion of the story that, if done well, will provide some kind of message—the takeaway for the reader. Usually one sentence, the payoff, or takeaway, should imprint in the mind of the reader exactly what this story has been about; touching the heart, satisfying the emotions that this piece has been resolved. This often is done by way of a quote. As with the opening, though, the quote selected must not only be a good quote, but it must be the absolute best choice of endings for this particular story. With respect to structuring the one-two punch (or *alley-oop*) of the closing, consider an anecdotal summary that leads to a concluding quote, or a sentence through which you tie up everything. This works especially well when it tracks the opening in some way. In fact, the most effective article structure will employ something of a circular construction of opening and closing. The closing will relate back to the opening in such a way as to connect the theme from beginning to end in a tangible way, in effect, bookending the point of it all.

The *GQ* piece on the social and economic collapse of Greece—illustrated above by the Chris Heath passage of the free-for-all among Greek lawmakers— provides a setup that begins as follows:

> Hope persists that Greece's grim unraveling can be reversed. For its people's sake, of course, but maybe for ours. How sure can we be that there is anything happening today in Greece that could not also, someday not so far in the future, happen here in America?

The writer is summing up the theme of the piece that began with the parliamentary slugfest anecdote illustrating just how things appeared to be falling apart in the government itself. He moves from this setup to another anecdote, a report of someone stealing a bridge in Greece, ending with the quote of a dismissive police officer.

> "All over Greece," he explained, "there are people doing that."

The quote effectively provides the payoff, which is the pervasiveness of the problem in Greece. Working together with the setup, the takeaway is a warning about the effect on the American economy.

In the Kanye West story in *TIME*, the writer sets up with an anecdote shared by "Late Registration" co-producer Jon Brion that sums up the point of the story about West's determination to meld middle-class values and hard-edged hip-hop rhythms.

> "Kanye looks at me, and he goes, 'You know that saying You can't be all things to all people? Well, seriously, why not? I want to be all things to all people.'" Brion waited for a moment, then burst into laughter. "I knew he wasn't kidding, and he's smart enough to know that wanting to be loved by everybody is probably really bad for your mental health, but at the same time his point was, you know, why not try?"

Then the writer finishes with the payoff:

> You never know. He just might succeed.

With that, we get the point of the story, which has focused on West's ability to beat the odds and the doubts about his cultural fit that were set out in the beginning of the story.

With the right structure for your article, you not only will organize your material in a logical way, but you also will ensure that your reader continues to move through the entire piece. With a tightly coordinated opening and closing, you also will ensure that the significance of the material is communicated and that the point of it all endures.

WRITER'S WORKSHOP

Here is a suggestion for you to apply a central point of this chapter as you begin to develop and refine article structure.

This might be referred to as the "Vision Test." When you have developed a draft of an article, make notes in the story's margins indicating "A" for anecdote, "F" for facts, "E" for example, and "Q" for quote. Take a look at your marginal notes and see if you can visually detect a balance of weight and material. Consider the alternating pattern of marginal letters. This will give you a good visual assessment of your AFEQ, your balancing and pacing of the story. How effectively have you structured this piece, based on the alternating pattern? How might you move some elements around in order to achieve that balance? There is no particular order for the elements. We use AFEQ because it is easy to remember and master. But the important thing to remember is the usefulness of making a regular practice of doing this vision test of AFEQ for best affect when it comes to reader impact.

Chapter Eight Review

ASSIGNMENT DESK

1. Select a magazine article, preferably a feature of 3,000 words or more. After reading this piece, examine the various elements of structure in much the same way we suggest with the AFEQ vision test. Consider the balance of elements. How does it check out?

2. Take that same article and write a summary of the theme, pointing to how it is established in the opening (lead and nutgraf), and reinforced in the closing (setup and payoff). Does the writer effectively set out the theme in the opening and relate it back through the closing in a way that creates takeaway value for the reader?

3. Consider alternative openings and closings you might choose for this story and explain why you think your choices might be more effective.

4. Return to the alumni magazine exercise from Chapter 7. Consider how you might structure your story on the renovation of the football stadium. Map out a few sections, imagining how you might alternate the presentation of anecdotes, facts, examples, and quotes.

▶ KEY TERMS

- copy
- nutgraf

▶ SUGGESTED READING

Dranov, Paula. "Protect Your Breast Health Now: The latest findings on what really works to reduce your risk," *Ladies' Home Journal*, October 2005.

Dunn, Jancee. "Natural Selection," *Vogue*, December 2012.

Kaplan, James. "A Life That Matters," *Parade*, June 10, 2007.

▶ WEB RESOURCES

http://www.time.com/time/magazine/article/0,9171,1096499,00.html "Why You Can't Ignore Kanye," by Josh Tyrangiel. *TIME*, August 29, 2005.

http://www.gq.com/news-politics/newsmakers/201212/fall-of-greece-gq-december-2012 "Live on TV: The Fall of Greece," by Chris Heath. *GQ*, December 2012.

9 Structure II: The Mortar for Storytelling Blocks

▶ INTRODUCTION

In addition to the very visible structural elements of good writing we discussed in Chapter 8, there also are a number of factors that, while they are not necessary readily observed, still work together to form a critical part of the structure of a magazine article. The late award-winning journalist and Temple University Professor Hiley Ward referred to these elements as part of the "invisible structure" of magazine articles. If anecdotes, facts, examples, and quotes form what observers have referred to as the building blocks—the bricks—of good structure, then the elements we discuss here might be considered the mortar that is used effectively to fix those more visible pieces in place. Here we consider those additional elements of magazine storytelling, without which the structure likely would not hold together. Through a number of examples, we will show how the language used, the rhythm of the presentation, and the transitions play a vital role in solidifying the framework of a story. We also discuss the importance of the authoritative voice of the writer as a significant factor in this process.

Getty Images / Tripod

▶ THE ELEMENTS

Here we are talking about certain structural components of magazine storytelling that are not so easily identified for the kind of marginal marking we did in the Chapter 8 exercises.

These are elements like language, rhythm and pacing, and the authoritative writing voice. If considered and produced effectively, the reader should not be aware of these elements as she is reading. But she should have a sense that there is something holding the story together; something that arguably facilitates her movement through it, and certainly makes it less likely that her experience with the article will be interrupted. The one unifying point in connection with these elements is that they keep the presentation smooth and flowing in a forward movement.

In that connection, a conversational style is the most readable. It also has a certain logic. Thinking the article through as a conversation helps you to order the material very naturally, moving from one of the storytelling building blocks to the next and so on. Pacing is important. You must maintain a good flow in your presentation of the facts and details. Don't hit the reader with too much at once. Handle this material in easily managed portions of information. Weave them into the fabric of the story. This is where the visual test suggested in the last chapter will be useful. If you were to step back from the piece and simply look at the structure of it, how balanced would it appear to be with respect to the AFEQ—the presentation of anecdotes, facts, examples, and quotes? Even before you re-read the work, this visual assessment will give you a pretty good idea of the pacing of your article.

Still, in order to make this process work effectively, there are decisions that must be made early on in determining just how much information is required to tell the story. It starts with sorting the information you have gathered in the course of your research.

In this regard, keep your eye on the ball. At every stage of the writing process—from preliminary research to the pitch to the substantive research and interviewing to the actual writing—you must always be mindful of what this story is all about. And with that, you always are considering your market—the magazine, the audience. What is the shape of a typical piece like yours in your magazine of choice? What have your editors asked you to include? What would your readers expect to receive? This continuous consideration will help to keep you in the right frame of mind in maintaining a balanced, well-paced presentation.

If you have maintained this focused writing mindset, then your research and interviews should reflect what is essential to the piece—this story, this magazine, this audience. Even if you have gathered far too much material to include, you can begin to pare it all down by taking a critical view of it all. This is accomplished by maintaining a unified theme or focus and using certain elements of good storytelling. First, you must stick to the core ideas. What are those essential points that should be made? In answering this question, you automatically will discard a great deal of secondary information. Again, in this first stage of your review, consider what the reader will need to know in order to comprehend your subject. Of course, that consideration depends on the characteristics of the reader. But if you have taken the steps we suggested early in the process, you already should know this reader very well. You will understand in very deep ways just how to frame a conversation with him; how much he brings to the reading experience in terms of prior awareness; how much you will need to provide in order to bridge that prior knowledge with the ultimate knowledge the reader will have at the end of the reading experience—the takeaway value.

In addition to the volume of material you include to tell the story, it is important to consider how the elements of the story also touch the reader. And here, we mean those elements of the story that touch the reader most deeply. Touching the reader requires that you involve the emotions as well as the intellect. In order to accomplish this, you must include the human element in your balanced presentation. As we have written, quotes certainly add an important dimension—the human voice—to your piece. Examples of the facts also can be used to show how information impacts people. But the anecdotes—the mini-stories—also help establish a sense of connection with the reader. Here is where the reader will touch and be touched. Here is where you can cause a reaction in the reader that will result in a personal investment in the story, making the reader want to keep moving through it. Here again, the alternating blocks of storytelling elements—anecdote, fact, example, quote—work together to tell the story, but also to balance the telling of the story in ways that will keep the reader moving through it at a comfortable pace.

Balancing background   What happens when it is necessary to provide background information that covers a long period of time or a wide area or range of ideas? The first suggestion is to carve up this material and weave it throughout the fabric of the piece. In clothing design, a plaid pattern is repeated in ways that create balance and reinforce theme. The same is true with your magazine writing. To the extent that you can take portions of the historical information, or geographical information, and present it in segments throughout your story, you not only will cover the subject, but you also will keep the focus on your theme.

There are those times, though, when you will want to provide only a digest of the essential information that is needed to enhance reader understanding. Writer Peter Jacobi has suggested the technique of "compression" in order to accomplish this and keep the presentation balanced. Compression is where you can work a little storytelling magic. This technique allows you to cover a lot of ground in a little bit of space. It resolves a perpetual writing dilemma. If context is important for our understanding of the facts, and background information is critical to setting context, then how much background is enough; how much is too much? The compression technique is effective in covering quite a bit of ground in a relatively small amount of space. As Jacobi has recognized, the compressed presentation often is used to present elements of time and place. With respect to time, we are talking about a chronology of events—a sequence that might be necessary to include for reader comprehension. Consider the following passage from Joshua Green's November 3, 2005 *Rolling Stone* article, "The Enforcer," on then Congressman Rahm Emanuel:

> For years, Emanuel was the political brains of Bill Clinton's White House. Intense to the point of ferocity, he was known for taking on the most daunting tasks—the ones no one else wanted—and pulling off the seemingly impossible, from banning assault weapons to beating back the Republican-led impeachment. "Clinton loved Rahm," recalls one staffer, "because he knew that if he asked Rahm to do something, he would move heaven and earth—not necessarily in that order—to get it done."
>
> Now, as head of the Democratic Congressional Campaign Committee (DCCC), Emanuel has taken on his biggest challenge yet: to win back the House of Representatives after more than a decade of Republican control.

This passage provides a good illustration of several points we will make, but for now note how effectively the writer handles quite a bit of background material in such a way as to add much-needed context to the story that will follow. The reader now gets the point—in only the third paragraph of the story—that Rahm Emanuel is (was) just the person to take on the serious political challenge of the moment facing the Democratic party. Through the crisp, efficient handling of this background material, the writer has maintained a sense of balance and pacing that are consistent with the *Rolling Stone* voice. It is what the magazine's audience would expect. And the writer has saved room to develop the theme through more pertinent contemporary anecdotes, facts, examples, and quotes.

Similarly, with respect to place, information might be needed about a specific location—a school, a neighborhood, an entire city or country—for deeper understanding of a person, a group, or even an entire culture, depending on the story being presented.

In her April 2011 *National Geographic* article, "The Acid Sea," writer Elizabeth Kolbert sets the stage for a discussion of the setting for ongoing study of the effects of carbon dioxide on the ocean by taking us on location, and then quickly taking us into the story.

> Castello Aragonese is a tiny island that rises straight out of the Tyrrhenian Sea like a tower. Seventeen miles west of Naples, it can be reached from the somewhat larger island of Ischia via a long, narrow stone bridge. The tourists who visit Castello Aragonese come to see what life was like

in the past. They climb—or better yet, take the elevator—up to a massive castle, which houses a display of medieval torture instruments. The scientists who visit the island, by contrast, come to see what life will be like in the future.

In short order, we learn about the location of this place, as well as a bit of its history—just enough to appreciate the exquisite contrast between past and present and the conflict that will become the theme of this story.

Here, again, we must keep our eye on the storytelling objective. How much of a chronology is needed in order to understand the present circumstances? How much of the history or physical appearance of place is needed to understand the people or the issue at the center of it all? In visualizing this technique, it is useful to think of film presentations. The classic boxing movies can help to illustrate this point. Often what you will see is something of a montage that includes a racing locomotive, spinning newspaper headlines, and a series of knockout punches. This compression technique was used so often in film storytelling as to become cliché, but the point of it is worth noting here. It helped the film director—the storyteller—cover a period of time and space in the story to move the viewer forward without getting bogged down in lengthy and boring sequences. Similarly, the reader will need only a concise presentation of certain elements of background in order to "get" the point of the contemporary moment.

The important thing to keep in mind here is that maintaining the right balance between background information and the rest of the story becomes one of those invisible structural elements that work effectively to hold the story together—and keep the reader's attention on the story that is unfolding at a comfortable pace.

In addition to volume, balance, and pacing of material that is presented, there also are specific elements of the "mortar" that can be used to hold your storytelling structure together. Let's take a look at these elements and how they work to great effect.

Words   Language is important in communicating the story, in conveying meaning. In this connection, though, your choice of words and the way in which you shape the presentation of the words that are chosen will have great impact on the meaning conveyed. Words also must be considered a vital part of the structure of your story. The choices made with respect to words that are selected will create a sense of solid structure for the story.

In this regard, imagery is important. We want people to read our stories, but most importantly, we want people to experience the stories. How do you share the experience with the reader? We can start by using words that create images in the readers' minds. Words that involve the senses—touch, sight, hearing, smell, taste—will accomplish this. Involving the senses in your description puts the reader in the scene, creates images that engage. When you enter a restaurant or a bakery, there are smells that instantly breathe life into the moment. In fact, the best advertising a bakery might utilize is a ventilation fan that blows out into the street. It is seductive. Consider how you might capture this experience for your reader. Similarly, if a bar has the stale smell of beer on the floor, what story does that convey? A locker room, badly in need of a shower; an assisted care facility with the smell of incontinence, the smell of antiseptic in the air, also will tell stories about place, condition, and people that ultimately will situate your reader in that place, under those conditions in ways that help to experience it all. Audrey Petty understands the power of the word. Petty, an associate professor of English at the University of Illinois at Urbana-Champaign, thought very carefully about the words she used in her highly regarded December 2005 *Saveur* magazine essay, "Late-Night Chitlins With Momma." In describing her experience with food and family, Petty used language that evoked Southern culture, and childhood memories of chitlins in her mother's kitchen. "The smell was pervasive—vinegary and slightly farmy." Although she described the unique smell, the choice of the word "farmy," a child's word, creates an immediate sensory experience in the reader, as well as that empathy—that connection to childhood the writer is trying to convey.

This immediacy is a very powerful way to engage the reader, to keep the reader moving forward through the story. Thus, the descriptive use of words can become a vital element of your storytelling structure.

Sound of words   The sound of the words you use also can have a subliminal impact on the reader. Most writers understand that words can be heard even when read silently. And let's face it, the sound of words can have positive and negative effects on us as we read/hear them. Some words simply sound better than others. Think about words that have such an effect on you. And then think about the words you are selecting for your own storytelling. How might they *sound* to the reader as she works her way through your story? In addressing this point, some writers suggest doing something of a "sound check" on your writing. You can read passages of your story aloud to hear how the language sounds and to determine the effect it has. Certainly, you can do this silently as you would any other story you read, only now paying close attention to the way the words come across to you. But you also can read aloud, making the words audible in a real sense and considering whether the language choice works effectively. Does it resonate? Does it jar you? Which word sounds better in the context of story, magazine, and audience? If the word is jarring to the reader, then that reaction will cause the reader to hesitate, even if only for a moment. The effect of that is to be taken out of the story. If the aim is to facilitate the movement through the story with a continuous flow, then an alternative word choice would be in order. Rhythm and pacing are key considerations in this regard.

If too many ponderous words are resulting in a series of stops and starts, then there might be better choices to make. Why use the word "aberration" when "flaw" works just as well?

In this connect, it is important to avoid jargon in your exposition. Certain bureaucratic language might amount to a **term of art** in a particular profession, but it does not amount to artful writing. Clearly, some language is better left to corporate releases and annual reports and government documents. Hopefully, you'll know it when you hear it in your sound check.

TERM OF ART:
Language that has special meaning in a particular area, such as the law.

Of course, if a term of art is necessary in conveying the point of a story, then make sure you give that term definition by way of more accessible alternative language or examples. And here, conveying the point of a story might require that you show the shape and dimension of a character. The language a person uses will say a great deal about that person, so including even technical expressions in quotes by that person will help the reader feel the person. Still, it is important to clarify the meaning of the words and terms even in this context.

In addition to word sound, there is word meaning. Often there are word choices that might appear to have similar definitions, but have dramatically different meaning to the reader. Choosing the right word for the right meaning is an important part of the process. This process of **semantic differential**, developed by psychologist Charles E. Osgood in the 1950s, is a method for determining the meaning of words to individuals. In contemporary practice, it is used mostly in advertising in choosing those words that are likely to cause the most positive reaction in consumers. But there are considerations in this area for writers, too, given that writers choose words in order to elicit a particular kind of response in the receiver. Just as, in the classic example, a particular smell might be described as an aroma or a stench depending on the meaning we want to convey, the word choice in every context will mean something to the reader. What do you want it to mean?

SEMANTIC DIFFERENTIAL:
The measurement of the meaning of words to individuals.

Quotes   As discussed in the last chapter, quotes are essential to good magazine writing. They give substantive information, color, warmth, and life. They tell something of the human, emotional aspects of the story. They say something about the person talking, whether in a personality piece or not. They advance the story as a structural matter. Just like dialogue in fiction, some substantive element in the quote adds to what came just before and leads to what's coming next. For these reasons quotes must be selected very carefully and strategically. By this, we mean that quotes certainly should flow logically in the presentation. But they also must be edited for strategic storytelling purposes. That is not to say that we are encouraging the manufacture or manipulation of quotes. Instead, we are urging consideration of that precise segment of the interview that is needed at a given point in the story. Often there is quite a bit of verbal throat clearing in conversations and it is our responsibility—we writers—to spare the reader from these extraneous passages.

There is a need first to anchor quotes with a setup, a lead-in with the preceding paragraph. To do this, it is helpful to consider paraphrasing a portion of the quote, which can be used in the setup. As you review passages from the interview with an eye to placement in the story, consider moving from the general to the specific, or the specific to the general. For example, in a story about a history-making election you might have the following quote: "I recognize the historical significance of my position, and the responsibility I have as a result of that. After all, I am the first woman ever elected to the U.S. Senate from this state." The challenge for the writer here is to determine the essential point that is being made and the best way to make that point, with impact and in a way that connects one part of the story with the next, while avoiding the unwieldy structure of this long passage. So, in paraphrasing, we can consider a lead-in that moves from a general point to a specific one that carries the story forward and adds more meaning:

> Senator Brown recognizes the significance of her position. "After all," she says, "I am the first woman ever elected to the U.S. Senate from this state." She also recognizes the responsibility she has as a result of that election.

What results here is a seamless structure that bridges everything leading up to the quote and leads us into the next story segment, which should deliver on the promise that is made to inform the reader just what that responsibility of Senator Brown might be. Note how Joshua Green handles a factual lead-in to a colorful quote regarding the tough leadership of Rahm Emanuel in his *Rolling Stone* piece, summarizing Emanuel's merciless drive.

> When he joined Clinton's campaign team, he reportedly introduced himself by standing on a table and yelling at the staff for forty-five minutes. "We joke that someone should open a special trauma ward in Washington for people who've worked for Rahm," says Jose Cerda, a veteran staffer.

Consider how to make the quotes more efficient in terms of their length, but also more effective as structural components that connect everything else in the story.

Words of attribution   In magazine writing, attribution is written in the present tense for the most part. Remember, magazines are periodicals, not daily newspapers. Most of what is published in a magazine context is not necessarily fixed in time. Instead, it reflects ongoing feelings, beliefs, and convictions. So, as in the Senator Brown example above, "she says" makes that point clear. The senator always is aware of the fact that she is the first woman to achieve this milestone. Of course, we must distinguish those cases where we are citing a specific quote at a particular point in time, as with a news conference, or some other event. Here your attribution would be in the past tense to clarify that you are citing an historical moment. So, had Brown made that comment at a political fundraiser, and the point of the quote is to establish what was said then, the past tense would be the appropriate way to go.

Thus, writing attribution in the present tense provides a sense of currency. But what about the actual words of attribution? Should we use **color verbs** (e.g. maintains, proclaims, declares, insists, claims), or stick with a more neutral "says"? Clearly, the color verbs can be quite a bit more descriptive. They can help you cover a lot more narrative ground in less space than a full descriptive sentence or two. They also can be distracting to the extent they call too much attention to themselves. This will take the reader out of the story and slow the pacing. On the other hand, using "says" repeatedly can get monotonous.

One possible alternative is to use what are referred to as **beats** in fiction writing. A beat is a device used to avoid the monotony of "says" and the distraction of overblown color verbs like "laments" in your attribution. Beats are used to narrate dialogue in fiction. The point here is to use descriptive narrative to break up quotes. Note how the various forms of attribution can alternately convey meaning or, if overdone, distract.

> "At first, she took the marriage seriously," he says.
>
> "At first she took the marriage seriously," he recalls.
>
> "At first she took the marriage seriously," he laments.
>
> He glanced at their wedding picture on his desk. "At first she took the marriage seriously."
>
> He paused to weigh the next words, how dramatically things had changed for them. "At first she took the marriage seriously."

In the first three passages above, we move through attribution that increasingly adds to our understanding of what is being conveyed. But the final attributive word, "laments," arguably attracts too much attention. It just might cause the reader to pause for a moment to contemplate. A contemplative moment by the reader is a moment that is lost in the storytelling process, in the pacing of it all. It always is best to avoid contrivance in your storytelling effort.

In the last two references, we see how beats can add something to the narrative of the piece, expanding the dimension of the story even while they spare us the repetition of attribution. They can take up more space, but also can help you tell more story, or *show* more story, as we discuss in the next chapter. Take care, though, not to overdo it (or overwrite it), as the last example gets dangerously close to doing. As one of our editors used to caution all the time, "You are writing to express, not impress." Don't try to wow readers with how brilliant you are. Tell the story, and keep the reader engaged by the storytelling and you will have done your job successfully. Ultimately, you have to decide what you want to evoke in the reader and how best to accomplish that end without being noticed—especially by your editor.

Mike Sager remembers a particular story conference when he was a staff writer for the *Washington Post*. He and his immediate editor, Walt Harrington, were meeting with a deputy to Bob Woodward, arguing for alternative attribution. "I was trying to put dialogue in a story," Sager recalls. "And Woodward's deputy wanted me to put in things like 'he said, she said' and Walt said 'Tom Wolfe used this kind of literary device in the *Washington Post* years ago.' Bob Woodward's deputy said 'Tom Wolfe was fired from the *Washington Post.*'" And the outcome? "We trimmed it down."

Always check with your editor, or make sure you are familiar with the presentation style of the magazine before you try something that might not be accepted, no matter how good a storytelling technique it might be.

Transition   This is a very important part of storytelling that, again, cannot be seen, but certainly is missed if it does not exist, or if it is not executed properly. The point is to write one seamless story. You certainly do not want to call attention to separate elements—as between an anecdote and a section of background—with jarring breaks. It is imperative that you have smooth transitions. Smoothing out transitions most often is done through the use of conjunctive words. (Words like: accordingly, although, besides, consequently, furthermore, however, and therefore). Additionally, there are **transitional terms** (like: at the same time; for example; in addition), and even more subtle "directional" transition words (like: instead, or still).

Even more effective is the creative use of language that serves to link one paragraph to the next. Note how writer Alexis Jetter uses language as connective tissue in her November 2005 *Reader's Digest* story on a near miraculous medical procedure titled "The ER Drama You Won't Believe." Here, we list only the first lines of several successive paragraphs to give you an idea of how she connects it all.

"The approach was simple."

"Mobility was key."

"There was a danger, however."

"And there was one other catch."

[. . .]

"Unlike most of them, Marcos Parra was in remarkably good shape."

"More astonishing, no veins had ruptured."

"And as a surgical specimen, Parra had another quality that made him well suited for the new technique."

"But there was no time to delay."

With her creative use of language, the writer is able to use transitional words and terms sparingly, yet establish a sense of motion that moves the reader forward with a pace that is well suited for a human interest story. She does this with effective use of language in the new paragraph that refers to a point just made in the preceding paragraph. The result is a connecting link that bridges each thought in the kind of seamless flow that makes for a good read.

Ultimately, these are literary devices. Their purpose is to help tell a story and move the story forward logically, smoothly. These devices are most helpful in holding everything together when they do not call attention to themselves. Indeed, these are the vital elements of structure that are scarcely noticed at all.

Voice   Among the "scarcely noticed" elements of structure that can be most effective in storytelling is voice. As a writer, you develop a style that becomes something of a signature of your writing. It is something people can begin to recognize as your voice. It is important to make sure that voice is authoritative. When done effectively, that authority rings through your copy in a way that infuses it with credibility and serves to hold together all the other elements. It becomes a significant structural element.

This authority begins with the research. As we have advised, there well could be a tremendous amount of research that is conducted just to prepare for the interviews you will arrange. That does not mean that every detail of your research has to work its way into your copy. Indeed, as we have advised, you likely will not have the space to include such a heavily factual presentation in the story and, even if you did, the effect on the reader would be numbing. But the weight of this research and your depth of understanding of the issue resulting from it will resonate. In the beginning, it will show in the confidence you bring to your interviews. You will begin to sound like an expert yourself in facilitating the conversation with your sources, which will net even better quotes. It also shows in your presentation. You will find it increasingly unnecessary even to attribute certain factual points you make in your story. Your depth of knowledge of the subject matter will show that certain aspects of the story are widely known in the particular field. Thus, as you set out your exposition, you will come across as the expert you have become in the course of your research. Just knowing what you know is going to shape your writing in a way that gives it much more credibility, builds confidence in the reader that you know what you are talking about, and, as a result, keeps the reader moving forward. The key here is to work your research seamlessly into the fabric of the narrative. We'll see more of this as we discuss story development in greater detail.

WRITER'S WORKSHOP

Here is a suggestion for you to apply a central point of this chapter as you begin to develop and refine article structure.

In the last chapter, we suggested a Vision Test. Here, we are suggesting a "Sound Check." Take a completed draft manuscript and read it. Aloud. Notice how the words flow, how they sound. Consider whether longer sentences can be shortened, and whether shorter ones might be a bit longer. What about the words of attribution? Do they sound right? Can you substitute narrative "beats" to create more immediacy of setting? The bottom line is that you should feel the rhythm of the language and rebalance where the words are not flowing comfortably, with smooth transitions and words that do not attract too much attention. This is where those elements of Professor Hiley Ward's invisible structure come to life.

Chapter Nine Review

ASSIGNMENT DESK

1. Select a magazine article of about 2,500 words.

2. Make notes of the transitions that are used in a selection of 10 to 15 paragraphs, and especially note the transitional terms used.

3. Consider how you might substitute connective language, as we point out above in the "ER" story by Alexis Jetter in *Reader's Digest*.

4. Now look at the language used in the article. Consider how the word selection helps to move the story forward. Do you stumble over any word choices? How might you smooth out these stumbles with substituted language?

5. Finally, look at the words of attribution. As we suggest in the Writer's Workshop box above, consider whether "color verbs" or narrative "beats" might add a dimension to the story that helps the flow.

▶ KEY TERMS

- beats
- color verbs
- semantic differential
- term of art
- transitional terms

▶ SUGGESTED READING

Jacobi, Peter P. *The Magazine Article*. Bloomington, Indiana: Indiana University Press, 1991.

Ward, Hiley H. *Magazine and Feature Writing*. Mayfield Publishing Company, McGraw-Hill Higher Education, 1993.

Jetter, Alexis. "The ER Drama You Won't Believe," *Reader's Digest*, November 2005.

▶ WEB RESOURCES

http://www.rollingstone.com/politics?rnd=1141682869671&has-player=unknown
   "The Enforcer," by Joshua Green. *Rolling Stone*, November 3, 2005.

http://www.zingermansroadhouse.com/2011/12/14/late-night-chitlins-with-momma/
   "Late-Night Chitlins With Momma," by Audrey Petty. *Saveur*, December 2005.

10 Self-Edit

▶ **INTRODUCTION**

In an important way, once a draft article is produced, the real work begins. As award-winning Chicago playwright and magazine freelancer David Barr often says, "I'm a pretty decent writer, but I'm a great editor." Editing is where you make the tough choices about what will work and what will not. You also have a chance to make sure you have a complete story. The self-edit process is the stage where everything really comes to life. Here we discuss the important steps that must be taken by the successful freelancer in tightening and (in some cases) even loosening up the copy to maximize reader impact. Planning this stage is essential. This is a process that calls upon the writer to be brutally honest in self assessment—cutting some of the best lines in the story, if need be, and finding additional material that might be required to complete the story. Ideally, the self-editing process should track on multiple levels to make sure your piece is "clean." In other words, you must make sure you have good coverage, the story is a good read, and it is error-free. We will show how important this review can be in making sure factual information and context are comprehensively provided, and, as important as all else, that you have established and supported your theme. Among the other areas covered in this chapter is the nature of the collaboration between contributor and editor. This working relationship creates demands, which we will discuss. Deadlines are vital in this connection to give editors time to work with contributors on conceptual edits, ensuring that the scope of the assigned article that is produced is

> **LEARNING OBJECTIVES**
>
> 1. Discuss the importance of taking a critical look at your first draft.
>
> 2. Show the critical steps that must be taken to polish the article.
>
> 3. Demonstrate the documentation that is important to provide editors.
>
> 4. Discuss the important considerations to make in planning for this stage.

what the editor envisioned. An important part of the production process in working with line editors and fact checkers is making sure research records (source material citations and interview notes and contact information) are maintained in an organized fashion for submission to the editor.

▶ THE RIGHT ATTITUDE

Editing and revising are two very important functions of this whole process. To do it most effectively, you first have to revise your thinking about it all. Up to this point, you have been working as a writer, dedicated to research, interviewing, and writing the piece you pitched and were assigned. But now you have to abandon that proprietary interest—that notion you own this thing; that it is a part of you—in order to take a cool, dispassionate, detached look at it all. The process will be a lot easier if you don't start out trying to be a great writer on your first pass. As we suggested at the top of this chapter, the best attitude to have is that your first draft is not carved in stone. It is, after all, digitized, which means it is changed easily with just a few keystrokes. So, try to approach the self-edit process as you might do with someone else's copy, assessing what is working and what needs to work. This is the time for critical self-appraisal. This is the time for evaluation. What is the most suitable structure for the piece? Have you already accomplished that best architecture? What is missing? What is needed to complete this story? Are there additional anecdotes that might enliven it? Are there additional facts that will support it? Are there more examples that will clarify it? Are there more quotes that will humanize it? You must be open to the answers that come to you. The point is that, certainly, you want to be a good writer. But, as Barr suggests, at this stage, you really want to become a great editor. In so doing, you become an even *better* writer. The measure of that quality is on the page. You can determine what goes on that page before your line editor ever sees the copy. Indeed, you must do so. Your goal is to turn in "clean" copy. By that, we mean a story that requires no further sourcing or documentation; one that reads well, consistent with the style of the magazine; and one that has no grammatical or typographical errors.

▶ GREAT EDITORS: A COLLABORATION

Magazine editors agree that the best writers they work with are the ones who are open to the collaborative process. Conversely, of course, the best editors are those who know how to collaborate in bringing out the best of the writer without taking a heavy hand in rewriting the story. If you approach the task with the right frame of mind, you will have done a lot of the editor's work before she ever sees your manuscript. The first step is to approach your copy objectively (or, as objectively as possible). So, when it comes to your writing, don't love it. In fact, don't even *like* it. That is the only way you will be able to make the tough choices you invariably will have to make about what stays in and what is cut from the story. You must work as a technician, one who knows what it takes to make the story better. That doesn't necessarily mean making it shorter. That doesn't necessarily mean making it tighter. As we have seen, sometimes anecdotal narrative can strengthen a story by involving the reader. But well-crafted anecdotal material can take space to develop. As a result, this element makes the story longer.

You must be willing to make all revisions necessary, even if certain segments of the writing sounded great when you first wrote them. In fact, maybe these passages have to go now precisely *because* they sound terrific. The writing might be so good that it attracts too much attention to itself, taking the reader out of the story. It might cause her to pause, even if only to appreciate the artistry. That pause obviously will break the rhythm of the story that should carry her through it from beginning to end. So, as you review the entire story, sometimes even the good stuff has to go precisely because it is too good. It might seem unnecessary. It might seem out of place, wrong. The key here is that you simply cannot be wedded to anything until it's done. And it is not done until you have gone through a few considerations.

▶ THE PROCESS

The self-editing process calls upon you to consider first and foremost what makes for good storytelling. This is where you take a long hard look at your work as an outsider might do. Ideally, there are a couple of key considerations to be made in your review. Coverage and presentation are vitally important. You want to make sure your story coverage is complete and consistent with the theme.

THE PRODUCTION PROCESS

Typically, the magazine production process involves multiple departments within the organization, including the editorial department, the research department, the art department, and—increasingly these days—the Web department. In this way, all considerations regarding presentation across *platforms,* will be made in the most effective and efficient way possible. The following is a summary of the way it all works at most magazines. It is vital for the writer to understand your connection to this dynamic process.

1. **The freelancer pitches a section editor** or, in some cases, a section editor will approach a writer she knows with an assignment.

2. **The editor and the writer work together on story development,** at times in multiple conversations or email memos to determine the precise angle

on the story, illustration ideas, including photo possibilities, and whether the piece will live in the feature well or the front-of-the-book.

3. **If the piece will be designated for the front-of-the-book piece,** then the consideration likely will turn to how the information will be conveyed. Front-of-the-book pieces well could be presented as all text, all graphic, or mostly graphic with a little bit of text.

4. **The editorial and art team begin to discuss presentation,** to determine how the story might look on the page.

5. **Once all these determinations are made**, the writer has clear direction to begin conducting research, scheduling interviews, as needed, and producing the first draft of the piece.

6. **When the draft is submitted,** the assigning editor reviews mostly for the scope of coverage to determine whether every aspect of the story is being presented, as agreed in the initial discussions. Now, on review, new information might be needed based on unexpected discoveries in the course of the writer's research or interviewing. Is there anything more that is needed; holes that should be filled; new perspectives that should be included in the interest of being accurate, fair, and balanced?

7. **In reviewing the draft, the assigning editor might consult with the research department** to determine the scope of the discourse on a particular subject. What is being said, and who is saying it? The editor then can make a judgment on whether the draft meets the expectations of his readership—what his audience would want or need to know about this subject.

8. **The editor will submit notes to the writer** resulting from this preliminary review. Then the writer will produce another draft or two, addressing the points made in the notes.

9. **If the draft is too long for the space assigned,** the writer often will be asked to trim it down to size. Sometimes the editor will make specific suggestions about sections that can be shortened.

10. **Once the length is established, the fact-checking begins.** Typically, the fact-check and copy editing teams of staff editors and interns will identify and verify every fact asserted in the piece, correct spelling and grammar, and make style-specific changes based on the particular voice of the magazine. While magazines vary on fact-check requirements, some might require as many as three sources for verification. Spelling also is confirmed, especially for proper nouns.

11. **The writer takes part in this process** when asked to consult with line editors who have questions. But, even before that, the writer must submit all research documents, including:

    • a complete source list with contact information

    • interview notes and recording transcriptions

    • a list of cited materials

    • any other official documents.

    Note in the fact-checking guidelines for *Chicago* magazine writers the level of detail required for submission of supporting materials.

12. **Finally, after everything checks out** and has been thoroughly copy edited, the piece is ready to move forward. The web staff will review for **repurposing** to determine how short or long the web version will be, whether hyperlinks will be included, what graphic elements or animation to include, and whether there is suitable audio or video recording that was generated in the reporting of the particular story or might be drawn from related materials to add dimension.

REPURPOSE:
To present material produced in one medium, such as printed text, in a different medium, such as digital or audio-visual.

Coverage   The central issue here is whether you have kept your promise. Have you written the story you set out to write? Have you covered all dimensions of the story you discussed in your pitch, as revised in consultation with the editor, and as developed over the course of everything you discovered in your reporting? Here is where you want to check all your documented facts, the background you have included for context. The point is to ensure that you have done everything you need to do to substantiate your premise. Consider whether there are sources to be added, and if there is a need to follow up with the ones you already interviewed. Sometimes things will be revealed to you in the course of conversation, sometimes in the course of reviewing notes and transcripts of interviews. Make sure you have left no pertinent questions unanswered.

Fact-checking Guidelines for Writers

To all writers:

In an effort to make the fact-checking process as smooth and thorough as possible, we ask that you submit an organized and clearly marked packet of source materials backing up your article.

We'll need the following information. Please use this as a checklist:

____ **An annotated copy of your story.** Indicate in the margins or in footnotes where each piece of information comes from and where it can be found in the packet.

____ **A complete source list.** Include names, phone numbers, and email addresses for all sources, named and unnamed. Note the date and format (e.g. by phone, in person, or via email) of each interview with your sources.

____ **Your interview notes and/or tape transcriptions.**

____ **All background material cited in the article.** Include books, articles, studies, reports, etc. Don't rely on memory or something you heard. We need documentation.

____ **Court documents.** If your story involves a criminal or civil lawsuit, you MUST submit all pertinent court documents. Don't simply refer us to the lawyers. This is especially important if you quote directly from legal documents—court testimony, affidavits, depositions, police reports, or other legal briefs. You should clearly mark the quoted sections with tabs and highlighter.

You can expect a few calls from the fact-checker during the editing process. If you have not submitted the proper materials, you will be asked to do so. Thank you in advance for your help.

Chicago magazine
Chicago Home + Garden   www.chicagomag.com

As much as anything else, you want to make sure you have threaded your theme throughout the story. We easily could have placed this reminder in the "Presentation" discussion below, because it is a function of stylistic writing. But the theme also is a substantive element of your story. It goes to coverage. If done well, you will show how every other substantive point that is made actually reinforces the theme you have set out early on in the story. In fact, keeping this point in mind will help you greatly in determining those elements of your substantive material that should remain in the story, and those you really do not need. Everything must advance the central point of the story. The theme—that unifying element of the story—should be infused in every other element. Keep asking yourself: What is this story about? What is it really all about?

Presentation   As with gourmet food, in magazine writing, presentation arguably is everything. Think here about the structural elements we discussed in Chapter 8. If key presentation elements—the copy blocks—of your work are not present, or well balanced, or welded together firmly, then you will need to work on them. Here we are talking about the components of good writing. As indicated, good writing is a function of both the elements of presentation, such as your authoritative voice, style, word choice, pacing, and also the structure of presentation—the lead, nutgraf, expository building blocks, and the summary and conclusion at the end. You may even decide that the "story" is not a narrative piece at all, but something best suited for "high-concept" presentation, featuring data that is displayed graphically on the page or animated in some form for presentation on the web or on a tablet.

The key is to be objective and subjective all at once. Keep a healthy distance. Maintain detachment from the words. Keep your ego out of it. Then ask: Does it read like something you would want to read? Award-winning pop producer Kenny "Babyface" Edmunds once said in a magazine interview that he knows he has a recording hit when he can imagine hearing the newly recorded tune on the radio. Run your own creation through the "Babyface" test. If on review it looks like an article you would buy a magazine to read or would capture your attention on a website, then you've got a hit. So, can you see your story on the cover of a magazine or as the lead **element** on the homepage of a magazine's website? Can you see it anywhere inside the magazine? Set your standards high and then work to meet those standards.

▶ BALANCING THE STRUCTURAL ELEMENTS

So, obviously, when you consider the elements of a text-driven story, you want to make sure you are writing in a clear and well-paced way that keeps the reader moving through the story. But you also want to make sure the story is well constructed. How well does the story hold up logically, thematically? How cleanly, how smoothly does the story flow from one element to another? Have you incorporated enough of those "invisible" elements—the well-considered transitions that can hold things together—as recommended by Hiley Ward? What about your voice? Does it ring with authority? What about your pacing? Look at the story on the page. Can you see the balance among elements—the anecdotes, facts, examples, and quotes?

Lead   In this connection, the presentation review starts with your opening. Does the lead bring the reader into the story? Does it effectively set a tone? As you might recall from our earlier discussion of the lead, you know that the choice of style for the opening—whether summary lead or anecdotal lead—is completely up to you. But you must decide on what works best to set up the story that is about to unfold, as well as "hook" the reader. In evaluating the choice you have made during your self-edit, consider the approach that is most appropriate for the story, and the approach that is consistent with the presentation of the magazine and the expectations of the readership. For example, you will not want to limit yourself to a short summary lead in a story that relies on extensive narrative anecdotes. Start out with a narrative that not only is attention grabbing, but also sets up the style of presentation.

Nutgraf   What about the nutgraf? What is the angle of the story? What is the theme? What is this story really about? Consider these questions first, and then take another look at your nutgraf to determine how effectively it sets it all out. As important as anything else, consider how well this section of your story flows from the opening to the body of the piece. Does it move naturally, logically to the rest of the story? Keep in mind the structural function of the nutgraf. It must serve that all-important "bridge" effect, connecting your opening to everything else, and making the reader want to move on. But also keep in mind the substantive function of the nutgraf. In addition to forming a bridge from the lead to the body of the story, it also must clarify what the story is all about. It must establish the theme.

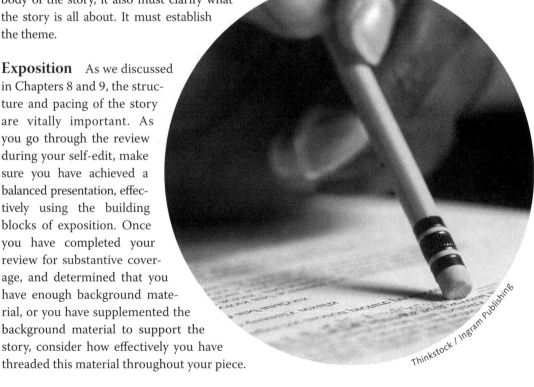
Thinkstock / Ingram Publishing

Exposition   As we discussed in Chapters 8 and 9, the structure and pacing of the story are vitally important. As you go through the review during your self-edit, make sure you have achieved a balanced presentation, effectively using the building blocks of exposition. Once you have completed your review for substantive coverage, and determined that you have enough background material, or you have supplemented the background material to support the story, consider how effectively you have threaded this material throughout your piece.

How well do you balance the presentation of background as against quotes, examples, and anecdotal information? In terms of pacing, how effectively have you timed the placement of the alternating components—the building blocks—of the story? The "vision test." Also, make sure your transitions from one element to the next are smooth and seamless. The "sound check."

End Remember that the best endings will relate back to the opening in some way. The ending should resolve the issue that was established in your lead and nutgraf, and then—if done right—has been threaded throughout the story. Again, the ending should give the reader a sense of satisfaction. Consider the vitally important "takeaway" value. What is it that you want the reader to get from the story? Have you provided it? Consider the structure of the ending. It should be developed in two parts:

- A **setup** of the conclusion tying everything together, perhaps returning to the opening anecdote.
- A **payoff** that forms the ultimate takeaway. One sentence can be enough. And, if that one sentence is a quote, make sure it is the best closing line available. Not just the best quote. But the best *closing*. And it is the best closing if it nails the theme.

AHA: THE SELF-EDIT CHECKLIST

In the rush to meet your deadline, invariably some things might not occur to you until it is too late to address them. This is why you should plan for a careful review period in your overall schedule. We suggest you at least take an **AHA** moment of reflection and then proceed with a methodical checklist. AHA is our acronym for critical questions you can ask yourself in three areas once you have developed a draft. Does the piece **Attract**, **Hold**, and **Awaken**? These concepts track the beginning, middle, and end of the basic structure of your story. Does it attract attention with an opening that sets up the story and establishes the theme? Does it hold onto the reader in the development of the theme—holding the story together—over the course of the expository middle? Finally does it awaken something in the reader, something new by way of information or understanding? Is there some attainment? Keeping these broad concepts in mind as you go through the following checklist will help you polish the story in the most effective way to produce that "AHA" moment to the reader.

LEAD
- Hook the reader.
- Set up the story that is about to unfold.

In making your choice, consider:

- The approach that is most appropriate for the story.
- The approach that is consistent with the established presentation of the magazine and the expectations of the readership.

NUTGRAF
- Make sure you bridge the lead and the body of the story.
- Make sure you clarify what this story is all about; establish the theme.

EXPOSITION
- Structure and pacing of the story are vitally important.
- To achieve a balanced presentation, effectively use the building blocks of exposition:
  - Background
  - Quotes
  - Examples
  - Anecdotes.
- Make sure your transitions from one element to the next are smooth.

END
- Remember that the best endings will relate back to the opening in some way.
- The ending should resolve the issue established in your lead and nutgraf:
  - The ending should give the reader a sense of satisfaction.
  - Consider the vitally important "takeaway" value.
  - What is it that you want the reader to get from the story?

The ending should be developed in two parts:

- A **setup** for the ending, tying together everything in the story:
  - A return to the opening anecdote can work here.
  - Ideally, the summary should be shorter than the lead.

- A **payoff** that forms the ultimate takeaway for the reader:
  - One sentence can be enough.
  - If you use a quote, make sure it is the best closing line available.

▶ PROOFREADING

Let's be clear: the work *must* be proofread. Typos, misspellings, grammatical problems must be found and corrected before submitting the story. Many writers, editors, and commentators suggest that this is best done as its own separate pass. In other words, after you have completed your review for coverage and presentation, making all changes you determine are needed, then you should do a final read-through only to search for errors. This approach makes a lot of sense as a practical matter. Invariably, if you are trying to check for substantive coverage elements (thinking about whether you need to conduct follow-up interviews), or you are trying to move a quote to break up a long section of background material to improve presentation, then you could miss an errant typo or a stray punctuation mark. Performing your own proofread in a separate pass gives you a chance to focus only on catching all those embarrassing mistakes. Here you will do a line-by-line edit for typos and misspellings, and you must do a careful read for grammatical problems. Some writers depend on spellcheck and grammar review programs, but this is not wise. Spellcheck will not make a correction if you have the right spelling but have selected the wrong version of a word. Most grammar programs don't account for style variations, and writer's voice. Only you know what you want to say and how you want to say it. A careful review will get it right.

WRITER'S WORKSHOP

Here is a suggestion for you to apply a central point of this chapter as you begin to conduct your self-edit.

The time needed to complete the self-edit process successfully should be factored into the timetable you set for the production of the entire article. No less than a day should be preserved, but preferably a week for all the points you want to cover. Journalist and University of South Florida journalism professor Rick Wilber suggests that writers plan on three passes through the manuscript. One would be for the structural review. A second would be for stylistic presentation. And a final pass would be for the proofing and copy editing. We agree that this careful self-edit process is a methodical way to ensure you turn in clean copy. But it also requires that you plan sufficient time to complete the process successfully. Look back over the checklist and consider how much time you need for follow up with sources, or even to contact new sources for additional information. This part of the process adds considerably more time to the purely mechanical process of editing and proofreading. Just as the entire self-edit process should come before the editor reviews and makes suggestions, the timetable planning should come even before you agree on a deadline with the editor.

Chapter Ten Review

ASSIGNMENT DESK

1. Consider a magazine story you want to pitch.

2. As you go through the suggestions we made in Chapter 6, summarizing the information you want to include, listing the preliminary sources you want to interview, begin to process the amount of time it reasonably might take to complete the task.

3. Put together a timeline for your magazine assignment. Start with the deadline. Even if you don't have the assignment yet, you can start with a date just for purposes of calculating.

4. Work your way back through all the elements of the process, including the self-edit, writing, interviews, and background research.

5. Determine your ideal self-edit period of one week and determine how much time you will need to complete the assignment (and all its phases) successfully.

When you are asked by an assigning editor how much time you will need to complete a story, you will have a reasonable answer. Or, if you simply are given a deadline date, you will know what it will take to process everything.

▶ KEY TERMS

- AHA
- element
- pay off
- repurpose
- setup

▶ SUGGESTED READING

Harrison Smith, Sarah. *The Fact Checker's Bible.* New York: Anchor Press, 2004. A complete guide to the art and craft of fact checking.

Navasky, Victor; Cornog, Evan. *The Art of Making Magazines: On Being an Editor and Other Views from the Industry:* New York: Columbia University Press, 2012. Navasky and Cornog compile essays by a variety of editors, writers, art directors, and publishers, who discuss the importance of things like fact checking and copy editing.

Wilber, Rick. *Magazine Feature Writing.* New York: St. Martin's Press, 1995. A guide to preparing and writing magazine articles.

▶ **WEB RESOURCE**

http://www.nationinstitute.org/files/managed/Nation%20Intro%20to%20Fact%20
Checking.pdf   Fact-checking guide for *The Nation* magazine, provides helpful
tips for both writers and fact-checkers.

Literary Non-fiction: Storytelling at Its Best

▶ INTRODUCTION

As many writers will attest, showing goes a long way toward telling. In fact, showing has more impact than simply telling. In literary non-fiction, we use the best elements of fiction writing—**character**, voice, **theme**, **conflict**, and, ultimately, **resolution**—to inform and energize true stories in ways that draw us into the immediacy of the narrative, to reveal to us; effectively to show us. Through lucid and detailed descriptions, we experience the atmosphere, hear the sounds, smell the aromas, and see the sights of the surroundings of our subjects.

In this chapter, we look at constructing stories, as writer Tom Wolfe has suggested, by moving the reader through carefully framed scenes—effectively placing the reader in the story. We illustrate the power of narrative and its demands for detail and for **immersive reporting**. We also discuss the criticism of this form in ways that will guide contributors away from the potential pitfalls: composite scenes; manufactured quotes; and imagined **interior monologue**.

In the end, even narrative-driven stories must be factually accurate. The story is in service of the factual occurrences. The facts are not reshaped to fit a **narrative arc** or build the tension through a **rising conflict**.

IMMERSIVE REPORTING: Research and reporting based on personal experience with a subject, resulting in a deeper understanding of that subject.

INTERIOR MONOLOGUE: The inner voice of a character, sometimes imagined by the writer and presented as if the character were thinking aloud.

NARRATIVE ARC: The flow of a story from the introduction, through the exposition or rising conflict, to the resolution.

RISING CONFLICT: A series of incidents, events, or personal conflicts that build dramatic tension in storytelling. Also known as "rising action."

▶ OVERVIEW

Many people relate long-form narrative with the mid-twentieth century work of journalists like Tom Wolfe, Gay Talese, and Hunter S. Thompson, writers associated with a type of literary non-fiction dubbed the "new journalism" by Wolfe in his 1973 anthology of the best examples of the form. Wolfe and his contemporaries sought to shake up journalism by breaking conventional rules. They didn't shy away from writing in the events they recorded and writing about them in the first person. They treated their subjects like characters in a novel, focusing on their hopes, fears, and motivations, in addition to what they said. More importantly, they wrote from a distinct point of view and not merely like detached observers of people and events.

Wolfe was pretty emphatic in his declaration that the new journalism was a significant advancement in American letters. In truth, the new journalism wasn't entirely new. There were plenty of precursors, including late nineteenth and early twentieth century journalists such as Stephen Crane and Lincoln Steffens—writers who also employed a number of novelistic techniques and defied journalistic convention.

Many young people who are drawn to this "new journalism" are attracted by their mistaken impressions of what long-form narrative is. They have read (or at least heard of) the elegantly written, absorbing treatises crafted by the likes of Wolfe, Talese, Joan Didion, and Susan Orlean. In these pieces they see the compelling characters, dramatic story lines, and lilting language that make the articles read more like fiction than journalism, and they assume that the key to these writers' effectiveness is all in the writing. While it is true that the prose in some of the best long-form narrative pieces is as graceful as that in the most fascinating novels, the key to these pieces is the sharp detail that powers the story and illuminates character. For literary journalists, there is great storytelling opportunity in even the finest details. If writing were physics, then literary nonfiction would be the quantum mechanics of the field—focusing on the subatomic particles of life; the essential things that make up the world; the smallest things that can have the biggest meaning and impact.

In essence, it is the immersive reporting that distinguishes long-form narrative, not merely the innovative use of language. It can serve to illuminate the significant issues of the moment, or search for that relatable thread in the lives of celebrities or even find the larger significance

Gay Talese

Getty Images

in stories about everyday lives. Each case involves an incredible amount of digging with a purpose. "Literary journalists are boundary crossers in search of a deeper perspective on our lives and times," notes Norman Sims, professor of journalism at the University of Massachusetts, Amherst, in his introduction to *Literary Journalism*, co-edited with Mark Kramer.

That perspective is presented often in the small stories, the "intimate journalism," as advanced by Walt Harrington, former staff writer for *The Washington Post Magazine*. "The goal of intimate journalism is simple," notes Harrington, a professor of journalism at the University of Illinois, Urbana-Champaign. "It is to understand other people's worlds from the inside out, to understand and portray people as they understand themselves. Not the way they say they understand themselves but the way they really understand themselves," he writes in his edited work, *Intimate Journalism: The Art and Craft of Reporting Everyday Life*.

Tom Wolfe

Getty Images / Redferns

Though it is true that the best practitioners of the form do indeed use writing techniques borrowed from their fiction-writing counterparts (and also true that many of these non-fiction writers have tried their hand at fiction), make no mistake about it, with the documentary goals defined by Professors Sims and Harrington, long-form narrative must be rooted in facts—copious, scrupulously reported facts. That is one part research, one part interview, and one part observation—which sometimes can become the dominant part. As practitioners are quick to tell you, there is a fundamental difference between being told something and simply watching it happen.

Yes, some novelists who trafficked in non-fiction—notably Norman Mailer and Truman Capote—are known to have played fast and loose with the truth. But contemporary journalists who have made their names in this genre tend to be obsessive in their devotion to relaying factual accounts. Alex Kotlowitz, author of *There Are No Children Here* and a regular contributor to *The New York Times Magazine*, recounts how he collected the details that fleshed out *In the Face of Death*, his July 2003 *NYT* story about a capital murder trial that had taken place three years earlier. Kotlowitz began the piece with a detailed description of the vicious murder at the heart of the story. To recreate the scene, he conducted an extensive interview with the young man on trial for the crime and pored over court transcripts and police reports that described the scene. The result was vivid passages like this:

> After they left, Beers lifted himself off the floor and shuffled out the door to a pay phone, where he again collapsed. He died under a dangling phone, rivulets of blood running from his head.

For scenes in which there was no detailed record, Kotlowitz went to other lengths to capture detail.

> I went to the courthouse and would sit in that same courtroom. I went to the exact same jury room where they were empaneled to get a feel for what it must have been like to be a part of those deliberations. I took notes on things like how big the rooms were, what the table looked like, what the chairs felt like. I talked to the jurors about what it felt like to be there. I wanted to paint a very clear picture of what it was like to be in that room.

The result is description that is almost cinematic in its recording of the proceedings:

> Courtroom No. 4 is modest in size. The jurors sat along one wall, slightly elevated, in low-back swivel chairs. The witness stand and the spectators' gallery, which seats 50 and was nearly filled every day, mostly with families and friends of the victim and Gross, were within a few feet of the jury box. A number of the jurors complained of feeling cramped. At one point, a couple of them asked if some of Beers's relatives could be moved to another part of the gallery; they could feel the presence of the men in the first row.

But gathering detail is only half the challenge in developing a good long-form narrative story. The most difficult part of this process actually may be finding the story itself.

▶ WHAT MAKES A GOOD LONG-FORM NARRATIVE STORY?

When John Mecklin speaks to young people about finding stories that are suitable for long-form literary treatment, the former editor of *Miller-McCune*, a national public policy magazine, reads to them from a book that he maintains is a perfectively structured narrative: Dr. Seuss's *The Cat in the Hat*.

Hearing that *The Cat in the Hat* is a perfect narrative is startling to students at first, but as Mecklin explains it, this little children's book has all the elements one should look for in a long-form narrative piece. It has protagonists—Sally and her brother—who are buffeted by the whirlwind events set in motion by the antagonist, the chapeau-wearing feline of the title. But more important for a topic deserving long-form treatment, the story has rising action. As the cat's antics grow increasingly wilder, the tension in the story rises, and it is the heightened anticipation of what will happen next that draws the reader deeper and deeper into the story. Will Sally and her brother get caught with the cat in the house? Will they clean up the mess the cat has made before mother gets home? This mounting suspense is the essence of narrative and the essence of a long-form narrative story.

But how do you know in advance that a story has that kind of narrative potential? Often, it is difficult to see the long-form narrative potential in a story that is unfolding in real time as the writer is reporting it. Many writers (and documentary filmmakers) heighten the odds of finding a story with narrative potential by latching on to a controversy—some contentious topic or spectacle—that may have opposing sides whose stories may unfold in dramatic fashion as the reporting progresses. Once they have a sufficiently compelling controversy, the writer attempts to home in on a central character or characters on either side of the controversy; one who will provide the lens through which the events are viewed.

Just as often, long-form writers begin with a character, an individual whose battle with some forces gives the story the rising action it needs to make a compelling long-form narrative. It is then up to the reporter to vividly reconstruct events in a way that makes an absorbing narrative. A good example of this is "Lucky Jim," Elizabeth Gilbert's harrowing account of the litany of incidents that transformed Jim MacLaren from a strapping former college football player to a one-legged triathlete to a wheelchair-bound quadriplegic. The article ran in the May 2003 issue of *GQ*.

Without the benefit of having witnessed any of the horrific episodes in MacLaren's life—like the time a New York City bus plowed into him, leaving him with one leg or the time eight years later when he was mowed down by a speeding car when he was participating in an Ironman competition in California—Gilbert captures these moments and builds reader anticipation to learn more about MacLaren's plight. Even though the scenes are told in flashback, the detail is riveting:

> He never saw the 40,000-pound bus that ran the red light on 34th Street and demolished him. Nor does he have any memory of the paramedics who scraped him off the sidewalk (certain he was already a corpse) and delivered him to Bellevue Hospital. The next thing Jim remembers—after disappearing into a coma for eight days—is waking up in intensive care and learning that his left leg had been amputated below the knee.

In the next episode, set during a race, Gilbert builds on the tension established in the first:

> Suddenly Jim heard the crowd gasp. He turned his head to see what was going on, and there was the steel grille of a black van heading straight toward him. He realized he was about to be hit by a goddamn car.

[…] This time Jim vividly remembers being hit. He remembers the screams from the crowd. He remembers his body flying across the street and smashing into a lamppost headfirst, snapping his neck. He remembers riding in the ambulance and being aware that he could not feel his limbs …

The narrative often can be used to connect us to an issue of importance by way of an individual's impacting personal story. The human interest angle is what drives many stories published in *Readers' Digest*. As with many publications, *RD* also has used celebrities as the point of that connection, as the magazine did in the September 2004 story on actress Terri Garr, written by Lynn Rosellini.

The tingling began in her right foot. Then, jogging in New York's Central Park, Teri Garr stumbled. […] Before long, she felt a stabbing pain in her arm.

That was 1983, and Garr was at the peak of her career.

[…]

Finally, in 1999, she got a definitive diagnosis: multiple sclerosis.

Notice how the writer effectively has woven a number of facts derived in research and interviews to provide a sense of connection to the subject—Garr—that connects us to the effects of MS, in a way that lends the story universal appeal. This should be the aim of any writer attempting the narrative form.

▶ LITERARY NON-FICTION ELEMENTS

So what are the elements of this form? They are the same storytelling elements that bring fiction to life. Among the leading ones are:

1. Character
2. Theme
3. Conflict
4. Voice
5. Resolution.

Character   In fiction writing, the story always starts with the character. The character is established, and the reader identifies with that character and all that the character wants to achieve—the motivation. People connect with other people in non-fiction storytelling, too. To the extent that the literary writer can infuse the story with the human element, she effectively will produce a story that will resonate and captivate. The reader will be in empathy with the main character. The key here is paying attention to those aspects of human character that not only tell the reader who the person is, but why the person figures so prominently in the story. In other words, the writer must find that aspect of the "character" that illustrates the central point of it all—the theme.

Theme   This is the story. This is the answer to the question, what is the story all about? In literary form, that story can unfold as a single flowing narrative. It can proceed in a straightforward chronology, or with chunks of narrative that move between contemporary and flashback elements. In either approach, the imperative is to make sure that every aspect of the story continues to reinforce in the reader's mind what the story is all about. In fiction, that point is set out in the dramatic question. What is the character trying to achieve? What does the character want? That is the character's motivation. Similarly, when a real-life personality is driving a work of literary non-fiction, the writer must consider what aspect of the person's life will illustrate the point of it all.

SEBASTIAN JUNGER AND THE FORENSICS OF STORYTELLING

The literary non-fiction form of magazine writing has been used quite effectively in presenting dramatic accounts of issues of great public significance. The celebrated October 1999 *Vanity Fair* article, "The Forensics of War," by Sebastian Junger is a riveting example of such an effort, illustrating for readers the true impact of the Balkan conflict and particularly U.S. and NATO engagement. This story—the winner of a National Magazine Award in 2000—is an example of immersive reporting, highly detailed research on background factual information, as well as the very human stories that help connect us to the meaning of it all. Consider how Junger begins this journey with a detailed account of a killing that places readers right there in the scene, and then uses that scene—infused with background—to illustrate the full dimensions of the violent conflict.

> No one knows who he was, but he almost got away. He broke and ran when the Serbs started shooting, and he made it to a thicket before the first bullet hit him in the left leg.
>
> It must have missed the bone, because he was able to keep going—along the edge of a hayfield and then into another swath of scrub oak and locust. There was a dry streambed in there, and he probably crouched in the shadows, listening to the bursts of machine-gun fire and trying to figure out a way to escape. The thicket stretched uphill, along the hayfield, to a stand of pine trees, and from there it was all woods and fields leading to the Albanian border. It didn't offer much of a chance, and he must have known that.
>
> He tied a sweater around the wound in his thigh and waited. Maybe he was too badly hurt to keep moving, or maybe he didn't dare because the Serbs

were already along the edge of the field. Either way, they eventually spotted him and shot him in the chest, and he fell backward into the streambed.
His killers took his shoes, and—months later, after the war ended—a fellow
Albanian took his belt buckle and brought it to the authorities in Gjakovë. It
was the only distinctive thing on him, and there was a chance that someone
might recognize it.

Clearly, Junger was not on the scene as an eyewitness of the events he includes
in his opening narrative to set up his piece focusing among other things on the
retaliation by the Serbs for an attack by the Kosovo Liberation Army. But the
detail that unfolds here results from the kind of intense background research
and interviews that are fundamental to this kind of textured rendering, a hallmark of literary non-fiction writing. In fact, the use of "forensics" in the title
may foretell a framing of this piece as both scientific analysis—not unlike a
criminal investigation—and compelling argument, the two distinct contemporary meanings of the word. But the writing itself just might serve as its own
justification, an argument for the methodical approach that made it possible;
an illustration of the forensics of storytelling.

Conflict   Once the writer has established what the character is out to
achieve, there also must be a sense of the obstacles that stand in the way.
Here these obstacles can be created by another person (the nemesis, or
antagonist, in fiction), or circumstances. In any event, the obstacles create
a sense of conflict. That conflict and the way in which it will be resolved
will move the story forward. Developing the conflict effectively creates that
rising action that is so important in maintaining the suspense that keeps
readers moving forward.

Voice   In fiction, there are times when writers will use the omnipotent narrator, who is everywhere watching the action and explaining it all to the reader.
The voice can range from the edgy slang of the hardboiled noir novel to the
lilting prose of high-end literary form. That narrator also can be the main
character, speaking to us in first person. Often, writers of literary non-fiction
(magazine pieces) will adopt a voice that reflects the central character—or
personality of the story—in a way that reinforces the personality. Ultimately,
that narrator's voice is your voice. It is defined by its tone, the use of language
(slang or perfect grammar), sentence construction, and even punctuation.

Resolution   Clearly, the reader moves through a story in order to find
out how it ends. To the extent that the tension builds with a form of rising action, or conflict—the introduction of progress and setbacks along the
way—then the reader continues to be engaged in order to reach that conclusion, that all important takeaway value.

In working with these elements, it also is important for the successful writer to consider how best to develop them. For example, good

characters have dimension. They are not all good, nor are they all bad. The writer of literary non-fiction will want to show the full range of qualities in writing about people. This involves probing interviews that sometimes go off topic just to explore certain character traits or background information.

▶ LITERARY NON-FICTION PROCESS

As you can see, good non-fiction employs many of the techniques of short fiction, except, of course, the fiction part. We must keep in mind that the stories we write for magazine publishing are expected to be real; they are expected to be factual. That is why so much emphasis is placed on the reporting—or fact-gathering—component of this form. There is great pressure on the writer to become immersed in the story, spending many hours researching even the smallest details and focusing on probing interviews that sometimes can require days of full access to sources. The result, though, is rich storytelling that engages and entertains the reader, even while informing.

Narrative detail   These stories must provide description. This description, in turn, is highly detailed. But here, the *quality* of specific details will outweigh the *quantity*. The accomplished writer in this form will provide the detail that is necessary to tell, or *show*, the story. What does a particular hand gesture say about the character you are revealing? And what does that character say about the issue she is illustrating? This is what must be kept in mind as you absorb all the details in your work. And, obviously, that work involves research, interviews, and the writer's observations. In this way, you will be able to provide description of place and situations as well as people and character. With respect to people, there are a number of details to capture, including speech, appearance, and manner. What does the voice sound like? Capture real-life dialogue as Professor Harrington suggests. How are the sentences phrased? Is there a tendency toward vulgarity? "It creates the sense of life happening before readers' eyes," Harrington writes. These details also tell something about the person's confidence, style, and irreverence. Does the person dress casually or formally? Is that apparel selection appropriate for the meeting? Does the person gesture when speaking, avoid eye contact, seem to take in everything in the room? Anything that can be observed can be analyzed in telling the writer what the words of an interview might otherwise try to conceal. These are the kinds of observations that make the person come alive. But, for storytelling purposes, they only come alive to breathe life into the story. Everything—every detail, every nuance, every sound, every smell—should be in service of the story. All description should be considered only to the extent that it moves the story forward.

A BURNING PASSION

As with the original practitioners of the New Journalism, literary non-fiction in contemporary magazines sometimes will experiment, taking risks with the style of presentation. When he was assigned to cover the aftermath of a devastatingly destructive canyon fire in California, Mike Sager, writer-at-large for *Esquire* magazine, decided to adopt a presentation built around alternating scenes, much like a feature movie. Although writing in scenes is characteristic of literary journalism, the approach Sager adopts in this piece takes that approach to another level. Here he talks about the process that unfolded, starting with the first trip out to the devastated canyon to meet the victims. The result of his work, "Is Something Burning?" was published in the February 2004 issue of *Esquire*. Embedded in Sager's contemplations are guidelines of a sort in handling the kind of immersive background work for accuracy and detail and context that are crucial to this storytelling form.

When I was assigned a story about all of those people who lost their houses in a canyon fire, I said I would ride out there.

I'm a general assignment reporter. Just give me my orders and I go. It was nice that this was not far from home. It was bad because I was suffering from asthma that had been aggravated the year before on a different assignment. You go where they send you is how I look at this job. That way I bring fresh eyes.

I'm not one of those journalists who spends time looking through phone books. I don't do that. Coming up at the Washington Post, there'd be a big crime or a fire, and I'd have to go to the Criss Cross Directory that listed people's phone numbers by address and I'd have to cold call all these people. "Sorry to bother you at a time like this but . . ." I also used to have to call more than 30 different police jurisdictions around DC several times a night . . . So I don't love the phone.

I drove out to the scene of the fire to look around first. And . . . surprise . . . I came across all these people hanging out at the crossroads where the mailboxes for the rural community were all grouped. An impromptu gathering of some of the victims. It was serendipitous; the karma of finding people. So once I had the connection to the people, I knew I had something to write about.

I am shy and don't like to travel or meet people. Which makes it hard for a journalist. This has informed my style of interviewing. I don't push at first.

I don't ask a million questions. I don't even know what questions to ask going in. I'd rather hang around and get the feel for things first. I'm not in that much of a rush to get started, and I think that helps my subject. It's like old-fashioned dating. I take things slow.

So when I came upon the survivors, I just played it cool. I wasn't ready to start interviewing that moment. What you need first is someone to interview. I handed out my card. I asked if people would be interested to talk, and if I could send them samples of my work so they could make an informed choice. I feel like that way everything comes off more human. I mean, these people had been through a lot.

When it does come to interviewing, you can also apply the rules of dating. Look into their eyes. Nod your head to acknowledge you're listening. Smile and be understanding. People want to be heard. They want to tell you things. I think they also want a little attention. I listen well. I witness. I minister.

When people are telling good stories, you of course hear them and try to explore the good story to its fullest. But there are dozens and dozens of scenes I did not use. When I'm interviewing people I'm just trying to bring them out. Report first. Write second. Reporting is about your subject. Writing is about you. Two different mindsets.

I like knowing stuff and putting it all together. The simple truths of this entire story are that man keeps rebuilding in the path of fire, and that these fires are part of the natural order of nature.

* * *

In the conception of executing this story, I was shooting for a sort of homage to the movie "Poseidon Adventure." That was the ultimate disaster movie. I liked the way it went from character to character, advancing the story over several different fronts. Most times in my career my stories focus way down on one single character, and there are supporting players. For this story there were groups of characters, strings of storylines that came together. Everyone's experience was different, but there was a universality and a time line that tied them together.

I always use a cinematic approach. But I never know what it'll look like when I'm interviewing. When I'm interviewing I'm collecting all the pieces. After I transcribe and review the notes and the research, certain scenes just naturally start floating to the top.

You can't build the piece until you've done all the research. After that, I identify the scenes that pop out the most as being symbolic, and also scenes that contribute to a sort of general story arc I want to tell. At that point, there are usually more phone calls involved. I get back to the person or persons in the scene and drill down a little farther.

The time line was the ultimate journalist's nightmare. Because the night of the fire was the night of daylight savings time. At some point that evening, everybody was supposed to fall back, turn their clocks back one hour.

So, as I was reporting the story, I had to establish with everyone what time they did things, so I could make the strings of stories go together accurately. But the challenge quickly became this: When you're telling me the time you did something, had you turned your clock back yet or not?

It was a funny litmus test of different personality types. Some people change their clocks *before* they go to bed and some people after. And some people totally forgot. And so I had to create a separate timeline for every group of people I met. And that had to be established before I could do anything.

* * *

We live in a multi-media age. I'm working in a medium that uses 26 letters to convey all. Luckily we can recombine the letters into infinite words that evoke, inform, entertain. The more evocative my writing, the deeper into human truths I can drill, the more a reader will be moved.

Quotes   When it comes to quotes for narrative presentation, we must consider not only what is said, but also what is meant by what is said. Here, good quotes also are measured by what they say about the person speaking. They should illuminate the persona as much as they relate facts. So, good quotes—the ones that reveal something—also move the story forward. That is how, in the literary form, they become the vital building blocks of the story.

THE PERFECT QUESTION

At news conferences with public officials, reporters often compete with one another for the memorable question of the day—the one that generates the headline for the following day in the traditional news cycle. But it is rare when a question elicits a response that adds to the cultural lexicon.

That was the case with Sebastian Junger in 1993, when he was working on a book about the Halloween Nor'easter of 1991 that sank the *Andrea Gail* killing all six crew members. True to literary non-fiction form, Junger plumbed the depths of the personal lives of the crew members and conducted substantial research to become an expert on the weather conditions that converged on this 100-year storm. In the process, he interviewed the late Robert "Bob" Case, the National Weather Service meteorologist in Boston, who was a leading expert on hurricane forecasting and analysis.

There are a couple of versions of the way things unfolded during the course of Junger's 1993 interview with Case. The version we like best helps to illustrate one aspect of the craft of the literary journalist in probing, analyzing, contextualizing, and reframing, often all in the space of a single interview. Case described the convergence of tropical moisture from Hurricane Grace with the warm air of a low-pressure system and the cool air of a high-pressure system as creating the "perfect situation" for the formation of the devastating storm that resulted.

Junger considered that characterization—"perfect situation"—and, according to the story that is most often credited, said to Case, "So, this was a perfect storm."

The title of the book and film adaptation was only the beginning. By 2007, "Perfect Storm" had become such a popular term for convergence and coincidence in just about every context that it made the top of the list that year of overused words and phrases compiled by Michigan's Lake Superior State University in Sault Ste. Marie.

Perfect storm that year was joined by "surge" and "post-9/11."

Never mind that. Clearly, Junger struck a cord in the public psyche. The takeaway here (not to put too fine a point on it) is the transformative impact of the convergence of the elements: immersive reporting, meaningful context, interpretation, and evocative writing.

Setting   Scene also is key to good non-fiction storytelling. It is important to place characters in a context. Set the scene with vivid descriptions of surroundings. What do the significant places in the story look like? What do they sound like? What do they smell like? This involves scrupulous note taking. Keep in mind that these observations are made not only to put the reader in the immediate scene, but also to advance the point of the story. So, not every detail about setting will be important. But those that add to our understanding of the central character and the motivation and conflict will be essential. In this connection, the more the reader feels a part of the location, the more he will experience the drama of the story and its impact. The point of describing the surrounding scene and circumstances in this form is, again, to add something to the reader's understanding of the character and what the character means to the ultimate story that is unfolding. So, description of the sights, smells, and sounds can do a couple of things. First, it lends to the immediacy of the presentation. It places the reader right there with you and the subject. The more the reader feels a part of the scene, the more she will feel the impact of what is unfolding. Second, the way the subject interacts with the setting can be revealing. Again, everything observed in the course of gathering information should be considered for meaning. That interaction also can connect to another area of detail.

"IS SOMETHING BURNING?"

Consider the opening scene of the February 2004 *Esquire* story "Is Something Burning?" excerpted below. As he indicates in the companion box, Sager uses the slow burn of the drama (starting out with an exquisite understatement-of-a-question) to hook readers on the elements of character and scene in what will become a full-scale conflagration of a narrative that went on to be awarded "Notable Essay" in *Best American Essays, 2005*. Note the tremendous amount of research that already is apparent in this opening scene, and how Sager uses the narrative beats as an alternative to traditional attribution to effectively move the story forward.

Bob Younger whispered into his wife's ear. There was alarm in his voice. "Honey, wake up."

[. . .] "I must have dozed off," Sandra said. She sat up, gathering her wits. "What time is it?"

Bob looked at his watch, then thought about it a moment. Tonight was the time change: fall backward. Had he changed his watch?

"1:05," he said definitively.

Sandra sniffed the air. Her brow wrinkled. "Is something burning?"

"There's a glow on the horizon. Over the hills, to the northeast."

They'd just spent $10,000 clearing brush. "Did you call the fire department?" she asked.

"Lakeside had a recording: 'Please call back during business hours.' I finally got a human at Barona. He said there's a fire up near San Diego Country Estates."

Sandra frowned. After nineteen mind-numbing years in the suburbs, they'd only recently moved to Wildcat Canyon. She counted her blessings every day: coyotes and deer, hawks and hummingbirds and rattlesnakes. Fragrant sage, thorny cactus, stately oaks. Huge granite boulders, rounded over the eons by wildfire and erosion, peeking out like dinosaur eggs from thick nests of impassable brush. To the east was El Capitan mountain; to the west, the San Vicente Reservoir, a breathtaking basin of deep-blue water surrounded by undulating foothills that stretched off in all directions, a no-name range. The sunsets were mesmerizing; you could see the Pacific twenty miles away. At night, a million stars—you could see the lights of Tijuana. The sunrise bathed the sky in extraordinary light, a lovely pastel shade of peach. The previous owner had gone so far as to custom blend the stucco to match.

"How far away is that?" she asked.

"About fifteen miles as the crow flies. Some hunter got lost in the Cleveland National Forest. He lit a signal fire."

She rolled her eyes. "So what do we do now?"

Bob stroked his beard. "The Barona guy said not to worry. He said we should go back to bed."

Each scene progresses pretty much in that established format. Sager weaves together a tremendous amount of background research as interior monologue intercut with dialogue between the characters. There is an immediacy in that. It draws the reader in, places him right there in the scene. As the story builds through the use of rising action, we virtually smell and feel what is going on.

As he discusses in the companion box above, Sager decided on a "disaster movie" approach for this story about the largest fire in California history and the deadliest wildfire in US history. By the time it was extinguished on November 3, 2003, the fire (which began on October 25) had burned 280,278 acres (at one point burning an estimated 5,000 acres an hour), destroyed 2,820 buildings (80 percent of them homes), and killed 15 people. Whipped up by Santa Ana winds, it was only one of 15 wildfires reported in Southern California during this period, an event that would be called the "2003 Firestorm."

Action   People are not static creatures. But what do their movements suggest about them? If a person gestures wildly or makes very calculated movements that punctuate the words, these things have meaning, too. The style of walk. Emotional flare. Smiles. Grimaces. What can you make of movement that makes something of your story theme? How do other people move through your story? How do they respond to your subject? How does your character respond to the wait staff, and other patrons in a restaurant? These details say a lot about the makeup of the person. In this connection, consider that you are painting a portrait of the subject. As a number of writers have suggested, imagine that no photos will accompany the story. How would you render a picture that helps the reader visualize the person?

SO, YOU WANT TO BE IN PICTURES: MAGAZINE STORIES THAT HAVE GONE HOLLYWOOD

Given that long-form, literary non-fiction magazine articles often employ the same techniques that make for effective screen treatment—theme, character development, rising conflict, and resolution—it is not surprising that a number of magazine stories have been adapted as films. What follows is a list of some of these films, which is surprising only in its scope.

- "Adaptation," based on "The Orchid Thief," a book by Susan Orlean, which was based on her January 23, 1995 article of the same title published in *The New Yorker.*

- "Almost Famous," based on "The Allman Brothers Story," by Cameron Crowe, December 6, 1973 issue of *Rolling Stone.*

- "Argo," based on "How the CIA Used a Fake Sci-Fi Flick to Rescue Americans From Tehran," by Joshuah Bearman, *Wired,* April 24, 2007.

- "Coyote Ugly," based on "The Muse of the Coyote Ugly Saloon," by Elizabeth Gilbert, *GQ,* March, 1997.

- "Dog Day Afternoon," based on "The Boys in the Bank," by P.F. Kluge, *Life* magazine, September 22, 1972.

- "Fear and Loathing in Las Vegas," based on "Fear and Loathing in Las Vegas" (Parts 1 and 2), by Hunter S. Thompson, *Rolling Stone,* beginning November 11, 1971.

- "In Cold Blood," a book by Truman Capote, which was based on his series published in *The New Yorker,* beginning with "The Last To See Them Alive," September 25, 1965.

- "The Insider," based on "The Man Who Knew Too Much," by Marie Brenner, *Vanity Fair,* May, 1996.

- "Shattered Glass," based on "Shattered Glass," by Buzz Bissinger, *Vanity Fair,* 1998.

- "Saturday Night Fever," based on "Tribal Rights of the New Saturday Night," by Nik Cohn, *New York,* June 7, 1976.

(Includes additional material from the "List of non-fiction works made into feature films," Wikipedia)

Chapter Eleven Review

ASSIGNMENT DESK

1. Read the "Is Something Burning Story" (accessible through the link listed below).

2. Consider and analyze the structure of this narrative piece, particularly the scene-by-scene, chapter-by-chapter progress of it all.

3. How would you describe the rising conflict here? How effective are the transitions from one scene to the next?

4. Consider the depth of reporting. How effectively does the writer balance the presentation of material here? What about the voice of the characters? How does the use of alternative attribution work in this presentation? Does it help to introduce more story into the story? Does it help with the pacing of the presentation?

5. What is the takeaway, the theme that is established and will endure in that payoff at the end of the story?

▶ KEY TERMS

- character
- conflict
- immersive reporting
- interior monologue
- narrative arc
- resolution
- rising conflict
- theme

▶ SUGGESTED READING

Boynton, Robert. *The New New Journalism: Conversations with American's Nonfiction Writers on their Craft.* New York: Vintage, 2005. Boynton conducts interviews with 19 writers who ruminate on a range of issues, from how they find stories to how to conduct interviews.

Harrington, Walter. *Intimate Journalism: The Art and Craft of Reporting Everyday Life.* Thousand Oaks: Sage Publications, 1997. This primer on the craft of feature writing includes practical tips on the conceptualization, reporting, and writing of compelling human interest stories.

Sims, Norman. *The Literary Journalists.* New York: Ballantine Books, 1984. A collection of writing and interviews with some of the twentieth century's best practitioners of the craft of narrative non-fiction.

Sims, Norman; Kramer, Mark. *Literary Journalism*. Ballantine Books, 1995. Updated version of Sims' 1984 collection of stories and interviews.

Wolfe, Tom. *The New Journalism*. New York: Picador Books, 1973. Wolfe's anthology and exultation of the work of his peers, including Joan Didion Truman Capote, George Plimpton, Joe Eszterhaus, and Hunter S. Thompson.

▶ WEB RESOURCES

http://longform.org/ A website dedicated to providing showcasing the best in long-form non-fiction writing.

https://www.atavist.com/ Home of the media and software company that offers a platform for long-form non-fiction journalism and multimedia storytelling.

http://www.esquire.com/features/ESQ0304-MAR_FIRE "Is Something Burning?," by Mike Sager, *Esquire*, February 29, 2004.

http://www.vanityfair.com/magazine/archive/1999/10/kosovo199910 "The Forensics of War," by Sebastian Junger, *Vanity Fair*, October 1999.

http://www.wired.com/magazine/2007/04/feat_cia "How the CIA Used a Fake Sci-Fi Flick to Rescue Americans From Tehran," by Joshuah Bearman, *Wired*, April 24, 2007.

http://www.rollingstone.com/politics/news/fear-and-loathing-in-las-vegas-19711111 "Fear and Loathing in Las Vegas," by Hunter S. Thompson, *Rolling Stone*, November 11, 1971.

http://www.newyorker.com/archive/1965/09/25/1965_09_25_057_TNY_CARDS_000280568 "The Last To See Them Alive," by Truman Capote, *The New Yorker*, September 25, 1965.

http://www.gq.com/news-politics/newsmakers/199703/elizabeth-gilbert-gq-march-1997-muse-coyote-ugly-saloon "The Muse of the Coyote Ugly Saloon," by Elizabeth Gilbert, *GQ*, March 1997.

http://nymag.com/nightlife/features/45933/ "Tribal Rights of the New Saturday Night," by Nik Cohn, *New York*, June 7, 1976.

http://books.google.com/books?id=5VYEAAAAMBAJ&pg=PA66&source=gbs_toc_r&cad=1#v=twopage&q&f=false "The Boys in the Bank," by P.F. Kluge, *Life*, September 22, 1972.

http://www.newyorker.com/online/blogs/culture/2013/02/the-wired-origins-of-argo.html "The Wired Origins of 'Argo,'" by Nicholas Thompson, *The New Yorker*, February 22, 2013.

http://en.wikipedia.org/wiki/List_of_non-fiction_works_made_into_feature_films "List of non-fiction works made into feature films," *Wikipedia*.

12   The Profile: Where Life Stories Come to Life

▶ INTRODUCTION

People care about other people. And people stories have impact. In this chapter, we show the elements that are essential to the well-crafted profile. Each story must have some distinctive meaning in a particular moment to give it a publishable hook. It must have a compelling theme that provides value-added effect. Detailed description is vital. And it must touch the reader in ways that help form a connection to the subject. Here we will walk through the approaches to good profile writing ranging from the interview story to the day-in-the-life narrative. The key to the effective profile, we will show, is the revelation—the untold story—which emerges from the unguarded moment we reach when we are allowed full access to our subjects. But the interview story, particularly the Q&A, also will get attention here. We will discuss the best examples of the form as presented in *Vanity Fair, GQ, The New Yorker, Esquire, New York* magazine and, of course, *Playboy,* with discussion of the construction and editing of the Q&A to provide an engaging flow of a good conversation.

▶ OVERVIEW

The profile is more than just a biographical sketch of an individual who happens to be making headlines or is in some way emblematic of the news. It is a story, a story that provides insight into character, motivations, or personal endeavors. And it is a story that has engaged readers for quite some time.

The profile is an editorial staple of American magazines. *The New Yorker's* founding editor Herbert Ross often is credited with developing both the concept and the rubric for the classic biographical profile. Current editor David Remnick in his introduction to *Life Stories*, a collection of some of the magazine's most notable profiles, has a different view of the origin. "If a Profile is a biographical piece—a concise rendering of a life through anecdote, incident, interview, and description (or some ineffable combination thereof)—well, then, it's a little presumptuous to stick Ross at the front of the queue," writes Remnick. Certainly *The New Yorker's* incisive examinations of such celebrated early twentieth century figures as Ernest Hemmingway, Henry Luce, and Isadora Duncan set the standard for rendering amazing lives as amazing magazine stories. But virtually every publication, regardless of platform (digital or print) or editorial emphasis (sports, fashion, lifestyle, or epicurean), features stories about people with whom the audience might identify or whom the audience might idolize, either because they are masters of a practice or icons of an industry.

We all have read great profiles. The form is so pervasive and familiar that many novice writers underestimate the skill and effort it takes to pull off an engaging piece. The biggest mistake that inexperienced profile writers make is failing to invest enough time in the reporting. Because profiles are principally the life story of an individual, fledgling writers tend to think that crafting a profile is as simple as spending a couple of hours with the subject and transcribing the recorded interview. The articles that result from such brief encounters, however, are pithy at best. They read like dull Wikipedia entries.

Contrary to what some believe, an exceptional profile requires more than drive-through reporting. Even a Q&A, the most stripped-down version of the profile, requires immersion into the life and works of the subject. Ideally, you should interview the subject over several sessions and find opportunities to observe her in action—in an environment that provides you with insight into her world. Those observations provide the color and context that enliven profiles.

Not every subject is cooperative, however. Of course, there are the rude subjects whose "cooperation" amounts to little more than monosyllabic responses grunted over a 90-minute lunch. Sometimes, however, you might not get the chance to do even *one* interview, let alone several. Many subjects resist the intrusion of writers into their natural habitats. Celebrities, in particular, are shielded by a phalanx of public relations reps whose sole job is to prevent exactly what journalists prize the most—that unguarded moment with their client, the exposure that potentially will yield what they might consider embarrassing, quotes or anecdotes, and what you and the readers would consider deeply revealing moments. As we suggested in the last chapter, these are exactly the kinds of revelatory and illuminating experiences the literary journalist seeks.

These obstacles are not necessarily impenetrable barriers to the creation of a good profile. Even with an obstinate or heavily armored subject, a good journalist can find ways to craft an appealing story that illustrates something about that person's character—craftsmanship; something about the work ethic. Certainly, the writer does not want to serve merely as another cog in the public relations machinery. Instead, it is vital to the craft that the writer always be alert to the story that unfolds before your very eyes. Think about it. Even the bad attitude or the refusal to cooperate can show something about a person. What does it say? Does it reflect a mood that will pass? If so, what are the conditions that are causing it at that moment in the subject's world? If it is something much deeper and more enduring, then what does it say about the person's character?

One of the most famous examples of a stellar profile written without the cooperation of the subject is Gay Talese's seminal examination of the life and career of Frank Sinatra, which appeared in the April 1966 issue of *Esquire* magazine. It serves to illustrate the kinds of considerations we raise here.

THE ELUSIVE PROFILE SUBJECT

As we discuss, there are those times when, despite all the hard preliminary work by a writer, the subject of a profile just refuses to cooperate. "Frank Sinatra Has a Cold" published in the April 1966 edition of *Esquire* is hailed by journalists, journalism instructors, and others who study the art of magazine writing as one of the greatest profiles ever written. Yet it does not contain a single quote from Sinatra. He refused to be interviewed for the piece. Without Sinatra's cooperation, Talese was forced to paint a portrait through three months of observations of the singer in various public and private settings and by chronicling in great detail the efforts of his retainers to keep Talese at bay. The result is a vivid account of Sinatra's world.

In this classic piece, note how writer Talese uses that reluctance in setting up a profile of Sinatra that is quite revealing.

> Frank Sinatra, holding a glass of bourbon in one hand and a cigarette in the other, stood in a dark corner of the bar between two attractive but fading blondes who sat waiting for him to say something. But he said nothing . . .

Talese weaves an opening narrative that tracks the list of annoying distractions for Sinatra at the moment he describes—press criticism, probing of his personal life, a film project that was adding to his sullen mood, and, not least of all, his fragile voice just days before he would have to sing. Then, the reveal.

> Sinatra was ill. He was the victim of an ailment so common that most people would consider it trivial. But when it gets to Sinatra it can plunge him into a state of anguish, deep depression, panic, even rage. Frank Sinatra had a cold.

Sinatra with a cold is Picasso without paint, Ferrari without fuel—only worse. For the common cold robs Sinatra of that uninsurable jewel, his voice, cutting into the core of his confidence, and it affects not only his own psyche but also seems to cause a kind of psychosomatic nasal drip within dozens of people who work for him, drink with him, love him, depend on him for their own welfare and stability.

A Sinatra with a cold can, in a small way, send vibrations through the entertainment industry and beyond as surely as a President of the United States, suddenly sick, can shake the national economy.

In Talese's narrative, even Sinatra's refusal to cooperate becomes part of this story in a way that says so much about him in this particular moment. The refusal to talk—something so relatively trivial—becomes something much larger, something representative of the man himself. Talese uses it as an opportunity to gaze deep into the soul of the man, analyzing every aspect of his life at that moment—a moment of possible mid-life crisis.

While this piece is illustrative of the possibilities for creative writing even in the face of uncooperative sources, don't fall into the trap of thinking that clever writing will mask the holes in an underreported profile. Too many lazy or ineffectual writers cite "Frank Sinatra Has a Cold" as the basis for their half-hearted reporting efforts. But, like any piece of solid journalism, a good profile requires industriousness and lots of sourcing, all of which are on full display in Gay Talese's work.

▶ GETTING STARTED

Attack your profile the way you would any other story—by doing a ton of research before you actually sit down to interview your subject. Get a copy of her official bio or resume and study it for insight into her personal and professional journey. Read any previous articles in which the subject was featured or quoted or which the person actually wrote. Try to learn as much as you can about her field of endeavor. Don't feel that you have to master the field. Try to learn enough so that you can engage with your subject on a level that demonstrates you've made an effort to get to know about her and her work. But don't be afraid to ask for clarification or elaboration about elements of the work you don't understand. The fact that you've attempted to learn about the field will endear you to your subject and generally makes people more understanding when you probe them about areas you don't understand. They are far less tolerant, however, when they suspect that you've done no homework. There is an added benefit of asking these questions. In providing answers, the subject will reveal more than just the facts. Character traits are revealed even in the manner of speech. You might see the person's passion for an idea, or depth of knowledge about related areas. You might find a person who has no real understanding of the subject at all, but merely has been coached.

Negotiate for as much time with your subject as possible, but be careful about suggesting several sessions of all-day interviews. Your subject will be put off by what seem to be liberties taken with her time. Few people realize how much access a writer really needs to flesh out a full-bodied profile. And these days, with publicists ferociously blocking for their high-profile clients, access is incredibly difficult to come by. Try to move yourself in the person's world a little at a time. One of the authors was writing about the actor Billy Dee Williams in connection with his role in "The Empire Strikes Back." The conversation started at a press event on the 20th Century Fox studio lot. It continued as Williams began walking to the commissary for lunch with studio executives. And it continued even as Williams sat down to lunch. The writer—who always believed it is better to ask forgiveness than to ask permission—acted as if he had been an invited guest to the luncheon. And, since he had walked in with Williams, no one even asked whether that was the case. Often this "hanging around" time is negotiated.

Typically, you will begin the interview process by asking for an initial conversation and the opportunity to observe the person in a setting that provides you with a more complete picture of her life. Perhaps there is a meeting you can attend and, like a fly on the wall, simply observe. Perhaps there is a leisure activity. Maybe there even is time you can spend with the family. Even a photo opportunity provides another chance to observe and to learn something about the person. One of the authors was profiling Barack Obama during his successful run for the U.S. Senate and attended the studio photo session for the cover shoot. There was the future president, standing with his wife, Michelle, wind machines blowing, and Frank Sinatra serenading in the background—just to set the mood. Suddenly, during a brief pause in the action, Barack Obama took his wife in his arms and started dancing with her. The moment was included in the story to make a point about the driven couple. After twelve years of marriage, and nearly twelve months of a driven campaign, they still were in love.

It is that "hanging around" access that produces a story, as Professor Norman Sims relates. Something even more revealing than anything the person can say is what you can observe and interpret, as we can see in the box.

FULL ACCESS PASS: FROM THE BASKETBALL COURT TO AIR FORCE ONE

Writer Michael Lewis was granted an unprecedented six months of access to President Barack Obama for his October 2012 *Vanity Fair* piece, "Obama's Way." In an interview with "Today" host Matt Lauer, Lewis said this access to the President on Air Force One, in the presidential limousine, and even on the basketball court, "let me get to know him." And it shows even in this brief excerpt.

At nine o'clock one Saturday morning I made my way to the Diplomatic Reception Room, on the ground floor of the White House. I'd asked to play in the president's regular basketball game, in part because I wondered how and why a 50-year-old still played a game designed for a 25-year-old body, in part because a good way to get to know someone is to do something with him. I hadn't the slightest idea what kind of a game it was. The first hint came when a valet passed through bearing, as if they were sacred objects, a pair of slick red-white-and-blue Under Armour high-tops with the president's number (44) on the side. Then came the president, looking like a boxer before a fight, in sweats and slightly incongruous black rubber shower shoes. As he climbed into the back of a black S.U.V., a worried expression crossed his face. "I forgot my mouth guard," he said. Your mouth guard? I think. Why would you need a mouth guard?

"Hey, Doc," he shouted to the van holding the medical staff that travels with him wherever he goes. "You got my mouth guard?" The doc had his mouth guard. Obama relaxed back in his seat and said casually that he didn't want to get his teeth knocked out this time, "since we're only 100 days away." From the election, he meant, then he smiled and showed me which teeth, in some previous basketball game, had been knocked out. "Exactly what kind of game is this?" I asked, and he laughed and told me not to worry.

That full access also can lead to embarrassing moments for the subject. Even worse. Michael Hastings was granted full access by General Stanley McChrystal for his July 8, 2010 *Rolling Stone* story "The Runaway General." During the time Hastings spent observing and interviewing McChrystal in his role at the time as U.S. commander in Afghanistan, the general made a series of harshly critical remarks about President Obama and senior members of the administration. McChrystal wound up resigning his post as a result of the flap.

Lucy Liu

Getty Images

Remember a good profile is not just a chronology of someone's life or an advertisement for an upcoming book, movie, or television show. A good profile places that individual's life or work in some context. For example, in "Karl Lagerfeld, Boy Prince of Fashion," the award-winning profile of the iconic designer, which appeared in the February 6, 2006 issue of *New York* magazine, writer Vanessa Grigoriadis crafts a story that is not merely a paean to Lagerfeld's fashion empire but a probing look at what keeps the septuagenarian going. It paints the designer as a "terrific pop cartoon" whose desire to remain young and relevant keeps him jet-setting and trend-setting long after many men his age have retired. While the story certainly traces the arc of Lagerfeld's lengthy career, it also attempts to get beneath Lagerfeld's glossy veneer in an effort to divine what fuels the designer's drive. To get at that thesis, Grigoriadis' line of questioning needed to probe the impetus for Lagerfeld's work. "I work only from feelings and motivations and creations and needs and opportunities," the designer tells Grigoriadis.

▶ DETAIL: THE KEY TO VIVID PROFILES

While anecdotes recorded during your interview will illuminate key moments in your subject's life, the detail you collect during your time with the subject is what will truly enliven your piece. It is important—if a bit tricky—to pay attention to and make note of lots of little telling details observed during your time with the person. What color is her hair? How does she wear it? How is she dressed during the interview? Be specific. Don't use hollow adjectives (i.e. "She's dressed casually"). Use precise language and concrete detail ("She's wearing a loose-fitting white T-shirt and well-worn Calvin Klein jeans"). The use of color and brand names not only paints a picture in the reader's mind, it establishes something about the subject. The fact that she is wearing designer jeans is a statement worth noting. One of the authors once asked the late Mamie Till Mobley, the mother of Emmett Till, about a dress she was wearing in a black and white newspaper photograph. She was taken aback. She never had been asked that question before. The writer recognized that there could be a story about that dress—the one she was wearing the day in 1955 when she claimed the body of her 14-year-old son—the victim of a Mississippi lynching. With each response, he asked more questions to learn about the dress, its color, when she bought it, whether Emmett had liked the dress when he was still alive, and what she was thinking about when she decided to wear it to greet his body at the train station. It was a revealing moment that opened the door to many more by way of the close bond that was formed.

Other interview questions about cowboy boots that a former Illinois appellate court judge was wearing, or why he only used a first initial and not his full name, revealed an aspect of the rebelliousness of the late R. Eugene Pincham, whose hard-riding, kick-ass attitude made him refuse to tell southern Whites his first name. It was the only way he could garner racial respect.

This excerpt from Bill Zehme's award-winning account of the humiliating fall of former *Chicago Tribune* columnist Bob Greene, which appeared in the April 2004 issue of *Esquire*, illustrates how bits of personal detail shed light on character.

> He wore the same uniform he forever favored prior to life in exile: faded jeans, penny loafers, cotton shirt with sleeves rolled, tie tugged loose and no jacket other than his weathered beige Burberry trench coat. As ever when out, he carried his battered leather briefcase—"that goddamned briefcase," as one of his friends puts it. He was a man of routine whose routine had ceased to exist . . .

Green had been "fired" from the *Tribune* after it was revealed that he had inappropriate contact with a teenage girl. During Zehme's profile, we encounter Greene shortly after his dismissal. He is a broken man, but still clings to hope for redemption and a return to fame. The detailed personal description Zehme employs shows Greene still defined himself by the clothes and accoutrements that marked his professional life. The description not only paints a picture of Greene, it shows him clutching to the shards of a shattered career.

Also take note of your subject's mannerisms. How does she sit? How does she walk? How does she talk? Again, it's important to try to get an opportunity to observe your subject in a natural habitat. You want to see how she interacts in her usual environment, not an artificial setting like a restaurant, unless it's a restaurant the subject frequents and where "everyone knows her name," so to speak.

One caveat: Be careful about using overly sexual descriptions of women that could be construed as degrading or objectifying them. There is a fine line between description that paints a compelling picture and detail that is merely prurient. Avoid descriptions of anatomy that are used gratuitously. That doesn't mean you can't describe body type or other physical attributes. Simply think about the purpose for those details. Notice how *New Yorker* media writer Ken Auletta describes the appearance of *New York Times* Executive Editor Jill Abramson in his 2011 profile:

> Abramson, who is fifty-seven, wore a white dress and a black cardigan with white flowers and red trim. Her usually pale complexion glowed from summer sun, but there were deep, dark lines under her eyes. As she entered the Times Building, she waved to the security officers and greeted colleagues in the elevator, something that she had usually been too preoccupied to do. The vast newsroom was quiet—the place does not really come alive until about ten-thirty—but there was a hint of apprehension. The few reporters at their pods silently watched their new boss as she walked by.

It is not an entirely flattering description, but it provides a rich picture of Abrahamson's professional style, conservative, but not the male version of the power suit. It also provides an insider's view of her morning routine. Auletta does not linger on aspects of Abrahamson's appearance that have nothing to do with the story he is attempting to tell—one about the first woman to assume what some consider the premier post in American journalism. Detail and color have to be used judiciously and with purpose. It shouldn't be scattered in to show off your writing style. It must be employed in the service of the story you are attempting to tell.

▶ FINDING YOUR ANGLE

The hardest part of crafting any feature is finding the angle or focus. That is true even for a story that, ostensibly, is about an individual's life. As we have discussed in earlier chapters, you must determine precisely what the story is about. Is it just a personal story or is there an angle or element beneath the personal story that really is the focus? The best profiles will use the personality as a foundation for something more.

Begin by thinking about the news. Why is this individual in the news? What accomplishment or enterprise makes this individual worthy of featuring? Is her new movie or book about to be released? Is she running for public office? Has her firm passed some significant milestone? Has she been elevated to a high-profile position? These achievements are often what place individuals on the media radar. They provide a news peg. But the lives of other—lesser-known—people are also worthy of highlighting. A topic in the news—homelessness, unemployment, war, a technological development—may make some individuals interesting profile subjects because of the larger issue they represent. A view of their lives provides readers with deeper insight into the issue and humanizes it in a way that helps readers connect. It is much more effective than merely writing about an issue without showing the human impact.

Beyond issues and achievements, a profile is about what makes this particular individual tick and about that aspect of their lives that will resonate with an audience. A profile of the actress Julia Roberts that appears in *Entertainment Weekly* might focus on her latest movie and her film choices. For *More*, a lifestyle magazine aimed at women over age 35, a profile of the actress might focus on how she juggles motherhood and film work, particularly at an age when many women in Hollywood find movie roles harder to come by. Both treatments will mention the "news"—the fact that Roberts has a new movie that is about to be released—but each will take a different, audience-appropriate angle.

An angle may begin to surface when you're doing your preliminary research. You amass information about Roberts and her young family and decide that readers of *More*—largely women who are balancing career and family—would be most interested in discovering what sacrifices Roberts has made as she wrestles with similar choices. The line of questioning will explore Roberts' daily routine (hopefully you'd have some opportunity to observe her in that routine), but, in tracing Roberts' life, might also explore what experiences in her life influenced her parenting style. The detail and anecdotes we collect and use will be at the service of that angle. Consequently, it may not be important to know who her favorite elementary school teacher was unless we suspect that teacher also influenced Roberts' parenting style.

In his 2006 profile of country music star Merle Haggard, author Chris Heath builds the story around what it's like to be in the orbit of one of the last men standing among country's angry old guard, guys like the late Waylon Jennings and Johnny Cash. On the surface, the primary reason for "The Last Outlaw," which appeared in the November 2006 issue of *GQ*, is the release of Haggard's new album, but its subtler angle is its glimpse into the inner sanctum and opportunity to trace his path from juvenile delinquent to one of the grand old men of country music.

One paragraph lays out the news and rationale for the story:

> This fall Merle Haggard will release a new album. I don't think anybody is quite sure how many have come before it; his first came out in 1965, and by 1974 he was already releasing the thirtieth (called, with delightful insouciance, *Merle Haggard Presents his 30th Album*). Within them, he has laid down one of the last great catalogs of country-music songs. Most of the best he wrote himself, songs that did perhaps the hardest and most wonderful thing a song can do—join together a handful of simple, commonplace words in a way that somehow makes them new and true and eternal, their wisdom and poetry hidden in plain sight.

A few paragraphs later, Heath lays out the angle and suggests the journey on which he will take readers:

> As Merle Haggard sits there in his favorite rocking chair, facing a giant flat-screen TV silently showing the news, it is stirring to think how far he has traveled, not just through time, but through history.

Here, Heath prepares readers for the sweep of events in Haggard's life that he will cover in the next 3,000 words.

The thing to remember is that your story is about a life, yes, but it also is about much more. It is about some deeper understanding of the person and the world in which she resides. It is about how this person became the individual we meet today and those issues in her life that resonate most with our audience. They resonate because of some universal aspect, some representational quality of it all, something you discover through your research, interviews, and observations. In fact, an important feature of great profile writing also is finding that universal element in the subject's story—that aspect of the life to which everyone can relate. Love and loss and love. Triumph over adversity. Resolving some conflict, as we pointed out in the last chapter on narrative. And here, that conflict does not necessarily have to be one that is caused by some external force, such as a person or circumstance. It can be a conflict that is internal. It can be a fear or other emotional setback, one that poses a dramatic question about the prospects of success. Clearly, such a question, such a conflict, is resolved in the course of the storytelling, as well as in life. But that is the theme, or angle. Keeping your angle and focus in mind will prevent your profile from being either a dull bio or a rambling mess.

▶ CLASSIC PROFILE STRUCTURE

Many profiles adhere to the same structure as the one we outline in Chapter 8. Some call the format cliché; we like to think of it as classic. It is particularly useful in organizing the profile. Let's review the elements in this diagram of a very traditionally organized profile, writer Adam Sachs' treatment of actor Ryan Reynolds for the June 2011 issue of *Details* magazine.

It begins with a particularly spicy quote before dropping the reader into Reynolds' orbit, in this case the South African location where he is filming his current movie. We quickly establish his bonafides as a bankable movie star and the fact that his latest blockbuster is about to be released. That's the news peg. There is more buildup to pique the reader's interest in reading about Reynolds before we reach Sachs' nut section and thesis, which culminate in a paragraph that makes the point "that offscreen he is just a guy" Sachs informs, portraying Reynolds as "self-deprecating," and a "guilelessly, legitimately, put-you-at-ease nice dude of a guy."

While it is not the most original angle, it helps to organize and focus the story. The background—Reynolds' actual life story—is brief. Sachs doesn't belabor Reynolds' childhood in Canada or his rise to stardom. That's all been chronicled before. Besides, it's not the point here. This profile paints a portrait of the movie star who's supposed to be a regular guy, so Sachs powers through the background and devotes more space to a chronicle of his time with Reynolds in South Africa and the anecdotes and quotes that support his thesis. He maintains temporal coherence in the exposition, however. He doesn't jerk the reader around in time. The anecdotes are arranged in chronological order, allowing the reader to feel as though he's experiencing Sachs' jaunt with Reynolds in real time.

Sachs dutifully covers the tabloid fodder, notably Reynolds' divorce from the actress Scarlett Johansson. But even that is used to validate his thesis, pointing out that Reynolds "accepts the public scrutiny and media meddling as occupational hazards."

The kicker, in classic fashion, returns us to the present while hinting at Reynolds' future.

> That's his business, but more to the point, he seems content to be his own man for a while and wait to see where the next adventure takes him. "I'm

very happy not to be in a relationship right now. That's okay. I didn't plan on it, that's for sure . . . but that's okay."

Without question, the extensive interview (or series of interviews) with the subject of the profile is vital to the fully developed story. But that full "hanging around" access also is important. Just observing situations without engaging in an interview can be helpful in getting the full dimension of the subject story. But additional sources are important in exploring the subject, too. Often these sources—friends, family, and associates—will be interviewed before the interviewing with the subject begins. These source interviews can reveal anecdotes and pieces of the personality that flesh it all out. But they also can be interviewed after at least one of the main interview sessions with the source. This gives the opportunity to follow up on things that were revealed by the source, and to come back to the source with the reaction of his friends, family, and associates.

▶ ALTERNATIVE STORY FORMS

As we discussed in Chapter 11, many editors and writers are experimenting with the classic form, employing techniques that borrow heavily from fiction and break many of the rules of conventional journalism. The effort is designed not only to entertain, but to surprise readers who some editors suspect have grown weary and suspicious of the traditional format. One of the most controversial recent examples is writer Edith Zimmerman's profile of Captain America star Chris Evans, "American Marvel," which appeared in the July 2011 issue of *GQ*. Zimmerman abandons many journalistic conventions in this chronicle of her "date" with Evans. She describes in great detail her flirtations with the actor:

> Since we're both single and roughly the same age, it was hard for me not to treat our interview as a sort of date. Surprisingly, Chris did the same, asking all about me, my family, my job, my most recent relationship. And from ten minutes into that first interview, when he reached across the table to punctuate a joke by putting his hand on top of mine, Chris kept up frequent hand holding and lower-back touching, palm kissing and knee squeezing. He's an attractive movie star, no complaints. I also didn't know how much I was supposed to respond; when I did, it sometimes felt a little like hitting on the bartender or misconstruing the bartender's professional flirting for something more. I wanted to think it was genuine, or that part of it was, because I liked him right away.

Zimmerman describes her flirtations with the actor in great detail and is very cheeky about it.

> We both drank too much and said too much. I never opened the notebook of questions I had brought with me.

Passages like these provoked a great deal of controversy and howls of "unprofessionalism" from the journalistic community. Yet, in her unconventional way, Zimmerman does cover classic profile territory.

> His face is a lot friendlier, toothier, smileyer in person than it is in, say, the smoldery/serious billboards of him and Evan Rachel Wood for Gucci's new Guilty fragrance.

And while the story meanders through this "date," Zimmerman clings to the chronology of the evening and manages to relay a lot of information about Evans, his upbringing, and his life as a budding star, which is what one expects to get from a profile.

As mentioned, after its publication there were the protests from readers and journalists alike about Zimmerman's approach, and the article's suitability for a men's magazine (many thought it more appropriate for women's lifestyle magazines like *Cosmopolitan*). The buzz highlighted how well-read celebrity profiles are and how passionately people feel about the form.

CHAPTER: A section of a narrative-driven story that can have its own internal theme and chronology, even while connected to the overall focus of the story.

A story that skirts the line between traditional and alternative is Chris Jones' moving tribute to the late film critic Roger Ebert, "Roger Ebert: The Essential Man," which appeared in the March 2010 issue of *Esquire*.

It is classic in that it begins in Ebert's world—in a screening room where Ebert and his wife are watching the Pedro Almodóvar film "Broken Promises"—and brings the reader full circle at the end, with a snippet of Ebert's review of the film. In the 6,000 words in between, Jones chronicles Ebert's devastating battle with throat cancer and the myriad surgeries that have left him with no chin and no voice, at least, no speaking voice. Jones' thesis is that despite the fact that Ebert can no longer utter a sound, his words and reviews continue to pour out at a frantic pace.

Roger Ebert

The piece employs the **chapter** format that is common in narrative structure. Each chapter in the profile charts one aspect of Ebert's life journey and the path that led him to being the last of the highly recognizable (and influential) newspaper film critics. Each chapter has its own focus. One, for example, is just about Ebert's surgeries, another charts his rivalry and partnership with fellow critic Gene Siskel, another explores what life is like for the one-time bon vivant who is now fed through a tube.

99581126 (Ebert): Courtesy of Featureflash / Shutterstock.com

The chapters themselves are not arranged in a particular order, but within each chapter Jones sticks faithfully to the chronology of events related to that chapter's theme or focus. The whole story rests on this thesis:

> Now his hands do the talking. They are delicate, long-fingered, wrapped in skin as thin and translucent as silk. He wears his wedding ring on the middle finger of his left hand; he's lost so much weight since he and Chaz were married in 1992 that it won't stay where it belongs, especially now that his hands are so busy. There is almost always a pen in one and a spiral notebook or a pad of Post-it notes in the other—unless he's at home, in which case his fingers are feverishly banging the keys of his MacBook Pro.

▶ THE *THROUGH LINE*: CONNECTIVE TISSUE FOR THE STORY

THROUGH LINE: A line of dialogue or narrative that sums up the theme and can be woven through the story.

Even when a writer employs an alternative story structure, she needs a device to connect the disparate elements and propel the narrative. That device often is referred to in fiction writing as the **through line**. It also is referred to as the thread, the spine, or, as Nancy Lamb calls it, "the driving force" of a literary work.

Reportedly first suggested by fabled actor and stage director Constantin Stanislavski as a method for internalizing characterization, the through line is a frequently recurring reference—the theme summed up in a line of dialogue or narrative—that can be woven through the story, reminding the reader of the thesis and/or providing chronology in a story that does not appear to be organized chronologically.

MOTIF: A recurring element in a story that can be created by use of language or imagery.

Writer Chuck Wendig has identified several forms of through line, including those that refer to and build upon character, plot, **motif**, and language.

Take, for example, Chris Jones' Ebert profile, referenced above. Though the chapters of this piece seem to appear in no particular order, the theme that connects the chapters is Jones' focus on Ebert's attempts in the last years of his life to remain prolific and keep his words flowing despite the ravages of throat cancer, which took away his voice and most of his lower jaw. So, the references to hands—writing, typing, gesturing—and the detailed description of them can be considered a motif that reminds the reader of Ebert's attempt to continue "speaking."

Other writers have used elements like the innings of a baseball game or the author's encounters with the subject to propel the narrative of a story. Think of the through line as a literary signpost that runs along the story so that neither the reader nor the author loses the way.

▶ THE INTERVIEW AND Q&A STORY

While the fully developed—researched, interviewed, and sourced—profile is the standard, there are other forms of presentation of the personal story that, if done right, also can be quite revealing.

The interview   There are times when magazines are interested in a single source story on a particular subject. Often this is the approach when there is something of a news peg with a personality: a new CD or film; perhaps even a new development in the person's life, like a marriage or baby. The interview story is a profile of sorts in that it covers a slice of the person's life. It is based largely on a single interview with the source. Sometimes this sort of interview story will be written as something of an "as told to" piece, where the writer will use the voice of the subject in weaving together a narrative that is composed by the writer based on the interview and additional research. Note this technique, as used by writer Amy Paturel in "Skin Cancer & You" published in the June 2005 issue of *Marie Claire*. Paturel adopts the voice of her subject, 30-year-old clothing company founder "Melissa," in telling the story of her experience with skin cancer. "I grew up being cautious about the sun. I have fair skin and strawberry blonde hair, and my mother was ultra-careful about skin cancer." The entire narrative piece is written in this voice—of the subject—as we learn of her surprise discovery and the cautionary note for others. The details of the life clearly have been obtained through interviewing, yet written here in the first person. It can make for a compelling presentation.

Q&A   This kind of mini profile, a format first introduced in 1962 by *Playboy* as the now fabled *Playboy* interview (see box), is pretty much what its characterization suggests. A block of copy will be used to introduce the piece, providing biographical background and some information on the news peg for the story. Then it will proceed with some form of "Question"

Scarlett Johansson

99885125 (Scarloj: Courtesy of Helga Esteb / Shutterstock.com and "Answer" by the writer and the source. But, this does not mean that the entire story is nothing more than a glorified transcript dump. The interview is edited before it is published and the questions and answers usually are rearranged to create some kind of thematic flow.

Consider this excerpt from the Q&A with the actor Scarlett Johansson by Holly Millea in the September 2005 issue of *Cosmopolitan*.

Cosmo   You've pulled off some mature roles in the last few years. Why do you think you're so convincing as an adult?

Scarlett   I was only 17 when I did "Lost in Translation," but I felt grown up. I had just graduated from high school and had decided to continue to do what I've always wanted to do—make movies.

The interview continues in this way building on the theme set in the opening, focusing on Johansson's "confidence and sophistication" in various aspects of her life—acting, romance, politics.

THE *PLAYBOY* INTERVIEW

The Q&A magazine interview format was an innovation of *Playboy* magazine. It was initiated in the September 1962 issue with the eye-opening interview of jazz great Miles Davis by journalist Alex Haley. "In high school I was the best in music class on the trumpet but the prizes went to the boys with blue eyes," Davis says in the interview. "I made up my mind to outdo anybody white on my horn." Thus, *Playboy* not only launched an impacting new magazine feature, but it also began to carve out space in the volatile national dialogue on race and social justice. Haley, who went on to win a special Pulitzer Prize in 1977 for his tremendously successful book, *Roots*, would become the go-to interviewer for the magazine, at a time when many African American journalists were not given such opportunities outside the African American press. Haley took on such other significant *Playboy* interview subjects as civil rights leader Martin Luther King, Jr. (the longest interview granted by Dr. King), Black Muslim leader Malcolm X at the peak of his militancy (Haley later co-authored *The Autobiography of Malcolm X*), boxing great Muhammad Ali, "Tonight Show" host Johnny Carson, and American Nazi Party leader George Lincoln Rockwell, who famously participated in the interview with a gun on the desk.

Over the years, the *Playboy* Interviews have become a signature feature of the magazine presenting revelatory moments with such notables as Frank Sinatra, Bernadette Devlin, Steve Jobs, Raquel Welch, Gene Siskel, Roger Ebert, Joan Baez, John Wayne, Mae West, and Milton Friedman. The list goes on. Over the years, many guys have insisted that they pick up the magazine for the articles. The high level of probative magazine journalism presented by way of the *Playboy* Interview certainly could make that a more credible claim.

A hybrid of the interview and Q&A approaches has been advanced by *Esquire* with its "What I Have Learned" department, an innovation of the magazine's writer-at-large Mike Sager. This one-pager in the magazine presents a slice of life of a personality, based on an interview and compiled by the magazine writer, as if recounted by the subject. Note in this passage from Sager's February 2001 *Esquire* session with comedienne Roseanne Barr how elements of the interview are assembled to create the sense that Barr actually is talking to the reader:

> **I hate sex**. I'm done with it. I tell my husband he should go have sex with other people, but he never does. I don't know why. Probably because I told him to. Whatever you tell men, they always do the opposite.

Asking the probing questions, editing, and even translating, while maintaining the voice of the subject can be tricky stuff. But it is pulled off in this format in ways that reveal character—exactly what a profile is supposed to do. This is the interview, by the way, led to a startling revelation that Sager was able to pitch for a larger profile on Barr and her multiple personality disorder!

Whatever form the profile takes, it provides an exciting opportunity for writers to interact with subjects, search for a theme that emerges in a life story, and relate that theme to some universal element that connects with readers. That can be all the more satisfying when it is executed in literary style, as we discuss in the next chapter.

WRITER'S WORKSHOP

Here are suggestions for you to apply a central point of this chapter as you begin to develop article ideas.

Once you've done your preliminary research and set up your interview(s), it's time to formulate your questions. In addition to the suggestions we made in Chapter 7, consider a line of inquiry that may help you develop a thesis or angle for your story.

Don't use your interview time merely to get biographical data that can be gleaned from a resume—date and place of birth, first job, or the like. Yes, you will need to gather that information, but interspersed with the questions about biography should be questions that build on the theme you suspect you'll be pursuing. Be careful, however, not to get so tied to what you think your thesis might be that you miss other interesting angles that present themselves during the course of the interview. You must be open to allowing the conversation to take you in unexpected directions.

Try to elicit anecdotes and detailed recollections about places and events from your subject. Rather than asking how your subject "felt" at a particular moment in her life, ask what she did. Remember, open-ended questions prompt the most expansive responses. "Were you happy on your wedding day?" or "How did you feel on your wedding day?" are not nearly as effective at generating an evocative response as "Can you describe your wedding day?" (see Chapter 7 on interviewing).

In preparing your questions, don't just create a checklist. You're trying to gain insight into what makes this person tick, what drives her creative process. You won't get there by running through your inventory of questions robotically. Of course there are questions that you will have to power through just to get the "facts." Be sure to write those down so you won't forget to collect or check those details (especially if you got background information from secondary sources). Have twice as many questions as you think you'll need. You don't want lulls in the conversation.

As we suggested earlier, think of the interview with your profile subject as a conversation, not an interrogation. Your objective here is to get your subject to reflect on her life, career, and accomplishments in a way that will provide your readers with greater insight about who this individual really is. The conversation is not entirely freewheeling.

Chapter Twelve Review

ASSIGNMENT DESK

1. You are to write a "classically structured" 1,200-word profile of one of your peers or classmates. The piece should have a clear angle or focus (expressed in a subtle, though easily identifiable nutgraf) and exposition that builds upon and supports that angle. It also should include appropriate description of your subject and his/her environs.

2. While you may use your judgment about what you want to explore in your interview and present in your written work, you should include certain basic biographical information (age, hometown, etc.) as well as personal and professional information that might help a reader get to know your subject.

3. Keep in mind that the profile should be thematic. As you conduct your interview and write this piece, consider what sets this person apart. What is it that makes this person's story worth telling? Ultimately, what is this story about? (What is it *really* about?) Is it, for example, about overcoming adversity? Is it about a turning point that led to an interest in writing? Is it about a lifelong addiction to hard work or commitment to public service? Once you have identified that key element, you should weave it throughout the biographical elements of this short profile. In other words, the personal and professional background information should be included in service of the larger story.

▶ KEY TERMS

- chapter (as used in magazine structure)
- motif
- through line

▶ SUGGESTED READING

Reed, Rex. *People are Crazy Here.* New York: Delacorte Press, 1974. A collection of profiles of show biz types by the acerbic former film critic.

Remnick, David. *Life Stories: Profiles from The New Yorker.* New York: Modern Library, 2001. A collection of 75 years' worth of *New Yorker* profiles, curated by Remnick, the magazine's current editor.

Tynan, Kenneth. *The Sound of Two Hands Clapping.* New York: De Capo Press, 1975. A collection of critical profiles of a wide range of celebrities by the British theater and film critic.

▶ **WEB RESOURCES**

http://6thfloor.blogs.nytimes.com/2013/04/18/the-long-celebrity-profile-endangered-yes-but-not-yet-dead/ Musings in the *New York Times* magazine about the current state of the celebrity profile.

https://www.byliner.com/anthologies/the-celebrity-profile-a-love-affair A paean to the celebrity profiles of old that appeared in *Byliner*, a web subscription website devoted to long-form narrative writing.

http://www.vanityfair.com/politics/2012/10/michael-lewis-profile-barack-obama "Obama's Way," by Michael Lewis. *Vanity Fair*, October 2012.

http://www.rollingstone.com/politics/news/the-runaway-general-20100622 "The Runaway General," by Michael Hastings. *Rolling Stone*, July 8, 2010.

http://www.writersdigest.com/whats-new/what-is-the-throughline-of-a-novel-and-why-its-important-you-have-one "What is the Throughline of a Novel? (And Why It's Important You Have One)," by Nancy Lamb. *Writer's Digest*, August 28, 2012.

http://terribleminds.com/ramble/2012/03/14/shot-through-the-heart-your-storys-throughline/ "Shot Through the Heart: Your Story's Throughline," by Chuck Wendig. Terribleminds blog, March 14, 2012.

http://www.slate.com/articles/life/longform/2012/11/playboy_interviews_conversations_with_frank_sinatra_steve_jobs_vladimir.html "Read Playboy . . . for the Interviews," by Max Linsky. *Slate*, posted November 26, 2012.

Service:
"Hey, I Can
Do That!"

▶ INTRODUCTION

Without question there is a service component of many of the magazine features produced these days. Breezy, information-packed, high-concept service pieces are also a staple of the front-of-the-book sections of most magazines and are a good way to break into bigger magazines. In this chapter, we will discuss the fundamental writing challenge of identifying a reader problem, concern, or issue that can be resolved by the contributor. This process is a vital point of connection for the readers of many magazines and websites. A glance at the news-stands, websites, and tablet editions of many magazines will demonstrate the wealth of publishing possibilities for emerging writers in the service area. In addition to providing a guide for constructing **how-to** pieces, we will demonstrate the rich storytelling possibilities available in introducing people to new products, services, lifestyle choices, or simply to new ideas about these things. We will show how important service articles are in providing information that shapes readers' lives, and how even the writer can be an expert in providing useful advice through this format.

▶ INSPIRATION: THE FUNDAMENTAL COMPONENT OF SERVICE PIECES

In the Pulitzer Prize-winning Broadway musical *A Chorus Line*, Mike, one of the performers who is auditioning for a spot in the titular chorus, sings of how he was inspired to go into show business after watching his older sister's early, albeit clumsy, efforts at tap dancing.

Service pieces—articles and departments that inspire readers to think "I can do that!"—are the essence of many magazines and websites. That is why this is probably one of the most popular types of articles. There is a big market for articles that tell people how to do things. Hence, the "how-to" format for many pieces in this category (see box). Service was encoded in the editorial DNA of a lot of media properties at inception and it is the force that keeps readers coming back. So, for some magazines, like *Real Simple*, service pieces are not merely how-to stories. They can be much more comprehensive. They provide the blueprint for helping readers act and think in less complicated, life-changing ways. For readers of an aspirational magazine like *Martha Stewart Living*, service is as much about celebrating "the art of creative living" as it is about actually being creative.

Whether it's the *Better Homes and Gardens* "I Did It!" column, with its soft-sell approach to domestic enhancement, or *Men's Health*'s "Belly Off! Club," with its monthly challenge to chisel rock-hard abs, service pieces engage and convince those who fall under their spell that readers can accomplish all the feats the editors lay before them. That many of those readers and website visitors may never actually play out those editorial fantasies is beside the point. Service stories are about presenting ideas that *seem* possible—getting readers to say: "Hey, I can do that!"

▶ SOLVING READER PROBLEMS

Many magazines consider service pieces as a staple. They provide exactly what they are promising to provide: service. They can introduce readers to products, professional assistance, and lifestyle choices. They even can offer up advice for self-help on emotional or physical issues. Indeed, service is considered one of the pillars of the contemporary magazine.

Think of service stories as problem-solving for a magazine's audience—often in advance of the realization by readers that they even had a problem. The problems can be personal (about fashion, fitness, relationships), professional (how to get a job or promotion), recreational (the best vacations, the sleekest running shoes). Look at the covers of most major lifestyle, fashion, epicurean, health & fitness, shelter, travel, or city and regional magazines and you will find them blaring with cover lines promoting the service pieces inside: "The Jet-Setter's Guide to Fitness," "Perfect 4-minute Makeup," "The Smartest Car and 40 Other Breakthroughs," "Where to Find the Best 5 Bars, Gastropubs and Liquor Stores for Craft Beer."

Your charge as a would-be contributor is to discern what the aspirations and activities of these readers are and develop story ideas that will help enjoy and achieve them or at least dream of enjoying and achieving them.

Remember, service stories needn't (and probably shouldn't) be didactic, making readers feel bad about what they can't do or have. The magazine experience is about inspiring readers to believe that this activity, this goal, this information is within reach. The information should make them feel smarter and more capable. While it is true that women's lifestyle magazines are flogged for promoting unhealthy and unrealistic body images and touting relationship advice that some find dangerously antiquated, the service pieces these magazines peddle are based on the real issues confronted by women in the targeted demographic. Were the editors not connecting with the audience on these issues, it is unlikely these giants would continue to dominate the magazine marketplace, even in the digital age when many other kinds of publications are dramatically losing readers.

HOW TO THINK ABOUT HOW-TO

In the most popular approach, the service piece provides news you can use. The "how-to" format is the standard. You've seen the cover lines at the checkout counter. How to: make money; save money; spend money; lose weight; gain weight; be more attractive; cope; and live healthier, more fulfilling lives. But service increasingly is becoming much more broadly defined. Traditionally, "How To" actually was included in the title. Gradually, we began seeing magazines play the numbers game in multiples of five. The 5, 10, or 15 Best Ways To Do (fill in the blank). More often these days, we see odd numbers on the covers. Without question, the 101 Ways, 7 Tips, 9 Things, or 13 Ideas will grab attention right away, just because odd numbers tend to do that. They are, well, *odd*, especially in a world already conditioned to mark anniversaries in fives. The number 13 is one of the most attention grabbing, given its traditional association with something negative. Turning it into a positive is a good way to draw readers in. The odd number also (in sort of an odd way) suggests a certain credibility, which translates into reliability in the information provided. In other words, the editors really did think about pulling together a list of the absolute best suggestions on a given topic and didn't whimsically round up the number of suggestions just to contrive a Top 10 list.

The important thing to consider is that, conceptually, "How To" still provides the subtext for the piece, no matter how it is framed. That is true even if the words "How To" don't appear anywhere in the title. They are certain to appear in the editor's mind. And they should appear in the mind of the writer.

A lot of young writers stress about not having the expertise to produce authoritative how-to articles. It has been said that experts are not born; they are developed. We would like to suggest that what's really needed to craft a good how-to is not so much expertise in doing the thing you're writing about (though that certainly helps). It is more a matter of curiosity about the activity; deep, detailed reporting about how it's done; and the ability to relay that information in tight, bright, easy-to-follow instructions. (In an ideal world, the writer would give those instructions to someone else and have her follow them before publishing.)

It is the sharp, detailed reporting that lends authority and credibility to the how-to. Even if the skill or activity you're writing about is one that you have performed or participated in thousands of times, it can be helpful to consult a wide array of other experts who can offer another perspective on how it's done. But, when thinking about breaking into magazines with how-to pieces, don't discount the expertise you actually do have.

We all have hobbies and interests that will lend credibility to our effort at how-to writing. You may be a lifelong roller blader. Think about the how-to story on this activity that might fit into a lifestyle or fitness magazine. Care and maintenance of the in-line skates. Safety gear. The best roller blade routes in the U.S. You collect vinyl records? Pitch a story to a magazine about repairing scratches or storing the discs to prevent warping. What about the best techniques and latest equipment for dubbing and preserving these collectibles? We all have a modicum of expertise in some domain—other than writing and reporting—that could lend itself to a fascinating how-to story. College students, for example, often have to navigate circumstances that are rife with problems that must be resolved. Internship strategies and decisions. Moving from one apartment to another. Sports activities, health and fitness, nutrition for people with demanding schedules. Sleep deprivation. All these are areas that are central to student life. How do you translate the things that you experience into problem-solving service stories for others? Hobbies, recreation, bargain hunting, coupon clipping. Promote those interests when you're pitching yourself and your story idea to a prospective editor.

The important thing to keep in mind is that you, the writer, can become the expert—either because you are writing about something you have perfected through years of practice (How To Pack For a Weekend Getaway), or because you have done an expert job of reporting—reading the documents, talking to the experts, evaluating their books.

Once you have a sense of who these readers are, consider what sorts of advice and inspiration they seek from the magazine you'd like to pitch. It helps to consider the magazine's editorial "pillars," the topics and issues that are at the very core of what the editors consistently deliver each month. But also consider its mission. What is this magazine seeking to do for its readers?

Take the case of *O, The Oprah Magazine.* The tagline of the Winfrey brand is "live your best life," a sort of clarion call for *O*philes who admire the celebrity and want to emulate her. After all, she has inspired with her story, trumpeting her triumphs over a number of adversities (including poverty, sexual abuse, and weight) and seizing control of *their* lives. Each *O* story, therefore, whether it is a short front-of-the-book department or a feature, offers a blueprint for life-changing transformation. The advice here is always simple and in plain-speak:

"Ignorance is not bliss where money is concerned," warns Winfrey pal and financial guru Suze Orman in her advice column.

"You should love somebody not because you 'should', but because he 'deserves it'" cautions Dr. Phil McGraw, another of Winfrey's longtime confederates and contributors.

While you may not have the authority or celebrity of Suze Orman or Dr. Phil, you can think about stories that serve up Winfrey's "live your best life" ethos. For example, one recent issue featured a short piece about the renewed connections a young woman made to her mother and grandmother by joining a knitting circle. It served both the *crafty* side of the *O* audience with its discussion of the joy and technique of knitting, and it incorporated the magazine's overarching sense of finding inner peace and happiness with your loved ones. For the *O* audience, it was a service piece on multiple levels.

Service pieces can be completely aspirational as well, as long as they communicate authority and speak to the values the audience holds. Let's face it, few in the audience of *Martha Stewart Living* really have the time to sew their own duvet covers or weave placemats out of thatch they culled from a nearby marsh. But having those ideas placed before them in *MLS*, the bible of creative living, is motivation enough to at least consider the possibility that they *might* someday tackle such a project, and that's satisfaction enough.

The advice in a service piece, no matter how challenging the project, has to make the enterprise seem within the *realm* of possibility for the readers of this magazine or website, which means the instructions must be clear and the advice has to inspire confidence. The reader should leave the piece thinking that she can accomplish this feat, even if she never will.

SERVICE STRUCTURE

The basic structure for the how-to service piece is, in a word, simple. The standard approach in structuring this article is first to grab attention with a concise lead. It can be in the form of an anecdote, a shocking statistic, or merely the statement of an issue. The point is to set out the problem that needs to be solved in summary fashion.

Here is an example of a setup from "5 Ways to Break a Downward Spiral," by Gabrielle Leblanc, published in the October 2007 issue of *O*:

> Sometimes a funk can equal more than the sum of its parts. For instance, you wake up to discover there's no milk for your coffee, the highway is backed up so you're late for work, and you're sinking into another bad—and worsening—day.
>
> You don't have to go there . . .

In quick summary fashion, the writer has set out the problem and in a smooth transition to the nutgraf, begins to establish that there is a solution. The solution then unfolds through the five suggestions, with explanations.

Often, like this piece, the service article will progress through a series of recommendations or solutions, point by point. Include an example as needed, but the paragraphing in this form is short and the language straightforward. Always keep in mind that this is a resource story. Readers are going to want to get right to and breeze through the information you are providing. If you have fixed on a real need, then they are going to have a real need to figure out how to meet that need. Often writers will employ bulleted points or short paragraphs that outline the steps that should be taken in order to resolve the problem. Subheads will tend to help organize this presentation in the form of imperative statements, like Walk Every Evening; Substitute Carrot Sticks for Potato Chips; Warm Up First. Conceivably, a reader could read the subheads and get a quick summary of the advice offered. This is the approach taken by writer Jasmine J. Parker in the piece "Erase Student Loan Debt," published in the August 2012 issue of *Essence*. Parker opens with an overview of the problem that is set to connect with a readership that ranges from college students and recent grads to relatively young parents who might be looking ahead to college demands for their children. She outlines the problem she has identified as rising costs of college attendance that is resulting in a larger debt load for the current generation of college students and their families "struggling to pay off loans to meet college costs that have risen 900 percent since 1978, according to the College Board." She goes on to expand on the scope of the problem, citing authors of books on the subject, along with other research. Then, in a companion text box titled "4 Ways To Gain Control of Your Debt," there are the bulleted blurbs in two sections:

COLLEGE STUDENTS
- Seek free funding.
- Borrow federal first.

COLLEGE GRADUATES
- Find a job that repays the debt.
- Seek debt consolidation.

Each tip includes a paragraph of related information.

If experts are included, some short quotes might be incorporated. But keep them short. Experts can be quoted, just not quoted often in the piece. Remember, by the time you have completed your research, you have become something of an expert yourself. That authority should show in your writer's voice.

While some how-to articles will simply conclude with the end of the last paragraph tip, it is nice to frame a conclusion—space permitting—that can simply restate the benefits of following the proposed steps.

▶ FRONT-OF-THE-BOOK: CHUNKS, CHARTICLES, AND OTHER HIGH-CONCEPT FORMATS

Take a look at the front section of virtually any lifestyle magazine and most websites and you will find loads of service pieces, packaged in columns and departments that focus on everything from grooming to gadgets. These departments provide a wonderful entry point for writers who are new to the industry and new to a particular magazine. But to successfully pitch to, and ultimately write for, these departments, you must get the lay of the land.

One thing you'll notice about the departments in many contemporary magazines is that they often are not rendered as narrative stories. Many magazine editors—fully aware of the many demands on their readers' time and attention—now prefer writers to take a **high-concept**, highly graphic approach to departments, breaking the information into easy-to-read boxes or **chunks** of copy that enable readers to grasp material quickly.

HIGH-CONCEPT: A story idea that can be pitched in relatively simple, straight-forward terms.

In *Chicago* magazine's "Arena" section, for example, new artists, restaurants, businesses, and upcoming events often are presented in **charticles**—deeply reported, tightly written text boxes—that abandon conventional narrative structure.

CHUNKS: Information fragments that can substitute for shorter articles.

Even articles that years ago would have taken a classic narrative approach now get charticle treatment. In the February 2012 issue of *Chicago*, an Arena piece by political editor David Bernstein maps out the personnel changes on Barack Obama's campaign team from the point of his initial bid for the presidency in 2007 up to his reelection campaign in 2012. It begins with a brief (100 words) intro that is not unlike an anecdotal lead in a traditional narrative piece. But the bulk of the "article" is a colorful one-page graphic with tiny floating "head" shots and mini bios of the members of the 2008 and 2012 Obama campaign teams aligned in two columns with arrows indicating who's in and who's out on the staff. The bottom of the page is arrayed with Obama campaign paraphernalia from both 2008 and 2012.

CHARTICLE: A combination of short text and mostly graphic material that can take the place of a fully developed article.

It is a service piece for politics junkies who thrive on knowing who's who in Washington. But rather than delivering this information in a wordy, wonky narrative, it is given broader appeal—and provides an even greater service to those who might be indifferent to politics—by presenting the information in a clever chart.

Before you attempt to pitch a high-concept piece, read back issues of the magazines to get a sense of the kinds of graphics-driven service pieces the editors seem to like. Pay very close attention to the design. You needn't be a designer yourself to imagine how you might deconstruct the information and present it graphically. Look to other magazines and websites for ideas and inspiration about how to present the material in an alternative storytelling form. Websites are particularly helpful, since it was the short-text, heavy graphic format of digital publishing that, in many ways, drove the move to high-concept in print.

THE TOP 3 MUST-HAVES FOR YOUR HOW-TO

The biggest roadblock new writers confront in successfully pitching a how-to is that they fail to follow a simple freelance checklist of things that must be considered in every short service piece.

1. **Make sure you know the magazine.** You must have a clear idea of the magazine's niche and focus, as well as the audience demographics, in order to know whether the service piece you are pitching will be of interest.

2. **Make sure the idea is new.** You must have a good idea of the history of the target magazine and any of its competitors to determine whether your idea or any similar idea already has been published.

3. **Make sure your information really is useful.** Here is one area where you absolutely must provide a takeaway for the reader. News she can use. One observer has stated that the writer of service pieces is something of a teacher. As you think through your piece, consider whether you have taught the reader anything. Test the ideas on your own focus group of people who can be objective.

Follow this checklist and you will improve your chances of breaking in with a winnable how-to story idea.

Thinkstock / Hemera

The key to making this deconstructionist approach to service pieces work is to think through the components of the article. Is it a guide to an upcoming event that can be broken down by moments in the day or the geography of the venue? Is it a new product piece that examines the features of the gear or gadget in minute detail. Think about the elements of the story that might lend themselves to good images.

For a Northwestern graduate student project, a writer was struggling for a way to give a service component to a short profile—a famous tailor from London's Savile

Row who was touring the United States. Rather than presenting the story as a perfunctory 500-word blurb about the impeccably turned out tailor, the writer added a high-concept service component, borrowing from the treatment for web design. The story featured a 200-word sketch of the tailor's life story superimposed over a three-quarter-length portrait of the tailor that covered the entire page. Framing the tailor's image were close-up cutouts of his haberdashery—his cuff links, the lapels of his suit, his pocket square. Each cutout included tips from the tailor about how the reader could emulate his classic bespoke style of dress.

It was a piece that combined great service with interesting graphic presentation. One could imagine this piece rendered digitally—in either a tablet or website—so that touching or clicking on an item of the tailor's clothing would produce a pop-up of that item with the tailor's voice explaining how to sport it properly. Perusing the web or tablet magazines for those kinds of story treatments can help sharpen your eye and imagination for high-concept presentation and enable you to craft pitches that will get editors' attention.

WRITER'S WORKSHOP

Here are suggestions for you to apply a central point of this chapter as you begin to develop article ideas.

Keep your eyes and ears open to the things you encounter every day and consider how you might shape your own service piece for publication. It is a good idea to start with something simple that is very much in your experience. Above, we discuss the weekend getaway and the apartment move. Sooner or later, many people are going to encounter these issues. How do you plan for such a getaway? How do you plan for the move? How do you do either in an efficient and cost-effective way?

One suggestion in determining your topic is to make an observation about something that could be a universal need, interest, or dilemma (like the move), and determine how you might frame it as a how-to. In so doing, match up your idea with a market by considering something of a "Who's Who" list: Who is affected by this problem or need? Who can help or advise?

Chapter Thirteen
Review

ASSIGNMENT DESK

1. Develop a list of three things you do all the time, whether it involves work, leisure, health, fitness, grooming, shopping, cooking, or merely going to class and to the library. As you develop this list, consider a problem or need that arises in connection with each item.

2. Review your list and develop lists of three things you do for each of the needs or problems on each list. Frame this new list in the form of suggestions to meet the needs or solve the problems you have identified.

3. Now take your lists and consider who might have an interest in the kind of advice you have developed. Consider this "audience" for each of your original three things in connection with a particular magazine or to several magazines this group might read.

4. Now develop a pitch for a how-to article based on one of the items on your original list.

5. Develop an outline for this how-to article with a summary opening, outlining the problem you are addressing and then listing the imperative subheads you would suggest for the paragraphs of advice you would provide.

▶ KEY TERMS

- charticle
- chunks
- high-concept
- how-to

▶ SUGGESTED READING

Evans, Robert Michael. *The Layers of Magazine Editing*. New York: Columbia University Press, 2004. Evans' editing manual also discusses the tone and style of service material.

Morrish, John; Bradshaw, Paul. *Magazine Editing In Print and Online*. New York: Routledge, 2012. Morrish and Bradshaw's examination of the magazine editor's art includes a look at the crafting of front-of-the-book service and how-to material.

▶ **WEB RESOURCES**

http://www.writersdigest.com/whats-new/write-a-how-to-article-in-6-easy-steps
The editors of *Writers Digest* offer quick tips on the construction of how-to articles.

http://www.writersdigest.com/writing-articles/by-writing-goal/improve-my-writing/thou_shalt_steal Freelance writer and *Writers Digest* contributor Linda Formichelli suggests ways to develop how-to ideas.

http://www.adweek.com/news/press/womens-service-mags-trade-housekeeping-style-147815 Adweek provides an overview of the changes taking place in the contemporary women's service magazines.

http://www.chicagomag.com/Chicago-Magazine/February-2012/Charting-Obamas-New-Campaign-Team/ "Charting Obama's New Campaign Team," by David Bernstein. *Chicago*, February 2012.

14 Arts and Entertainment

▶ INTRODUCTION

When it comes to arts and entertainment writing, it is imperative that you think expansively. The first thing for the aspiring freelance writer to consider is that there is a wealth of outlets for arts and entertainment writing that extends far beyond the celebrity-filled titles that take center stage on the newsstands. Without question, these magazines are the destination for many young journalists who aspire to cover music, film, theater, and the like. But, in addition to high-profile magazines like *Rolling Stone, Spin, Vibe,* and *Entertainment Weekly*, a host of publications—both new digital titles and legacy media—cover the broad range of activities and avocations that fall loosely under the category of arts and entertainment. In fact, thinking expansively about what constitutes "arts and entertainment" opens up a wide array of publishing possibilities for industrious writers. It's not all about stage and screen, or stargazing, for that matter. Taking a deep dive into any creative endeavor could be an aspiring arts writer's entrée into the field. And for the truly entrepreneurial, starting your own digital arts publication could be your ticket to developing a presence in this sphere. The key is to think as creatively about your publishing options as you do about the activities themselves.

▶ **THE FIELD**

Most people think of the "major" titles devoted to things like performing and painting when they consider where they might break into arts and entertainment writing. And to be sure, the number of titles devoted to individual artistic pursuits is vast. The landscape includes small, but venerable magazines like *Dance*, one of the premier publications of that field, *Downbeat*, long considered the bible of jazz, *Opera News*, a tastemaker in classical music, and *American Photo*, a showcase of photography and photographers. But the Internet is exploding with websites and webzines that are hungry for contributions from young writers and bloggers who know their stuff.

The thing to remember about the big, established titles is that few of them enlist new, unproven writers. Most only work with writers and bloggers with established track records. That is particularly true of a pop culture behemoth like *Rolling Stone*, but also true of some of the smaller niched titles like *Downbeat* and *Dance*. Breaking into these books requires cutting your teeth in smaller publications and websites that will enable you to build a body of work, and maybe even a following, that will attract the notice of editors up market. Which isn't to say that breaking into the big books is an impossible dream, but you can't set your sights on these destination titles at the outset of your arts and entertainment writing career. It will take some groundwork to get there.

You can plant the seeds at the more accessible magazines and websites that cover specific areas in this far-reaching realm. For music enthusiasts, there are webzines dedicated to every conceivable genre. Sites like *Pitchfork*.com (which covers independent and alternative rock) and *Bust* (a pop culture zine that covers the arts from a feminist perspective) have carved out their own identifiable spaces in the world of arts and entertainment coverage. Music writing can also be instrument-specific. Magazines like *Guitar Player* and *Modern Drummer* have loyal if limited followings and are in need of writers who know and love the instruments and can communicate effectively to an audience that shares that passion. They are very open to contributions from young writers, though they rarely pay novices.

Every art form has similar publications that are equally receptive to submissions from writers who are just getting started. Keep our earlier advice in mind: always chart out a path to your destination market. Be as resourceful and enterprising in identifying these markets as you are in recognizing good story ideas. And this process can begin right there on your campus. If your school has a magazine, pitch arts and entertainment pieces for that publication. If no magazine, then look to the alternative weekly. If no alternative, then the feature section of the campus newspaper. Somewhere there is an opportunity to demonstrate what you can do.

Additionally, your quest to get started in arts coverage needn't be confined to what is traditionally defined as "arts and entertainment." Think about art in broader terms and your prospects will also broaden exponentially. "Art" can include fashion and interior design. "Entertainment" can include dining out and the club scene. All of these areas have robust communities of websites and zines that need content. Art can also mean arts and crafts—everything from knitting to woodworking—which also have their own dedicated media outlets. Any pursuit that has a creative bent can be defined as art.

Think about your own hobbies—ones in which you're currently involved, or ones in which you dabbled—and you will find an opportunity to do some arts writing. You played cornet in the high school marching band? *Brass Musician* or *Halftime* magazine may help you launch your career in arts writing. "We're always looking for writers who know something about drum and bugle corps and marching bands," says *Halftime* founder and editor-in-chief Christine Katzman. "I like to think of this as a very specific kind of writing about the arts."

▶ GETTING STARTED IN ARTS & ENTERTAINMENT WRITING

In the pre-Internet era, breaking into writing about the arts was nearly as difficult as breaking into entertainment as a performer. There were far fewer venues and gatekeepers back then. And they were loath to use anyone but seasoned writers who had already produced a body of work at other well-known publications. It took considerable luck and perseverance to get even a foot in the door of most publications that featured arts coverage.

Today, aspiring arts writers have a much easier path. It still takes a good deal of preparation and perseverance to break in, but, with infinitely more publications—both digital and traditional print—as well as the opportunity to make a mark with your own blog or website, getting started in entertainment writing takes more individual effort than luck.

One of the first things a new writer should do is pick an area or two in which to specialize and learn all you can learn about the area. Whereas once journalists who were generalists were valued for their ability to parachute into any topic and learn enough to communicate its essence to a detached public, in this age of niche publishing, when audiences gravitate to media properties covering a topic for which they have an affinity, writers are appreciated for their depth in the subject. In other words, readers often have a grounding in the subject matter itself. They expect the writer to have even more. And they expect to be able to get up close, intimately engaging the subject matter as only you—the writer—can help them do. They expect a front-row seat and a backstage pass all rolled into your piece. Learning the topic

Thinkstock / TongRo Images

means developing a feel for its nuances—the changes that have occurred in the field, the differences in technique that distinguish practitioners. Learn about its key behind-the-scenes players.

In moving deeper into the arts and entertainment writing field, look at a number of publications that might include arts and entertainment features as part of their lineup. City and regional magazines are especially keen on these types of stories, central to their editorial mission. Not only are their readers consumers of entertainment, but they are consumed by it. Restaurants, bars, and nightclubs, in addition to museums and cultural offerings, as well as movies, stage performances, concerts, and dance recitals. New openings, new designs, new menus are all ripe subject areas. So, too, are behind-the-scenes narratives that add dimension to entertainment stories in this area. What does it take to put on a concert? Stage a plan? Pull a magic show out of the hat? What does it take to make a record? Produce a local indie film? Look at the popularity of the behind-the-scenes—"making of"—documentaries that are featured on channels like HBO. People are interested in these stories. What does it take to get through the night of a popular restaurant? From the perspective of the chef? The maître d'? A waiter? Maybe an intersecting narrative of all perspectives. Just look at the huge popularity of "reality" shows that present such stories. The point is to consider stories anyone might see, but then to consider further the stories that rise above those observations. These are the stories people will *want* to see.

As you build your expertise in the area, start pitching stories to small outlets first, then to larger venues as your portfolio grows. If you can't convince editors at the smaller magazines or websites that you're ready to take on assignments, start building a portfolio on your own blog or website. Showcase a variety of story types—reviews and profiles, as well as in-depth reported pieces that demonstrate your ability to dig into the topic as well as ferret out authoritative sources. Push the pieces out to your friends and relatives on social media and get them to comment, demonstrating that you attract a following and generate an online conversation.

Pay attention to the masters of the craft and imitate them. Good arts writers have a voice, whether it's that of *Rolling Stone* film critic Peter Travers or *GQ* food writer Alan Richman. Listen to the voices. First, Tavers on the release of "The Great Gatsby" in the May 9, 2013 issue of *Rolling Stone*:

> Shush. Listen. That's F. Scott Fitzgerald turning in his grave.

Or, Travers on the release of "Iron Man 3" in that same issue:

> This may sound like heresy, but I'm getting Robert Downey'd-out—at least as Iron Man and his alter ego, Tony Stark.

Or, Richman on the emergence of Portland as a food town in this excerpt from his "Cloudy with a Chance of Stinging-Nettle Flan and Tomato Coulis," published in the November 2012 issue of *GQ*:

> How did it happen? How did Portland, at best second-tier and certainly worse where food was concerned, ascend to its status as the most fascinating gastronomic city in America, the all-around champion in the category of food and drink? Bragging a bit, I can say that I pretty much predicted it would happen, foresaw that the American Northwest had the potential for culinary preeminence. I anticipated the vineyards, the farmers' markets, the abundant produce and seafood, the leisurely lifestyle, and above all the entrepreneurial spirit.

Learn to recognize how writers in various areas of arts and entertainment use language to paint word pictures that clearly communicate for specific audiences what they experienced while enjoying (or *not*) a performance on stage, onscreen, or in the kitchen.

▶ WHAT "WRITING ABOUT THE ARTS" REALLY ENTAILS

Everybody's a critic—or wants to be one anyway. (See critical arts reviews in Chapter 17.) Yet there is much more to writing about the arts than doing reviews and profiles. Yes, both are staples of magazines and websites dedicated to arts and entertainment, but if you really want to separate yourself from the pack of people trying to break into this arena, you must consider the multitude of other story types that flesh out the pages of these vehicles.

Much of arts coverage is devoted to the business of practicing an art, whether professionally or as a hobby. Every artistic endeavor has some sort of commercial transaction at its heart. Equipment and supplies are manufactured and purchased. Tickets to performances and showings are sold. And, in most instances, the art itself—whether it's film, fashion, or food—is placed on the market and offered up for public consumption. Good arts and entertainment writers pay as much attention to the business behind the arts as they do to the art and artists. Pricing and sales are as important a part of the arts as performances. Few aspiring arts writers think to pay attention to this area. The ones who do will be rewarded with story ideas that lead to assignments. For example, an April 2013 issue of *Guitar Player* magazine featured short pieces on a new line of Fender guitars and a new phase shifter, along with pieces on Eddie Van Halen's appearance on LL Cool J's "Authentic," and tour announcements by Peter Frampton and Steely Dan. A recent *TimeOut New York* feature clearly had costs as well as ambiance and mixology in mind when it included a range of offerings "From dives to cocktail dens and craft-brew havens to wine haunts," in its piece on the "50 best New York bars." And with Rolling Stones concert tickets for the band's "50 and Counting" anniversary tour going for more than $600 apiece in some venues, it should come as no surprise that *Huffington Post* ran a May 4, 2013 story on a late price slash for the Stones' Los Angeles show. The skyrocketing cost of live entertainment always will generate some interest.

Trends can be another important fertile source of story ideas. But the trend needn't be related to the arts. It also may be related to the artists. Keep an eye out for things that artists are doing, the things they are wearing. Consider writing not just about the object or action, but also about who manufactures or distributes it. Look for that story behind the story. We have seen what hip-hop artists are doing to adorn themselves with bling. *Ebony* magazine Senior Writer Margena Christian wanted to look beyond it all for an untold aspect of the story. She developed a compelling piece on "grills"— the expensive, jewel-encrusted bridges many hip-hop artists were having affixed to their teeth. Her story, which ran in the August 28, 2006 issue of *Ebony's* sister publication, *Jet*, didn't focus on the mere fact that rappers were festooning their mouths with $500,000 worth of diamonds and gold. She also spoke with some of the dentists responsible for creating these lavish smiles and described in intricate detail how the procedures are done.

"People think writing about entertainment is just writing about the performers, but there's a lot of behind-the-scenes stuff that goes on in entertainment that can make for even more interesting stories," Christian says.

Of course, the tried and true story forms, like profiles, remain a solid source of story ideas, but where young writers go astray is looking only at high-profile artists and performers as the subjects of their profiles. "The fact is, nobody is going to assign a new writer to a profile of an A-list celebrity," says *Entertainment Weekly* Senior Writer Dan Snierson. "The Justin Bieber, George Clooney, Taylor Swift stories are going to go to someone an editor knows will represent the publication well and can deliver the story. Those stories are not going to go to someone who's not already a known commodity to that editor."

But emerging writers can have success by pitching profiles of up-and-coming artists in the field. Look for unusual performers or practitioners of the craft who may not be on the radar of your editor, but who you may have unusual access to because of your proximity to them or due to some other alliance (One that does not pose a conflict of interest: You can't pitch stories about close friends or relatives without disclosing the nature of those relationships.)

Also consider stories about the multitude of other professionals who make it possible for artists to ply their craft, from managers and agents to producers and directors to the manufacturers who fabricate the tools of the artists' trade. Pitching these profiles demonstrates a potential contributor's depth of knowledge about the field and can lead to assignments with more high-profile subjects down the road.

Reviews are not entirely off-limits to new writers. Again, reviews of off-beat or unusual offerings are more likely to be assigned to a writer who is new to a publication. But reviews are not only evaluations of performers; you might consider product reviews as well. Everything from instruments to leotards is ripe for review, and virtually every publication and website has a section where products and equipment are evaluated, usually in small text blocks. Still, they are a good way to hone your critical eye—and get published by editors who are hungry for stories about the next hot item. Eric Gillen recalls a meeting with journalism students when he was Web Director, Hearst Men's Network, Hearst Digital Media. He was in charge of Esquire.com, among other titles, and during that meeting mused about the increasing number of people on the streets of New York City trading in their stereo ear buds for the new "Beats By Dr. Dre" headphones. What's up with that? "I told a room full of journalism students that idea, and no one pitched me on it. I gave them a great idea," he recalls. "Why didn't any of them go, like, 'opportunity'?" The point is that you should never let opportunities for potential trendy entertainment stories pass you by.

Many in the world of entertainment writing make a distinction between review writing and criticism. Reviews, generally speaking, are shorter, snappier critiques that provide the writer's endorsement or condemnation. In the shorthand of music journalists Greg Kot and Jim DeRogatis, hosts of the syndicated public radiocast *Sound Opinions,* a review is a writer's recommendation to either "buy it, burn it, or trash it." Think of review writing as the ultimate in service journalism. It is the writer's effort to prevent the consumer from plunking down hard-earned cash on a new offering or to encourage the patronage of a book, movie, play, restaurant, CD, concert, or exhibit. Though reviews are short, they should not be pithy. The art of the review is to convey a sense of the offering in this tight space while also providing a well-reasoned and entertaining opinion.

THE REVIEWS ARE IN

As we explain here and in Chapter 17, the critical review is both a summary of the salient points of the offering and a critical appraisal of it. Take this brief review by Jody Rosen of M.I.A.'s single "Space Odyssey" from the February 4, 2010 issue of *Rolling Stone*:

> Head trip alert, M.I.A.'s new song recorded in a day with producer Rusko and released on Twitter, forsakes her usual dance-floor-rattling clangor for dreamy psychedelia. Over a swirling mid-tempo beat, broken occasionally by the howl of an air-raid siren, M.I.A. chants a simple nine-note melody. The lyrics are a stoner's play-by-play. "Gravity's my enemy . . . I'm floating in the light-golden sea." The video—recorded on a webcam—is just as bare-bones and mesmerizing: get high like planes, indeed.

Note how Rosen packs vivid description and snatches of lyrics into this 76-word excerpt that clearly expresses how he feels about the cut. It is a wonderfully evocative recommendation of the song.

Now, consider this excerpt from Emily Nussbaum's critique of the comedian Louie C.K.'s sitcom on the FX channel, *Louie*, which appeared in the July 9 & 16 edition of *The New Yorker*:

> To his fans, Louis C.K. is more than just an artist. He is Lenny Bruce, he is Bob Dylan—the performer who serves the truth raw, not cooked. It's a reputation that could rankle, if the man didn't pretty much deserve it. If you're not familiar with him, Louis C.K. (short for Szekely) is the country's best standup. With a radical level of productivity (he generates an hour of new material per year, then discards it), Louis has built a confessional act that covers the birth of his kids, his divorce, and his rancorous arrival into middle age . . . In 2006, he created and starred in HBO's *Lucky Louie,* a bleak deconstruction of *The Honeymooners*, which won praise from critics but was cancelled after one season.

Here Nussbaum reaches back to compare Louis' work with masters across the artistic spectrum, including Bruce (standup), Dylan (music), and implicitly Jackie Gleason (the star of television's *The Honeymooners*). And she places Louis' current sitcom alongside his past show to provide insight into how his work has developed since that earlier outing. It is a trenchant examination of Louis' career as well as a review of his new offering.

Criticism combines both the recommendation aspects of a review with a deeper analysis of the artist and the art form. Criticism places the offering and the artist in context, comparing the new effort with the artist's past work as well as with other influential antecedents. Criticism references history, literature, and the towering figures in the genre. It is where the simple review fleshes out into an articulation of cultural and societal value.

Note how the writer Thomas Connors contextualizes an opening of an exhibition of works by Pablo Picasso at Chicago's Art Institute, establishing the late artist's Chicago connections in ways that resonate with the audience in this piece published January 14, 2013 in *Michigan Avenue* magazine:

> Chicagoans know their Picasso—or at least the 162 tons of steel standing tall in Richard J. Daley Plaza. But when that still-enigmatic sculpture was unveiled in 1967, its appearance was just the latest manifestation of the city's long relationship with the wildly inventive and mind-bogglingly productive artist.

Curators of museum exhibitions are storytellers. The best in their fields—and clearly, the best will work at places like the Art Institute of Chicago—know how to find the stories behind the stories of artifacts, as well as art. The writer who is interested in arts and entertainment would do well to analyze how curators craft stories. The lessons drawn from this experience can transfer to storytelling about the exhibitions, as we see with the *Michigan Avenue* preview piece, showing readers the historical significance of "Picasso and Chicago," an exhibition and a story that tracks the fascinating 100-year relationship of the artist and the city.

Arts and entertainment writing comes in many forms, not just reviews and profiles. Understanding the forms and where your best opportunities are for securing an assignment using that form is your ticket to entering this world.

Chapter Fourteen
Review

ASSIGNMENT DESK

1. Consider an area of entertainment you would be interested in covering in your campus community. This subject area can be a performance (dance, theater, or music), a release (film or music recording), a restaurant, or a museum exhibition.

2. Develop a story idea for a short piece for the front-of-the-book section of a magazine—an actual magazine or website. The article you plan can be a review (covering something that already has taken place) or a preview (an advance story on something that will take place). And it can be aimed at a campus publication.

3. Outline the elements of the story you will write, including any interviews you might conduct.

4. Develop a pitch to the relevant editor of the publication you have selected for your story.

5. This pitch is your one shot to impress the editor with your story-generating creativity, so while you are developing a single story idea, you also should have an idea of several other related possibilities. But here is the hitch: You may not pitch profiles (even of little-known artists).

▶ SUGGESTED READING

DeCurtis, Anthony. *In Other Words: Artists Talk about Life and Work.* Milwaukee, WI, 2005. This volume features articles and essays on a number of music and entertainment personalities by the prolific DeCurtis, whose work has appeared in a number of publications, from *The New York Times* magazine to *Rolling Stone.*

Ebert, Roger. *Your Movie Sucks.* Kansas City, MO: Andrews McMeel Publishing, 2007. A collection of some of the most scathing reviews by the venerable television personality and film critic of the *Chicago Sun-Times.*

Kael, Pauline. *I Lost It at the Movies.* London: Marion Boyars Publishing, 1965. This collection of essays by one of the twentieth century's most influential critics charts the genesis of her love affair with cinema.

Lane, Anthony. *Nobody's Perfect.* New York: Vintage Press, 2003. Essays, articles, and reviews by the *New Yorker* film and cultural critic.

▶ WEB RESOURCES

http://aafca.com/ Homepage of the African American Film Critics Association, an organization composed of reviewers who have a particular interest in creating a platform for movies with universal appeal to the African-American community, while highlighting films produced, written, directed, and starring persons from the African Diaspora.

http://www.mcana.org/ Website of the Music Critics Association of North America, an organization devoted to promoting high standards of music criticism in America.

http://filmmusiccritics.org/about/ Website of the International Film Music Critics Association, an association of online, print, and radio journalists who specialize in writing about original film and television music.

http://www.ofcs.org/ The website of the online Film Critics Society, an organization comprised of Internet-based film critics located around the world.

http://www.rollingstone.com/movies/reviews/the-great-gatsby-20130509 "The Great Gatsby" and http://www.rollingstone.com/movies/reviews/iron-man-20080515 "Iron Man 3," by Peter *Travers. Rolling Stone*, May 9, 2013.

http://michiganavemag.com/living/articles/aic-opens-picasso-and-chicago "AIC Opens 'Picasso and Chicago,'" by Thomas Connors. *Michigan Avenue,* January 14, 2013.

15 Sports

▶ INTRODUCTION

Writing about sports is more than just game coverage and stats-filled profiles. The personal travails of athletes and the dramatic backdrop against which sporting events often take place are great fodder for the kinds of rich narrative stories that fill many magazines. But what comes to mind for a lot of young writers when they consider where to pitch their sports-themed stories are the obvious titles, *Sports Illustrated*, *ESPN*, and the plethora of sports websites that clutter the Internet. Your interest in sports, however, can extend to publications and websites well beyond the narrow niche of sports or health and fitness titles and blogs.

As you attempt to carve out a place in sports writing for magazines, expand your perception of what a sports story is and where it will fit. These are stories that can appeal to a wide range of audiences, not just the fanatics and weekend warriors. Some are lifestyle stories. Others are stories about triumph over adversity. By thinking more broadly about the focus and audience for your sports story, you will open up a wealth of placement possibilities and storytelling options.

LEARNING OBJECTIVES

1. Consider the different categories of sports stories published by magazines.

2. Develop an understanding of the various types of stories within the sports categories.

3. Develop an understanding of the expectations of readers of sports stories.

4. Develop an approach to identifying and producing sports pieces for magazine publication.

▶ THE MARKETPLACE

For writers who are interested in writing sports stories, the opportunities just might be limited only by your imagination. Getting in the game depends on how you define sports, how well you can pull story ideas out of events that unfold, and how well you can pitch these stories to a wide variety of magazines. In other words, this is essential magazine writing. The first thing to consider when it comes to actual sports stories is that there are two basic categories. There are the games people play ("participant sports") and the games they watch others play ("spectator sports"). There can be some overlap. In the first category, for example, tennis and golf would be considered participant sports, but they also are games people watch others play. In taking the participant perspective, you would consider the service approach. Readers of golfing magazines want information on how to improve their game. Driving lessons, in a manner of speaking. But they also are looking for putting techniques. In tennis, improving on a serve or volley techniques certainly would be of interest. There also are running magazines that will look for features on diet, hydration, preparing for distance running, or challenging terrains. In addition to the service features in these magazines, celebrity profiles and events features also are included.

Another sub-group of the participant category are the magazines that play to a sense of adventure. There are hunting, fishing, and camping zines that also include a service orientation. But these magazines also can provide showcases for engaging narrative features that allow freelancers more room for creative expression.

The spectator sports are pretty obvious, with an emphasis on every aspect of team coverage, the players, the coaches, the owners, the performance, the deals, and the scandals, among other things. It has been noted by accomplished sports writers that every spectator sport actually has four seasons. There is the season in which the sport is played. There is the post season. There is the

Thinkstock / Digital Vision

recruitment season and there is the pre-season. Thus, there are potential stories for any kind of team sport all year round. The key to finding publishable stories here is in recognizing that readers want more than the basics.

▶ MORE THAN SCORES AND STATS

Sure, *Sports Illustrated* and a variety of sports websites recap games and provide their readers with a wealth of player statistics, but when you consider writing a sports story for most other magazines it is important to think first and foremost about the *story*. What angle can you hang this story on to heighten its appeal to an audience beyond the traditional readers of sports-themed publications and websites? Athletes, after all, are people—albeit people blessed with incredible physical ability. How they came to make the most of those gifts is often the stuff of compelling profiles.

It's not just the big-name athletes who garner lots of coverage who have interesting backstories. Often the most absorbing stories are those of athletes who are rarely showcased in major media and are off the radar of the general public. For example, in the run-up to the 2012 Olympics in London, considerable ink and airplay was devoted to the trials—Olympic and otherwise—of over-exposed media darlings like swimmers Michael Phelps and Ryan Lochte, and hurdler Lolo Jones, who set websites aflame when she confessed her celibacy. Even gymnastics, which is all but ignored by the media except in the off-years, sits squarely in the glare of the spotlight when the Olympic games draw near. Gymnast Gabby Douglas, who had received little media notice prior to her stunning triumph in the trials, became one of the Games' poster girls. That was due partly to her performance, but also to the heart-rending personal story about her decision at the tender age of 14 to leave the bosom of her close-knit family in Virginia to live and train in Iowa, half a continent away.

Beyond the glamour sports, the struggles of Olympic athletes and would-be Olympic athletes are stories made for narrative treatment and other magazine storytelling forms. Consider rhythmic gymnastics—the all-female sport where the athletes twirl ribbons and toss apparatuses like hoops and Indian clubs while twisting, turning, and jumping. Rhythmic gymnastics is the lesser-known sister of artistic gymnastics, where the athletes like Mary Lou Retton and Nadia Comaneci tumble on and off of apparatuses like the balance beam and pommel horse. While artistic gymnasts garner considerable attention in Olympic years, the stories of the sacrifices and struggle—the injuries and personal setbacks—of the rhythmic gymnasts rarely penetrate the media bubble beyond the tiny websites that cover the sport, and, of course, those scene-setting profiles the networks include in their Olympics coverage.

It is important to note that within this world are tons of stories that would make fascinating reading for women's lifestyle magazines like *Glamour*,

Cosmopolitan, and *Marie Claire*. In addition to stories about their diets and training regimens, a close look at the grooming techniques of these highly coiffed and intricately made-up athletes could make interesting copy for fashion titles and even the books and websites that appeal to teen girls.

Just as compelling as the stories of athletic triumph are the ones about the failures of an athlete or a coach; failures and the way they persevered (or failed to recover) in the wake of those defeats. When tennis star Todd Martin blew a two-set lead to MaliVai Washington in the 1996 Wimbledon semi-final, the stories of Martin's disappointment and grace in defeat provided wonderful illustrations of his character and also served as fascinating discussions of what can go wrong in the sometimes unpredictable sporting arena. The match itself was made for narrative treatment, with dramatic moments that mirrored the rising action and tension of a novel. It is vitally important to remember that, at its core, sport is about more than stats and contracts and trophies. At the core, sport is about human challenge, about overcoming adversity, about winning against odds. It also is about character and dedication and will. Sports stories are very human narratives that have universal appeal and, accordingly, could be published in a number of markets besides those specifically aimed at sports enthusiasts.

Certainly, they fit the format of sports magazines. The fall from grace of an athletic hero also makes for a good examination of human frailties and character flaws, as illustrated by the piece featured in the box.

THE OPENING PLAY

In 2001 George O'Leary was forced out of the head coaching job at Notre Dame—a post he held for all of four days—when revelations surfaced that he had fabricated many of the credentials on his resume, including claims that he was a college letterman and had earned a master's degree in education. In an insightful 2002 piece in *Sports Illustrated*, Gary Smith uses line items from O'Leary's resume to provide the chronology for the piece. He traces the little fibs that grew into big lies as the story's narrative through-line.

Smith sets up his theme with an opening anecdote that recounts a time 23 years ago when one of O'Leary's early bosses caught the fibs on the coach's resume and shrunk away from the opportunity to confront him about them.

> Could he have averted the personal catastrophe that lay in silent wait for George for the next 23 years, gathering, girding? What would you have done? . . .

> "Here. Take one. Read it. It's George's curriculum vitae. Not the bogus one claiming that he lettered in football for three years at the University of New Hampshire and holds a master's degree in education from New York University. Not a bare-bones list of jobs and duties. A man is so much more than that—doesn't *vitae* mean 'of life'? Then you can decide. Then you'll have the right to make Luca's choice."

The story spins out like a brilliant little morality play, with O'Leary cast as the Jay Gatsby-esque anti-hero who fabricates a pedigreed past to gain acceptance in coaching's upper echelon. In that regard, the story is less about sports and more about the crises of confidence and other foibles that cloud a career. And that makes it a suitable story for any number of magazines.

▶ WORLDS OF POSSIBILITY

You should also think of sports stories as an opportunity to peek behind the scenes of a rarely explored world. "Sports" encompasses a wide range of physical activities, many of which receive scant media attention. While there are tons of small websites and specialty publications devoted to some of the more obscure sporting endeavors, they rarely get coverage in mainstream publications. But these sports, in addition to being replete with interesting athletes whose dedication to the endeavor is fueled more by love than compensation, are often fascinating activities that make for interesting reading in their own right. The key to enticing the readers to enter these little-known worlds is finding the character on which to center your story.

Even traditional redemption stories—stories we already think we know well—can take on a different hue when a skillful magazine writer has the time with the subject and the space to challenge the conventional narrative that has begun to take shape around the subject.

Following his spectacular return to professional football after serving three years in prison for his involvement in a dog-fighting scandal, Philadelphia Eagles quarterback Michael Vick was enveloped in a public relations blitz that trumpeted his remorse and rehabilitation. Writer Will Leitch helped us see through it all in his September 2011 *GQ* profile of Vick (see box).

CUTTING THROUGH THE HYPE

The sports hype machine was humming with Philadelphia Eagles quarterback Michael Vick's return to the NFL, following his prison release. In his September 2011 *GQ* profile of Vick, writer Will Leitch cut through the public relations blitz surrounding the superstar to get a revealing look at Vick post-prison as the following excerpt illustrates.

> For a long time thereafter, he played the humble, stoic good citizen. You will recognize this Vick from all those court appearances during the dogfighting trial—head down, chastened, all traces of his famously brash and arrogant personality smothered. Every facial expression came with an implied thought bubble: *I am a remorseful man.*

> Suffice it to say, Michael Vick no longer looks sorry. That Vick swagger, the charisma that once made the famously individual-averse NFL promote him as if he were Michael Jordan (remember "The Michael Vick Experience"

commercials?)—that Vick is back. It's this version of Vick that I encounter during a three-hour photo shoot, a few weeks after the commencement speech. I'd been so used to Vick looking forlorn during public appearances over the past three years that I didn't anticipate how bold he'd be in person. Many athletes are reluctant to take their shirts off for photographers, which has always struck me as odd. (If I looked like an athlete, I'd take my shirt off to go to the gas station.) But Vick is shirtless before the photographer even asks.

In this story, like any good magazine profile, Leitch attempts to look beneath the public relations veneer to present a more nuanced portrait of Michael Vick, one that examines the resentment Leitch detected simmering beneath his penitent facade. Here, too, we have a story that is less about sports (it appeared, after all, in a magazine that is largely about fashion) and more about the reconstruction of a celebrity's shattered image.

▶ FOLLOW YOUR PASSION

An athlete of some sort lives within each of us, even those of us who were perennially the last picked for the teams in gym class. Think broadly about your own athletic activity and interests and you will find sports stories—loosely defined—within them. Did you jump rope as a kid? The world of jump rope competitions is another of those domains where mainstream media coverage—other than novelty appearances on talk shows—has been negligible. Say you like juggling? The eye-hand coordination required to keep tennis balls and a trio of apples aloft is similar to the skill it takes for a number of other athletic pursuits. Thinking about the mechanics and agility that it takes to master these games and tricks is another way to tease out novel sports stories. The point here, of course, is not to turn these ideas into story suggestions. Not necessarily. No, the point is to recognize the connection between what you know and what you might turn into stories.

Some of us had semi-successful prep careers in sports we may have abandoned or only participated in recreationally but continue to follow. Use that interest and still-burning passion to promote yourself to editors at publications—even big-name publications—that may devote little space to the sport.

When writer William Carey was an intern at SI.com, the *Sports Illustrated* website, he knew he had little chance of writing features about any of the big sports the magazine covers. But Carey, a distance runner in high school, felt he had a decent shot at convincing the editors to let him write about cross-country track at the prep level if he found a feature-worthy story. He found one in the form of Lukas Verzbicas, a high school cross-country star from Carey's home state of Illinois who blazed trails and busted records throughout his brief prep career (he graduated from high school in three years). Verzbicas, a native of Lithuania, was a true cross-country phenom. He broke the national high school record in the 5,000 meters twice, besting himself the second time. And he won five national running titles in a three-month sweep.

But what set Verzbicas' story apart were two compelling elements: first was his quest to become only the fourth high schooler in history to break the four-minute mark in the mile. Second was his flirtation with a somewhat different event—the triathlon. The fact that a distance running prodigy like Verzbicas would risk injury and lose focus to concentrate on a different event seemed like heresy to the elders of the elite running world. The tension of both facets of Verzbicas' life and career, combined with his somewhat exotic heritage, made for a story even SI.com readers could engage with despite their indifference to the sport.

Carey's pitch of the idea and the fascinating aspects of Verzbicas' life, coupled with Carey's intimate knowledge of the sport, resulted in a richly detailed 5,000 word portrait of the runner, which debuted on the SI.com website on June 10, 2011.

"It helped that I was a runner both in the writing of the story and in the fact that I was allowed to do it in the first place," Carey recalls. "Because of my background, I could really convince the editors that this was an important story. They had never heard of Verzbicas. But I knew the kinds of things to highlight in his story that would help them see that it was worth giving an intern a shot at writing it."

Call upon your passions to help you develop ideas and stories, particularly in those sports the mainstream media often ignore.

Thinkstock / iStockphoto

▶ SPORTS AS A CULTURAL PHENOMENON

The world of sports touches upon many aspects of popular culture, from fashion to music. Athletes influence far more than the way we think about and view their sports. What they wear, what they say, what they listen to, eat, and drink not only reflect the zeitgeist, but can affect it all, as well, causing major shifts in the cultural landscape. (Consider the widespread acceptance of men with shaved heads à la Michael Jordan or the prevalence of tattoos in every sport.)

Wesley Morris, the former Pulitzer Prize-winning film critic for the *Boston Globe*, offers a prime example of how to look at sports through a different lens. In his "The Sportstorialist" columns for Grantland, the sports and pop culture website backed by ESPN, Morris comments on the sartorial hits and misses of athletes from around the sporting world. With biting humor and a sharp eye for the fashion forward and the fashion clueless among the sporting set, he offers a unique look at athletes' on and off-the-field mien. Take this tart assessment of tennis star Roger Federer's getup for the 2012 Wimbledon championships:

> The most self-consciously fashionable man in any sport—a man who, three years ago, wore a military jacket to his epic championship battle against Andy Roddick; who often has Anna Wintour seated in his friends box . . . that man was forced to dress stylelessly, like a mortal, like a junior programmer, like a mook . . .

Morris evokes both sports and fashion to great effect. Grantland describes itself as a site where pop culture and sports intersect, and Morris' column illustrates that connection perfectly. He demonstrates that sports writing can be as much about the accoutrements of the sports as it is about Xs and Os. Clearly, thinking outside of the box score can help you carve out a place for yourself in this subfield.

▶ SPORTS AS BUSINESS

Sports are more than mere games. They're also big business. Even "amateur" athletics is awash in money for coaches, equipment, travel, apparel, and time on the court, rink, or field. Who makes money in sports and how much money is spent is an under-reported and little understood aspect of the sporting world. That means it's also an aspect full of story possibilities.

Typically, when we think of the business of sports, we think of the fat contracts of big-name athletes or the gate receipts and ticket prices of major sporting events or the cost of a minute of advertising airtime during the Super Bowl. As interesting as those statistics are, there are many more areas of business related to sports and sporting events that go unnoticed or unremarked upon. For example, it is presumed that the big revenue college sports—men's basketball and football—are the cash cows that generate millions of dollars for their schools. And while that may be true in many high-profile Division 1 schools, further down the athletic food chain, the cost-benefit analysis of maintaining a first-class football or basketball program provides a murkier picture. An examination of the financing of these programs at state schools—where the records are public and accessible—would provide an interesting look at the assumptions surrounding college sports.

Similarly, the world of professional sports is supported by a coterie of businesses, from concession stands to parking lot companies whose fortunes can rise and fall with the success or failure of the team. Some of the businesses exist, in part, through contractual arrangements with municipalities and county governments; others are offshoots of the team. In any event, their financial relationships and business models remain a mystery to most fans. Stories that unpack and demystify these relationships make for excellent explanatory journalism, the kind that fills the pages of publications like *Businessweek* and *Crain's*. Of course, Dallas Mavericks owner Mark Cuban gets a lot of play in *Texas Monthly*, given his public persona and expansive business investments—both in and out of sports.

The bottom line is that sports reporting for magazines needn't be confined to the traditional venues or traditional stories. Thinking about "sports" in a broader light opens a wider range of reporting and publishing possibilities.

COMING ON STRONG

In the July 23, 2012 edition of *The New Yorker,* author Burkhard Bilger takes readers on a journey into the realm of international strongman competitions—the contests featuring beefy mesomorphs who haul, heave, and hurl any manner of heavy objects. The central character in Bilger's treatise ("The Strongest Man in the World") is Brian Shaw, a six-foot-eight-inch, four-hundred-and-thirty-pound gargantuan from Fort Lupton, Colorado who is one of the sport's most towering figures, both in terms of accomplishment and physical stature.

The story, which is both a profile of Shaw and the world of strongman competitions, essentially has two nutgrafs. The first one focuses on the profile of Shaw and establishes his credentials as the sport's leading light:

> He has since deadlifted more than a thousand pounds and pressed a nearly quarter-ton log above his head. He has harnessed himself to fire engines, Mack trucks, and a Lockhead C-130 transport plane and dragged them hundreds of yards. In 2011, he became the only man ever to win the sport's two premier competitions in the same year. He has become, by some measures, the strongest man in history.

In the second nut section, found just a few graphs later, Bilger explains the world in a bit more detail:

> Strongman events tend to be exaggerated versions of everyday tasks: heaving logs, carrying rocks, pushing carts. Awkwardness and unpredictability are part of the challenge. When I visited, Shaw was coaching his lifting buddies in the Super Yoke and the Duck Walk. The former harks back to the ancient strongman tradition of carrying a cow across your shoulders.
>
> Using Shaw's biography and an historical take on the developments that turned this one-time carnival act into a sport with an international cast of competitors, Bilger takes readers on a journey that introduces them to the characters and quirks that have made these events a programming staple on ESPN television. The "sporting" world is filled with such competitions, each with its own set of compelling figures who would make interesting reading—for fans and neophytes.

▶ THINK DIGITALLY

The digital sphere also opens all sorts of possibilities for would-be sports writers. While the websites of destiny publications like *ESPN* magazine and *Sports Illustrated* may be a stretch, a wealth of digital-only publications offer opportunities for writers looking to break into this realm. Virtually every team (college and pro) or sport (professional and amateur) has an online magazine or fanzine catering to its most ardent followers. While the quality of the writing and editing in these vehicles can vary wildly, contributing to these publications is a good way to develop a following and deepen your digital footprint, which is also a good way to attract the attention of editors higher up the food chain.

High in the digital sports pecking order are two websites backed by large organizations—Deadspin and Grantland.

Deadspin, founded in 2005 by prolific writer Will Leitch, is owned by New York-based Gawker Media, parent of a host of sites that cover a variety of interests, including Gawker (pop culture), Gizmodo (technology), Kotaku (video games), Jezebel (women's interests), Jalopnik (cars), and Lifehacker (tips for living in the digital world). Deadspin, like all sites in the Gawker universe, has a decidedly irreverent tone and has gained significance and a considerable following for its exposes of leading sports figures, most notably its revelation in 2013 that Notre Dame's All-American linebacker Manti Te'o's alleged girlfriend did not exist.

Deadspin's small full-time staff is augmented by a stable of regular contributors who blog and provide commentary and recaps of major sporting events and personalities of the day in addition to critiquing the performances of the leading figures and media in sports journalism. Writing and blogging for

Deadspin requires sports knowledge, of course, but also a willingness and ability to look beyond conventional wisdom or narrative tropes to explore ideas that others may be missing.

Grantland was founded by former ESPN.com writer Bill Simmons, one of the early phenoms of Internet sports writing who, before he was recruited to ESPN, built a considerable following with his website Bostonsportsguy. com. Moving to ESPN.com as a columnist in 2001, his reputation and readership continued to grow. In 2011, Simmons launched Grantland, named for a pioneering early twentieth century sportswriter revered for his lilting narrative style. Simmons wanted Grantland to elevate sports writing beyond traditional game coverage to include more analysis, social commentary, and long-form narrative.

As the example of Sportstatorialist columnist Wesley Morris indicates, Grantland writers bring sports knowledge and knowledge of intersecting domains to the editorial mix. That is evident in the roster of contributors, which includes not only sports writers and sports figures like Jalen Rose, but also people like political writer Charles P. Pierce, journalist and social critic Malcolm Gladwell, and writer/editor/essayist Dave Eggers.

Like the destination print publications, high-profile digital vehicles like Grantland and Deadspin may be a bit out of reach for novice writers, but searching these sites can help you think of new ways to approach your sports writing career and see new story possibilities that can land you in sports websites a tad further down market. They might even spark ideas for your own blog.

"I always recommend that people start their own site and then get better," notes Will Leitch, who left Deadspin to become a contributing editor at *New York* magazine in 2008, just three years after founding the sports blog. "Show it to ESPN Nation or Yahoo, or sportingnews.com. There are a lot of places. The one nice thing is that even though there are a lot more sports bloggers and sports writers than there used to be, there's always a hunger for more."

Without question, thinking broadly and creatively about what constitutes a sports story can expand your options and lead you to the destination publications to which many young sports writers aspire.

Chapter Fifteen
Review

ASSIGNMENT DESK

1. For this assignment, you first will identify an athlete on one of the college teams to profile.

2. Given the fact that most athletic divisions bar student athletes from granting interviews, this assignment has an added complication: you will write the profile without interviewing the main subject. Instead, you will rely on your background research, observations, and interviews with others.

3. Make a list of the three people (besides the athlete) whom you will interview.

4. Keep in mind that this assignment falls at the intersection of profile writing and sports. With the profile, you will want to identify a theme, some aspect of the person's life that can be threaded throughout your story. Something that tells us something about the person, and maybe ourselves. In that connection, think about sport as an area of writing that is larger than the subject matter. While you can focus on sport as such, consider, too, some human interest aspect of this story. Yes, it is about an athlete, but what else?

5. Write a piece based on your research, observations, and interviews that does not exceed 1,000 words.

▶ SUGGESTED READING

Halberstam, David; Stout, Gary. *The Best American Sports Writing of the Century.* Boston, MA: Mariner Books, 1999. The late historian, Halberstam, and prolific ghostwriter, Stout, collect a wide range of brilliant examples of great American sports writing, from Gay Talese's brilliant 1966 profile of Joe DiMaggio to a package of six pieces all devoted to Muhammad Ali.

Smith, Gary. *Beyond the Game: The Collected Sports Writing of Gary Smith.* New York: Grove Press, 2001. A collection of 15 profiles by one of America's most celebrated sports writers.

Wilstein, Steve. *Associated Press Sports Writing Handbook.* New York: McGraw-Hill, 2001. Veteran AP sportswriter Wilstein offers tips for aspiring sports writers of all stripes and all media.

▶ **WEB RESOURCES**

http://www.gq.com/sports/profiles/201109/michael-vick-gq-september-2011-interview "The Impossible, Inevitable redemption of Michael Vick," by Will Leitch. *GQ*, September 2011.

http://deadspin.com/5432171/the-best-best-american-sports-writing-of-the-decade Deadspin blogger Ben Cohen's musings on the best sports writing of the first decade of the twenty-first century.

http://sportsillustrated.cnn.com/vault/article/magazine/MAG1025474/index.htm Gary Smith's National Magazine Award-winning profile of George O'Leary, the Notre Dame football coach who was summarily ousted when the discrepancies on his resume were revealed.

http://deadspin.com/ Homepage of the scrappy and snarky website that is helping to change the sports media landscape.

http://www.grantland.com/ Homepage of the ESPN-backed sports and pop culture website that explores the sporting world in many dimensions.

16   Travel

▶ INTRODUCTION

Travel articles offer a great opportunity to break into print. There are quite a few potential outlets for stories. These must be balanced against the many writers trying to get in. Just as we have seen in other contexts, there are travel stories everywhere. Take a tour of the travel magazines, the in-flight publications, and even magazines with their own specialized distinctive non-travel focus, and you will discover how each magazine market considers travel and travel-related features that are consistent with the interests of the reader. And your ability to serve these interests just might be a matter of opening your eyes to seeing and your mind to thinking creatively. Even a short personal or professional trip can yield a good travel story idea. Attending an out-of-town wedding, or a family reunion, or a business meeting can create opportunities to discover new stories, or fresh angles to develop into new stories. Always be on the lookout for these travel story possibilities—whether on a weekend getaway, a luxurious resort vacation, or right there on the bus ride to work through historically significant, ethnically rich communities.

LEARNING OBJECTIVES

1. Consider the various types of travel stories.

2. Show how travel and travel-related stories exist everywhere.

3. Show how to develop the right approach to connect with readers.

4. Point out those things to document as you prepare the story.

▶ PUBLISHING POSSIBILITIES

Quite a few publishing possibilities exist in the area of travel writing, given the wide range of types of travel and travel-related markets that are available. In this category, we find everything from magazines that focus on particular

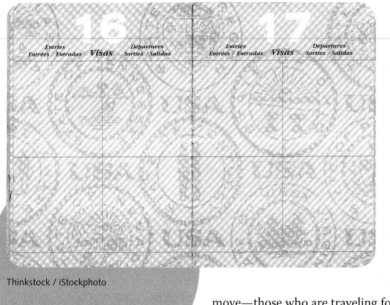

Thinkstock / iStockphoto

types of activities, like *Camping Today*, to those focusing on modes of transportation, like *AAA Going Places*, and those focusing on specific regions, the *Southern Traveler*, even specific places, like *Aruba Nights*, and specific activities and indulgences, like *Spa*. In-flight magazines, like *American Way* (American Airlines), also look at a broader range of stories that include personalities, trends, and new offerings that appeal to people on the move—those who are traveling for pleasure and business. But *destinations* are the bread-and butter of travel and travel-related magazines. Some in-flight magazines, like *Spirit* (Delta Airlines), tend to look at destinations along their routes. Fair enough. Given the international reach of the airline, there certainly are plenty of story possibilities in each destination. But the point is that destinations—from the popular places to the remote—are the core of this category.

Of course, the destination in travel writing is the travel magazine itself. *Travel & Leisure* and *Condé Nast Traveler* are the leaders in the field. They tend to rely on a proven and familiar stable of writers. As with any other market category, though, these magazines, too, will consider a fresh voice in the front-of-the-book sections. Proving worthy of this consideration is a matter of setting a writing strategy that takes you on this path. Many magazines include regular travel features. Newspapers also have special travel sections—particularly in the Sunday editions—that not only are written by freelancers, but often are written in a magazine style. Clearly, people who have a grounding in this style have a leg up in getting their work published. But there are points of entry for the emerging writer.

The explosion of Internet titles presents a world of opportunity for aspiring travel writers. Unlike the legacy print publications, the newer digital travel vehicles are often more willing to take a chance on novices. Some, like *Wild Junket* (http://www.wildjunket.com/) and *Vagabundo* magazine (http://www.vagabundomagazine.com/), are designed to exploit the rising interest in adventure travel and exotic destinations. Others, like *In Travel Magazine* (http://www.intravelmag.com/), take a more eclectic approach, featuring photography and articles from a wide variety of destinations (*In Travel's* interactive map covers the entire globe). Still others, like *Black Soul of America* (http://www.soulofamerica.com/), a culture and travel magazine aimed at African Americans, cater to a well-defined audience with a plethora of content offerings.

A good place for novice travel writers to start is Travelwriters.com, a network of travel writers, editors, and members of the public relations community. The site serves as a digital meeting place for writers, editors, PR agencies, tourism professionals, convention bureaus, and tour operators. Writers register to become members and upload their resumes and writing samples for access to news about press trips and opportunities to contribute to a variety of publications, both digital and print.

While digital outlets often do not pay as handsomely as many of the more established legacy publications, they provide great opportunities for travel-writing newbies to break into this genre. Make sure you are clear about the ethical standards maintained by some of the bigger players in this sphere, many of which require writers to disclose (or decline) any and all freebies they are offered. Make sure you understand the rules of the publication, whether digital or print, and be sure to play by those rules when you take on or pitch an assignment.

▶ GENERAL APPROACH

There are several approaches to travel writing. Broadly speaking, the majority of stories in this category fall into several areas: getting there (modes of travel), staying there (accommodation), and being there (all the sites, attractions, and activities of the destination). Additionally, there are thematic stories that are travel related largely because the stories are set in distant places. In most cases, writers also should be able to address the very practical aspects of travel, as they might do in service stories. There also are the stories (dealing with personalities and trends) that tend to appeal to the traveling class.

While many stories can have a relation to some travel interest, people tend to think of travel stories as focusing on a particular place people might want to visit. But even the focus on a particular destination still has certain requirements that have to be met. This means doing more than simply providing a sightseeing tour.

Requirements   Keep in mind that travel stories are meant to inform. Information is crucial. People turn to these pieces because they need information about places they want to visit. They turn to these pieces because they are looking for travel ideas. But they also are looking for information about the place—information that can heighten awareness and interest.

Descriptions of the locale and all its features will be most important in satisfying this need.

Additionally, readers look to the travel story as a resource (as well as a good read) in deciding to take a trip and in planning how to get there and what to do when they *are* there. Given this high level of reader reliance, the information must be accurate and up to date. In other words, it simply must be factual.

As we can observe in surveying some of the best examples of this type of writing, there is a service ("How to") component of the travel piece. In some stories, this can be more apparent, as with articles that identify travel-related problems (airport security screening, hotel bookings, local dining decisions). But accomplished writers of the destination story always will anticipate issues that travelers might have to sort, and will provide the solution. Thus, details are vitally important.

With all the other substantive requirements, we still must keep in mind what a number of editors and commentators have advised: that a good travel piece also must entertain. By entertain, we don't mean make you laugh. Not necessarily, although there are some that well could give you a giggle. That is fine if that kind of approach is suitable for the particular magazine. But a good read is a form of entertainment. So the point here is that these stories should read well, engage the reader, and be a source of satisfaction in the mere reading experience itself—let alone for the information and guidance provided. That is the entertainment value.

▶ FUN IN THE TOPICS

For the most part, general travel stories will be too simplistic for most magazines. For example, it is likely that a general travel story on the Bahamas already has been done. Practically everywhere! But a thematic piece is quite a different matter. The best casinos in the Bahamas. World-class dining in the Bahamas. Or, better yet, "how to avoid eating like a tourist in paradise" with an eye to the personal travel budget and personal interest in soaking up local culture all at once. Interesting front-of-the-book pieces we have seen include a survey of the best gourmet vegan restaurants across the country, or restaurants with the best "rock star" chefs around the world. The point is that you need to have a hook that will reel people in. *Chicago* is among the many city and regional magazines that have done travel pieces aimed at the busy lifestyle of a readership that often might need to figure out a weekend getaway more than an extensive trip to some faraway destination. It's easier to arrange a couple of days off than a couple of weeks. Area spas, bed-and-breakfast offerings, covered bridge tours, antique safaris, all are stories that can resonate with such a readership.

IN-FLIGHT: *AMERICAN WAY*

Typical of in-flight magazines, *American Way* (the official organ of American Airlines) provides its audience of passengers with a slice of culture, sites, and experiences in wide-ranging areas. While the articles engage reader attention, they also have the ancillary benefit for the airlines of stimulating travel interest and, you guessed it, more airline bookings. For the freelance writer, there are opportunities for story assignments that, as we have written, can arise right in your own backyard. Past front-of-the-book pieces have included "Golf Reservations" (Native American tribes moving from casinos to golf resorts); "Made-To-Order" (custom-made goods online for home delivery); "Where's the Beef?" (top-rated gourmet vegetarian restaurants around the country); and "A Little Slice of Zest" (looking at the new popularity of yellow, from $22 lemon shaving gel to a $175,000 yellow Lamborghini).

The magazine also serves as a showcase for narrative form, even while using celebrity stories as the point of departure. Take a look at the opening for this August 2007 cover story on actor Kyra Sedgwick's Costa Rica journey, written by Mark Seal.

> Kyra Sedgwick wanted something different, something exciting. She and her husband, Kevin Bacon, and their two teenage children, Travis and Sosie, were tired of lazy days on Caribbean beaches that seemingly all of Hollywood had discovered. "The decision was mine," she says. "I wanted to make us go on an adventure vacation."

The piece, based on an interview with the actor, takes us on an eco-friendly tour of the country that is both thematic and illustrative of the kinds of activities other interested travelers might experience.

▶ INFORMATION GATHERING

Because people rely on the information, the writer has to make sure to take all necessary steps to capture that information. As everyone advises, travel writing can require a tremendous amount of detail, which means that the travel writer must take a great deal of notes and collect any and all documents that might provide the information that will help bring a place to life in the presentation. Obviously, then, this task is not limited to facts. It also extends to impressions. As the editors of the 90 percent freelance-written *Aruba Nights* urge in *Writer's Market*, "Let the reader experience the story; utilize the senses; be descriptive; be specific." Whatever the nature of the travel story you are writing, it is vital to capture the essential quality of the locale—helping the reader experience the place with vivid visual descriptions, the visual portrait, the reflections on the things you might hear walking the streets, or even the smells that surround and seduce you. For example, on a trip to Puerto Vallarta, one of the authors stayed in the southern section of town, rather than at the resort hotels to the north. Each morning he awakened to the sounds of clanging pots and pans, the smells of meats and vegetables and corn tortillas being prepared. This experience awakened the flavor of the place and enabled him to develop a deeper appreciation of the customs and practices of the people who lived there. These are the kinds of experiences to share with readers. Remember: "Let the reader *experience* the story."

Additionally, as mentioned above, there are the service requirements, which create tremendous reporting demands on the writer. This can be a very practical kind of consideration, including information on hotel accommodations, quality, costs, and service, as well as dining recommendations and cultural offerings. General price comparisons are all important matters of interest to readers. Relative value also will be significant. Without question, this kind of reporting involves a great deal of note taking and "collecting" while on the ground. No matter how effectively you have done your background research before landing in some exotic place, there is much more to learn just being there.

It always is enlightening to learn how the locals see themselves. And this is true whether you are visiting Okracoke Island off the North Carolina coast, or Cape Verde Islands off the coast of Africa. There is a great deal of local culture, history, and lore that can be found in the brochures, books, magazines, and other published materials found on site. While there is no substitute for the writer's own impressions, it also is vital to obtain all the background information that might not be available anywhere else. Some writers, editors, and commentators even recommend a sort of restaurant carryout: the *menus* (if you can get away with them, that is, if you can get permission to get away with them). Good advice, in that, as has been suggested, these takeaways can provide a good note-taking aid, allowing you more time to focus on other things while you are in the country; things like the ambiance of a place that can help the reader "*experience*" it all much more deeply.

Having an eye for such detail is a key to the success of travel features. Here is where your narrative techniques can become quite useful—not only in engaging the reader, but also in having a satisfying writing experience. Often, you will find that travel writers can be very subjective, which makes sense, given the need to capture impressions of the places being presented. The travel narrative can be quite engaging, captivating reader attention, even if people have no intention of ever visiting the place being described. Here is where the entertainment value can be so important. People will read a travel story just to have the *experience* of being there. That is the task of the writer. The entertainment value. Again, there is reliance on immersion reporting by the writer. You really become absorbed in the environment. Spending time in the south end of, say, Puerto Vallarta—with the locals—in addition to the resort hotels to the north. That level of absorption shows in the presentation, which allows you to place readers right there in the scene. They smell the food in the early morning of Puerto Vallarta and, as a result, they experience the culture.

▶ THEMATIC STORIES

Some magazines build travel stories around a particular theme. As we mentioned, the city and regional magazines like the fresh, creative approaches to the great weekend getaway story. There also are seasonal pieces that can provide useful local and regional travel opportunities. Apple orchards in fall. Vineyards in summer. You must key the story to specific thematic requirements and make sure to place the emphasis on service—identifying a travel problem for the reader and resolving it by anticipating and answering the questions. Sometimes this works to great effect.

⏻ ARABIAN NIGHTS: *CONDÉ NAST TRAVELER*

Known for its sweeping narratives, *Condé Nast Traveler* writers engage readers in ways that provide entertaining reads, even if people are not at all planning to travel to far-flung places, as with the case of Susan Hack's August 2006 piece on travel to the Middle East. In this story, she develops a narrative that places us in scenes that are as vivid as they are contextual—demonstrating some of the political realities of the region that, at the time, was experiencing a significant rise in international travel.

"Arabian culture and tradition are synonymous with generosity, hospitality, and all-around warmth," gushes the brochure for the new Emirates Palace in Abu Dhabi. So I am vexed after driving across the desert to have sand-colored tanks turn me away. A machine gun-wielding soldier at the gate explains that the geniality is temporarily on hold because the rulers of Bahrain, Kuwait, Oman, Qater, Saudi Arabia, and the United Arab Emirates—emirs, kings and sultans all—have commandeered the place for their annual Gulf Cooperation Council meeting.

Hack goes on to describe the tremendous tourism development that had taken place in the region, while helping us experience the culture and sites on her own engaging tour.

▶ STRUCTURE

It is important to provide useful information; what people need and will want to read. First, there is the lead. Often the lead will provide some sort of anecdote to set the stage and engage the reader in the story. The lead also must tell what this story is all about. It should provide some sense of the setting of the place. Right up front, we need to know where we are.

The main body of the story can progress in a couple of ways, depending on the narrative arc you want to set. In a sense, as some observers have

Thinkstock / Jupiterimages

advised, you can approach the storytelling as something of a tour guide, moving through a planned itinerary organized either by time or by location. In using a time sequence to move the reader through the story, it has been suggested that the writer can set up the "tour" as measured by days or weeks—moving, in effect, from moment to moment. In organizing by location, the writer will craft a narrative that will move the reader from place to place. This approach is something like the work of a Club Med GO—a Gracious Organizer, or activities planner. You—the writer—are the planner, and you map out your plan for the reader to follow.

The challenge is to do all this activities "planning" while writing descriptions that are so vivid as to place the reader in the story, setting scenes, revealing remarkable discoveries. And you carry us along with you. Provide glimpses of history and culture of the place. As one editor has commented: "I'm an archeologist. I'm on a dig."

This, again, is where the entertainment element comes in. Even if the reader never makes the trip, she should feel as if she's been there just because she's read your piece. At the same time, she will long to be there for the same reason. There is something of a dichotomy of the travel writer: a split focus. On the one hand, it has been advised by travel editors and writing experts that you must think like a traveler—a tourist, if you will. On the other hand, they say, you must think like a travel agent. If you think like a traveler, you will see this new world with fresh eyes. With the wonder and excitement of a visitor seeing it all for the first time. And that will show in the energy and enthusiasm of your presentation in a way that connects with readers who can identify with that first time experience. That is the first part. But now, the second part. If you think like a travel agent, then you will not be seeing things for the first time. You will have enough background, enough experience to hit the ground running. You will be well informed. You will know what to look for. It is a balance of experience that informs the story, and excitement that makes one want to have the experience—all over again. So, the combination of techniques is a winning one, connecting with the reader as a "fellow traveler" amazed and excited about the experience; guide the reader as an expert knowledgeable about how to get the most enjoyment and value out of the experience.

▶ TRAVEL AT HOME

One key in travel writing is a sense of enterprise. You don't have to go to exotic places to write appealing and marketable travel stories. As we have written in other contexts, often the greatest opportunities are those close to home. What are the things you see around you that might inspire someone else from outside your community to want to plan a trip there? What are the things within a day's drive that might be of interest right here in this area to people who live in your town, but have not thought about venturing out simply because no one ever showed them how? Antiques, auction houses; museums; outlets; historic sites; parks; rivers; lakes; covered bridges; events; balloon races; Civil War or Revolutionary War battle reenactments; inns; bed and breakfast spots. Your story could be a single point of interest; it might be a collection of activities and sites.

▶ TRAVEL-RELATED STORIES

Here we consider stories that fall into a travel context, but are not necessarily focusing on aspects of a particular destination. These are enterprise stories that are travel related. A number of magazines will look at such issues from time to time. Which airlines are safest? Which carriers have the best on-time records; passenger services? Where is the best place to sit on the plane (or the place where you are likely to get off quickly, or have the most legroom)? What about the treatment of luggage, and additional charges? What is the latest development with respect to airport safety? What about local hotel concerns? A *Chicago* magazine special report "Surviving O'Hare: How to get the most out of the airport you can't avoid" combined enterprise reporting with a service approach to provide a guide that was of great interest to the magazine's high-flying readership.

AN AIRPORT SURVIVAL GUIDE

Chicago magazine often features travel and travel-related stories for its readership. Sometimes these pieces can be in the form of special packages on weekend getaway ideas and points of interest within a short drive of the city. Sometimes, there are the reports that dig even deeper into issues of interest.

In the February 2001 *Chicago* magazine feature "Surviving O'Hare," Robert Kurson takes us on a journey that is both service-oriented and something of an expose. Note how he opens the piece with a summary lead that sets up the value of the airport, as well as its cultural connection to fast-paced Chicago travelers—also known as the *Chicago* magazine demographic.

> If Chicagoans can be said to share a single experience, that experience is O'Hare International Airport. O'Hare winds its way into our most meaningful days and times, a concrete constant while Chicago lives hurtle forward. When a child is born, a business deal is sealed, a parent dies, O'Hare often figures into the day, a passageway for people to important places at important times. Chicago escapes itself through O'Hare—and returns the same way.

He goes on to show why most busy travelers hardly have time to assess the effectiveness and quality of the service provided at O'Hare, before setting up the format of the unique presentation in this article.

> You can know this O'Hare, it turns out, without changing your routine or spending an extra minute at the airport. You just need to know where to look.

The writer then outlines the approach the story will take, walking the reader through a typical trip to and through the airport, pointing out all those familiar things the reader will see for the first time. For the *Chicago* magazine audience, such a piece becomes a compelling must-read.

▶ PERSONAL COMMITMENT

Travel writing is something of a passion for people who get published frequently. While a scan of the *Writer's Market* guidelines will show that most of the consumer magazines listed under "Travel, Camping & Trailer" do not pay exceptionally well, there can be great opportunities for experienced writers to see exciting places and for enterprising new writers to develop a portfolio. Travel budgets at most magazines typically might be limited to the experienced writers with whom editors have worked. But there also can be very satisfying break-in possibilities for emerging writers who are enterprising enough to see travel and travel-related stories all around them. As we mentioned earlier, many stories in this area can emerge during trips that are planned for other purposes. If there is any need for preliminary fact gathering, though, it is likely that you will pay your own way.

ON THE *VERGE*: MAKING YOUR STUDY ABROAD EXPERIENCE COUNT

Among the many publications that either focus on travel or include travel as part of the regular lineup of articles that readers are most interested in reading, many are freelance friendly. But there is one that also is welcoming to young emerging writers. *Verge* magazine (60 percent freelance writer) is aimed at a younger demographic (ages 17–40) comprised of people who are committed to making a difference in their studies and general travels abroad. It is the "magazine for people who travel with purpose," the editors insist in *Writer's Market*. "It explores ways to get out and see the world by volunteering, working and studying overseas."

Thus, the editors are interested not just in stories that are based on your own personal experience in areas of international volunteerism (whether in the context of internships, study abroad, or other opportunities), but also stories that profile people ("doing something different and making a difference doing it"), or that focus on a special program having impact, or even local cultures in disparate areas.

Verge magazine pays on publication. According to the editorial note: "Editorial content is intended to inform and motivate the reader by profiling unique individuals and experiences that are timely and socially relevant. We look for articles that are issue driven and combine an engaging and well-told story with nuts and bolts how-to information."

Sometimes there are **fam trips** that can be made available to writers. These "familiarity" trips—or fam trips—often are provided free of charge by travel ministries and local tourism boards and bureaus for travel agents who then can urge more travel by clients to certain locations.

FAM TRIPS: Free travel provided by travel ministries to travel agents and sometimes travel writers to encourage promotion of tourism.

But writers, too, have been known to take advantage of these **junkets**. Of course, this raises an ethical question. Do you accept such a freebie? No strings attached. While usually there is no requirement that you write a positive piece, the *expectation* still might be overwhelming. In January 2010, Gawker Media writer Foster Kamer wrote about issues arising in connection with two freelance writers for *The New York Times* regarding questions of whether travel was being provided by sources. The *Times*' rule on junkets is pretty clear: "In connection with their work for us, freelancers will not accept free transportation, free lodging, gifts, junkets, commissions or assignments from current or potential news sources." Best to check with your editor. Some publications might not even ask. But a number of publications are incorporating ethical clauses in their writers' contracts (see Chapter 20). You have to certify that you have not accepted anything of value from a source, and that "fam" trip just might be interpreted as a thing of value.

JUNKET: Free travel provided for a specific purpose, such as an event.

WRITER'S WORKSHOP

Here are some suggestions for you to apply some of the central points of this chapter as you begin to develop travel article ideas.

As with everything else we have discussed in terms of content, think of travel stories as broadly as the planet, and as narrowly as the market you are targeting. The subject certainly will be destination oriented, but then what? Consider points of interest. Consider how to take advantage of those points of interest. Think about the service component of travel pieces. Keep a list of prices, admissions fees, operating times of certain events, travel time on the ground between Point A and Point B. Think of yourself as a tour guide. How would you plan the itinerary, day by day? This means that, if you travel to the places you want to feature, you will have to take copious notes. Document all of the pertinent facts listed above. But also take notes of your impressions, of the culture of the place. Don't overlook the narrative possibilities. What can you note that will place the readers right there in the scenes with you?

Chapter Sixteen
Review

ASSIGNMENT DESK

1. Consider your hometown as a travel destination. Make a list of three story ideas with this objective in mind. How would you pitch these three story ideas? Will the focus be on the destination? If so, will you point to the locale as a good idea for a weekend getaway? What would the attractions be for someone to visit? Will you instead consider some historical or cultural point of connection as your theme? Is there something about the people or the history that can serve as the point of departure for a publishable article? Is there a significant site or attraction that might be of interest? In that regard, is there some kind of compelling narrative possibility? Is there something about your locale that might be appealing as a weekend getaway? What are the local attractions? Is there historical significance? What are the outlets for entertainment and dining?

2. Review your list of these three story ideas and now consider the magazines that are likely to be interested in the stories. What will the editors expect in terms of specific focus and elements of the story? Will this be a feature or will it be a front-of-the-book piece? How do you shape the theme to address specific audience demographics and psychographics? How do you sharpen that theme by way of your proposed title?

3. Now compose a query pitching one of the stories and showing why it is of interest to the target market. Be sure to work in aspects of the first two assignments as you make your best case for publication of your piece.

4. Even though you have thought very carefully about the first market and the tie-in of your story idea to that audience, consider how you might adjust the angle for a more specialized audience. If your initial story pitch was aimed at a travel magazine, then think about pitching to a magazine with a different focus, but one that will publish travel from time to time, aimed at its specific audience needs.

▶ KEY TERMS

- fam (familiarity) trip
- junket

▶ SUGGESTED READING

George, Don. *Lonely Planet's Guide to Travel Writing*. New York: Lonely Planet, 2009. A how-to guide that provides new travel writers with such practical tips on everything from how to conduct pre-trip and on-the-road research to effective interviewing techniques.

Turner, James. *The Writer's Handbook Guide to Travel Writing*. London: Pan Macmillan, 2004. A guide that offers practical advice to budding travel writers; also includes interviews with leading writers and editors.

▶ WEB RESOURCES

http://www.travelwriters.com/ Website of a member organization that connects travel writers and editors.

http://www.wildjunket.com/ Website focusing on adventure travel and exotic destinations.

http://www.vagabundomagazine.com/ A digital and print magazine that features a wide range of destinations.

http://www.soulofamerica.com/ A culture and travel website that features destinations and events aimed at an African-American audience.

http://gawker.com/5439277/the-new-york-times-junket-ethics-firings-futile-embarrassing *The New York Times'* "Junket Ethics Firings: Futile, Embarrassing," by Foster Kamer. Gawker Media, January 3, 2010.

17   Essay

▶ INTRODUCTION

In this chapter, we will discuss the various forms of essays, including the critical arts reviews, socio-political opinion columns, and personal reflections. We will present approaches to considering solid critical essays, including book, film, and music reviews. We also will explore the areas of social, political, and economic commentary in ways that make this form accessible.

Finally, we will show the power of the personal essay to make observations about rather routine occurrences, and then draw **inferences** that have much larger consequence. In this connection, we will include examinations of structure—moving from an anecdote or the observation of something relatively mundane into discussion, context, and finally a conclusion that ultimately will connect with the reader in ways that are familiar and fresh all at once. When done well, the result is elevating for the reader. We reach that final "A" in our AHA checklist from Chapter 10, for there is an awakening, a sense of attainment that can be quite satisfying to the reader. It also can be most rewarding to you in tuning your writer's voice—clearly transferable to other areas of magazine writing. And that is the point here. You will take your magazine writing ability to the next level.

LEARNING OBJECTIVES

1. Have an understanding of the magazine essay and its several forms.

2. Have an understanding of the impact of essay writing among readers.

3. Begin to see topics for your own personal essays in everyday occurrences.

4. Begin to develop an approach to writing a personal essay.

5. Sharpen your own writer's voice for all your magazine article writing.

INFERENCE: A reasoned and logical conclusion derived from an observation, occurrence, or idea.

▶ KNOWING IT WHEN YOU SEE IT

Essay writing is among the more challenging forms of non-fiction. It can demand a great deal from the writer in terms of writing skills and even research, although some essays can be written without much research at all. That is because, unlike other forms of writing—even other forms of magazine writing that require a great deal of enterprise in conceptualizing—the essay often is the most original form of magazine writing. Even though it can be based on research and interviews, it requires that the writer step outside such constraints to express a point of view. The accomplished essayist must be able to observe, contextualize, and draw inferences to make sense of logical, thoughtful connections to the observations in order to give readers fresh, new insight into a topic—whether that topic is a concert performance, semi-final basketball game, or a gaggle of geese flying in the wrong direction as the seasons change. As we will see, some of the best essays have used points of departure from everyday occurrences in order to weave captivating discussions of larger issues—political, economic, social, and on.

While research and quoting sources is helpful in virtually every form of writing, as stated above, neither is imperative in order to write a great essay. Indeed, the essay can be written without ever citing a source, though the bedrock journalistic principles of accuracy and truthfulness still apply. Even opinion must have a rational basis in fact. The hallmark of the good essay is the personal reflection. "If examining everyday life is your goal, every place is your laboratory," Walt Harrington writes in *Intimate Journalism*. That observation is as important to consider in essay writing as it is in literary non-fiction. The key is to be able to recognize a good essay topic when you see it. Once you do, you will come to see subjects that are worthy of your writing attention everywhere you look. The goal is to take the observation, the inferences it spawns and the essay inspired by it all, and to find for it a home. On the pages of a magazine. In the memories of the readers.

▶ ESSAY TYPES

While essays can take on a number of forms—including fictionalized narratives used to illustrate a point—it is generally accepted that magazine essays fall into three broad categories: there are critical arts reviews; opinion pieces, focusing on political, economic, or social issues; and personal reflections. Clearly, there are no bright lines separating creative work among these categories, as there often can be political dimensions of critical reviews or personal essays, and reviewers and commentators often are injecting their essays with personal observations and opinion. But it is helpful to start in this area thinking about these major categories and what usually is expected by editors and readers.

Critical arts reviews   This form of essay already should be familiar, as a result of your exposure to newspaper reviews or from watching televised reviews of concerts, arts releases, sports events, and cultural openings. The critical review can focus on a new film, a television show, the opening of a play, the release of a book, a new musical recording or concert tour, a sports development or performance, even a new restaurant or nightclub opening. But, while the critical review in a magazine can take up any of this subject matter, its approach will be different from newspaper or television coverage, owing to the unique nature of magazines, their available space, and, of course, the expectations of a more demanding and highly targeted readership.

So, the critical review in a magazine provides the writer with the opportunity—if not the obligation—to do more than a newspaper review that tends to focus strictly on appraising the event, the book, film, or CD release. Instead, the magazine essay will use that event—providing a review of the book, film, or CD—as a mere starting point for something much larger. The critical essay—or review—in a magazine will provide a wide-ranging discussion of an entire context for understanding the particular work. It illuminates the field of work by critiquing the particular piece under consideration. An example of this might be a critique of a murder mystery, a novel. The essay will include a lengthy discussion of other relevant murder mysteries in that specific area. It also might include a discussion of the origins of

Thinkstock / iStockphoto

the genre. Or even a discussion of the merits of the genre. Take, for example, *New Yorker* film critic David Denby's review of Australian filmmaker Baz Luhrmann's 3D version of the F. Scott Fitzgerald novel *The Great Gatsby.* Denby begins his essay not with his impressions of the film, but with a biographical sketch of Fitzgerald:

> The tale of Fitzgerald's woeful stumbles—no great writer ever hit the skids so publicly—is suffused with varying shades of irony, both forlorn and triumphal. Fitzgerald was an alcoholic, and no doubt his health would have declined, whatever the commercial fate of his masterpiece.

Denby places the film in context by considering the genesis of its source material. Thus, the critical essay, the review, will evaluate a particular work (writing style, clarity). But it also will critique the substance of the work in a context that gives much more meaning to the review. Having set the reader up with his short portrait of Fitzgerald, Denby seamlessly moves into his examination (in this case an evisceration) of Luhrmann's cinematic treatment:

> Lurhmann whips Fitzgerald's sordid debauch into a saturnalia—garish and violent, with tangled blasts of music, not all of it redolent of the Jazz Age. (Jay-Z is responsible for the soundtrack; Beyoncé and André 3000 sing.)

Often the critical review in magazines will go further still. In many ways, the late Pauline Kael set the standard in this area with her wildly influential film critiques published in *The New Yorker*, and other magazines. But the award-winning Kael at times would use the film review as the platform for commentary on a larger social issue (see box). Her work influenced a whole generation of film critics-essayists—and even screenwriters and directors.

PAULINE KAEL AND FILM VIOLENCE

The late Pauline Kael was widely known for her film critiques published in *The New Yorker* and, earlier in her career, in such magazines as *McCall's* and *The New Republic*. A great influence on other film critics (including the late Roger Ebert) and on the entire field of film criticism, Kael often would use the film review as the platform for commentary on a larger social issue. In effect, as Kael shows in her commentary on the effects of film violence in the excerpts below from "Stanley Strangelove," January 1, 1972 edition of *The New Yorker*, the accomplished critical essayist recognizes that art certainly can imitate life, but even more significantly, it also can reflect and illustrate certain compelling aspects of life. In the end, as Kael suggests, life just might imitate art. Note how she sets up the piece, zeroing in right away on the seductive quality of the violence presented in the film.

> Literal-minded in its sex and brutality, Teutonic in its humor, Stanley Kubrick's "A Clockwork Orange" might be the work of a strict and exacting German

professor who set out to make a porno-violent sci-fi Comedy. Is there anything sadder—and ultimately more repellent—than a clean-minded pornographer?

Kael then goes on to nail the theme of her piece, which is one part critical review of the film and several parts critical assessment of the cultural impact of film violence.

> The trick of making the attacked less human than their attackers, so you feel no sympathy for them, is, I think, symptomatic of a new attitude in movies. This attitude says there's no moral difference.

Even while she is assessing a quality of the picture negatively, she also balances her review by pointing to skillfully executed elements of it in a way that continues to punch the theme of the critique.

> This picture plays with violence in an intellectually seductive way.

Finally, Kael concludes by using "A Clockwork Orange" to illustrate what she sees as a disturbing trend in filmmaking that reflected a shift away from earlier rationales for using violence. She also once again punches up the impact on viewing audiences.

> practically no one raises the issue of the possible cumulative effects of movie brutality. Yet surely, when night after night atrocities are served up to us as entertainment, it's worth some anxiety. We become clockwork oranges if we accept all this pop culture without asking what's in it. How can people go on talking about the dazzling brilliance of movies and not notice that the directors are sucking up to the thugs in the audience?

In addition to arts coverage, the critical review also can focus on entertainment venues, such as restaurants, clubs, and museums. New openings or new offerings can serve as the point of departure for a critical review that will compare, contrast, and critique service and preparation, as well as ambiance (restaurants); drink specialties, prices, and clientele (clubs); and story framing (museums). As with all critical reviews in magazines, context still is important. For example, restaurant reviews will tend to be thematic, presented in the context of similar fare, or focusing on the work of noted chefs, or fixing on appeal among cultural sub-groups. Club reviews will look at the larger context of nightlife in specific settings. Museum exhibitions can go into greater detail about the underlying story that is presented in, say, an historical presentation on Ghengis Khan and the implications in a contemporary period of warfare, or an artistic presentation on the intersecting influences of Impressionist painters Paul Gauguin and Vincent van Gogh, when they briefly shared a house and studio in the south of France in 1888. Or, as with the Art Institute of Chicago, an exhibition that tells the "story" of Picasso's Chicago connection, which was significant. "Picasso and Chicago," Thomas Connors wrote in *Michigan Avenue* magazine, celebrates "the city's link to a man who reshaped the way we see art."

Clearly, as an essay form, the critical review is full of rich storytelling opportunity, even while it creates the chance for the expression of point of view, and even harsh critique.

Opinion   The magazine essay long has been used for socio-political commentary. Indeed, entire magazines, such as *The Nation* and *National Review*, are devoted to perspective. Recently, *Newsweek* and *TIME*—recognizing the difficulty of publishing news magazines on a weekly cycle in an age of virtually instant news coverage and development online—retooled in order to provide more commentary on the world's events (before *Newsweek* made another transition, abandoning its print edition and publishing only online).

Similar to the critical review of arts and entertainment, the opinion piece often will take a specific issue and discuss it in a context that provides much greater meaning for readers. This context usually is provided by a discussion of the historical development and contemporary significance of the issue, and a comparison or contrast with other similar issues. Also, similar to what we will discuss in shaping a personal essay, the opinion piece can take an apparently small occurrence (by way of an anecdotal observation) and draw much larger implications. Whatever the approach taken by the writer, the opinion piece will be thematic, setting out some kind of a thesis statement, weaving in the context (historical or contemporary comparisons and contrasts), and reaching a conclusion that ties together the central points of the theme. The point of commentary, though, is to have impact on consciousness and public opinion. When commentator Fareed Zakaria wrote about the controversy surrounding a proposed Islamic community center in lower Manhattan (see box), his objective was to reframe the volatile issue in order to positively affect American attitudes toward Islam. But personal reflective essays also can have a profound effect, even arising from similar sets of circumstances.

FAREED ZAKARIA, "BUILD THE GROUND ZERO MOSQUE," *THE DAILY BEAST*

Fareed Zakaria was named by *Esquire* in 1999 as "one of the 21 most important people of the 21st Century." He hosts an international affairs program on CNN, "Fareed Zakaria GPS," and is editor of *Newsweek International*, responsible for all of the magazine's overseas coverage. He also writes a regular column for *Newsweek*, which appears in *Newsweek International* and periodically in the *Washington Post*. He is an award-winning writer and author of several books on public policy, including *The New York Times* bestseller *The Future of Freedom*. As you can see in the following setup of this commentary, carried by the online publication *The Daily Beast*, Zakaria takes the emotionally charged issue of the proposed Islamic community center planned for a site near the footprint of the former World Trade Center, and carries readers to a new understanding of the consistency of support for the community center and global U.S. policy. He appeals to reason, rather than emotion, setting up his essay as an argument for a new strategy aimed at discrediting radical interpretations of Islam, rather than attacking the religion more generally.

> Victory in the war on terror will be won when a moderate, mainstream version of Islam—one that is compatible with modernity—fully triumphs over the worldview of Osama bin Laden.

The effect of Zakaria's piece, which is key to the success of well-crafted sociopolitical essays, is to reach the reader with common points of connection that can be used to transport her to new awareness.

Reflection

In a way, the term "reflection" is both descriptive and a bit misleading all at once. As the name suggests, this is a form of writing that provides an opportunity for the writer to reflect on something—typically an event or an experience of the writer or the writer's observation of something. Given its nature as a personal reflection, it can be just that—personal. But even while it also will tend to reflect a common theme in public awareness (if done well), it also can spark some aspect of that awareness in the inferences that are drawn.

As stated, this essay form springs from an event, experience, or an observation that can lead to deep reflection that is tied together thematically. Resolving a family crisis. Overcoming a debilitating accident. Sharing the joy of a child's first piano recital, or Little League no-hitter. But, if done well, this reflection piece can have deep meaning for an entire audience of readers. That is because the writer of the personal reflection starts off with an **inciting event**—anything that might be readily observable or experienced by anyone in the audience of readers.

INCITING EVENT: In storytelling, that event that sets everything else in motion.

Then the writer begins to draw inferences from that event, experience, or observation, often using the best forms of **analogy**, to point to some larger significance, making a point that might not have been apparent at the beginning of the piece, but is recognizable to the audience in something of an "aha" moment. Watching two groups of racially distinct teenagers provided Pulitzer Prize-winning writer Michiko Kakutani with the basis for her highly regarded *New York Times Magazine* essay, "Common Threads" (see box).

ANALOGY: A comparison drawn between two things that might appear dissimilar, transferring the meaning of one to the other.

MICHIKO KAKUTANI, "COMMON THREADS," *THE NEW YORK TIMES MAGAZINE*

Pulitzer Prize-winning writer Michiko Kakutani has been considered one of the leading literary critics in the country. Both respected and reviled, she was noted by the online *Slate* magazine for her "estimable intelligence," even while the magazine referred to the "smoke rising from the page" whenever her name is mentioned in print (a clear reference to the unfavorable reaction to her unfavorable book reviews).

In a February 16, 1997 *New York Times Magazine* essay, Kakutani wrote about something that caught her attention outside the Museum of Natural History in New York City: the fact that all of the young people—homeboys and prepsters alike—milling about were dressed in an identical uniform of designer wear.

The irony here, as she points out, is that the Ivy League appearance is being sported by an urban contemporary crowd—a cultural expression, which is as much about longing as it is about artistic commentary. It is "an earnest yearning after the American dream," she writes. On the other side, hip-hop in its sanitized pop radio format—as opposed to the more threatening "gangsta" rap—provided white suburban kids a point of connection to authenticity and everything—including the clothes—of urban life. The point she makes is a compelling one: that the two polar opposites have met somewhere in the middle as a result of marketing—pop culture, lifestyle, and, yes, the look.

At an age when nearly all kids feel powerless, the class war becomes a kind of looking-glass world. Rich white kids, guilty about their privileged lives and fearful of being wimps, equate power—and authenticity—with the street-smart, badman swagger of the homeboys, while poor black kids, facing dead-end jobs and unemployment lines, equate power with money and bourgeois comforts. Everyone looks in the mirror and covets what the other side has—or, at least, the clothes the other side is wearing.

Below, James Fallows turns a sexist term on its head to make a point about gendered attitudes and behavior in "Throwing Like a Girl" (see box). Writer Audrey Petty used the childhood memory of her family's cultural connection to food to write a moving essay, "Late Night Chitlins With Momma," for *Saveur*, a highly regarded piece that serves to deconstruct racial stereotype (see box). And Pulitzer Prize winner Anna Quindlen uses the same World Trade Center attack (as Fareed Zakaria discussed in his political commentary) as the point of departure for a different kind of essay—one with a more personal, rather than political theme—in "A Nation's Fear of Flying" for *Newsweek* (see box).

JAMES FALLOWS ON "THROWING LIKE A GIRL," *THE ATLANTIC*

In his much-celebrated August 1996 *Atlantic* essay, "Throwing Like a Girl," writer James Fallows uses observations of opening pitches thrown out by former President Bill Clinton and former First Lady Hillary Clinton as his point of departure. But Fallows, who served as a speechwriter for former President Jimmy Carter and editor of *U.S. News and World Report*, uses these observations to draw inferences about the shaping of gender roles in American society. Notice here how Fallows, a five-time National Magazine Award finalist, describes the opening pitches in great detail so as to create an everyday visual for the readers, but then he does something much more.

MOST people remember the 1994 baseball season for the way it ended—with a strike rather than a World Series. I keep thinking about the way it began. On opening day, April 4, Bill Clinton went to Cleveland and, like many Presidents before him, threw out a ceremonial first pitch. That same day Hillary Rodham Clinton went to Chicago and, like no First Lady before her, also threw out a first ball, at a Cubs game in Wrigley Field.

Fallows proceeds through a narrative description of the first pitches by the president and first lady through a comparison of the photo images of each that were published the following day. His observations at first appear to be provocative as they key in on the form of Bill Clinton as compared with the apparent awkward stance of Hillary Clinton—a pose that has been used as part of the sexist lexicon that has characterized gendered difference. He then turns the whole piece on its head, by showing the reader the deeper social meaning of it all.

The phrase "throwing like a girl" has become an embattled and offensive one. Feminists smart at its implication that to do something "like a girl" is to do it the wrong way. Recently, on the heels of the O. J. Simpson case, a book appeared in which the phrase was used to help explain why male athletes, especially football players, were involved in so many assaults against women. Having been trained (like most American boys) to dread the accusation of doing anything "like a girl," athletes were said to grow into the assumption that women were valueless, and natural prey.

Clearly, Fallows intends to grab attention right away with the use of a highly offensive reference. He then takes the reader on a journey of revelation in an essay that reveals itself as an incisive comment about the way we socialize our children—the subtle and not so subtle ways we teach them to be "boys" and "girls" and then, by implication, how we attach meaning to these labels.

AUDREY PETTY AND THE LATE NIGHT FAMILY CONNECTIONS

Audrey Petty is an associate professor of English at the University of Illinois at Urbana-Champaign and former head of the Creative Writing Program there. She saw an opportunity in producing this essay, which was published in the December 2005 issue of *Saveur* magazine, and in *Best Food Writing*, 2006. It was a chance to explore African American folkways through something so familiar to the culture—food, and to be more precise, *chitlins*. Petty, a self-described "first generation Northerner," said recently that this work also was "an opportunity to develop a different relationship with my parents," both from the South, who figure prominently in the reminiscence. There also was the chance to show the profound cultural unifier that exists in food and can make chitlins a lot more than merely a late night event.

We usually shared them in the wintertime, Momma and I. Negotiations regarding their appearance began weeks in advance, around the dinner table. My mother would tell my father she was considering fixing chitlins for the holidays. My father would groan, twist his mouth, and protest in vain.

With that, Petty establishes the ritual that has been common in some African American households, but also begins to lay the groundwork for the family relationship that is solidified by the relationship with food. That point of departure allows her to carry the reader even further into a presentation that illustrates quite a bit about the African American experience.

> I once believed that my father didn't like chitlins because of how they smelled. That was his core complaint, but as I got older, I began to contemplate my father's childhood and I formulated a more complex theory. My father had eight brothers and sisters; his father was a miner and a preacher and his mother was a domestic worker (a fact I discovered only this year). I assumed that Daddy rejected chitlins as suffering food—a struggling people's inheritance.

As seen in the best of essay writing, Petty punches her family theme in the end, by relating back to the bonding between she and her mother, established in the beginning of her piece.

> She doesn't have to ask me twice; we have a date for chitlins this coming December.

ANNA QUINDLEN, "A NATION'S FEAR OF FLYING," *NEWSWEEK*

Pulitzer prize-winning writer Anna Quindlen is known for her inspiring empathetic personal essays. She began the trend-setting technique, dubbed by critic Lee Seigel derisively as the "Quindlen Effect," with her "Public Private" column in *The New York Times*. She carried it over to her bi-weekly essay for *Newsweek* magazine, where "A Nation's Fear of Flying" was published on August 20, 2006. True to the form of the reflective essay, Quindlen starts this piece off with an observation that connects with readers right away, and then begins weaving in inferences that will set up her point.

> The citizens of New York, who live in the spiritual home of the skyscraper, now fear the office tower and the high-rise. In San Francisco they build structures that are earthquakeproof. But there's no structural steel, no reinforced foundation, that can ward off fear.

In the end, she circles back to the opening reference to the skyscraper, once a symbol of ingenuity and power, transformed by fear into something entirely different.

> Metal detectors, random searches. No toothpaste in that carry-on. Safety is a useful illusion, as modern—and as vulnerable—as a skyscraper.

An important consideration with the reflective essay is that the writer takes the reader on a journey from something familiar to the reader, something the reader could have observed for herself, to a conclusion that can resonate with the reader in a familiar way, but a way the reader still needed the writer to identify for her.

Note how Tom Junod sets up his celebrated September 2003 *Esquire* magazine essay "The Falling Man" focusing on the publication of one disturbing photograph as the platform for a discussion of a compelling aspect of the 9/11 attacks on New York's World Trade Center.

> In the picture, he departs from this earth like an arrow. Although he has not chosen his fate, he appears to have, in his last instants of life, embraced it . . .

Junod's description is vivid, pointing to details that heighten the tragic irony of a moment that is at once horrific and illustrative.

> There is something almost rebellious in the man's posture, as though once faced with the inevitability of death, he decided to get on with it; as though he were a missile, a spear, bent on attaining his own end.

Junod goes on to weave together such unifying themes as grieving and human dignity in death, along with journalism ethics in the search for the "falling man's" identity, finally concluding:

> At fifteen seconds after 9:41 a.m., on September 11, 2001, a photographer named Richard Drew took a picture of a man falling through the sky—falling through time as well as through space. The picture went all around the world, and then disappeared, as if we willed it away. One of the most famous photographs in human history became an unmarked grave, and the man buried inside its frame—the Falling Man—became the Unknown Soldier in a war whose end we have not yet seen. Richard Drew's photograph is all we know of him, and yet all we know of him becomes a measure of what we know of ourselves . . .

Connecting with the reader, as Junod has done quite effectively here by tapping into universal themes, is a hallmark of the best reflective essay writing.

It will become apparent as you read published essays in this area that there is no special expertise or research or interviewing necessary to write an effective piece. It is vital, though, to connect the observation to a conclusion through logical inferences and analogies that will cause the reader to make the connections willingly, and, ultimately, to reach that "aha" moment.

Chapter Seventeen Review

ASSIGNMENT DESK

1. Think again about the elements of the opinion essay and those of the personal reflection. Read the Fareed Zakaria essay on the Islamic community center and Anna Quindlen's piece on fear of flying after the 9/11 attacks. Identify three ways the Zakaria opinion piece incorporates personal essay techniques; identify three ways the Quindlen personal reflection piece might incorporate social commentary techniques. Consider these overlapping qualities as you handle the following exercises.

2. For this assignment, you will spend time in a public place, perhaps the central student union, a bookstore, a coffee shop on your campus, or some high traffic place outdoors. The point is to place yourself in a position to observe human behavior. Jot down at least three observations, things you might have seen a hundred times before, but now see as representative of something else. For each of the three observations, consider the significance, by drawing an inference. What does it all mean? Now write down one line explaining that meaning. For example, one observation you might make is the fact that two people are sitting together in the coffee shop, but they are talking or texting on their mobile phones. The ironic significance, or inference, you might draw from that is how disconnected from human contact we can be in a digital world of connectivity. Outside, you might see someone pushing one of those traffic signal buttons and waiting to stop the cross traffic in order to cross the street. The significance or inference you might draw from this is the impatience we have to get nowhere important. Come up with your own list of observations and inferences that might be drawn from them.

3. Here you will write a personal essay. Take one of the observations you made in number one above and craft a personal essay from the inferences you drew based on that observation. Keep in mind that you want to make logical connections between the thing you observed and the inferences you make to something larger. In considering the possible meaning of the observation, you will cause the reader to walk away feeling enriched and enlightened, finding some clarity in the pattern you observe.

4. For this assignment, you will write a critical review. Take a look at the television listings. Select a dramatic series, situation comedy, or documentary report. Remember that the point of the critical review for magazines is not only to critique the overall quality of the work under consideration, but also to contextualize that work. So, how does the television production you have selected fit into the body of similar works? If a dramatic series, a detective show, then you should

consider other such shows to reach a conclusion about whether this one measures up, or even exceeds the other works. Of course, there could be some other aspect of the production you choose to examine. For example, how does the treatment of women or LGBT community members fuel stereotypes or deconstruct them? How does the treatment of violence in a cop series serve to desensitize us to such violence in real life? (Note again how Pauline Kael treated this issue in the excerpt of her review of "A Clockwork Orange.")

▶ **KEY TERMS**

- analogy
- inciting event
- inference

▶ **SUGGESTED READING**

Franzen, Jonathan. *How to be Alone.* New York: Picador, 2003. Cultural criticism and personal reflections from the National Book Award-winning novelist and essayist, whose work has appeared in *The New Yorker* and *Harper's*.

Hitchens, Christopher. *Arguably.* New York: Twelve, 2011. In this wide-ranging collection of essays, Hitchens, a contributor to *Vanity Fair, Slate,* and *The Atlantic,* offers his musings on everything from conflict in the Middle East to Harry Potter.

Sedaris, David. *When You Are Engulfed in Flames.* New York: Little Brown, 2008. A collection of 22 sardonic essays by the quirky *New Yorker* contributor.

▶ **WEB RESOURCES**

http://www.newyorker.com/arts/critics/cinema/2013/05/13/130513crci_cinema_ denby "All That Jazz," by David Denby. *The New Yorker*, May 13, 2013.

http://www.visual-memory.co.uk/amk/doc/0051.html "Stanley Strangelove," by Pauline Kael. *The New Yorker*, January 1972.

http://michiganavemag.com/living/articles/aic-opens-picasso-and-chicago "AIC Opens 'Picasso and Chicago,'" by Thomas Connors. *Michigan Avenue*, January 14, 2013.

http://www.thedailybeast.com/newsweek/2010/08/06/the-real-ground-zero.html "Build the Ground Zero Mosque," by Fareed Zakaria. *The Daily Beast*, August 6, 2010.

http://www.nytimes.com/1997/02/16/magazine/common-threads.html "Common Threads," by Michiko Kakutani. *The New York Times Magazine*, February 16, 1997.

http://www.theatlantic.com/magazine/archive/1996/08/throwing-like-a-girl/306152/ "Throwing Like a Girl," by James Fallows. *The Atlantic*, August 1996.

http://www.zingermansroadhouse.com/2011/12/14/late-night-chitlins-with-momma/ "Late Night Chitlins With Momma," by Audrey Petty. *Saveur*, December 2005.

http://www.thedailybeast.com/newsweek/2006/08/20/a-nation-s-fear-of-flying. html "A Nation's Fear of Flying," by Anna Quindlen. *Newsweek*, August 20, 2006.

http://www.esquire.com/features/ESQ0903-SEP_FALLINGMAN "The Falling Man," by Tom Junod. *Esquire*, September 2003.

18 B2B: The Ultimate Service Journalism

▶ INTRODUCTION

The glossy publications available on newsstands and at grocery store checkout counters are what most people think of when they hear the term "magazine." But relatively few people are familiar with the wide-ranging segment of the industry where the bulk of the titles reside—the sphere known as business-to-business or **trade magazines**.

More than two-thirds of the roughly 11,000 magazines published in the United States are in the business-to-business realm. They range from tiny, highly specialized publications like *Plate*, a 5,000-circulation magazine that goes mainly to executive chefs of white linen restaurants, to huge well-known vehicles like *Billboard*, the bible of the music industry. While the general public rarely gets a glimpse of these titles (most are only available to industry executives who must "qualify" in order to receive a subscription or gain access to their websites), these publications are extremely important to the men and women who depend on them for news and information about the laws, trends, innovations, and innovators in their fields.

Often criticized as being mere shills for the industry-specific goods and services advertised on their pages and on websites, trade magazines (many of which are distributed free of charge to qualified readers) do indeed maintain close relationships with advertisers. The very name of this sector of the industry—business-to-business—suggests how close that relationship

LEARNING OBJECTIVES

1. Be introduced to the realm of specialized business or trade magazines.

2. Learn what makes a good trade magazine article.

3. Learn about careers in trade magazines—pros and cons.

4. Develop a *revise* letter that demonstrates your understanding of how to appeal to the audience of a trade magazine.

is. These titles connect business advertisers to the managers and executives who make purchasing decisions for their companies. To many, the strong advertising-editorial connection in the B2B sphere is prima facie evidence of compromises to the editorial integrity and autonomy of the publications. However, similar charges could be leveled against highly niched consumer magazines, particularly those in categories like fashion and beauty (*Vogue, Elle, Lucky*), shelter (*Traditional Home, Old House Interiors, Better Homes & Gardens*), and hobbyist books (*American Photo, Sound & Vision, Skiing*) where showcasing designs, trends, and new products is one of the primary editorial objectives. But just like the product-driven consumer magazines, trade magazines are valued for their authority and insight into the fields and endeavors they cover.

Developing the expertise to write with authority for trade magazines (and highly specialized consumer magazines, for that matter) is not as daunting a proposition as many young writers believe. And it is a skill aspiring magazine writers are well advised to consider adding to their arsenal.

▶ THE CASE FOR A CAREER IN TRADE MAGAZINES

Few young journalists launch their careers with the intent of working for publications like *Plumbing & Mechanical* or *Lawn & Landscape.* But there are several reasons why aspiring magazine writers *should* consider work in the B2B sphere. One of the primary reasons is that there are more opportunities to work in trade than consumer magazines simply because there are far more trade magazines, nearly twice as many as consumer magazines. And while many categories of B2B magazines experienced a good deal of shakeout due to the twin firestorm of the digital revolution—which siphoned off both advertisers and readers—and the housing bust—which decimated hordes of titles devoted to building and construction—many more continue to thrive. They have embraced new technology and use a variety of digital tools to engage their audiences and advertisers across multiple platforms.

In addition to having far more titles to serve as a source of potential employment for aspiring magazine writers, the trade magazine world also offers opportunities for more rapid advancement. In the realm of consumer magazines, entry-level employees typically work as assistants to editors who are higher up the masthead. Their duties are largely clerical or administrative, though they are often tested with small editorial tasks designed to gauge their worthiness for bigger writing and editing assignments. In trades, which typically have much smaller staffs, entry-level editors immediately assume a good deal of writing and editing responsibility, including interviewing and writing about leading executives in the industry the magazine covers. The jobs also can immediately involve travel to trade shows and conventions, most of which are held in major cities around the country—and sometimes abroad.

The career of Laura Van Zeyl, publisher and editorial director of the lighting and design group at Scranton Gillette Publishing Co., a large trade magazine publisher near Chicago, provides a good example of rapid ascent and multiple opportunities available to writers and editors in the trade magazine world. Van Zeyl began her career as an associate editor covering lighting design for another trade publishing group. The job afforded her opportunities to travel to trade and design shows around the world and develop a considerable amount of expertise about the industry. "Starting at a very early stage in my career, I was going to design shows in London and Paris, New York and Las Vegas," Van Zeyl says. "I enjoyed seeing all the new designs. To me, it was like covering fashion shows only the designs I was covering were lighting designs."

Medioimages / Photodisc

Often young trade magazine writers are afforded opportunities to cover the exact same events—like fashion shows—alongside more senior writers from consumer magazines. For example, at New York Fashion Week—the twice-yearly showcase where clothing designers parade their new lines before celebrity editors, retail buyers, and members of the gliteratti—it is not uncommon for trade magazines like *American Salon* to allow younger writers in on their team coverage. At consumer magazines, only the most seasoned writers get coveted seats at these shows. In short, even the most junior writer at a trade magazine has the opportunity to do substantial work, including major features and cover stories, almost from her first day on the job.

▶ WHY MOST PEOPLE ARE HESITANT ABOUT WORKING FOR THE TRADES

There are a couple of reasons why most people—at least most people who don't know any better—recoil at the thought of working for a trade magazine. One, they think the topics these magazines cover are boring. And, two, they think the topics these magazines cover are too difficult for laymen to understand.

To the first point, writing about an industry—any industry—from the point of view of its senior managers can be fascinating. The thing to remember is that B2B writing is *business* writing. The readers of trade magazines, largely executives and entrepreneurs who are responsible for making their companies run more efficiently and profitably, are reading these publications with an eye on their bottom lines. Most young writers and editors who begin immersing themselves in the industry covered by the business magazines for which they work soon find themselves drawn to the issues and personalities.

Take, for example, Kathryn Rospond Roberts, a writer and editor who has built a 15-year career specializing in the coverage of heating, ventilating, and cooling (HVAC) systems. Roberts had no knowledge of the construction industry—let alone HVAC systems—when she took her first job at *Consulting-Specifying Engineering Magazine* right out of journalism school, but she quickly developed a keen interest in new, energy-efficient, and more environmentally friendly methods of heating and cooling large buildings as she learned more about the industry. As her reporting deepened and her knowledge grew, she gained a national reputation within the industry as one of the experts in the field and is frequently asked to appear on panels and at trade shows alongside HVAC contractors.

She finds the topic anything but boring. "Heating and cooling a building or home is something so basic that the general public doesn't really think about it very much," she says. "But once you start to delve into it, it's very easy to get sucked into how important it is to find ways to make our homes and offices comfortable in ways that don't do damage to the environment or waste energy."

As for the difficulty of covering topics in highly specialized industries, Roberts says journalism training equips most young writers to dive in and learn about very technical subjects.

"I am by no means an engineer or an architect," she says, "but I'm not afraid to ask questions and have people explain their work to me in a way that I can understand. So after a lot of years talking to engineers and contractors, I really have come to understand this work. And because I also have the luxury of talking to people all over the country, I really get the full spectrum of what's going on throughout the industry, which is probably why I'm considered an expert."

At many of the medical and highly scientific magazines, like *DVM Newsmagazine*, a publication aimed at veterinarians, only doctors and researchers write the most technical or peer-reviewed articles. The journalists on staff are responsible for crafting articles related to the business of running a medical practice or lab. These stories have a practical, news-you-can-use twist that is not beyond the scope of any industrious journalist who is willing to dive in and learn the industry norms, as well as its nomenclature. Becoming familiar with industry jargon is what many young writers find so intimidating about working in trades. Those who conquer that fear often find very satisfying and versatile careers.

▶ WRITING FOR THE TRADES

First and foremost, successful writing for trade magazines—like successful writing for a consumer magazine—requires an understanding of the audience the magazine serves. Many people confuse the specialized business press, the trade magazines, with the general business press, magazines like *Forbes, Fortune,* and *Businessweek.* While both the specialized business publications and their general cousins cover economic news and trends, as well as the captains of industry and other important business personalities, the consumer magazines are not deemed as must-reads for the business class. Though they are chock full of useful information, they are predominantly leisure publications that cover a wide swath of economic and business news.

Conversely, trade magazines are very narrowly niched, covering a specific industry or job title. We describe trade magazines as either vertically or horizontally situated within the marketplace. A **horizontal publication**, like *Folio*, the magazine for magazine professionals, is aimed at every executive who works within the industry, no matter what her title. A **vertical publication**, like *Circulation Management*, which is directed at the managers of subscriptions and newsstand sales, drills deeply into the issues affecting individuals who hold a specific job title. Knowing whether your audience holds virtually the same title or is spread across the industry can dictate what jargon you use and how you use it. Terms that are not universally understood across the industry will need to be explained, even if they are commonly used in one segment of the industry.

A common mistake made by journalists who are new to trade magazines is writing stories from a consumer perspective. Our training conditions us to think about how a particular issue will affect members of the general public. For example, in the throes of the housing crisis, a journalist writing for a consumer magazine would undoubtedly focus on underwater mortgages and foreclosures. A writer employed by one of the building magazines, say *Builder & Developer* magazine, might focus on the ways in which the contractors and home builders in its circulation of 25,000 are weathering the downturn in home sales, with special emphasis on tips for cutting costs and moving inventory.

The bottom line of most trade magazine stories is, in fact, the bottom line. Whether it is a profile or a trend story, the emphasis of a B2B article should be how this information will benefit the reader's company or improve her job performance. Think of trade magazine writing as the ultimate in service journalism. The information, therefore, should not merely be presented as a general examination of an industry issue. It should provide the reader with practical solutions to the problems the issue poses.

This is not to suggest that feature stories in trade magazines are not structured like features in consumer magazines. Trade features use many of the same writing techniques outlined elsewhere in this book, including anecdotal leads, colorful details, and salient quotes. But all of these techniques should be employed in the service of a story that illustrates how business problems can be resolved.

For example, a profile of Arkansas architect Marlon Blackwell in the September–October 2011 issue of *Residential Architect* not only showcases Blackwell's innovative designs and traces the arc of his successful career, it provides a blueprint for other small to mid-sized architecture firms that are struggling to survive in the economic downturn. The story is full of colorful language and beautiful photographs and might be suitable for a consumer magazine like *Architectural Digest*, but its focus is on running a successful architectural firm, not just the beautiful homes the firm designs.

▶ PITCHING TO THE TRADES

CONTROLLED CIRCULATION: Free subscriptions to select people on the basis of their professional status or position.

Freelancing for trade magazines can be difficult because these publications exist in worlds that are not readily accessible to readers who are not in the industry. Most trade magazines are not available on newsstands. They are distributed through a process called **controlled circulation**. Controlled circulation publications are provided to subscribers free of charge. Potential subscribers "qualify" for these free subscriptions by submitting a card to the publisher indicating that he or she has a particular job title (usually one in management) or is an executive in a particular industry. To qualify, subscribers typically must have budget-making or purchasing responsibilities, since these are the readers the advertisers in trades are most interested in reaching. **Verified circulation** is related to this concept, but the subscription also can be paid for by a third party—often another business that wants to advertise selectively in the publication.

VERIFIED CIRCULATION: Subscriptions are paid for by a third party, often to advertise to select markets.

STANDARD RATE AND DATA SERVICE: A print and database resource that provides profiles of publications by categories.

Because the publications themselves are not available on newsstands, aspiring freelancers for trade magazines will find it difficult to obtain issues that allow them to see the kinds of stories the magazine features. Some of these publications allow limited access to stories on their websites, which will clue freelancers in on the magazine's editorial approach. But unless a freelancer knows individuals who work in the industry, obtaining current or back issues of the magazines or full views of their websites will be a challenge.

One resource that may be helpful—though it, too, is not easily obtainable—is a database called **Standard Rate and Data Service** (SRDS). SRDS is a print and digital database, available through some libraries, that includes audience profiles and advertising rates for both "consumer" and "trade" magazines. In the print editions, there is both a consumer volume and one for B2B publications. Magazines are grouped by category. The digital database is searchable using keywords that describe the industry and audience. Each listing, in either print or digital, includes a publisher's profile describing the magazine, its audience, and its coverage areas. Many of these profiles also suggest the kinds of stories that fit the magazine's focus and niche. Indeed, these profiles will give a good idea of the magazine's bread-and-butter editorial offerings. Using SRDS will give freelancers some insight into how and what to pitch to a specific magazine's editors.

Determining what exactly to pitch requires putting yourself in the mindset of the industry executives who read this publication. Though many trade magazines use writers who once were involved in the industry to lend their stories a more authoritative voice, most editors find that it is easier to teach good writers and reporters how to communicate with industry professionals than it is to teach industry professionals how to write and report. So professional editors in this area are quite open to solicitations from writers who demonstrate that they can write for the audience.

As a layperson, don't think you'll be expected to know the industry from the moment you start reporting about it. Ask questions—lots of them if you're confused about terminology or processes. In most instances, people in the industry will be happy to explain their business to you. "Most people in these businesses don't have the opportunity to speak with a lot of reporters," says Kathryn Rospond Roberts. "They're flattered by the attention when a journalist calls and seems genuinely interested in their business and how it operates. They tend to be very patient and happy about explaining things to you."

One caveat about launching a career in B2B We would be remiss if we didn't point out that some people in consumer magazines look down on trade magazines, which often can make it difficult to move from the world of trades to the world of consumers. Conventional wisdom says four or five years in trades could make a switch to consumer magazines nearly impossible. But many writers and editors have successfully made the transition.

One of those editors who was able to parlay his time in trades to a career in consumers is Terrance Noland, editor-at-large at *Men's Journal* magazine. Noland began his career at a tiny 6,000 circulation trade magazine called *Construction Marketing Today.* Noland says the key to moving from trades to consumers is in knowing how to promote your work published in trade magazines. "What you want people in consumers to understand is that what you're doing in trades is business writing," Noland says. "It is writing for a very specialized business audience, but it is business writing nonetheless. If you can get people to wrap their minds around that, they can see the value and the versatility of the work you've done."

Still others say a career in this area is highly satisfying and they wouldn't, well, trade it. "I love working in B2B," says Laura Van Zeyl, publisher and editorial director at Scranton Gillette Publishing Co. "I love knowing that our audience really depends on the work we do. It's journalism that has an impact, and that's always what I wanted to do."

WRITER'S WORKSHOP

Here are some suggestions for you to apply some of the central points of this chapter as you begin to develop article ideas.

There are a few things to keep in mind in terms of benefits of freelancing for the trades. First, these publications are in need of content just as with any consumer publication. That demand, coupled with the relatively small number of available writers, creates great freelance opportunities. Start by setting a strategy just as you would with the consumer magazines. What are the paths that will bring you to your ultimate destination as a writer? That destination might be a particular magazine, or it could be a certain level of expertise, a specialty. If you are interested in writing about fashion, then consider the trades that will offer you the chance to gain highly marketable experience covering the industry. If you have an interest in cars, or banking, health care, or architecture, then there are trades that you should target in order to get the kind of experience that will move you forward. Second, because the B2B publications are so specialized, it is conceivable that you can write one article that can be sold to several markets with minor revisions. For example, if you have a piece you want to pitch on new human resource developments, there will be multiple publications that will be interested in a fine-tuned version of that story for their audience. So, while any given trade publication might not pay a considerable fee, you stand the chance to make up for it with simultaneous publication of your articles—if you strategize properly. Finally, look at the trades the same way you would consider developing a magazine pitch for any publication. Review the factors we discuss in the earlier chapters regarding the story development, pitch, and structure of your work. Then look at the special interests of particular fields, matching your talent to the need.

Chapter Eighteen
Review

▶ KEY TERMS

- controlled circulation
- horizontal publication
- Standard Rate and Data Service
- trade magazine (business-to-business publication)
- verified circulation
- vertical publication

▶ SUGGESTED READING

Drueding, Megan. "Top Firm: Marlon Blackwell Architect," *Residential Architect,* September–October, 2011; pp. 22–23.

Clinton, Patrick. *The Guide to Writing for the Business Press.* Lincolnwood, IL: NTC Business Books, The Business Press Educational Foundation, Inc., 1996.

▶ WEB RESOURCES

http://www.abmassociation.com/abm/default.asp Official website of the Association of Business Information & Media Companies (ABM), a non-profit organization composed of more than 200 business-to-business companies. ABM also sponsors the Jesse H. Neal National Business Journalism Awards, dubbed "The Pulitzer Prize of the business media," which showcases editorial excellence in business media publications (http://www.americanbusinessmedia.com/abm/56th_Annual_Jesse_H_Neal_Awards.asp).

19 Writing for the Web and Tablets

▶ INTRODUCTION

Many professionals in what has come to be known as the **legacy media**—old media, including longstanding print-based publications—continue to reel from the disruptions caused by the digital revolution. Despite all the hand-wringing about change, the explosion of websites and tablet editions of traditional magazines can provide some great opportunities for emerging writers. New media provide a wealth of opportunities to establish a publishing track record. While few of these digital outlets pay as well as their older, more established print counterparts (many, in fact, do not pay at all), they offer an entrée into a media world that once was closed to all but a select few who were invited to join the magazine writing club.

Some confuse writing for the web with technical writing or think that a level of technical expertise is involved. It certainly helps to know something about the possibilities that digital storytelling affords and the different ways in which audiences engage with digital as opposed to print content. But contributing stories to websites and tablets does not necessarily require a deep knowledge of coding or digital design (though developing that knowledge certainly would help you communicate better with web editors and designers).

Writing for websites and tablets does, however, require developing an eye for the visual aspects of storytelling—both video and photography. A digital journalist is a multimedia journalist. Sure, there are a few websites that

LEARNING OBJECTIVES

1. Develop an understanding for the differences between web and print audience engagement.

2. Learn what skills to add to your journalistic arsenal.

3. Learn to build your personal brand as a digital content producer.

LEGACY MEDIA: Traditional communications before the Internet, also known as old media—newspapers, magazines, radio, and television.

Getty Images

are largely text-based, but concentrating exclusively on writing and reporting without developing your video and still photography skills severely limits your prospects in this sphere. Success in the digital realm means demonstrating that you can do it all. Those who master **multimedia** will find a wide range of publishing opportunities open to them.

▶ SURVEY THE DIGITAL LANDSCAPE

MULTIMEDIA:
Communications across a combination of content types, or platforms, including video, audio, digital, photography, as well as printed text.

The web is a vast place—worldwide, as they say. But that doesn't mean entry-level writers should be overwhelmed. Like print magazines, web publications are **affinity media**, places where like-minded people with similar interests and avocations congregate. And just as in the world of print magazines, there is a website for every conceivable job, hobby, or demographic group. Finding a publication to which you might contribute really takes little more effort than plugging a topic into your web browser.

Think of your targets of opportunity as being divided into two broad areas—web-only publications and digital extensions of legacy media. The former ranges from well-known vehicles like *Slate, Salon,* and *The Huffington Post* to small, highly niched sites like *The Good Men Project, The Bleacher Report,* and *CafeMom.* Most of the content on these sites consists of blogs, personal essays, and opinion pieces that are riffs on the news of the day, in addition to aggregation of stories appearing in other media sources. But some sites also publish features, including in-depth original reporting.

On the legacy side, every traditional magazine has a website staffed by a relatively small team responsible for constantly seeding the space with content. "I like writing for the website of *Fast Company,*" says Greg Lindsay, who has written about business, air travel, and trends for a number of legacy media, including *The New York Times, Fortune, The Wall Street Journal,* and *Advertising Age,* among others. "I can write anything I want for my column for the website at *Fast Company,* because there's infinite space. They always need content," says Lindsay, who also maintains his own blog and, oh yeah, did we mention that he is a two-time Jeopardy champ?

Clearly, as Lindsay indicates, websites are voracious animals, so producers are always scrambling to feed the beast. Though they **repurpose** and upload a lot of stories and images from their print magazines, these brand extensions cannot be sated with print content alone, which is why website producers for these magazines are more inclined to take a chance on untested new writers than their counterparts on the print side. Still, as is the case with pitching to print editors, successful pitching to web producers requires developing an understanding of the audience, and pitching focused story ideas and knowing what it takes to deliver them for online consumption.

"Rule Number One: simpler is better," notes digital maven Eric Gillin. "Crisp captions, clear pictures, short paragraphs, sharp points, no wasted words, no long headlines, quick intros," says Gillin, who was able to build on his experience as a co-founder of the famously irreverent independent online magazine *The Black Table* (with A.J. Daulerio, Aileen Gallagher, and Will Leitch) to become web director, Hearst Men's Network at Hearst Digital Media. "Rule Number Two: be unexpected," he says "Don't cover something because someone else is doing it. Take risks, find a fresh angle, always surprise, but never bore."

Will Leitch agrees. "You have to give readers something new every time," he says. "That doesn't necessarily mean breaking news. The value of the scoop is not nearly what it once was. The minute you have a scoop, someone else—an aggregator site—has grabbed it and made it theirs in like five, ten minutes."

Staying alert, being creative and imaginative are vitally important. Bottom line, though, simplicity is key. "Right," Gillin asserts. "I need to be able to convey to you in a headline, and that headline might be on your mobile phone, it might be texted to you, it might be on the Twitter feed, it could be on your wall," he suggests. "It's divorced of context. You're just seeing the words. And so if you're just seeing these words, I need to simply convey to you that this story is worth reading and that it's interesting."

So, in conceptualizing stories and in executing clever and artistic titles with puns and openings with thoughtful allusions that might work well in print won't fly online. "If it's too hard to understand in a second, no matter where you are, no one's going to click on it. And you have to stand out from all the noise."

Just as reading back issues is essential to pitching print editors, before you pitch ideas to website producers you should thoroughly examine their offerings, clicking deep into the site to get a good sense of the kinds of pieces they favor under each of the tabs. Does the site consist primarily of blogs? What are the bloggers' credentials? Every post should have some ID of the author embedded

REPURPOSE:
Convert one form of communication to another, as with printed text to DVD.

somewhere in the layout. Does the site only seem to accept submissions from well-known authors and experts in particular fields or do the contributors appear to be "everyday" folks. Be forewarned: the more "everyday people" you find contributing to a site, the less likely it is that the producers actually pay for submissions. Some sites, like *The Huffington Post*, use a broad mix of highly credentialed and new writers/bloggers. Still, they pay relatively few of them.

Try to determine who the producers are attempting to attract. Really think about the point of view the site maintains. A site may appear broad and general, like *Slate* or *Salon*, but as you read through its posts, you'll note a decidedly left-of-center political perspective coursing through the articles and opinions. *The Good Men Project* clearly appeals to men, but its audience is largely young (21–34-year-olds), urban men who are in relationships. The tone and cultural references used throughout the site will provide clues to identity and characteristics of the audience.

▶ BUILD YOUR DIGITAL BRAND

Many websites will not enlist the services of a new blogger or content producer unless she already has a substantial digital presence. "In a way, writers are like entrepreneurs," Will Leitch contends. "You have to build your own brand. Build the thing that you do well, and then have someone buy it." Building your digital brand is not as complicated as it may sound. If you already have a presence on social media, you are well on your way to establishing that presence.

Every young writer these days needs a blog, a place on the web to push out content that displays wit and writing style and that can help develop a following. Your blog needn't be serious. It can be your musings about a hobby you're engaged in or a passion you hold. But your blog must be professional. Too many young people create a digital footprint—one that is easily accessible to anyone who Googles them. Too often, the footprint is filled with sophomoric or, worse yet, crude ramblings that are sure to offend any number of people. That is not the online presence you want to establish.

You want to establish in the minds of web producers that you can develop thoughtful content, packed with multimedia, that others enjoy as demonstrated

Thinkstock / iStockphoto

by the following you have amassed. Push the content out on your social media and get friends to comment on and "like" it. The more others engage, the more you demonstrate that you can drive traffic, which is what every web producer is looking for in a blogger or writer.

Use your blog to show that you understand **search engine optimization** (SEO). SEO is the art (some say science) of putting clues in your content that will be picked up by the antennae of search engines like Google or Bing and will help get your blog listed among the first page of entries when a user plugs the topic you are blogging about into her browser. Engineers at the search sites try mightily to prevent bloggers and other content producers from gaming their system and using sketchy methods of optimizing search, like stacking words in close proximity in their content. (**Keyword density** is one of the things that **algorithms** of search engines glom on to as they try to determine where to rank a site or blog in their listing.) But writing with an eye toward SEO is another way to demonstrate your understanding of web content development and of endearing yourself to web producers.

The bottom line is that, just as with any platform, long for legacy media, or short for new media, the more you write, the better you *will* write. "Good writing is good writing, no matter what format," Will Leitch insists. "I write the same way for my blog, for my column, for my features, for books, anything. I mean, for online, I might be able to embed video. But certainly when it comes to tone and voice, it's all at the same level."

SEARCH ENGINE OPTIMIZATION: The process of affecting the visibility of a site by strategically including key words that are likely to attract a greater number of unique visitors.

KEYWORD DENSITY: The percentage of times a word or phrase appears on a page compared to the total number of words on the page; used in generating higher search engine positions.

ALGORITHM: A set of mathematical instructions in computing designed to complete a procedure or solve a problem.

ONLINE BRANDING

Successful online writers often will take time to build their brand—an online identity—by blogging on specific subject matter at established sites and even by establishing their own sites.

One example comes from "Hip Hop Music, Pornography and the Guilty Pleasures of Good Men," an essay by Shawn Maxam posted on *The Good Men Project* site in June 2012. In it, he establishes his street cred as a fan of rap music, only realizing as he aged just how objectionable some of the content can be with sexist and homophobic references.

"Even 'conscious' rappers referred to women in derogatory terms," he writes, admitting to the attraction nonetheless. "The aggressive bravado spoke to me, even if I now cringe at most of the content."

The references here speak to men of Maxam's generation. They are offered without elaborate identification. Though some of the artists in his list are such ubiquitous pop culture icons that even the most out-of-touch baby boomer would recognize them, the piece speaks to a younger man's recollection of his adolescent idols and clearly distinguishes the audience of *TGMP*. In so doing, Maxam has established a connection with that audience through identification.

Vulture, an arts and entertainment website for pop culture junkies, also aims at a largely young, hipster audience, but its references can run the gamut from unapologetically au courant ("Tina Fey Closes Out Donald Glover's New Mixtape") to sweetly retro ("Andy Griffith, the No Muss, No Fuss Performer"). What binds this audience, regardless of age, is its intense dedication to film, television, and music, and the people who produce this entertainment. Some magazines also attract slightly different audiences to their websites than they do to their print products, and a still different audience to their tablet extensions than to their other platforms. The *Esquire* audience skews slightly older for print than the website, yet slightly older on its tablet edition than for print. "There's actually very little overlap," notes Eric Gillin. "I think it's something like five percent. So, five percent of the people who read the website read the magazine, and vice versa. So they're two very distinct audiences," he says. And that means adopting different strategies. "You have to think about these things less in terms of brands and more in terms of habits," Gillin advises. "Some people check the Web every single day and they don't really read a lot of magazines because they're always checking the Web." Knowing these habits goes a long way toward setting online writing strategy.

Paying attention to these audience variations is as key to pitching a website as it is to pitching a print magazine.

TAVI GEVINSON: TEENAGE STYLE ICON

The phenomenal career of Tavi Gevinson demonstrates how fashion tastemakers are made in the digital age. Inspired by the pages of *Vogue, Elle,* and *Harper's Bazaar,* Gevinson, who grew up in a Chicago suburb, started chronicling her musings about contemporary couture in a blog she started in her bedroom. The year was 2006, and Gevinson was 12.

From an early age, Gevinson had demonstrated her original sense of style. Even in third grade, she liked to visit thrift stores and pair her second-hand finds like lacey scarves and flowing skirts with penny loafers and Converse All-Stars. She decided to turn her passion for fashion into a blog. "I was just writing what I thought about the clothes that I saw," she told *Chicago* magazine in 2012. "I wasn't trying to be famous or anything. I was just amusing myself. Maybe I hoped I'd amuse my friends, but I really didn't know that anyone else would read it, let alone like it."

She called the blog "Style Rookie," and by the time she had reached the grand old age of 13, she was practically an Internet sensation attracting 25,000 unique eyeballs a day with her funny, quirky assessments of the runway looks she saw in magazines and in some of the online peeks at the Fashion Week unveilings from New York, Paris, and Milan. *Harper's Bazaar* took note of Gevinson's rising traffic numbers and hired her as a contributor. They jetted her off to runway shows in the fashion capitals of the world for a first-hand look at the clothes she once had only seen in magazines and online.

Before long, she was rubbing shoulders and making friends with the likes of designer John Galliano (who flew Gevinson and her father to Paris for his Spring 2010 show), and Laura Mullaevy of the Rodarte label, who mailed Gevinson clothes to photograph and review for her blog.

After blogging independently for two years, Gevinson was approached by Jane Pratt, the founder of *Sassy* and *Jane* magazines, to launch a magazine based on her blog. Though the partnership with Pratt fell through, Gevinson found other backers and *Rookie Magazine* made its debut in September 2011. The online magazine reached more than a million page views within six days of its launch. While Gevinson serves as editor-in-chief, Anaheed Alani, former fact-checker for *The New York Times Magazine*, serves as editorial director. The magazine, which covers fashion, art, and pop culture, has a variety of contributors, most of them established journalists, decades older than Gevinson. Yet, they must conform to the idiosyncratic tone and fashion point of view of the EIC.

While the jury is still out on whether Gevinson is an Internet flash-in-the-pan, her success thus far demonstrates partly how wit and passion can help launch a career. Mostly, it shows how wit, passion, a good idea, and a bit of online savvy can create online opportunities.

▶ UNDERSTAND THE DIFFERENCE BETWEEN THE PRINT AND DIGITAL AUDIENCE EXPERIENCE

Not only must you understand audience demographics when you attempt to write for the web, you must also gain a better understanding of the ways in which audiences interact with digital content and how that differs from the ways in which readers interact with print or tablet content.

We describe engaging with print content as a **lean-back** experience. The reader engagement study conducted by researchers in the Media Management Center of Northwestern University's Medill School of Journalism showed that readers of print magazines tend to view that experience as their "personal time out." It is a moment of reflection and self-indulgence, where they can lose themselves in the words and images while feeling smarter and being entertained. Print readers are believed to be more receptive to long blocks of text (though the web influence has certainly resulted in print stories becoming shorter and more dependent on graphic support).

The website experience is generally considered more active. Website visitors assume what is referred to as a **lean-forward** posture. The website user is often seeking information and wants it delivered quickly or she wants to access tools that will allow her to calculate, calibrate, or define the parameters of a personal goal or problem. She wants information delivered in interactive charts and photos and video that allow her to access it at her own pace, usually faster than she might gather it in a traditional print format. The infinite amount of space on the web means the user comes to expect a richer experience, with searchable content that enables her to find answers to questions raised by her engagement with it.

Narrative storytelling reigns in print. The writer and editor guide the reader through a linear path to the completion of the article or even the end of a photo essay. Storytelling for the web is anything but linear. The digital content producer cedes control of the path the user takes, allowing her to dictate how—or even *if*—she wants to get to some end point in the post. In addition, the content producer embeds links that allow the user to opt out of our site to survey content elsewhere on the web that might contribute to her understanding of the information we are presenting.

Developing content for the web means thinking through how the user will engage with it. Will she want this story told mostly through photographs with short text blocks? Does the story require building some sort of searchable database or creating tools that will allow the user to personalize the experience? Think about web stories not merely as static text, but as a dynamic, multimedia experience. Does it need video to help tell the story through pictures and sound? For example, in its coverage of the April 15, 2013 Boston Marathon bombing, *TIME* magazine augmented its weekly print cycle with constant updates online, including video from an eyewitness and tweets from readers. When it comes to showing what multiple platform presentation can do to augment print storytelling, *The New York Times* upped the ante with its coverage of the Boston Marathon bombing. The publication identified the runners who crossed the finish line at the time of the first explosion, interviewed them, and posted their audio interviews online.

The tablet experience is a cross between the lean-back experience of print and the lean-forward experience of a website. The physical act of holding the tablet almost replicates the print reading experience and seems to put readers in the same "time out" frame of mind and makes reading longer text blocks more acceptable. Yet the digital tools and multimedia extras that can be embedded in tablet content give it the interactive feel of a website.

Demonstrating your understanding of the differences between digital and print storytelling will elevate your pitches and help connect you to the producers you are querying.

THE BLACK TABLE: A LAUNCH PAD FOR TALENT AND CAREERS

It started in January 2003 as an irreverent site by and for some of the most talented writers around New York who were not having much luck getting published. By the time it ended only three years later, not only had more than 200 writers showcased what Gawker.com called "bold, hilarious and insightful writing," but the hunger and determination had paid off. Founding Fab Four A.J. Daulerio, Eric Gillin, Aileen Gallagher, and Will Leitch, digital rock stars to be sure, all wound up pursuing successful careers in New York media. Leitch joined up with Gawker as the founding editor of *Deadspin* and was succeeded by Delaurio, after Leitch moved on to become a contributing editor at *New York* magazine. Delaurio later would leave *Deadspin*, where, among other things, he had broken the Brett Favre sexting scandal, and became editor of Gawker. Gillin became web director, Hearst Men's Network at Hearst Digital Media, presiding over Esquire.com, among other brands, before moving on to Condé Nast, where he is director of product. Gallagher ultimately became an assistant professor at the S.I Newhouse School of Public Communications at Syracuse University (her alma mater), after sharing in several National Magazine Awards for her work as a senior editor for *New York* magazine online. *The Black Table* archives are still entertaining original and new fans with pieces like Leitch's posting, "President Bush's Wiretapped Conversations . . . Revealed!" or the one by Daulerio and Gallagher, "Hot Toys, Ruined Childhoods," posted just in time for Christmas 2005, and, of course, Becky Hayes' "Yes, I Have a Helper Monkey." But even more significant than the ability to look back is the appreciation of what can be gained in looking ahead and having the creativity and the wherewithal to make that vision real.

The tools you'll need   As we state above, you don't necessarily need to know how to do digital coding and animation to produce content for the web. But it is not enough simply to be a competent writer and reporter either. Today's web content producer must be proficient in all sorts of media—writing, still photography, and videography. A story that isn't accompanied by some sort of multimedia is practically useless to web and tablet content producers. So in addition to developing your understanding of the difference between web and print content, you must also develop your ability with multimedia.

This does not, however, mean that you need expensive, professional equipment to create useable content that you can upload with your text. But you should learn the techniques for creating photos and video that will hold their own on a website that does feature content by professional photographers and videographers. With the developments in digital technology that make shooting still pictures and video nearly fool-proof, consumer-grade equipment will suffice if you remember to film and record under the best conditions. If you've never done so before, you will now need to think about things like lighting and framing as you position your subjects to be photographed. You have to make sure you avoid backlight that will place your subject in a shadow. In framing, you have to understand the rule of thirds, to position your subject off center, and consider all the elements in frame. Do they contribute to the story that is unfolding, or do they distract from it? When recording sound—either for video or narrated slideshows—you will need to consider things like ambient noise that could ruin the quality of your audio. In fact, these days, whenever you record an interview even for print stories, you should consider additional applications for the audio that easily might be cut up and used in presenting outtakes from the session. Writing for online editions means thinking about storytelling on multiple levels and clearly requires proficiency with multimedia.

Take a class or an online tutorial to familiarize yourself with multimedia techniques. Work on developing an eye for pictures and a sense of whether a story would best be told as a narrative or a user-guided experience. Remember that as a producer of content for the web, you must no longer think of yourself as merely a writer. You must think of yourself as a backpack journalist, someone who can supply your editor with a variety of ideas and content that lends itself to various storytelling approaches.

WRITER'S WORKSHOP

Here are some suggestions for you to apply some of the central points of this chapter as you begin to develop online article ideas.

As you have seen in the chapter, writing for the web is as much about setting the right strategy as it is about perfecting your writing skills. Getting attention from editors requires that you show you get attention from readers. So, content should be shaped around attracting unique visits. Doing that means working in key words as well as substance into the work. Setting up your own blog is another key, as we saw with Tavi Gevinson and *The Black Table* online site team. Increasingly, blogging is providing a portal for emerging writers to sharpen their skills and to develop a following. So, the key part of the strategy to get more writing opportunities is, quite simply, to create them.

Chapter Nineteen
Review

ASSIGNMENT DESK

Take an article that you have written for traditional print presentation and consider how it might be rendered as a digital story. Does the story have data that could be animated or presented in an interactive chart or table? Could it be told as a slide show or enhanced with snippets of audio culled from your interviews? Write a memo for the section editor or articles editor of the magazine for which the piece was written suggesting how you think the article could be presented on either a website or tablet.

▶ KEY TERMS

- affinity media
- algorithim
- keyword density

- lean-back
- lean-forward
- legacy media

- multimedia
- repurpose
- search engine optimization (SEO)

▶ SUGGESTED READING

Thornburg, Ryan M. *Producing Online News: Digital Skills, Stronger Stories.* Washington, DC: CQ Press, 2010. A guide to skills necessary for developing compelling stories for digital presentation.

Ward, Mike. *Journalism Online.* New York: Focal Press, 2002. Book and companion website that serves as a primer for journalists who are just beginning to dip a toe in the digital waters.

▶ WEB RESOURCES

http://www.nytimes.com/interactive/2013/04/22/sports/boston-moment.html?_r=0 "4:09:43" *The New York Times*, April 22, 2013.

https://www.atavist.com/ Website of a media and software company that provides technology and a forum for digital and mobile publishing.

http://goodmenproject.com/ Webzine devoted to a variety of male lifestyle issues.

http://journalists.org/ Website of the Online News Association, nonprofit membership organization for digital journalists.

http://www.thestylerookie.com/ Blog that launched the internet career of teenage fashion icon Tavi Gevinson.

http://www.blacktable.com/archive2.htm *The Black Table* archive.

20 Legal and Ethical Considerations

▶ INTRODUCTION

In this chapter, we discuss practical considerations with respect to legal issues and ethical obligations. Regarding the legal issues, what should contributors consider in agreeing to take on assignments? Is there any room to negotiate rights acquired by publishers and what exactly does all the legal language of rights mean? When do "work-for-hire" considerations kick in? What about ownership issues for those contributors who are staff members at publications and take on assignments outside their assigned areas?

Additionally, we address the issues contributors might confront in the process of reporting their stories. Issues of **defamation** and **invasion of privacy**, as well as conflicts of interest, are taken up in ways that help contributors recognize and avoid potential problems, or even the appearance of impropriety. While legal and ethical considerations are taken up in their own specialized texts, our purpose here is to familiarize you with certain core principles that can create unique practical concerns in the magazine writing context.

In the area of ethics, there always are choices that are made in the conduct of your professional affairs. How you resolve the ethical dilemmas you face can do more than merely say something about your moral fiber. It also can have lasting impact on the lives of the people who have an interest in our work—directly and indirectly—and can affect how people view our entire profession. We consider some of these issues as well.

LEARNING OBJECTIVES

1. Develop a legal and ethical framework for doing your work as a magazine writer.

2. Develop an understanding of the legal limitations and potential liability of your work.

3. Develop an understanding of your rights in negotiating your freelance contract.

4. Develop a sense of the moral obligations you have as an ethical matter in balancing your rights and interests against those of sources and other stakeholders.

▶ LEGAL ISSUES

No matter how good a job you do in researching and writing your piece, problems do arise from time to time. There is a range of such problems. They can be relatively minor (as with a misspelled name), or a flaw in the attribution credit. They can be intermediate, as with a quote that is not quite accurate. They can be major, as with a factual error that creates difficulties for a source on multiple levels.

The consequences pretty much track this range of problems. The response to the minor problem likely would be an angry telephone call. The intermediate consequence is the demand for a correction or retraction. The major consequence is legal liability—exposure to protracted battles.

Thinkstock / iStockphoto

▶ DEFAMATION

DEFAMATION:
False statements about a person that injure the reputation, either through spoken word (**slander**) or through print (**libel**).

Causes of action in defamation arise when there is a false statement of fact that is published and winds up causing harm to a person's reputation in her community. Each of these elements has a whole body of legal decisions behind it, giving it even more meaning for specific factual settings.

"Publication" in the magazine context means any release to the public whether in the print or digital magazine article or even in the documents or emails that are generated while producing the article. In other words, it is important to watch what is stated in those query letters or pitches, and even in progress memoranda and emails. If a claim is filed, all these documents can be brought in and can provide further evidence against the writer and the magazine.

ACTIONABLE:
Giving cause for legal action.

Remember, the statements that are **actionable** are false statements of fact. A statement of fact simply is a declaration of information—something presented as objectively real. So, by its very nature, opinion is not fact. It is helpful to distinguish fact from opinion by using language like, "believes," "claims," or "views" in the attribution. It also is helpful to use words like "seems" or "appears" in exposition to separate a statement of fact from your own observation as the writer. Still, references can be actionable if only thinly disguised as opinion or observations, so it is important still to take all reasonable steps to document assertions or to frame them in a way that makes it clear that they are matters of opinion or unproved allegations.

Harm to reputation is shown by relatively objective standards, what is known as the "reasonable person standard." Calling someone corrupt or incompetent certainly would qualify as harmful, as most reasonable people—the kind we aim to select for jury duty—would agree. This can be particularly harmful to a person who is engaged in a profession that ordinarily would require integrity or a level of professional skill. Clearly, there are some risks of financial loss to a person subjected to false statements about dishonesty when honesty is a key requirement of the position held.

Establishing the identity of a person also is an essential element here. And that can be done even when you do not actually name the person. If you are referring to a rather discrete group, like the seventh battalion of the Whoville Fire Department, then the members of that relatively small group all can be identified merely with a reference to their squad. So, harm can be obvious or it can be shown by inference. Ultimately, truth is an absolute defense to a claim of defamation, since false statement of fact is the key first consideration in a defamation claim.

▶ PROTECTIONS FOR JOURNALISTS

The press is accorded certain freedom against government control under the first amendment of the U.S. Constitution against claims of defamation. Case law has added more definition to this protection, giving the press a little room even to make mistakes in the process of gathering and publishing information. *N.Y. Times* v. Sullivan gave us the standard that is applied to members of the press in covering public officials. **Malice** is not necessarily bad intent, but it is knowingly distributing false information. **Reckless disregard** is careless reporting or fact-checking. Increasingly, in a number of states, there is a **negligence** standard that can be applied where journalists fail to take reasonable steps according to standards of their own profession in covering ordinary citizens—people who are not considered public officials or public figures.

MALICE: Knowledge that information is false.

RECKLESS DISREGARD: Serious doubt that information is true.

NEGLIGENCE: Failure to exercise reasonable care, causing harm to others.

Most cases arise in the second prong of the *Sullivan* standard—reckless disregard. If your sources are unreliable, if you fail to double-check information, or if you rush to judgment when more thoughtful consideration and investment of time might have avoided a mistake, then there is a potential problem of negligence. If, as a result of this failure to exercise care, you or your editor actually doubt whether your work is accurate, then the problem becomes even more serious. Even if you don't have that doubt, but a jury of your peers thinks you should have because of all the surrounding circumstances, then the problem is worse still.

While the overwhelming majority of **libel** cases are dropped, settled, or dismissed before trial, the majority of those that go forward result in judgments against the media organization—and the writer. Awards for damages can range in the several millions of dollars.

The point here is that, even when news organizations prevail, it can cost hundreds of thousands of dollars in legal fees just to defend. And most magazines are going to pass along liability to you, the writer, with an **indemnification clause** in your contract. Since it is likely that you don't have your own independent insurance coverage for something like this, there is good reason to exercise care in producing your story. It starts with your approach to the craft. Responsible reporting is the beginning. You must be fair, accurate, and balanced. Give all parties a chance to respond. It also might be useful in this context, according to some accomplished writers, to review quotes for accuracy. One writer who does this is Mike Sager, writer-at-large for *Esquire*. He actually will share his manuscript with some people featured in his stories. He feels this eliminates potential problems, especially when dealing with people who are not normally in the public eye, and who are thus less experienced in media matters. Things often can look a lot more harsh in print or on a screen than a lay person realizes when offering comments during an interview. Sager believes he can defuse a lot of problems simply by the goodwill gesture of sharing beforehand. Of course, you also have to be willing to make the corrections, as needed.

It also is vital that the writer understands what is being offered in the mind of the source and, ultimately, what is being agreed upon when you tell someone that there will be a chance to review anything in the story. Are you agreeing to allow the source to check the accuracy of quotes? Are you agreeing to review rights of the whole story? If the whole story is being reviewed, does that mean the subject believes there will be approval rights?

Invariably, someone will see something that is just a wee bit objectionable. Everyone would agree that it is bad policy to grant editing rights to the subjects of your story. An *Ebony* writer once told a famous pop star that he would let her read his profile of her before it was published. She interpreted that as granting her a right of approval. The question for the lawyers focused on whether there was a contract between the two, where the interview was granted only on the condition that the star could approve the story in advance. A tremendous amount of time and considerable legal fees went into resolving that question in favor of the magazine. Clearly, these are troublesome areas—particularly on deadline with little time to spare—and the vast majority of writers will refuse, politely, to grant such rights. That said, it is not uncommon for writers to check the accuracy of quotes, often reading the quotes (and not the context, the surrounding paragraphs) over the telephone. As with all else, you must find your balance.

The point of all of this is that, given the relatively long period of time magazine writers and editors traditionally have had to background and verify

INDEMNIFICA-TION CLAUSE: Also known as a **hold harmless** clause, passes legal liability and the responsibility to pay legal costs from one party to another in a legally binding agreement.

for their print publications, the standards for accuracy here can be more exacting. In other words, a judge and jury will feel that magazine writers and editors, who can work on articles for several months, have much more opportunity to exercise care and get it right. Thus, it is important to factor into your production time frame enough space to check your work. Again, in the event of a problem, your case will be evaluated in light of the time that was available for you reasonably to verify or substantiate information.

As the writer of a magazine story, you also will be expected to continue playing a role in the entire process. In fact, such cooperation just might be required in a clause in your contract. Many publications proceed with caution. Within the editing/fact-checking process is a **pre-publication review** done by lawyers. If there are problems, or even questions, you as the writer can expect to be called upon to help resolve them. Often, this is just a matter of providing a reasonable answer or document.

PRE-PUBLICATION REVIEW: A legal review of articles prior to final production to check for any potential legal liability.

▶ FACT OR FICTION?

Whether or not we share quotes with subjects for review, as with Mike Sager, it can be tempting to clean up quotes to accurately reflect what a person said. A number of writers do this at times. Do we like that? Do we do that? Some writers are strongly opposed to sharing anything in a story with sources beforehand—even the source's own quoted material. And they let the quote stand as given.

It is important to consider these kinds of situations before you encounter them, so that you can develop your own standards. So, consider how you feel. Should it make a difference if a source made a grammatical error? Would you correct it then? What if you knew he would have said it differently if given a second chance—one you didn't provide? What if you know that what he said is not what he meant? What if it reflected poorly on him? What if it was a distraction to the reader to see such an error in print? What if what the source said affected that person's credibility? After all, ultimately, it is not accurate. Would you call him and read it to him; give him a chance to make a correction before publication? Is that better? To let him, in effect, edit the story?

The Supreme Court in Masson v. *New Yorker* (1991) ruled that quotes of a public official or public figure can be altered so long as they don't result in a material change in the meaning conveyed. The problem is that juries may be asked to act as editors to decide whether the words used convey the meaning of the official or figure. Is that something we can live with? The bottom line for most writers and editors is that we should make sure everything in quotes is exactly what the person said. If you want to maintain your purity and yet clean up what a source says, you can do it by paraphrasing, not by revising or inventing quotes.

▶ CONFIRM SOURCES OF INFORMATION

When it comes to achieving accuracy in the reporting of stories—the gathering of information—it is important to make sure your sources are the best possible sources of the information you are relying on. Is the building custodian the most reliable source, or is the school principal? That well could depend on whether the issue is a maintenance matter or a policy matter. Is the *National Enquirer* or *The New York Times* the most reliable research tool? That might depend on how a reasonable person feels about the reputation for accuracy of these sources. These are the kinds of considerations that can come up in court if there is a question about whether you took all reasonable steps in documenting the story. Choosing the right people to interview and the right documents to read are judgment calls. And, sometimes the answers to these judgment questions can be surprising. Even though the National Enquirer has a longstanding reputation for sensationalism (read, "unreliable"), there have been recent cases of provocative reports—such as allegations of marital infidelity against former U.S. Senator John Edwards—that, owing to the special brand of *National Enquirer* checkbook sourcing, have been, well, right on the money. Again, the question comes down to what a reasonable journalist would do under circumstances similar to those you faced in reporting the story.

In quoting your sources, know what communications are provided some protection for the writer to use just because of their nature and the circumstances surrounding release. Certain public records and proceedings usually are safe to quote. Among these are police arrest records; sworn witness testimony in court; lawmaker comments in the Congressional chamber. But take care to distinguish those cases from ones based on statements made by lawmakers in news conferences. These are not protected and had better be accurate if quoted. It was with this knowledge that a former *JET* magazine editor once quipped in a conversation with a congressman that the lawmaker should read a news release into the Congressional Record before the editor would run quotes in his magazine. And, obviously, in cases of unproven charges, care must be taken to clarify that claims only have been "alleged" and should not be referred to as actual facts—in other words, assertions that something has, indeed, happened.

INVASION OF PRIVACY: Interference with a person's reasonable right or expectation to be left alone, usually by publicizing private affairs or casting a person in a false light.

▶ INVASION OF PRIVACY

Know when you are crossing the line and invading someone's reasonable expectation of privacy. Privacy is the legitimate interest of any citizen to be left alone, left to the quiet enjoyment of his life. This right, though, can give way to the legitimate interest of the media in reporting matters of public interest. The question is when is a private citizen, in fact, a public figure for matters of coverage? When are a public figure's private affairs considered to be legitimate matters of public interest? If a person is involved in a matter of public concern, if a public official's private matters impact public concerns, then there arguably is a more limited zone of privacy for these individuals because of the impact on the public. This is the type of issue that gets vetted by the magazine publisher's lawyer. But you will help the pre-publication review process considerably by taking care to consider what most people might see as reasonable.

▶ ETHICAL DECISIONS

All ethical considerations come down to a matter of values that come to bear on moral choice making. Every decision you make as a writer, or as an editor, involves a host of values. By values here, we mean a consideration of what is desirable. Information. Exclusive information. Reliable exclusive information. Reliable exclusive information obtained with integrity.

As you closely evaluate these factors, you can see that somewhere along the line, these values are going to create conflict. Exclusive information sometimes requires great speed in obtaining, processing, and releasing. There is a need to beat the competition. If we go too fast, are we cutting short our fact checking? Are we therefore sacrificing reliability? And this tension can exist even in the magazine world where, arguably, there is more time to process everything.

Ultimately, the values of journalists should include fairness, accuracy, balance, and meaningful context. And these values are set against our multiple loyalties to the magazine that is paying us; to the reader who is relying on us for reliable and accurate information; to our profession, whose members are judged by our work; and to ourselves and our reputations and our career opportunities. Problems can arise when these loyalties conflict. The conflict is not always as obvious as in cases where a writer has a financial stake in a company included in the story. If loyalty to our media organization (the magazine) means beating the competition to give a competitive edge, and beating the competition means cutting corners in verifying information and rushing to judgment, are we creating a conflict with our own loyalties to ourselves, failing to maintain integrity, credibility? Are we not creating a conflict with our loyalties to the readers, failing to provide reliable and accurate information? Are we not creating a conflict with our loyalties to our profession, failing to maintain public confidence in the field of journalism? In valuing exclusive information, are we not sacrificing some measure of the range of loyalties we should maintain as an ethical matter? How far are we willing to go in fact gathering; in document review? How far are we willing to go in getting sources to open up? There is no enforceable code of conduct for journalists. There is for lawyers and doctors, where licenses to practice are at risk. For journalists, there only are guidelines on appropriate conduct.

The Society of Professional Journalists has a Code of Ethics. It provides, among other things:

- that journalists should avoid all conflicts of interest;
- that journalists should protect confidential sources;
- that journalists should avoid plagiarism;
- that journalists have a responsibility to the public; and
- that they have an obligation to the public's right to know.

In considering these points, we should be mindful of the ethics of reporting and the ethics of writing. (At the end of this chapter, we have listed links to codes of ethics that are pertinent to the work of journalists. We urge you to review these principles.)

▶ ETHICS OF REPORTING

In addition to overstepping with information gathering, a key area of ethical concern is in the area of conflicts of interest. Often this arises where there is the question of relationships with sources. There is a potential for conflict of interest especially when sources offer gifts and services. Most magazines have express policies that prohibit writers from accepting anything.

For freelancers, something approaching an ethical pledge just might be included in the terms of the contract. Newspapers like the *Chicago Tribune* and *The Washington Post* go to great lengths to cover this area.

Ownership of stocks and real estate   Some magazines prohibit ownership of interests (stocks) in certain companies to be written on by writers. There are other examples of lines drawn by publishing companies.

Public speaking   Increasingly, writers are getting nice fees for speeches. It is important to avoid even the appearance of conflict by avoiding such arrangements with associations you might cover as a writer.

Political participation   Many Supreme Court justices over the years have been known not to vote at all. Journalists feel strongly about maintaining their non-aligned status, although few will do so at the extreme of the Supreme Court justices. Bob Woodward came under fire for maintaining a relationship with the George W. Bush administration that appeared to some to be too friendly, although he would argue that he handled the reporting for his books with integrity and professional distance. There is a difference, he would argue, between having a cordial and professional relationship (that is conducive to good sourcing) and having a close and personal relationship (that might cloud your judgment).

Identifying with the story   B2B magazines often depend on the industries they cover for advertising. As a writer, it is important that you maintain an objective distance. Here is an area with a potential conflict of loyalties—to the publisher and to yourself and the journalism profession.

Identifying with the source   There is a tension in this area. We know we get better stories when we have friendly interactions. We tend to try to cultivate these in interview situations. They are best when they flow like conversations. But when do we cross the line between interactions and relations? Truman Capote befriended one of the murderers he wrote about in developing *The New Yorker* stories that became the book (and later the film) *In Cold Blood*. Are we comfortable with that? Putting aside the issue about being friends with a convicted murderer, is it okay to make friends in getting the story? Would Capote have gotten it otherwise? Do we care whether he got it or not? Doesn't it depend on the frame of mind of the source? Does he fully understand the scope of the interaction? Is he speaking to a friend? Is he speaking to a reporter? In stories we cited in Chapter 12, was there an ethical problem that arose from the very hanging around access we value for revealing quotes and actions? In the Michael Hastings *Rolling Stone* story, "The Runaway General," did General Stanley McChrystal know that everything he said or did could wind up in the story? Did he feel that there were times when he felt he was speaking off the record? Should the writer make it clear that everything is fair game when the access is negotiated? Should the source assume that anything said can be held against him in the court of public opinion? This kind of situation arises quite often in cases of journalists who have close relationships with officials or celebrities. The question becomes whether they each have the same understanding of what is going on at any given moment. Is the official or celebrity talking with a friend, while the journalist is talking with a source? If there is no meeting of the minds, so to speak, then there well could be a meeting of the lawyers.

On the other hand, some pure-at-heart journalists are highly critical of agreeing to too much in negotiating access. What about the deal reportedly struck by writer Michael Lewis for six months of access to President Barack Obama for Lewis's *Vanity Fair* story, "Obama's Way," we featured in Chapter 12? Should we grant elected officials approval rights over quotes to be used in a story? What happens if an official wants to edit out something we feel should be included as part of our duty to the public to provide fair, balanced, and accurate information? On the other hand, what about our duty regarding national security in a case where an inadvertent quote by a public official could cause harm? Ultimately, who should judge in these cases—the reporter and editor, or the source?

VOGUE MAGAZINE ON SYRIA'S FIRST LADY AND AN ETHICAL DILEMMA

In "Asma al-Assad: A Rose in the Desert," a 3,200-word story published by *Vogue* in February 2011, noted writer Joan Juliet Buck characterizes the wife of Syrian strongman Bashar al-Assad in glowing terms. She came to regret that characterization with the Arab Spring that came within months of publication, followed by the brutal crackdown and wholesale slaughter of protestors in Syria by Bashar al-Assad. *Vogue* was the target of ridicule by critics of the article and later removed the piece from its website. Buck later wrote in the August 6, 2012 edition of *Newsweek* how she believed she was "duped" by Asma al-Assad and her public relations representatives. Even that piece garnered criticism for Buck.

Notice here how Buck begins her original story in a voice that is consistent with the *Vogue* emphasis on style and positivity.

> Asma al-Assad is glamorous, young, and very chic—the freshest and most magnetic of first ladies. Her style is not the couture-and-bling dazzle of Middle Eastern power but a deliberate lack of adornment. She's a rare combination: a thin, long-limbed beauty with a trained analytic mind who dresses with cunning understatement. *Paris Match* calls her "the element of light in a country full of shadow zones." She is the first lady of Syria.

> Syria is known as the safest country in the Middle East, possibly because, as the State Department's Web site says, "the Syrian government conducts intense physical and electronic surveillance of both Syrian citizens and foreign visitors." It's a secular country where women earn as much as men and the Muslim veil is forbidden in universities, a place without bombings, unrest, or kidnappings, but its shadow zones are deep and dark.

This piece raises a number of ethical issues, which critics were quick to point out, and which led ultimately to Buck's *Newsweek* confessional, titled "How I Was Duped by Mrs. Assad." In her *Newsweek* essay, Buck sees a different Syria than the one she described in her *Vogue* piece. "The name itself sounded sinister, like syringe or hiss," she writes.

While Buck discusses her misgivings about doing the Asma al-Assad story to begin with, asserting that this should have been an assignment for a political reporter, and while there were a number of others—journalists and public policymakers—who missed some of the early warning signs of official Syrian terror, there also appear to have been a series of ethical missteps in the handling of the *Vogue* story from the very beginning.

In many cases, story framing (locking a writer into a positive approach), the "handling" by public relations representatives, and the lack of sourcing all can lead to a lack of balance and, as in this case, a story that reads as an apologia and ultimately requires a public apology.

▶ ETHICS OF PRESENTATION

Sometimes a story can have impact on an issue, but also on the people involved in the issue. Somebody might lose a job for talking freely. Worse, in certain situations, someone might lose liberty or even life for talking freely. Should you care? Is there a larger good? Does that make it okay? To an extent, we should care and we should make sure the writing does not distort to the point where people are affected unnecessarily. The question is not just the public right to know, but whether all details are part of a story necessary for public understanding. The issue is whether questionable material is material to the story. One writer recalls checking a provocative quote by a source—a military officer—that revealed the officer's anxiety about going into a conflict zone. The source asked that the quote be left out. He would have to lead men into battle, he explained, and they had to have absolute confidence in his will to lead, to fight, and, if called upon, to lay down his life for his troops. Quite a humanizing quote that wound up getting cut. Was the value of this glimpse of humanity worth the consequences? The writer thought not.

Among the greatest ethical challenges arises in image presentation. With all of the technical innovations at our disposal these days, it is tempting to manipulate photographs to represent what we want them to represent, rather than what actually was captured in the moment. Sometimes this consideration is made where the composition of the photograph is a bit less than perfect, or where the scene might be a little too gory for presentation. *The Atlantic* was criticized for its posting of a photograph of a man depicting his horrific injuries (he had lost his legs) resulting from the April 15, 2013 Boston Marathon Bombing. The initial decision to post the photograph without alteration was based on the consideration that it depicted the reality of that moment, as difficult as it was to view.

Some have asserted that a photograph (not unlike the words on a page or screen) is an interpretation of reality and can be manipulated by the author—the photographer—to present that creative interpretation. The better argument is that magazine presentation is a form of journalism and photography in journalism must be guided by the same principles of accuracy as with the published word. Photographs are historical documents and we must be mindful of the story these photographs will relate to future generations about the reality of our moment. The National News Photographers Association has developed a Code of Ethics providing guidance in this area.

Even so, there is room for creative manipulation in cases of the "photo illustration" where it is made clear to the reader that the photo image has been manipulated in order to make an editorial point. The critical consideration here is that the reader is aware of the "interpretation" and is not confused about whether the representation is real or not.

▶ PERSONAL CONCERNS

Copyright   A major concern for any writer is how to protect your work. This first comes up for freelancers very early in the game. In other words, how do you protect your work, your idea, from being stolen by an editor?

The first thing you should know is that **copyright** provides some measure of protection for created works, but not for ideas. Certainly not for titles.

Protection for the story   Your story is protected as soon as it is written and printed or posted on the Web. The law is written so that copyright protection kicks in when a work is created and in tangible form. Copyright notice, symbol, and registration are required to give notice to the world that this work is protected to enable you to sue for damages if someone infringes. Log onto the Library of Congress copyright website for forms, information, requirements on registration. Payment of a fee is required at the time you deposit copies of the original work along with a completed form.

Ideas   Generally, editors are not going to steal your ideas. One reason editors prefer queries is that there is an orderly process for submission and response. There are a few people in the chain of review and assignment. This provides a sort of protection for the magazine against frivolous lawsuits. By extension, it provides protection for you as the writer. It sets up a system that makes it less likely that ideas will be taken. If you have a good story idea but are not given the assignment, some editors will pay a nominal fee for the idea. Some will negotiate, but they are under no legal obligation to do either. "I like this idea, but I can't give the assignment to you. Someone else usually handles this area. We'll make sure we get you another assignment." Generally, that means send another query. But, in the event someone steals your idea, you have no recourse. The exception is where the idea gets translated so closely to the story you have developed—down to the actual flow of ideas—or translated so closely to the detailed outline you have submitted that it arguably is a copyright infringement.

▶ RIGHTS

The issue about which most writers are concerned is who owns the story once written and submitted. Typically, you will receive a contract. If you don't receive a contract, you will want to send a letter setting out your understanding of the terms. Basically, if you want to retain specific rights, then they must be negotiated. Ordinarily, the publisher will want to buy all rights. But what does that mean? Rights set out the scope of use to which the publisher is entitled. There are **first serial rights**, **second serial rights**, rights for presentation on the web and in tablet form, and all rights.

First serial rights   The magazine buys the rights to publish your story one time. It usually applies to North American publishing rights. That means the United States and Canada. Sometimes first serial rights can mean worldwide rights. This is a point that should be clarified, as there are English language speaking countries where publishers will buy rights to published material. If these rights are tied up just because they weren't clearly spelled out, you as the writer wind up losing money. The contract will set out a certain period for the exclusive publishing right whether North America or the world. In other words, during this period, the publisher has the exclusive right to publish in the territory designated. It is important to note that, if you sign such a deal, you have given up your own right to publish in specific locations. In effect, the ownership of your story has been transferred for a set time and a set geographical area. After that period, all rights revert to you.

Second serial rights   As the term suggests, these are rights to publish a second time. Some magazines are interested in previously published material. *Reader's Digest* historically was a leader in second serial rights in previously published articles the magazine would republish for significant fees. There is a similar concept in the context of the trades where the same idea and pretty much the same story can be published in multiple magazines. The basis for this practice is the increasing specialization of magazines. Because magazines are aimed at targeted markets, there is at least a possibility that a magazine will be interested in sharing a previously published story with its readership. Best to check to make sure if the contract is silent on this point.

All rights   Obviously, here you are selling your piece forever. Magazines increasingly want more rights so that they will be able to repurpose your story and publish it indefinitely on the Web or in a tablet app. The difference among all these rights is that there is a fee schedule that should match the rights that are being purchased. Second serial rights will pay less than first serial, which will pay less than all rights. At least, that is the way it should work. Current law states that unless a publisher sets it out in writing, it will be assumed that a writer is not selling all rights. Whatever the arrangement, it's best to have it all in writing. Some overzealous lawyers will insert language like "all rights in perpetuity throughout the universe." So, if you think you ever might want to publish your article on Mars, better read the fine print—and renegotiate.

Work for hire   This consideration goes to publication rights in the works produced by employees. The typical example is where you are being paid to write. It comes up when you are a regular contributor, or you are on staff. The publisher owns the copyright in all your writing for the magazine. The gray area arises when writing an article is not what you were hired to do. You might be a junior editor. You might be an office mail clerk. Even though you are working for the magazine, writing is not your primary responsibility. It might not be your responsibility at all. The publisher might argue that your poetry or your short story fiction or your non-fiction profile of Brad Pitt is a **work for hire**. If the publisher prevails, then the publisher owns all rights. Of course, you will get a fee, but no right to say anything about future publication of the article or anything within the article. Clearly, you will have another point of view and a different argument to make. The bottom line is that it is best to have an understanding ahead of time. And, just as all things are negotiable, if you see the very publication of your work as its own form of compensation, you might want to consider just how strenuously you pursue these issues.

Other copyright issues   Who owns the rights to the material you use within the story? For the most part, here we're talking about other published material. Better to find out in order to use material in most cases. And this applies to Internet sourcing as well. Often, fair use applies. Fair use allows the use of copyrighted material without permission, under set circumstances. Comment, education, criticism, reporting. The use must be reasonable. What constitutes reasonable depends largely on the amount of material reproduced and the effect of that use on marketability of the copyrighted material. The volume of material and its originality are factors. While there is no bright line, when in doubt it is best to get permission.

Releases   The magazine likely will rely on you to get all releases, whether for photo images or for interview excerpts. Make sure anyone depicted in a photo signs a release. Avoid using the photo in your story if it was shot for a different purpose. The consent just might be limited to that original purpose.

**IMPLIED CON-
TRACT:** A legally enforceable agreement that arises because of circumstances, or conduct of the parties.

Anonymity   If you promise, then it may be considered a term of the interview agreement. In other words, the interview is granted with anonymity in mind. Release the name, and you are in breach of that **implied contract**. Your credibility also is on the line. If you release the names after promising not to do so, then no one will want to talk with you.

WRITER'S WORKSHOP

Here are some suggestions for you to apply some of the central points of this chapter as you begin to consider the business arrangements for your story.

Record keeping is vitally important for freelance writers. Review the information we discussed in Chapter 10 related to materials that will be required by the research and fact-check team at the magazine. But you also should keep a file of everything you used in preparing to write the story. All notes, recordings, and documents should be kept for a minimum of five years, which would cover the statute of limitations in most jurisdictions. Keep in mind, though, that some magazines will have editors keep records on stories for seven or even ten years. Apart from these concerns, you also will want to keep records of your expenses for tax purposes. Consult an advisor, but consider everything you spend in connection with writing the story as a potential tax deductible expense. All non-reimbursed travel, accommodations, mailing, photocopying, and similar expenditures need to be documented. These records also should be kept for at least five years, as a matter of IRS requirements.

Chapter Twenty
Review

ASSIGNMENT DESK

1. You are assigned to write a profile of a famous film star. You have covered her before and she feels comfortable enough with you to invite you to be her weekend guest at her posh Beverly Hills mansion. Do you accept the invitation? Consider all the possibilities and explain the reasoning behind your response.

2. You are a music critic for a popular entertainment magazine and have just scored an exclusive with a number one recording artist who is about to drop a new product. His publicist grants the interview on condition that you allow her to read the article before it is published. What do you do? Consider all the possibilities and explain the reasoning behind your response.

3. You are working on a major public affairs story on government failings in disaster relief. You have just been given a provocative revelation by a source, who insists on remaining on "deep background." She tells you that if her name is attached to the revelation, she will lose her job. What do you do? Consider all the possibilities and explain the reasoning behind your response.

4. Review the Joan Juliet Buck excerpt on Syria's first lady presented in the box on p. 306.

How would you characterize the ethical issues presented by the story? What steps might you take as a magazine writer to avoid the pitfalls you have identified?

▶ KEY TERMS

- actionable
- copyright
- defamation
- first serial rights
- hold harmless
- implied contract
- indemnification clause
- invasion of privacy
- libel
- malice
- negligence
- pre-publication review
- reckless disregard
- second serial rights
- slander
- work for hire

▶ SUGGESTED READING

Christians, Clifford G.; Fackler, Mark; Richardson, Kathy Brittain; Kreshel, Peggy J.; Woods, Robert H. *Media Ethics: Cases and Moral Reasoning*, 9th Edition. Boston: Pearson, 2011. Provides contemporary cases and framework for development of moral reasoning in sorting real-world ethical dilemmas in media.

Moore, Roy L.; Murray, Michael D. *Media Law and Ethics*, 4th Edition. New York: Routledge, 2011. A presentation of media law and principles, providing a helpful connection between legal understanding and moral reasoning.

▶ WEB RESOURCES

http://www.journalism.org/resources/ethics_codes Ethics Codes, A Listing, Pew Research Center's Project for Excellence in Journalism.

https://nppa.org/code_of_ethics National Press Photographers Association Code of Ethics.

http://www.spj.org/ethicscode.asp Society of Professional Journalists Code of Ethics.

http://www.thedailybeast.com/newsweek/2012/07/29/joan-juliet-buck-my-vogue-interview-with-syria-s-first-lady.html "Syria's Fake First Family," by Joan Juliet Buck. *The Daily Beast*, July 30, 2012.

Appendix

Title: All That Jazz
Publication: *New Yorker*
Cover Date: 2013-05-13
Creator: DAVID DENBY
Page: 78

▶ ALL THAT JAZZ

BY DAVID DENBY
"The Great Gatsby."
RON KURNIAWAN

Leonardo DiCaprio and Carey Mulligan in Baz Luhrmann's new movie.

When "The Great Gatsby" was published, on April 10, 1925, F. Scott Fitzgerald, living high in France after his early success, cabled Max Perkins, his editor at Scribners, and demanded to know if the news was good. Mostly, it was not. The book received some reviews that were dismissive ("F. SCOTT FiTZGERALD'S LATEST A DUD," a headline in the New York *World* ran) and others that were pleasant but patronizing. Fitzgerald later complained to his friend Edmund Wilson that "of all the reviews, even the most enthusiastic, not one had the slightest idea what the book was about." For a writer of Fitzgerald's fame, sales were mediocre—about twenty thousand copies by the end of the year. Scribners did a second printing, of three thousand copies, but that was it, and when Fitzgerald died, in 1940, half-forgotten at the age of forty-four, the book was hard to find.

The tale of Fitzgerald's woeful stumbles—no great writer ever hit the skids so publicly—is suffused with varying shades of irony, both forlorn and triumphal. Fitzgerald was an alcoholic, and no doubt his health would have declined, whatever the commercial fate of his masterpiece. But he was a writer who needed recognition and money as much as booze, and if "Gatsby" had sold well it would likely have saved him from the lacerating

Notice how Denby sets up his critique of the Luhrmann film by referencing the genesis of the source material. This sort of contextual detail is the hallmark of criticism and elevates this piece far beyond a simple "review."

public confessions of failure that he made in the nineteen-thirties, or, at least, would have kept him away from Hollywood. (He did get a fascinating, half-finished novel, "The Last Tycoon," out of the place, but his talents as a screenwriter were too finegrained for M-G-M.) At the same time, the initial failure of "Gatsby" has yielded an astounding coda: the U.S. trade-paperback edition of the book currently sells half a million copies a year. Jay Gatsby "sprang from his Platonic conception of himself," and his exuberant ambitions and his abrupt tragedy have merged with the story of America, in its self-creation and its failures. The strong, delicate, poetically resonant text has become a kind of national scripture, recited happily or mournfully, as the occasion requires.

In 1925, Fitzgerald sent copies of "Gatsby" to Edith Wharton, Gertrude Stein, and T. S. Eliot, who wrote thank-you notes that served to canonize the book when Wilson reprinted them in "The Crack-Up" (1945), a miscellany of Fitzgerald's writing and letters. All three let the young author know that he had done something that defined modernity. Edith Wharton praised the scene early in the novel when the coarsely philandering Tom Buchanan takes Nick Carraway—the shy young man who narrates the story—to an apartment he keeps for his mistress, Myrtle, in Washington Heights. Wharton described the scene as a "seedy orgy." With its stupid remarks leading nowhere, its noisy, trivial self-dramatization, the little gathering marks a collapse of the standards of social conduct. In its acrid way, the episode is satirical, but an abyss slowly opens. Some small expectation of grace has vanished.

Notice how Denby returns to the scene mentioned above. The reader now has historical context for this description of Luhrmann's cinematic treatment of the scene.

I thought of Wharton's phrase when I saw the new, hyperactive 3-D version of "The Great Gatsby," by the Australian director Baz Luhrmann ("Strictly Ballroom," "Moulin Rouge!"). Luhrmann whips Fitzgerald's sordid debauch into a saturnalia—garish and violent, with tangled blasts of music, not all of it redolent of the Jazz Age. (Jay-Z is responsible for the soundtrack; Beyoncé and André 3000 sing.) Fitzgerald's scene at the apartment gives off a feeling of sinister incoherence; Luhrmann's version is merely a frantic jumble. The picture is filled with an indiscriminate swirling motion, a thrashing impress of "style" (Art Deco turned to digitized glitz), thrown at us with whooshing camera sweeps and surges and rapid changes of perspective exaggerated by 3-D. Fitzgerald wrote of Jay Gatsby, "He was a son of God—a phrase which, if it means anything, means just that—and he must be about His Father's business, the service of a vast, vulgar, and meretricious beauty." Gatsby's excess—his house, his clothes, his celebrity guests—is designed to win over his beloved Daisy. Luhrmann's vulgarity is designed to win over the young audience, and it suggests that he's less a filmmaker than a music-video director with endless resources and a stunning absence of taste.

Notice, too, how excess—the fictional Jay Gatsby's and the filmmaker Baz Luhrmann's—becomes a theme of this piece.

The mistakes begin with the narrative framing device. In the book, Nick has gone home to the Midwest after a bruising time in New York; everything he tells us of Gatsby and Daisy and the rest is a wondering recollection. Luhrmann and his frequent collaborator, the screenwriter Craig Pearce, have turned the retreating Nick into an alcoholic drying out at a sanatorium. He pulls himself together and, with hardly any sleep, composes the entire text of "The Great Gatsby." He types, right on the manuscript, "by Nick Carraway." (No doubt a manuscript of "Lolita by Humbert Humbert" will show up in future movie adaptations of Nabokov's novel.) The filmmakers have literalized Fitzgerald's conceit that Nick wrote the text—unnecessarily, since, for most of the rest of the movie, we readily accept his narration as a simple voice-over. Doubling down on their folly, Pearce and Luhrmann print famous lines from the book as Nick labors at his desk. The words pop onto the screen like escapees from a bowl of alphabet soup.

When Luhrmann calms down, however, and concentrates on the characters, he demonstrates an ability with actors that he hasn't shown in the past. Tobey Maguire, with his grainy but distinct voice, his asexual reserve, makes a fine, lonely Nick Carraway. He looks at Leonardo DiCaprio's Gatsby with amazement and, eventually, admiration. As Nick slowly discovers that his Long Island neighbor is at once a ruthless gangster, a lover of unending dedication, and a man who wears pink suits as a spiritual project, some of the book's exhilarating complexity comes through. (The love between Nick and Gatsby is the strongest emotional tie in the movie.) DiCaprio, thirty-eight, still has a golden glow: swept-back blond hair, glittering blue-green eyes, smooth tawny skin. The slender, cat-faced boy of "Titanic" now looks solid and substantial, and he speaks with a dominating voice. He's certainly a more forceful Gatsby than placid Robert Redford was in the tastefully opulent but inert adaptation of the book from 1974. DiCaprio has an appraising stare and he re-creates Fitzgerald's description of Gatsby's charm: that he can look at someone for an instant and understand how, ideally, he or she wants to be seen.

More context: Denby compares DiCaprio's depiction of Jay Gatsby to Redford's, a subtle display of film knowledge.

As Daisy, the English actress Carey Mulligan makes a good entrance, with nothing but her hand lofted over the back of a couch and a tinkling voice to accompany it. Mulligan is not elegantly beautiful, but she's a touching actress, and, when Tom and Gatsby fight over Daisy, her face crumples and her eyes tear. Mulligan makes it clear how much Daisy is a shaky projection of male fantasy. The men struggle to possess her; she doesn't possess herself. As the brutal Tom, the Australian actor Joel Edgerton is so unappealing that Daisy's initial love for him seems impossible, but Luhrmann makes the climactic fight between Tom and Gatsby a genuine explosion—the dramatic highlight of this director's career.

The rest of the movie offers fake explosions. Luhrmann turns Gatsby's big parties into a writhing mass of flesh, feathers, dropped waists, cloche hats, swinging pearls, flying tuxedos, fireworks, and breaking glass. There are so many hurtling, ecstatic bodies and objects that you can't see much of anything in particular. When the characters roar into the city, Times Square at night is just a sparkle of digitized colors. Luhrmann presumably wants to crystallize the giddy side of twenties wealth and glamour, but he confuses tumult with style and often has trouble getting the simple things right. Gatsby and Nick have their crucial meeting with the criminal Meyer Wolfsheim, but the director, perhaps not wishing to be accused of anti-Semitism, cast the distinguished Indian actor Amitabh Bachchan as the Jewish gangster. This makes no sense, since the gangster's name remains Wolfsheim and Tom later refers to him as "that kike."

Will young audiences go for this movie, with its few good scenes and its discordant messiness? Luhrmann may have miscalculated. The millions of kids who have read the book may not be eager for a flimsy phantasmagoria. They may even think, like many of their elders, that "The Great Gatsby" should be left in peace. The book is too intricate, too subtle, too tender for the movies. Fitzgerald's illusions were not very different from Gatsby's, but his illusionless book resists destruction even from the most aggressive and powerful despoilers.

▶ NEWYORKER.COM/GO/FRONTROW

Richard Brody blogs about movies.

Title: Natural Selection
Publication: *Vogue*
Cover Date: 2012-12-01
Creator: JANCEE DUNN
Page: 258

▶ **NATURAL SELECTION**

WITH THE VALUE OF ORGANICS CALLED INTO QUESTION, **JANCEE DUNN** REPORTS ON WHEN AND WHY GOING GREEN MATTERS.

The news was enough to make organic devotees hang up their Whole Foods eco-bags: In September, a group of Stanford researchers sparked an uproar when they reviewed 237 studies and concluded that organic food had no nutritional benefit over conventionally grown food. All those years of sifting through barrels of mottled apples (and paying more, to boot) were for naught?

Not exactly. Putting nutrition aside (and the inarguable fact that organic food tastes better), the way these two groups of food are produced has the biggest impact on our health. Most significant, organic produce does not contain synthetic pesticides, which are linked to a horde of maladies from Parkinson's to Alzheimer's. Dana Boyd Barr, Ph.D., a research professor at Emory University's Rollins School of Public Health, coauthored a study last year with UC Berkeley that found that prenatal exposure to organophosphate pesticides—widely used on food crops—is related to lower IQ scores in children. And organic food might even be the ultimate all-natural cleanse: In an Emory study, Barr and a team of researchers found that when children's conventional diets were replaced with organic food, the harmful chemicals in their systems almost disappeared. "An organic diet can actually wash out the pesticides," she says.

Indeed, organic food is notable for what it *doesn't* contain. Organic dairy must not have bovine growth hormones; organic meat (which, incidentally, has higher levels of omega-3s) must be free of antibiotics, which have given rise to antibiotic-resistant "superbugs" in humans. Organic food cannot include artificial dyes, sweeteners, or preservatives. Nor can it be irradiated (zapped with radiation to kill pathogens) or genetically modified.

And let us not forget that organics are better for the planet. Factory farms are among the world's most toxic and prodigious polluters: Recently scientists at UC Berkeley found a direct link from increased synthetic fertilizer use over the past half-century to an alarming rise in atmospheric nitrous

This *Vogue* magazine article is a good illustration of the benefits of mining news reports and even academic studies for potential magazine articles.

Note how Jancee Dunn uses a sharp summary opener to grab our attention with a news hook and then segue to the nut-graf with a provocative question.

Nice transition here, using the answer to the question in the previous graf to add a vital piece of the "invisible" structure while setting up the nutgraf.

Now Dunn effectively is filling in the gaps of the Stanford study, setting up the point of her short piece: that there are a number of ancillary benefits of organic food that are missed in looking strictly at comparative nutritional value.

oxide, a major contributor to climate change. As Barr says, "Anything that puts fewer harmful chemicals into our environment and in my children's bodies has to be a good thing."

▶ CLEAN EATING

Thin-skinned produce retains high levels of pesticides, even after a thorough wash. Opt for organic apples, blueberries, nectarines, strawberries, celery, peaches, and grapes.

Organic beef and dairy products have lower residues of pesticides and chemicals, and are free of antibiotics.

Greens retain high levels of chemicals, so it's best to buy organic lettuce, spinach, mustard greens, kale, collard greens, and Swiss chard.

—JILLIAN DEMLING
FOR MORE BEAUTY NEWS AND FEATURES, GO TO VOGUE.COM.

FARM TO TABLE
AN ORGANIC DIET MAY BE THE ORIGINAL ALL-NATURAL CLEANSE.

Here is an effective quote likely using material from the interview as a critical part of the setup. Whether the information in the sentence preceding the quote was also quoted material or the product of the writer's background, consider how this presentation gives us an effective one-two-punch of a payoff.

Dunn ends on a quote, but consider how this quote actually serves as a good takeaway for the reader and ties into the point of the piece that is established above. That point is that there is value in organic foods that doesn't necessarily show up in comparative studies of nutritional benefits alone.

Title: Stanley Strangelove
Publication: *New Yorker*
Cover Date: 1972-01-01
Creator: PAULINE KAEL
Page: 50

▶ STANLEY STRANGELOVE

Literal-minded in its sex and brutality, Teutonic in its humor, Stanley Kubrick's "A Clockwork Orange" might be the work of a strict and exacting German professor who set out to make a porno-violent sci-fi comedy. Is there anything sadder—and ultimately more repellent—than a clean-minded pornographer? The numerous rapes and beatings have no ferocity and no sensuality; they're frigidly, pedantically calculated, and because there is no motivating emotion, the viewer may experience them as an indignity and wish to leave. The movie follows the Anthony Burgess novel so closely that the book might have served as the script, yet that thick-skulled German professor may be Dr. Strangelove himself, because the meanings are turned around.

Kael minces no words. Right from the start of this review, she signals to the reader what her assessment of this film is.

Burgess's 1962 novel is set in a vaguely Socialist future (roughly, the late seventies or early eighties)—a dreary, routinized England that roving gangs of teen-age thugs terrorize at night. In perceiving the amoral destructive potential of youth gangs, Burgess's ironic fable differs from Orwell's "1984" in a way that already seems prophetically accurate. The novel is narrated by the leader of one of these gangs—Alex, a conscienceless school-boy sadist—and, in a witty, extraordinarily sustained literary conceit, narrated in his own slang (Nadsat, the teen-agers' special dialect). The book is a fast read; Burgess, a composer turned novelist, has an ebullient, musical sense of language, and you pick up the meanings of the strange words as the prose rhythms speed you along. Alex enjoys stealing, stomping, raping, and destroying until he kills a woman and is sent to prison for fourteen years. After serving two, he arranges to get out by submitting to an experiment in conditioning, and he is turned into a moral robot who becomes nauseated at thoughts of sex and violence. Released when he is harmless, he falls prey to his former victims, who beat him and torment him until he attempts suicide. This leads to criticism of the government that robotized him—turned him into a clockwork orange—and he is deconditioned, becoming once again a thug, and now free and triumphant. The ironies are protean, but Burgess is clearly a humanist; this point of view is that of a Christian horrified by the possibilities of a society turned clockwork orange, in which life is so mechanized that men lose their capacity for moral choice. There seems to be no way in this boring, dehumanizing society for the boys to release their energies except in vandalism and crime; they do what they do as a matter of course. Alex the sadist is as mechanized a creature as Alex the good.

Very high in the review Kael dispenses with the plot summary, complete with background on the author of the source material.

Stanley Kubrick's Alex (Malcolm McDowell) is not so much an expression of how this society has lost its soul as he is a force pitted against the society, and by making the victims of the thugs more repulsive and contemptible than the thugs Kubrick has learned to love the punk sadist. The end is no longer the ironic triumph of a mechanized punk but a real triumph. Alex is the only likable person we see—his cynical bravado suggests a broad-nosed, working-class Olivier—and the movie puts us on his side. Alex, who gets kicks out of violence, is more alive than anybody else in the movie, and younger and more attractive, and McDowell plays him exuberantly, with the power and slyness of a young Cagney. Despite what Alex does at the beginning, McDowell makes you root for his foxiness, for his crookedness. For most of the movie, we see him tortured and beaten and humiliated, so when his bold, aggressive punk's nature is restored to him it seems not a joke on all of us but, rather, a victory in which we share, and Kubrick takes an exultant tone. The look in Alex's eyes at the end tells us that he isn't just a mechanized, choiceless sadist but prefers sadism and knows he can get by with it. Far from being a little parable about the dangers of soullessness and the horrors of force, whether employed by individuals against each other or by society in "conditioning," the movie becomes a vindication of Alex, saying that the punk was a free human being and only the good Alex was a robot.

The trick of making the attacked less human than their attackers, so you feel no sympathy for them, is, I think, symptomatic of a new attitude in movies. This attitude says there's no moral difference. Stanley Kubrick has assumed the deformed, self-righteous perspective of a vicious young punk who says, "Everything's rotten. Why shouldn't I do what I want? They're worse than I am." In the new mood (perhaps movies in their cumulative effect are partly responsible for it), people want to believe the hyperbolic worst, want to believe in the degradation of the victims—that they are dupes and phonie and weaklings. I can't accept that Kubrick is merely reflecting this post-assassinations, post-Manson mood; I think he's catering to it. I think he wants to dig it.

This picture plays with violence in an intellectually seductive way. And though it has no depth, it's done in such a slow, heavy style that those prepared to like it can treat its puzzling aspects as oracular. It can easily be construed as an ambiguous mystery play, a visionary warning against "the Establishment." There are a million ways to justify identifying with Alex: Alex is fighting repression; he's alone against the system. What he does isn't nearly as bad as what the government does (both in the movie and in the United States now). Why shouldn't he be violent? That's all the Establishment has ever taught him (and us) to be. The point of the book was that we must be as men, that we must be able to take responsibility for what we are. The point of the movie is much more *au courant*. Kubrick has removed many of the obstacles to our identifying with Alex; the Alex of the book has had his personal habits cleaned up a bit—his fondness for squishing small

Kael was masterful at ferreting out the subtext in both screenplays and performances.

And she places the film in the context of the time in which it was made. These references were culled from the headlines of the time.

Note the social commentary.

animals under his tires, his taste for ten-year-old girls, his beating up of other prisoners, and so on. And Kubrick aids the identification with Alex by small directorial choices throughout. The writer whom Alex cripples (Patrick Magee) and the woman he kills are cartoon nasties with upper-class accents a mile wide. (Magee has been encouraged to act like a bathetic madman; he seems to be preparing for a career in horror movies.) Burgess gave us society through Alex's eyes, and so the vision was deformed, and Kubrick, carrying over from "Dr. Strangelove" his jokey adolescent view of hypocritical, sexually dirty authority figures and extending it to all adults, has added an extra layer of deformity. The "straight" people are far more twisted than Alex; they seem inhuman and incapable of suffering. He alone suffers. And how he suffers! He's a male Little Nell—screaming in a straightjacket during the brainwashing; sweet and helpless when rejected by his parents; alone, weeping, on a bridge; beaten, bleeding, lost in a rainstorm; pounding his head on a floor and crying for death. Kubrick pours on the hearts and flowers; what is done to Alex is far worse than what Alex has done, so society itself can be felt to justify Alex's hoodlumism.

The movie's confusing—and, finally corrupt—morality is not, however, what makes it such an abhorrent viewing experience. It is offensive long before one perceives where it is heading, because it has no shadings. Kubrick, a director with an arctic spirit, is determined to be pornographic, and he has no talent for it. In "Los Olvidados," Bunuel showed teen-agers committing horrible brutalities, and even though you had no illusions about their victims—one, in particular, was a foul old lecher—you were appalled. Bunuel makes you understand the pornography of brutality: the pornography is in what human beings are capable of doing to other human beings. Kubrick has always been one of the least sensual and least erotic of directors, and his attempts here at phallic humor are like a professor's lead balloons. He tries to work up kicky violent scenes, carefully estranging you from the victims so that you can *enjoy* the rapes and beatings. But I think one is more likely to feel cold antipathy toward the movie than horror at the violence—or enjoyment of it, either.

Kubrick's martinet control is obvious in the terrible performances he gets from everybody but McDowell, and in the inexorable pacing. The film has a distinctive style of estrangement: gloating closeups, bring, hard-edge, third-degree lighting, and abnormally loud voices. It's a style, all right—the movie doesn't look like other movies, or sound like them—but it's a leering, portentous style. After the balletic brawling of the teenage gangs, with bodies flying as in a Western saloon fight, and after the gang-bang of the writer's wife and an orgy in speeded-up motion, you're promised for more action, but you're left stranded in the prison sections, trying to find some humor in tired schoolboy jokes about a Hitlerian guard. The movie retains a little of the slang Nadsat but none of the fast rhythms of Burgess's prose, and so the dialect seems much more arch than it does in the book. Many of

Here she references Kubrick's earlier work. Critics should familiarize themselves with the canon of the filmmakers and actors in the work under review and provide some comparison and contrast.

For film buffs, Kael compares Kubrick to one of the art house masters. But the reference has enough clues and background to entice readers who might not be familiar with Bunuel's work and provides an appropriate illustration for those who are.

Note the specific description/criticism of Kubrick's technique.

the dialogue sequences go on and on, into a stupor of inactivity. Kubrick seems infatuated with the hypnotic possibilities of static setups; at times you feel as if you were trapped in front of the frames of a comic strip for a numbing ten minutes per frame. When Alex's correctional officer visits his home and he and Alex sit on a bed, the camera sits on the two of them. When Alex comes home from prison, his parents and the lodger who has displaced him are in the living room; Alex appeals to his seated, unloving parents for an inert eternity. Long after we've got the point, the composition is still telling us to appreciate its cleverness. This ponderous technique is hardly leavened by the structural use of classical music to characterize the sequences; each sequence is scored to Purcell (synthesized on a Moog), Rossini, or Beethoven, while Elgar and the others are used for brief satiric effects. In the book, the doctor who has devised the conditioning treatment explains why the horror images used in it are set to music: "It's a useful emotional heightener." But the whole damned movie is heightened this way; yes, the music is effective, but the effect is self-important.

When I pass a newsstand and see the saintly, bearded, intellectual Kubrick on the cover of *Saturday Review*, I wonder: Do people notice things like the way Kubrick cuts to the rival teen-age gang before Alex and his hoods arrive to fight them, just so we can have the pleasure of watching that gang strip the struggling girl they mean to rape? Alex's voice is on the track announcing his arrival, but Kubrick can't wait for Alex to arrive, because then he couldn't show us as much. That girl is stripped for our benefit; it's the purest exploitation. Yet this film lusts for greatness, and I'm not sure that Kubrick knows how to make simple movies anymore, or that he cares to, either. I don't know how consciously he has thrown this film to youth; maybe he's more of a showman than he lets on—a lucky showman with opportunism built into the cells of his body. The film can work at a pop-fantasy level for a young audience already prepared to accept Alex's view of the society, ready to believe that that's how it is.

At the movies, we are gradually being conditioned to accept violence. The directors used to say they were showing us its real face and how ugly it was in order to sensitize us to its horrors. You don't have to be very keen to see that they are now in fact desensitizing us. They are saying that everyone is brutal, and the heroes must be as brutal as the villains or they turn into fools. There seems to be an assumption that if you're offended by movie brutality, you are somehow playing into the hands of the people who want censorship. But this would deny those of us who don't believe in censorship the use of the only counterbalance: the freedom of the press to say that there's anything conceivably damaging in these films—the freedom to analyze their implications. If we don't use this critical freedom, we are implicitly saying that no brutality is too much for us—that only squares and people who believe in censorship are concerned with brutality. Actually, those who believe in censorship are primarily concerned with sex, and they generally worry about

Again, very concrete references to this scene and its scoring, contrasted with the source material.

It's important to note that at the time of its release, *A Clockwork Orange* was hailed by many critics as a masterpiece and Kubrick as a directing genius. Kael is acknowledging here that she was swimming against the tide, and she uses this critique to direct the reader to what she saw as the flaws and exploitative nature of the film.

violence only when it's eroticized. This means that practically no one raises the issue of the possible cumulative effects of movie brutality. Yet surely, when night after night atrocities are served up to us as entertainment, it's worth some anxiety. We become clockwork oranges if we accept all this pop culture without asking what's in it. How can people go on talking about the dazzling brilliance of movies and not notice that the directors are sucking up to the thugs in the audience?

Kael returns to the central theme of this review— the cavalier way in which Kubrick mixes sex and brutality and the duplicity of a film review board that heavily censors one while often turning a blind eye to the other. The review, therefore, becomes more than a critique of a film. It criticizes society and pop culture as well.

Index

Page numbers in **bold** refer to figures.

"When I think editing, I think 'core skills' –and this book delivers. *Contemporary Editing* helps to build a strong foundation for students with its laser focus on accuracy, ethics, mechanics and, perhaps most importantly, critical thinking. And its use is not limited to news editing. This is a toolbox, not a textbook."

Susan Brockus Wiesinger,
California State University, Chico

CONTEMPORARY EDITING

3rd Edition
by Cecilia Friend & Don Challenger

Contemporary Editing offers journalism students a forward-looking introduction to news editing, providing instruction on traditional newsroom conventions along with a focus on emerging news platforms. This comprehensive text provides students with a strong understanding of everything an editor does, addressing essential copy editing fundamentals such as grammar and style; editorial decision making; photo editing, information graphics, and page design; and new media approaches to storytelling. Throughout, the book focuses on how "the editor's attitude"—a keen awareness of news values, ethics, and audience—comes into play in all facets of news editing. This new edition offers expanded coverage of web publishing and mobile media, giving students solid editing skills for today's evolving media and news forums.

routledge.com/cw/friend-9780415892810/

paperback | 978-0-415-89281-0
ebook | 978-0-203-37032-2

Principles of
American Journalism

An Introduction

Stephanie Craft and Charles N. Davis

In a rapidly changing media landscape, what becomes of journalism? Designed to engage, inspire and challenge students while laying out the fundamental principles of the craft, *Principles of American Journalism* introduces students to the core values of journalism and its singularly important role in a democracy. From the First Amendment to Facebook, Stephanie Craft and Charles N. Davis provide a comprehensive exploration of the guiding principles of journalism—the ethical and legal foundations of the profession, its historical and modern precepts, the economic landscape, the relationships among journalism and other social institutions, and the key issues and challenges that contemporary journalists face. Case studies, discussion questions and field exercises help students to think critically about journalism's function in society, creating mindful practitioners of journalism and more informed media consumers.

routledge.com/cw/craft-
9780415890175/

paperback | 978-0-415-89017-5
ebook | 978-0-203-08191-4